D1062498

Paradise Lost

ALSO BY GILES MILTON

Non-Fiction
The Riddle and the Knight
Nathaniel's Nutmeg
Big Chief Elizabeth
Samurai William
White Gold

Fiction
Edward Trencom's Nose

Paradise Lost

Smyrna 1922

The Destruction of a Christian City in the Islamic World

GILES MILTON

BASIC
BOOKS

A Member of the Perseus Books Group
New York

Copyright © 2008 by Giles Milton
First published in the United States in 2008 by Basic Books,
A Member of the Perseus Books Group
Published in Great Britain in 2008 by Sceptre,
an imprint of Hodder & Stoughton

Books published by Basic Books are available at
special discounts for bulk purchases in the United States
by corporations, institutions, and other organizations. For
more information, please contact the Special Markets Department
at the Perseus Books Group, 2300 Chestnut Street, Suite 200,
Philadelphia, PA 19103, or call (800) 810-4145, ext. 5000,
or e-mail special.markets@perseusbooks.com.

A CIP catalog record for this book is available from
the Library of Congress
ISBN-13: 978-0-465-01119-3
LCCN: 2008921306

10 9 8 7 6 5 4 3 2 1

For Guy

Ex Oriente Lux (Out of the Orient, light)

The motto of Smyrna's Ionian University, due to open its
doors to all – irrespective of race or religion – in
September 1922

The strange thing was, he said, how they screamed every night
at midnight . . . We were in the harbour and they were on the
pier and at midnight they started screaming. We used to turn the
searchlight on them to quiet them. That always did the trick.

Ernest Hemingway, *On the Quai at Smyrna*

Contents

PART THREE: PARADISE LOST

List of Characters

British

David Lloyd George	Britain's pro-Greek Prime Minister
Arnold Toynbee	Historian; war reporter for the Manchester Guardian
Sir Harry Lamb	British consul-general in Smyrna, 1922
Reverend Charles Dobson	Anglican vicar in Smyrna, 1922
Grace Williamson	Nurse at Smyrna's English Nursing Home

Levantine

Magdalen Whittall	Fearsome matriarch of the Whittall dynasty
Herbert Octavius Whittall	Magdalen's eleventh child
Edward Whittall	Herbert's genial older brother
Edmund Giraud	Yachtsman and one of Magdalen's 91 grandchildren
Hortense Wood	Spinster and diarist; eyewitness to the events of 1922
Fernand de Cramer	Hortense's young nephew

American

Dr Alexander Maclachlan	President of American International College in Paradise
George Horton	American consul in Smyrna
Mark Bristol	American High Commissioner in Constantinople
Minnie Mills	Director of Smyrna's American Collegiate Institute for Girls

Asa Jennings	Employee of Smyrna's YMCA and director of rescue operation
Esther Lovejoy	Doctor who played leading role in humanitarian rescue

Greek

Eleftherios Venizelos	Greek Prime Minister and architect of the 'Big Idea'
Aristeidis Stergiadis	Greek governor of Smyrna, 1919–1922
Metropolitan Chrysostom	Greek religious hierarch and staunch nationalist

Turkish

Rahmi Bey	Pro-Allied Ottoman governor of Smyrna during the First World War
Enver Pasha	One of triumvirate ruling Turkey since 1908 Young Turk revolution
Mehmet Talaat Be,	Second member of triumvirate
Mustafa Kemal (Ataturk)	Leader of nationalist movement; creator of modern Turkey
Halide Edib	Prominent nationalist and close colleague of Kemal

Armenian

Dr Garabed Harcherian	Senior physician at Armenian National Hospital
Rose Berberian	Young Armenian eyewitness to the violence
Hovakim Uregian	Armenian eyewitness to outbreak of fire

Acknowledgements

The research and writing of *Paradise Lost* would not have been possible without assistance from people in many different countries. I am especially grateful to the descendants of the great Levantine dynasties of Smyrna – now scattered across the globe – who went out of their way to help me locate the unpublished letters and diaries of their grandparents and great grandparents. It should be put on record that the opinions expressed in *Paradise Lost* are my own and do not necessarily reflect the views of those who helped with my research, some of whom still live in the modern city of Izmir.

In Turkey, I owe a debt of gratitude to Brian Giraud, whose helpfulness, knowledge and network of friends and acquaintances opened many doors during my time in Izmir. He introduced me to Renée Steinbuchel, to whom I am most grateful for allowing me to photocopy the treasured last diary of her great aunt, Hortense Wood. Renée also supplied me with many of her family's letters, as well as the graphic despatches written by Fernand de Cramer. As far as I am aware, none of this important material has been used in any book previously written about the events of 1922.

Thank you to Daphne Aliberti for sharing her reminiscences about her Smyrniot forebears over a pleasurable coffee morning; to Willy Buttigieg, the British consul in Izmir, whose family have lived in the city for generations and who proved a fount of knowledge. He set up an interview with the nonagenarian Alfred Simes, for which I am most grateful.

Thank you to Esma Dino Deyer, daughter-in-law of Rahmi Bey, with whom I spent a fascinating afternoon at her grandiose villa. I came away with the impression that I had caught a tantalising glimpse of old Smyrna – the city as it was before the destruction. I also wish to offer my thanks to Bulent Senoçak; to Patrick Clarke, one of the last remaining Levantines still working in the fig trade; and to local journalist, Melih Gursoy.

In Greece, I am indebted to Michalis Varlas, Manager of the Genealogy project at the Foundation of the Hellenic World. He shared with me his research into Greece's venture into Asia Minor and introduced me to Petros Brussalis and other elderly survivors from the events of 1922. I am also most grateful to Stavros Anestides and the staff and librarians of the excellent Centre for Asia Minor Studies. Thank you to Daphne Kapsali for accompanying me to Athens and acting as interpreter and translator. All of the eyewitness accounts contained in the important Greek anthologies, *Exodos* and *Martyries* (full references can be found in the Notes and Sources) were translated by her. I also wish to thank the staff of the Gennadius Library in Athens, where many rare pamphlets (both Greek and Turkish) are held.

In North America, I wish to thank Marjorie Housepain Dobkin, who shared her Smyrna researches with me and whose excellent *Smyrna, 1922*, remains required reading. Thank you to Barbara Jackson for supplying me with Ian Wallace's reminiscences; and to John Hobbins of McGill University, Quebec, for his help and advice.

In Jerusalem, I wish to express my thanks to George Hintlian for his help and advice over the course of my research. He sent me a copy of the grim but fascinating eyewitness account written by the Armenian bishop of Smyrna, Ghevont Tourian.

In Switzerland, my thanks to Alexander Belopopsky for providing me with contacts in the Greek Orthodox world.

In Paris, thank you to Hervé Georgelin for sending me recently published French articles on Smyrna. His most recent publication, *La Fin de Smyrne*, is by far the best study of the pre-1922 cosmopolitan city.

In England, I wish to thank Yolande Whittall for her help and enthusiasm for my project. She put me in touch with many descendants of her extended family, including Betty McKernan, Maya Donelan and Brian Giraud.

I am most grateful to Victoria Solomonides of the Greek

Consulate in London for sharing her views on Aristeidis Stergiadis. Her PhD thesis on Smyrna – still, alas, unpublished – is required reading for anyone who wants to understand why the Greek invasion of Asia Minor was doomed to failure.

Thank you to Bruce Clark of *The Economist* for sharing his far-reaching network of contacts. His recently published book on the 1923 Treaty of Lausanne, *Twice a Stranger*, is an invaluable study of the population exchange.

Thank you to Ayça Duffrene of the BBC Turkish service for her help and advice and for putting me in contact with many distinguished Turkish families living in Izmir. Other thanks must be extended to Clovis Meath Baker, Frank Barrett, Wendy Driver, Father Alexander Fostiropoulos, Ara Melkonian - for translating Armenian documents – Tom Rees; and to Jessica Gardner and Charlotte Berry of Exeter University Library for allowing me to consult the Whittall archive.

Also, to the staff at the Institute of Historical Research; Colingdale Newspaper Library; the Imperial War Museum; the librarians at St Anthony's College, Oxford, and to the ever helpful staff at the National Archives in Kew, where much of the research for this book was undertaken; to the staff of the British Library and London Library, where a special mention must be made for Christopher Phipps, who produced the index for this book.

I wish to record my thanks to my late literary agent, Maggie Noach, who represented me for more than a decade and became a good friend in the process. She died suddenly in 2006, when the book was still in its early stages. Thank you, also, to my editor, Roland Philipps, who displayed such enthusiasm for the project, and to Lisa Highton, Heather Rainbow and Juliet Brightmore. I am most grateful to Paul Whyles for once again reading the manuscript and suggesting much needed changes.

Lastly, a huge thank you to my three girls, Madeleine, Héloïse and Aurélia; and to my wife, Alexandra, *pour tout*.

Magny, November, 2007

TURKEY AND

GREECE

Constantinople

Gallipoli

Panderma • Bursa

Chanak

• Izmit

Eskishehir •

Ang

A N A T O L

Aegean Sea

Piraeus •

• Athens

• Smyrna

Ushak

• Afyon Karahisar

• Aidin

T

Bodrum

Marmaris

Fethiye

CYP

Mediterranean S

SMYRNA PROVINCE

Ayvalik

Mitilini

Pergamum

Magnesia

Phokia

Menemen

• Kasaba

Smyrna
(Izmir)

Nif

Chesme

Aidin

Alexandria

Port Sa

EGYPT

| 0 | miles | 50 |
| 0 | kilometres | 80 |

GREECE : 1922

Black Sea

Caucasus

Samsun

Trebizond

jora

Mt Ararat ▲

Erzerum

I A

Sivas

Lake Van   • Van

U R K E Y

Mosul

S Y R I A

US

Beirut

• Damascus

ea

PALESTINE

TRANS-JORDAN

id

• Jerusalem

N
W   E
S

0   miles   200
0   kilometres   300

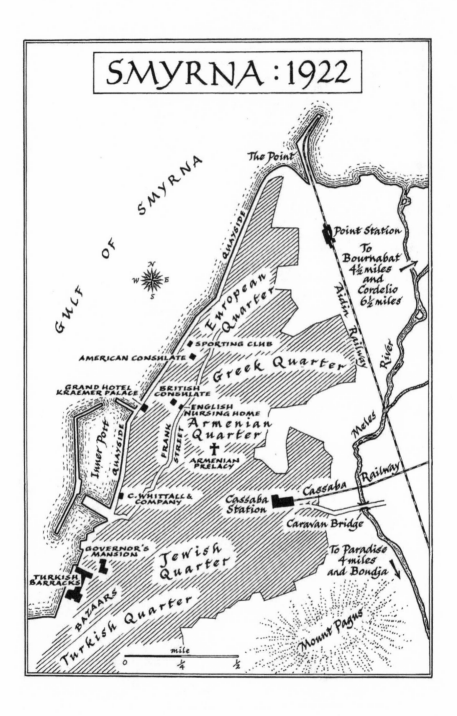

SMYRNA : 1922

The Point

GULF OF SMYRNA

European Quarter

Point Station
To Bournabat
4½ miles
and
Cordelio
6½ miles

Aidin Railway

River

SPORTING CLUB

AMERICAN CONSULATE

Greek Quarter

GRAND HOTEL
KRAEMER PALACE

BRITISH
CONSULATE

ENGLISH
NURSING HOME

Armenian
Quarter

ARMENIAN
PRELACY

Melas

Inner Port
QUAYSIDE

FRANK STREET

C. WHITTALL &
COMPANY

Cassaba Station

Cassaba Railway

Caravan Bridge

GOVERNOR'S
MANSION

Jewish
Quarter

To Paradise
4 miles
and Bondja

TURKISH
BARRACKS

BAZAARS

Turkish Quarter

Mount Pagus

mile

0   ¼   ½

THE GREEK MILITARY ADVANCE

Black Sea

Constantinople

Sea of Marmara

Izmit

Panderma

Ayvali

Eskishehir

Angora

Kutahya

River Sakaria

Smyrna

Ushak

Afyon Karahisar

Aidin

Mediterranean Sea

| 0 | miles | 200 |
| 0 | kilometres | 300 |

- - - - - - GREEK FRONT, SUMMER 1919 — JUNE 1920

— — — — AUGUST 1920 — JUNE 1921

▬ ▬ ▬ ▬ LINE HELD BY GREEKS, SEPTEMBER 1921 — AUGUST 1922

▬▬▬ FURTHEST POINT OF GREEK ADVANCE, AUGUST — SEPTEMBER 1921

A Note on Sources

The source material for *Paradise Lost* has been gathered largely from unpublished letters and diaries written by the great Levantine dynasties who had made Smyrna their home. These writings, which were never intended for publication, were often written at speed and in the most desperate circumstances.

Although many of the Levantine authors held British nationality, they had never lived in Britain and often spoke six or seven languages. This gave rise to a delightfully quirky and eccentric style in their private musings. I decided against correcting their numerous grammatical errors. But I have standardised spelling, provided translations for Turkish words and phrases and supplied full names whenever the author uses initials.

There is currently no archive of the Smyrniot Levantine families and their heritage is in danger of being lost. It is the author's intention to deposit all the documents collected during his researches in Exeter University Library, which already houses a portion of the Whittall family records.

PART ONE

Paradise

Wheel of Fortune

The Turkish cavalry presented a magnificent spectacle as it cantered along the waterfront. The horsemen sat high in their saddles, their scimitars unsheathed and glinting in the sun. On their heads they wore black Circassian fezzes adorned with the crescent and star. As they rode, they cried out, '*Korkma! Korkma!*' 'Fear not! Fear not!'

Their entry into the city of Smyrna on 9 September 1922 was watched by thousands of anxious inhabitants. On the terrace of the famous Sporting Club, a group of British businessmen rose to their feet in order to catch a better view of the historic scene. From the nearby Greek warehouses, the packers and stevedores spilled out onto the quayside. 'Long Live Kemal,' they cried nervously, praising the man who would soon acquire the sobriquet Ataturk.

News of the troops' arrival quickly spread to the American colony of Paradise, where Dr Alexander MacLachlan, director of the American International College, was keeping a watchful eye for signs of trouble. He ran up the Stars and Stripes over the college building as a precaution and jotted down some contingency plans. Yet he remained sanguine in the face of the day's events. When the British consul, Sir Harry Lamb, had offered to help with the evacuation of American citizens, MacLachlan politely declined. 'I felt we were not taking any risk by remaining at our post,' he later wrote.

Throughout the course of the day, Smyrna held its breath. The Turkish cavalry's triumphant entry came at the end of a brutal, three-year war with Greece – a war fought on Turkish territory in which Britain, and other Western powers, had aided and armed the Greeks.

Now, it was feared that there would be a backlash. Smyrna was known throughout the world of Islam for having a majority Christian population and there were concerns that the newly victorious Turkish army would sweep into the city to unleash a terrible fury on the infidel inhabitants. This, after all, was a city whose gaze had long been turned westwards towards Greece and the warm waters of the Aegean. Smyrna had little in common with the barren hinterlands of central Anatolia from whence the Turkish cavalry had come. She had a Greek population that was at least twice that of Athens and the reminders of her great Byzantine heritage were to be found scattered throughout the city. In the candlelit gloom of her cuspidated churches, Orthodox priests chanted dirges for the soul of St Polycarp, martyred here in the second century. Even at that early date, Smyrna had an impeccable Christian pedigree. St John the Divine had named the city one of the Seven Churches of Asia Minor.

By 1922, its Christian population included Greeks, Armenians, Levantines, Europeans and Americans. Many feared that St John's apocalyptic vision of doom was about to come to pass. There were dark predictions of a return to the days of old, when conquering Islamic armies were sanctioned three days of pillage, following the capture of a resisting town.

Yet there had been no resistance to the Turkish army and few inhabitants could really believe that their city would meet with such a fate. Smyrna had long been celebrated as a beacon of tolerance – home to scores of nationalities with a shared outlook and intertwined lives. It was little wonder that the

4

Americans living in the metropolis had named their colony Paradise; life here was remarkably free from prejudice and many found it ironic that they had to come to the Islamic world to find a place that had none of the bigotry so omnipresent at home.

There was another reason why Smyrna's inhabitants were confident that the city would be spared. In the harbour there was the reassuring presence of no fewer than twenty-one battle-ships, including eleven British, five French and several Italian. There were also three large American destroyers, among them the newly arrived USS *Litchfield*. Everyone believed that these ships would deter the Turkish army from committing any excesses.

By mid-afternoon of that day, the population breathed a collective sigh of relief. It was clear that the doom-laden predictions were wrong. Smyrna had been spared. In the tranquil suburb of Bournabat, where the great Levantine dynasties had their mansions, there were many who felt that the sense of panic had been overblown from the start. Hortense Wood had spent much of the morning peering out of her drawing-room window at the passing cavalry. Now, she felt that the danger had passed. 'Perfect discipline and perfect quiet,' she noted in her diary. 'Not a shot was fired. And thus came the change from Greek to Turkish administration, in perfect tranquillity and against all expectations and apprehensions.'

She also felt vindicated. She had confidently predicted to her family that people were making a fuss about nothing and had insisted all along that Smyrna would fall peacefully into Turkish hands.

Others actually welcomed the arrival of the Turkish army after long days of uncertainty. Grace Williamson, an English nurse living in the city, was relieved and happy that it was all over. 'What a week we have spent!!' she wrote. 'There was hardly a bit of trouble . . . No shooting on the streets! Thank God.

Such a relief, everyone is inwardly delighted to have the Turks back again.'

What happened over the two weeks that followed must surely rank as one of the most compelling human dramas of the twentieth century. Innocent civilians – men, women and children from scores of different nationalities – were caught in a humanitarian disaster on a scale that the world had never before seen. The entire population of the city became the victim of a reckless foreign policy that had gone hopelessly, disastrously wrong.

The American consul, George Horton, witnessed scenes of such horror that he would carry them with him to the grave. 'One of the keenest impressions which I brought away from Smyrna,' he wrote, 'was a feeling of shame that I belonged to the human race.'

The *New York Times* put it even more succinctly. 'Smyrna Wiped Out', was its headline. It was not hyperbole; it was a bold statement of fact.

Smyrna's hundreds of thousands of refugees clung to the hope that the Western governments who had done so much to precipitate the crisis would now come to their rescue. But those governments displayed a shocking callousness towards their own nationals, choosing to abandon the refugees to their fate in order not to jeopardise the chance of striking rich deals with the newly victorious Turkish regime.

Amidst the suffering there were to be acts of supreme heroism – men and women who risked their lives to save those caught up in a nightmare beyond their control. One of these individuals would launch what was to prove the most extraordinary rescue operation of the modern age, even though it seemed as if a miracle would be needed to save the vast crowds before they were consumed by the unfolding cataclysm.

No individual was able to avert the even greater crisis that occurred in the aftermath of Smyrna's destruction. Almost two million people were to find themselves caught up in a catastrophe on a truly epic scale, one that sent shock waves across Europe and America and was to cause the downfall of two governments. As families were forcibly evicted from their ancestral homes – and 2,000 years of Christian civilisation in Asia Minor came to an abrupt end – a vibrant new country came into being. Ataturk's modern Turkish republic arose from the ashes of Smyrna.

The events of September 1922 are fast becoming just another chapter of history. Yet to a handful of people – all in their nineties – the destruction of Smyrna continues to haunt them every day of their lives.

'Now, how would you like to converse?' asks Petros Brussalis, ninety-three years of age when I visit him at his home in Athens. He speaks with an accent as crisp and old-fashioned as a Huntley and Palmer biscuit. 'Greek? French? English? My English is a trifle rusty these days.'

His enunciation is that of his Edwardian governess; his sentiments are those of a man who has never quite recovered from the loss of his childhood. 'Forget Constantinople, Alexandria and Beirut,' he says. 'Smyrna before the *katastrophi* was the most cosmopolitan place on earth.'

The city into which Petros was born was one in which fig-laden camels nudged their way past the latest Newton Bennett motor car; in which the strange new vogue of the cinema was embraced as early as 1908. There were seventeen companies dealing exclusively in imported Parisian luxuries. And if Petros's father cared to read a daily newspaper, he had quite a choice: eleven Greek, seven Turkish, five Armenian, four French and five Hebrew, not to mention the ones shipped in from every capital city in Europe.

The Brussalis family were well-to-do merchants whose offices stood in the heart of Smyrna. In the late afternoon, when the infamous *imbat* or west wind blew in off the sea, Petros's father and mother would dress up in their finery and join the evening *passeggiata* along the Aegean waterfront. The imposing banks and clubhouses that lined the quayside were tangible symbols of Smyrna's prosperity. The Sporting Club, Grand Hotel Kraemer Palace and Théâtre de Smyrne were built on such a grand scale that their whitewashed walls, glimmering in the sunshine, were visible for miles out to sea.

Amidst the grandeur there was intense human activity. Hawkers and street traders peddled their wares along the mile-long quayside. Water sellers jangled their brass bowls; *hodjas* – Muslim holy men – mumbled prayers in the hope of earning a copper or two. And impecunious legal clerks, often Italian, would proffer language lessons at knock-down prices.

'You saw all sorts . . .' recalled the French journalist, Gaston Deschamps. 'Swiss hoteliers, German traders, Austrian tailors, English mill owners, Dutch fig merchants, Italian brokers, Hungarian bureaucrats, Armenian agents and Greek bankers.'

The waterfront was lined with lively bars, brasseries and shaded café gardens, each of which tempted the palate with a series of enticing scents. The odour of roasted cinnamon would herald an Armenian patisserie; apple smoke spilled forth from hookahs in the Turkish cafés. Coffee and olives, crushed mint and armagnac: each smell was distinctive and revealed the presence of more than three dozen culinary traditions. Caucasian pastries, *boeuf à la mode*, Greek game pies and Yorkshire pudding could all be found in the quayside restaurants of Smyrna.

It was not just the Brussalises' noses that enjoyed the evening promenade. The arias of frivolous Italian operettas drifted out from the open-air bandstands while the honky-tonk of ragtime conveyed a message of fun from the more outré establishments. Consul George Horton, a contemporary of Petros's parents, recalled that each café 'had its favourite *politakia* or orchestra of guitars, mandolins and zithers and the entertainers grew increasingly animated as more and more wine was consumed'.

Horton had lived in many places in the world, but nowhere caught his imagination like Smyrna. It had the climate of southern California, the architecture of the Côte d'Azur and the allure of nowhere else on earth. 'In no city in the world did East and West mingle physically in so spectacular a manner,' he wrote.

The city was dominated by the Greeks. They numbered 320,000 and had a virtual monopoly on the trade in the sticky figs, sultanas and apricots for which Smyrna was so famous. They also owned many of the city's flagship businesses, including the two largest department stores, Xenopoulo and Orisdiback, which sold imported goods from across the globe.

It was in this first emporium, more than eight decades ago, that the young Petros Brussalis got his first taste of luxury. He remembers accompanying his mother and three haughty aunts on extravagant shopping expeditions that included obligatory pit-stops at these two stores. The Brussalis family lived in Cordelio on the far side of the bay. From here, a short ferry ride brought them to the city centre – an exciting adventure for a five-year-old boy, although Petros disliked being dragged from store to store by four chattering women, who insisted on dressing in fancy hats for their shopping outings. 'I didn't like it at all,' he recalls with half a smile. 'Even as a very young boy I thought it was beneath my dignity. Worse still, my aunts would give me their packages to carry.'

But young Petros's eyes would widen when his female entourage swept into Xenopoulo on Frank Street. '*Everything* was imported from overseas,' he recalls. 'Biscuits, big tins, chocolates, lemon drops. To this day I can remember the names of them all.'

The Greeks had left their mark on every walk of life. Smyrna boasted scores of Orthodox churches and almost as many schools. The young Aristotle Onassis was one of the many local Greeks who attended the famous Aronis School.

Many of the city's best hotels, brasseries and cafés were also run by Greeks, establishments like the Acropoli, Luxembourg and North Pole. Yet Greek ownership did not lead to an exclusively Greek clientele. The Frenchman, Louis de Launay, passed one café and recalled seeing 'green turbans, red fezzes, embroidered Armenian hats, pink on a black backing, and the gleaming glass of the hookah pipes'.

The centre of Greek business was on the waterfront, where the wealthiest merchants had their trading houses. One of these was Petros's godfather, a fig exporter who sold his fruit to merchants from far and wide.

'You'd hear every language under the sun on the quayside,' recalls Petros, 'and see ships from everywhere in the world. There were so many of them that they'd have to moor with their sterns to the quay.'

The harbour was indeed one of the great sights of Smyrna. There were thirty-three steamboat companies catering for passenger liners arriving almost daily from London, Liverpool, Marseilles, Genoa, Brindisi, Trieste and Constantinople, as well as all the principal ports of the Levant.

As merchandise and fruit was loaded onto the merchant ships, Petros's godfather would select the ripest and stickiest figs and present them to his young charge. 'I also remember him choosing one special crate which he presented each year to the King and Queen of England.'

Greeks could be found living right across the city; the European community congregated in their own quarter just behind the quayside. Alfred Simes, a sprightly ninety-seven when I met him, recalls street festivities taking place almost every night of the week. 'In the evenings, the maids would sweep the dust from the street and place armchairs outside the houses,' he says. 'Of course there were very few cars in those days. Everyone came out into the street after their supper and offered cakes and sweets to their neighbours and friends. At Christmas, we'd all sing carols in French, Greek, English and Italian.'

Frank Street was the principal artery that ran through the European quarter. It had been laid out long before the advent of the motor car and was very narrow – too narrow, even, to cope with the human traffic. Yet in spite of the bustle, heat, noise and collisions with donkeys and camels, it remained the city's most popular street for shopping. When Marcel Mirtil came here on his world tour in 1909, it was the hair salons that caught his attention. 'In sheer size, they were reminiscent of ballrooms.'

Here, too, were the city's principal banks – the Imperial Ottoman, Credit Lyonnais, the British Oriental and the Bank of Vienna. No fewer than seven countries had their own postal systems that worked alongside the Ottoman system. And there were several dozen maritime insurance companies.

One of Alfred Simes's earliest memories is standing on tiptoes at his bedroom window and watching a daily procession of bowlers, fezzes and homburgs passing along Boulevard Aliotti, the street where his family lived. 'The gentlemen of business were always so impeccably smart,' he recalls. 'They wore the finest tailored suits and hats.'

The European quarter's most ostentatious building was the Grand Hotel Kraemer Palace, with its gigantic foyer and capacious dining rooms.

> In the first salon, [wrote one French hotel guest] there was a group of English visitors, crimson with sunburn (it was a Thomas Cook tour, just returned from Jerusalem) ... There were Young Turks from an operetta, fezzes on their heads; an open bed spread out in a corner; exotic rugs

from Turkestan and Persia hanging on the walls; on a small table inlaid with mother-of-pearl were placed dirty plates, and one could hear constantly one of the waiters saying, '*Oui, Monsieur le Prince* . . .'

Baedeker's guidebook particularly recommended the hotel for its ice-cold pilsen beer imported from Munich. The Kraemer Palace also offered German newspapers and had the city's finest brasserie, serving such specialities as *sauerbraden* and *blanquette d'agneau* to a bustling international clientele.

English, Greeks and Germans coming and going; some [guests] wearing Hindu headgear, others in the latest fashions from London. The Thomas Cook tour was at the table; its guide at the head, making a little speech between each course. They were quite charming, these English, as pink as cooked lobsters with their straw sunhats, veils attached, and a vacant expression that is so characteristic of the English young things, who are always in the habit of going, 'Ooh!'

Adjacent to the European area of Smyrna was the vibrant Armenian quarter, home to another of Smyrna's wealthy communities. The Armenians, who numbered around 10,000, had a reputation for being diligent and conscientious. One of those who lived here – a doctor named Garabed Hatcherian – would later write a chronicle of his life in the city. 'After three years of hard work in Smyrna I had achieved a measure of success,' he recorded on the opening page of his notebook. 'I was doing well, having become the physician of a great number of wealthy families.' Similar sentiments are echoed time and again in the jottings of Smyrna's Armenians. They were indeed 'doing well' and they had learned to enjoy their bourgeois creature comforts.

The nearby Jewish quarter had traditionally been one of the

most squalid, but by 1909, when Marcel Mirtil visited, it had been modernised and given sanitation. It nevertheless retained the same picturesque quality that had charmed the travellers of the previous century. The women still wore traditional Oriental costumes and had a reputation for beauty, although to Mirtil's critical eye their girth was rather 'too opulent'. The Jews were equally at home doing business with Greeks or Turks. 'Extremely polyglot,' wrote Gaston Deschamps, 'they're able to speak Turkish with the Turks and Greek with the Greeks.' He was interested to note that among themselves they still spoke a dialect of Spanish, a legacy of their expulsion from Spain in 1492.

The Americans were rather more recent arrivals. They started to pour into Smyrna in the late nineteenth century and soon became one of the city's distinct communities. They lived for the most part in Paradise – a large colony on the fringes of the city – and founded important educational and humanitarian institutions, including the American International College, an Intercollegiate Institute, a YMCA and a YWCA. They also owned the Standard Oil Company, whose big steel drum could be seen at the far end of the quayside. The Americans employed many thousands of workers – especially the MacAndrews and Forbes liquorice firm – and were respected for their charitable endeavours.

They were ably represented by their gregarious consul, George Horton, who was at the centre of every social activity. 'Teas, dances, musical afternoons and evenings were given in the luxurious salons of the rich Armenians and Greeks,' he wrote. 'There were four large clubs: the *Cercle de Smyrne*, frequented mostly by British, French and Americans; the "Sporting" with a fine building and garden on the quay; the Greek Club and a Country Club near the American college with excellent golf links and a race course.'

Horton's easygoing nature and determination to enjoy himself earned him and his fellow Americans much popularity among the Smyrniots.

Foreign tourists arriving on the daily passenger liners were always taken to the picturesque Turkish quarter of the city, which sprawled up the rocky flanks of Mount Pagus. This area was the most overcrowded and dilapidated, a maze of makeshift houses, cafés, little stores and Muslim shrines.

The majority of the 140,000 people who lived here were artisans and craftsmen '[employed] in the manufacture of copper utensils, camel bells, horseshoes, locks, chains [and] drums for packing figs'. So wrote Sir Charles Wilson, author of *Murray's Handbook*, who added that these were the only Turks who still dressed in traditional costume. Visitors flocked to the souk in search of the fabled Orient, but even in the poorest part of town, they would find the same imported items that were on sale elsewhere in the city. Louis de Launay noticed 'all sorts of bits and bobs from Europe. Here, a stall resembling the Louvre, there, one that's more like Bon Marché. Boots that are "ready to wear"; Indian cottons from Manchester, elasticated bowties, Swiss watches; stall holders in frock coats and fezzes; buyers in Western dress.'

Although the Turks played a marginal role in the commerce of Smyrna, they dominated the politics of the city. The Ottoman governor of Smyrna was traditionally always a Turkish national and his primary task was to represent the interests of all the different nationalities who had made the city their home. A glance at the 1913 census reveals why his job was not easy. Smyrna's Christians outnumbered the Muslims by more than two to one; his was a majority Christian city in a resolutely Muslim world. To many Turks – and especially to government ministers in Constantinople – Smyrna had forever been the city of the infidel.

'*Vous êtes interessé par Rahmi Bey?*' said a clipped voice on the end of the telephone. 'You must visit me. Today. At four o'clock.'

I had come on the trail of the affable, irascible and benignly despotic Rahmi Bey, governor of Smyrna at the time when Petros Brussalis and Alfred Simes were still young boys. Rahmi's elderly daughter-in-law, the tantalisingly worldly Esma Dino Deyer, still lives in the Ottoman mansion that was for a brief period the governor's private residence. From the outside, it presented a picture of sorry decline. Newspaper-sized sheets of paintwork had detached themselves from the rendering and the latticed shutters were veiled in dust. But inside, its elegant marble atrium was redolent of a more refined epoch.

I was ushered into the principal drawing room, where an imposing portrait of Rahmi Bey hung above the fireplace. We sat in near-darkness, for the shutters were kept closed and showed no signs of having been opened for half a century or more. On the floor there were richly coloured carpets from Persia and Turkmenistan. On the settle there was a pistol and a scimitar.

'He was rich, extremely cultivated and spoke impeccable French,' said Esma, as she slotted a Balkan cigarette into an ivory holder. 'And his wife came from an old and distinguished Ottoman family.'

Rahmi was to prove a benevolently devious governor. His machiavellian politicking during the First World War ought to have cost him his life, yet once-secret papers in the National Archives in Kew reveal that Rahmi was always one step ahead of his masters in Constantinople.

Rahmi Bey, in common with many of the city's elite, lived in one of the elegant suburbs that formed a ring around the metropolis. These leafy districts, which had begun life as country villages, were popular with Smyrna's Levantine bourgeoisie.

The Levantines were by far the richest community in the area. Of European descent, but thoroughly versed in the ways of the Orient, they had lived in Turkey since the reign of King

George III. They, more than any other community, had helped to shape Smyrna in their own image – rich, cosmopolitan and of mixed blood and heritage. Their factories and mines employed all, regardless of race or nationality. And they had a concern for their workforce that was patrician in sentiment and philanthropic in outlook. In the dark days of the First World War, many of Smyrna's families would owe their continued existence to the Levantine magnates.

They had the largest financial stake in every commercial activity in the city. They controlled Smyrna's shipping companies, insurance agencies, mines, banks and all of the most profitable import-export businesses. Cotton textiles and carpets were two of the most important exports and had provided the foundations of their vast fortunes. Dried fruit, too, was hugely lucrative. The Levantines also imported many goods to Turkey, including coffee, sugar and furs.

Their businesses were on a truly grand scale. One of the Giraud family's trading wings, the Oriental Carpet Manufacturing Company, employed 150,000 people, many of them inhabitants of Smyrna. The Whittalls' business empire – which included a massive fruit-exporting enterprise – was even larger.

The majority of Levantines lived in Cordelio, Boudja or Paradise, three of the more expensive and sought-after garden suburbs. They were places of excitement in the early years of the twentieth century, for there was a frisson of danger that was not present in the city itself. When Petros was a young boy, brigands still haunted the snow-dusted peaks of Nymph Dagh that formed the backdrop to the port. And picnic excursions to Lake Tantalus, undertaken in a barouche with Greek bazouki players, could quite easily end in a shoot-out. Gwynneth Giraud, elderly matriarch of the Giraud clan, can still remember her grandmother recounting stories of a running gun battle in the grounds of their suburban mansion. As I sipped Earl Grey tea in the shade of a chestnut tree, she showed me where brigands had fired pot-shots at her grandfather more than 120 years earlier.

The Girauds lived in the spectacular Levantine colony of Bournabat, where all the most exclusive addresses were to be found. Lying some six miles from the city centre – and dominated by rambling villas and pleasure gardens – Bournabat was home to many of the great dynasties that had done so much to shape Smyrna.

The Giraud family, the Woods and the Patersons, along with many others, all lived in palatial mansions. All, too, commanded vast fortunes. But even among the very rich there was a strict hierarchy of power. There was one family in Bournabat that wielded more influence – and had done more to engender Smyrna's unique spirit – than their surrounding neighbours put together.

Tuesday, 11 March 1902

Dearest Mother,

These are most delightful people. Helen Whittall . . . came to fetch me at 11 and we journeyed up here together . . . Mr Whittall joined us and there were also troops of cousins, for they all live out here. The house is a great big place with high enormous rooms, set in a garden 200 years old, across which a line of splended cypresses runs. The old mother of the tribe, Mr Whittall's mother, lives here, a very old woman who kissed me when I came in. We lunched, after which we walked about in the garden gathering bunches of roses and violets. Mrs Herbert Whittall is a very nice sweet woman, and the girl Helen a dear. It was a stormy day with sudden bursts of rain and bright sun between, so we did nothing more until we had had a cheerful schoolroom tea, after which Mr and Mrs Whittall and I

went to see a brother of his, Mr Edward Whittall, who
is a great botanist and has a most lovely garden. He
collects bulbs and sends new varieties to Kew and is
well known among gardeners – an interesting man, too,
for he is the Vali's [the city governor's] right hand and is
consulted by him on all matters, a thing unbeknown
before, they say. But these people get on with the Turks.
The old sultan, uncle of Abdul Hamed, stayed in this
house; it is the only private house which has received a
sultan.

When Gertrude Bell visited the Whittalls of Smyrna in the
spring of 1902, she caught a tantalising glimpse of a private
world. The Whittall family had amassed a spectacular fortune
over the previous five decades. By the time King Edward VII
came to the throne in distant England, they wielded more influence than at any previous point during their long years in the
Orient. Sultan Abdul Aziz had indeed beaten a path to their
door, an extraordinary acknowledgement that such trading dynasties were helping to prop up the ailing Ottoman empire. He
arrived early and spent the entire day with the Whittalls, inviting
local notables to an audience in the large garden marquee. The
sultan showed particular interest in the family's private botanical garden and, 'at his own request, was ushered into the
Protestant Church at Bournabat, built by Mr Whittall some years
previously'. Upon his return to Constantinople, he sent his
Minister of Foreign Affairs back to Smyrna with brooches for
two of the Whittall ladies: 'a costly souvenir . . . set with large
brilliants and pearls'.

Almost forty years had passed since the sultan's 1863 visit and
the intervening time had only served to increase the family's
fortune. C. Whittall and Company had expanded to become
the largest Levantine-owned business in Smyrna. 'My Whittall
friends . . . have the bulk of the English trade in their hands,'

noted Bell, 'branch offices all down the southern coast, mines and shooting boxes and properties scattered up and down the S. W. coast of Asia Minor and yachts on the sea.'

Their principal residences were in Bournabat, which was connected by railway to the city. Each member of the family had his or her designated seat on the steam train. Such privileges seemed a part of the natural order of life. After all, the British owned and managed the railway.

Complex marriage alliances had enabled the family to strengthen still further their commercial grip on the metropolis. The Whittalls, Girauds, La Fontaines, Charnauds, Alibertis, Williamsons, Patersons and Reeses (among many others) were all intermarried and all had hundreds of cousins in common. Procreation came about as naturally and annually as the company profits. A brief glance at their family trees reveals extraordinary fecundity and an alarming cocktail of mixed blood. If a Whittall boy married a Giraud girl one year, then it could be expected that a Giraud boy would reciprocate in the year that followed.

The family also had a singular attachment to names, rendering their genealogy well-nigh unintelligible to outsiders. Take the two Whittall brothers, Charlton and James. Charlton's sons were named Charlton and James. And James's sons were named James and Charlton. When one of these Jameses had sons of his own, he named two of them Charlton and one of them James. In time, there were dozens of Jameses and Charltons, all of whom could claim descent from Charlton and James. A family tree recently compiled by a surviving Whittall runs to more than seventy pages and reveals the complexities of Smyrna's intermarried families. '[We] called everyone aunt or uncle to be on the safe side,' recalled one of the Whittall grandchildren in her memoirs.

Matriarch of them all was the formidable Magdalen Whittall, descendant of a pirate-prince, who ruled her family fiefdom with all the swagger of an Oriental despot. She was destined to remain as head of the family for fully twenty-nine years after the death of her husband. It was she who had welcomed Gertrude Bell to Bournabat; Bell described her as 'mother of the tribe'.

As indeed she was. Magdalen produced thirteen children, ninety-one grandchildren and 256 great-grandchildren – offspring who would together help to shape the character and prosperity of Smyrna. Magdalen, meanwhile, was doing her utmost to shape them. She imposed her will on them with a severity that continued to terrify them long after she had died. Brooking neither dissent nor disobedience, she abhorred any of her children who might dare to call into question her pronounce-ments on matters concerning the family. 'She ruled over them till the end,' recalled one of her great-granddaughters, 'and during most of her lifetime, her word was law.'

With her imposing manner and unshakeable belief in her own importance, she seemed to embody all the qualities and weaknesses of the Levantines of Smyrna. She expected daily visits from her offspring – for which she would sit in state in the garden of the Big House, awaiting their arrival – and she tolerated no excuse for non-attendance. They called her Old Dudu, a Turkish term of endearment that meant something akin to 'old parrot'.

Magdalen was accustomed to being accompanied by her personal *kavass* or bodyguard, a fearsome bandit who wore 'a scarlet sash-like belt wound three times round his waist and stuck with daggers and pistols and other fierce paraphernalia'. He was always dressed in an embroidered jacket 'over which silver chains hung in tiers round his neck, flashing in the sun with each movement he took as he guided the old lady to her deck chair'.

Magdalen's favourite party of the winter season was the Whittalls' annual Christmas dinner, held in the gilded ballroom of the Big House. It was attended by at least a hundred adult members of the close family and scores of children, all of whom could claim their bloodline from Magdalen. 'Her Christmas dinner was one of the events of the year,' wrote one of those children, 'and, surrounded by a court of her grown-up children, she received her guests with all the dignity of an Eastern potentate.'

Gertrude Bell was entranced by the formidable Magdalen and her extended family. Industrious yet carefree, their lives seemed a heady blend of patrician duty and footloose frivolity. 'The sons [are] young men now in various Whittall businesses,' she wrote. 'The daughters very charming, very gay. The big gardens touch on one another and they walk in and out of one another's houses all day long, gossiping and laughing. I should think life presents itself nowhere under such easy and pleasant conditions.'

At the time of Bell's visit, the elderly Magdalen's authority was approaching its apogee, yet her power was totemic rather than real. The day-to-day running of the Whittall business empire was in the hands of three of her eight sons: Richard, Edward and Herbert Octavius. Of these, it was Herbert who inherited all the spunk and ebullience of his mother.

He was 'stern and uncompromising' according to one member of the family; 'hard and uncompromising' according to another. Patrician in sentiment, with a strict sense of duty, he remained in Smyrna right up to the terrible events of 1922 and became an important source of information for the British government. His grandchildren joshed among themselves that the initials of his name spelled the word 'HOW', 'but no one added a question mark', recalled one, '[and] no one would have dared to make a joke of it, for he was a formidable man'. A photograph of him taken in about 1910 reveals his sang-froid. Unlike his brothers, smiling and genial, his piercing eyes stare directly and chillingly into the camera.

Herbert was the eleventh of thirteen children and in any other family might have contented himself with a modest career in the Church. Yet it was he, not his elders, who became the effective head of the company and he who inherited the Big House. It was a perfect reflection of his personality – grand, chilly and austere.

The house had first been acquired by old James Whittall in 1820. Since that time it had been greatly enlarged and embellished so that it now included scores of reception rooms as well as a gilded ballroom, vast dining room, drawing room and library. From these rooms, visitors had a spectacular view of the Magnesia mountains, the cone-shaped Bel Khave and the snow-capped Nymph Dagh, home to ibex and wild boar. Herbert Octavius, a voracious hunter, had the great entrance hall mounted with scores of trophies and stuffed animals. His grandchildren were particularly terrified of an adult black bear that stood guard by the front door, its front paws outstretched and its bare teeth exposed in a snarl.

They were equally scared of their great-aunts. Three of them – Jane, Blanche and Mary – always used to take their afternoon promenade together. 'They were all three widowed at that time,' wrote one of the grandchildren, 'and were dressed in black from head to foot. It was a strange procession. They walked in single file, hardly speaking to each other, having perhaps little in common except a united desire for exercise.' No less frightening was Aunt Coralie. 'Who she was I never knew, but once a year we had to parade in front of her. She had a famous talking parrot and she was reputed not to have washed her hair for years, but always to clean it with eau-de-cologne.'

Not every member of the family chilled the blood quite as much as Herbert Octavius and his widowed sisters. His brother Richard, a partner in the business, was 'open handed [and] of a genial gay disposition'. He was rarely parted from his beloved hookah pipe, which he smoked with as much enthusiasm as the native Turks.

Another of the brothers was Edward, a firm favourite with

the Whittall youngsters. His branch of the family lived in their own vast mansion, which stood just a few minutes' walk from the Big House. Yet there was a world of difference in the feel of the two places. 'It was a most lovable house,' recalled Edward's niece. 'It had the unstudied charm and graciousness which comes from the daily use of beautiful things, and it was alive and without pomp. It rambled all over the place and was madly inconvenient, needing a regiment of servants to keep it going.'

The drawing room and dining room opened onto the winter garden, making them rather dark, and the deep-red velvet curtains added to the impression of twilight, but there were ample treasures to brighten the gloom. 'The dining room shone with silver, and the old-fashioned pergne in the centre was filled with flowers which cascaded down on all sides.' For the children, the only person to be avoided was Marco the head chef, who presided over the kitchen like an autocrat. 'The only time I can remember him being really pleasant was one April Fool's Day,' wrote one of those children many years later, 'when he condescended to fry some cotton-wool in batter and serve it instead of brains to one of our uncles at breakfast.'

Edward Whittall's passion was gardening and he devoted long hours to his spectacular botanical garden that climbed up the hillsides in sweeping terraces. There were Judas trees and ginkgo trees, giant cypresses and cream-flowered magnolias. Giant chestnuts kept the great lawns in shadow during the hottest hours of the day, while turpentine trees added a spicy scent to the air. Swings were attached to the rose arbour. It was a paradise for the numerous young cousins who played here together, refreshing themselves on the juicy oranges and limes that fell from the trees.

Edward Whittall had many glasshouses in which he propagated rare and exotic specimens. He also had a large mountain garden on the slopes of Nymph Dagh, where he grew bulbs, as well as an orchard in the village. He sent tens of thousands of specimens to the director of Kew Gardens and had a tulip and fritillary named after him. 'Whittall is smiling all over the place,' reads one letter written by Kew's head gardener.

Such frivolous pursuits never took place in the neighbouring Big House, whose garden was formal and filled with 'rather dull shrubs'. Its most distinguishing feature was a long avenue of cypress trees that led to the wrought-iron entrance gates. These gates opened out onto the principal square in Bournabat – the meeting point of five roads, including the main thoroughfare into Smyrna.

Each of the Levantine houses had a Florentine-style loggia situated just outside the gates. This was where the elderly members of the family would gather in late afternoon in order to share gossip and pass on news. All would defer to the elderly Magdalen, who would be flanked by her bodyguard, 'staff in hand, [who] stood by her side like a guard of honour. The leaders of all the caravans passing through the village had to get off their donkeys and bow to her,' recalled one. 'If they neglected to do so, the *kavass* quickly taught them manners.'

The mansion that stood next to the Big House was owned by the Wood family, another formidable dynasty that lived under the patrician care of Mr Ernest. He was a starched and steely individual who, even by Edwardian standards, seemed to belong to another era. He saw it as his duty to take the ladies of the family for rides in his carriage and was punctilious in his observance of correct etiquette. 'No one quite equalled the flourish of these expeditions,' recalled one. 'The handling of the ladies, the correct disposal of their trailing skirts, the arrangements for the comfort of the pugs and the last-minute alterations of these all took time.' The pugs were a source of constant annoyance, as was Yanko, the stone-deaf coachman. 'Whenever Aunt Luisa wanted him to stop, she would batter him with the handle of her umbrella.'

There were many other eccentrics who had made Bournabat

their home. 'Uncle Frank' used to walk around the village with two loaded revolvers, which he would fire into the bushes whenever he was angry. Wallace Turrell was similarly explosive. '[He] was a lawyer by profession,' recalled Eldon Giraud, 'but never won a case as he always came to blows with the judge and would often be put in the same cells as the person he was defending.'

Although the Levantines were the most visible inhabitants of Bournabat, the village was also home to a large number of wealthy Greeks and Armenians – families like the Gasparians and Elmassians – who had elected to build their villas alongside those of the Levantines. The Whittall children mixed freely with the offspring of these families and often accompanied them to services at the local Orthodox church. Years later, one of those children could still recall the Greek priest 'with his long black robes, his stove-pipe hat and his long hair done up in a bun . . . [He] was an awe-inspiring figure'. She added that 'you could imagine him determinedly going up to heaven in a chariot of fire, whereas our quiet, sober little parson would have hesitated to summon a cab'.

The Greek priest was a close friend of the Whittalls and a regular visitor to the Big House. '[He] came to visit the servants and to bless the house at certain times of the year.' So, too, did the local Catholic priest, Père Innocent. '[He] was nothing if not worldly [and] came to breakfast with my uncle and to have long, philosophical discussions with him.'

The patrician families of Bournabat felt at ease in any society, whether Levantine, Greek, Armenian or Turkish. One of the Whittalls remembers her father undertaking winter business expeditions into the heart of Anatolia, dressed in a cloak and astrakhan hat, and looking much like a Turk. 'When he stayed in the houses of his Turkish colleagues, he merged into the surroundings and was perfectly at home. He was used to their ways and their conversations and was always treated as if he were one of themselves. Sitting cross-legged on the floor, he would eat from the communal dish.'

The working lives of the Levantines were punctuated by long hours of leisure and play. Boating was one of the most popular activities in Edwardian Smyrna and many families owned at least one yacht or yawl. The largest of these was a veritable leviathan, the 160-ton *Abafna* owned by Albert Aliotti, a descendant of one of Smyrna's richest families. The La Fontaines possessed three motor cruisers, as did the Whittalls, while the Giraud family owned a yacht and a motor cruiser. This latter craft was called the *Helen May* and was the plaything of Edmund Giraud, who was married to one of Magdalen Whittall's numerous grandchildren.

Edmund wrote a book entitled *Days off with Rod and Gun*; given that he spent nine months of the year pottering about on the *Helen May*, the days off must have occurred with considerable frequency. 'It was between 1908 and 1914 that Smyrna saw its happiest and most prosperous days,' he wrote, 'and during these few years of prosperity, yachting around Smyrna was at its best.' The yachtsmen would set off on Fridays and arrange an anchorage somewhere off the Turkish coast in order 'to shoot ashore, or to go fishing, or else simply to pass the time pleasantly in each other's company'. A photograph published in Edmund's book depicts them happily at leisure, decked in white flannels and boaters, and sniffing the stiff sea breeze.

Edmund and his friends often sailed to Long Island, which was situated in the middle of the bay. He so enjoyed these outings that in 1913 he conceived of a plan to buy land on the island and build himself a summer house. 'This, however, I found to be a difficult thing to do,' he wrote. 'In that small, isolated community, land was held as a family possession and rarely, if ever, sold. Selling land to an outsider was quite unprecedented.'

But like so many of the Levantines, Edmund was not really

an outsider. He spoke fluent Greek and had excellent contacts in the Greek community. After friendly negotiations, he acquired the land and constructed a cliff-top house with spectacular views across the bay. Henceforth, Long Island became a regular meeting point for all the Levantine yachtsmen of Smyrna.

Edmund's fortune brought many benefits to the village: he wired electricity to the fishermen's cottages and gave money to the community. In return, the villagers brought him gifts of fruit and vegetables. In the dark years that were to follow, they would have even greater reason to be grateful. Edmund's patrician sense of duty would help save the lives of many inhabitants on Long Island.

Boating was just one of many social activities enjoyed by the Levantines. The Whittalls, Girauds and their neighbours also enjoyed spectacular balls and parties in the early years of the twentieth century. In the spring of 1907, for example, Herbert Octavius's favourite club, the 'Sporting', hosted a gala-extravaganza with all-night dancing, music and theatrical interludes. It raised an enormous sum of money for the city's Israelite Orphanage and guaranteed the continued welfare of many homeless boys and girls. The charity gala's organising committee was typically Levantine in its composition: it comprised three Turks, one Greek, one Jew and one Armenian, along with representatives of all the European nationals of Smyrna.

Charitable evenings such as this were by no means unusual; Herbert Octavius was forever receiving letters of appreciation for his charitable work. And he, like all his business associates, poured his fortune into hospitals, nursing homes and orphanages.

Edwardian visitors to Smyrna remained puzzled by these Levantine dynasties, whose origins were as hybrid as the hyacinths that Edward Whittall cultivated in his glasshouses. One British vice-consul described them as 'more exuberantly patriotic than we allow ourselves to appear at home'. Yet they rarely visited their mother countries and, although the Whittalls chose resolutely English names for their sons, one side of their family was in fact Venetian in origin, descendants of the great Cortazzi dynasty. Other families in Smyrna were more open about their mixed origins. Many families had sons and daughters whose names – Polycarp, Hortense and Francesci – betrayed their convoluted bloodlines.

With their fluency in five or six languages and their extraordinary wealth to boot, the lives of these dynasties seemed untouched by the cares of the world. But unbeknown to Herbert Octavius or any of his neighbours in Bournabat, the Levantines were rapidly entering the twilight of their charmed existence. It fell to an outsider, an eccentric Englishman named William Childs, to warn them – and all the rest of Smyrna's non-Turkish communities – that they were living on borrowed time.

The Great Idea

The captain had met some oddballs in his time but this particular Englishman was stranger than most. William Childs was travelling along the Black Sea coast of Turkey accompanied by one large trunk of Cambridge sausages and dozens of tins of bacon.

When the captain enquired as to his passenger's line of business, he drew an even more startling response. Childs was not travelling on business. Rather, he was intending to walk across Anatolia, a trek that would take him across more than 1,300 miles of wild countryside. He had no desire to eat the 'native foods' during his travels, preferring to rely on his trusty sausages. He found that they set him up for the day, providing him with the energy for a long walk. No matter that his insistence on eating pork might offend Muslim sensibilities. 'I intended,' he wrote, 'to have good honest English breakfasts the whole way.'

Nor did he have any intention of trying to blend in with the local inhabitants; he was a firm believer in wearing his Englishness on his sleeve. 'The fact of being English,' he later wrote, 'was ever the most universal and respected recommendation I could possess.'

When Childs confessed that his voyage was being undertaken for the purposes of pleasure and recreation, the captain of the little mail packet began to fear for his passenger's safety. 'An

29

avowal of lunacy had been made to him . . .' wrote Childs, 'and he took it as a matter requiring immediate attention.' Childs did his best to explain why he wished to travel on foot but the captain remained unconvinced. '"Paris and Berlin and Vienna are for pleasure," he said, "but not this country." And he waved his arm towards the coast.'

Childs' plan was indeed eccentric, especially as he was setting off in winter, when the temperature was already well below zero, yet it was not entirely without logic. He saw that the world was rapidly changing and he wanted to visit the heartland of Anatolia now – in October 1912 – before the colourful old customs disappeared for ever. He had decided to travel on foot because he thought it would bring him into direct contact with the different races and peoples of the interior of the country.

But there was another reason why Childs was undertaking his voyage – one that he did not reveal to the captain. He was working as a spy, garnering intelligence for the British Secret Service. The government, fearful of Russian expansion into Anatolia, was also deeply concerned by German influence in Turkey. As the international climate grew increasingly tense, British ministers realised that they needed a more detailed report on Turkey's vast interior.

Childs never admitted his role as an undercover agent, although he dropped several hints in the book that he would later write. He suggested that his voyage had been provoked by more than idle curiosity and liked to refer to himself as 'an ever listening ear and watchful eye'. His industry seems to have impressed his bosses in Whitehall. Soon after his return to London, he was given employment in the secretive 'Room Four' of the Foreign Office, gathering sensitive information on Turkey and the Middle East.

Childs' account of his Anatolian voyage, *On Foot Through Asia Minor*, might have sold more copies if he had included the tales of banditry and abduction that he promised his readers. Yet even base metal occasionally glitters and Childs' dullness is not without sparkle. His prosaic tales of daily life in the hinterlands of the Ottoman empire are heavy with portent and reveal many of the underlying tensions that would soon tear the empire apart. As such, his book is a clarion of doom for the international city of Smyrna.

Childs' first stop was Samsun, a cosmopolitan Black Sea port that bore certain similarities with Smyrna. He had been ashore only a few hours when he caught his first glimpse of the troubles that lay ahead. He was taking refuge from the biting cold when a young boy approached him and asked for a contribution to the Greek navy. Childs was taken aback by such a provocative act but he soon learned that collections for the Greek military were a daily occurrence. The Greeks in Samsun 'look to Greece and contribute money in her aid, especially to her navy, with open-handed generosity, hoping dimly for the reconstitution of the Greek Empire with Constantinople for its capital'. Childs was told that they had raised more than £12,000 in the previous year – a significant sum of money.

Although he was not aware of it at the time, he had witnessed an event of quite extraordinary significance. More than four and a half centuries after the Byzantine empire was snuffed out by the forces of Mehmet the Conqueror, the flotsam and jetsam of that empire – Greeks left adrift in Ottoman Turkey – were casting their gaze westwards, towards the mother country.

Over the long years of Ottoman rule, many had lost touch with their patrimony. Some had abandoned their Christian faith and many more had forgotten how to speak Greek. When the English traveller, Sir William Ramsay, passed through Anatolia in the 1890s, he had been shocked to find entire communities that could no longer converse in their mother tongue.

By the time Childs was trekking over the lonely peaks of Anatolia, everything was on the point of change. Intellectuals from Athens had pushed deep into the countryside in order to teach communities about their Greek roots. Even the smallest Greek villages boasted a school that taught children the language of their forefathers. These schools were transforming the old way of life in rural Turkey. The country found itself with a new class of educated Greeks who were channelling all their energies into commerce, profit-making and politics – often at the expense of the Turks. 'The Turks have turned a blind eye to the painstaking efforts of the Greeks,' wrote Gaston Deschamps, 'little realising that the day would come when they would find themselves enslaved by those in their midst.'

Every village in Anatolia had a Greek grocery store that dominated the life of the community. As these grocers accumulated more and more wealth, they found themselves becoming banker and moneylender to their Turkish neighbours. 'The Greek grocer offers his services with one hundred per cent credit,' noted Deschamps, 'with the Turk's property as guarantee. In this way, he is skilfully managing to recover all the land that the infidel conquered from him.'

Parish priests spared no effort in reminding their flocks of their neglected heritage. 'Religion provides the link for all the Greeks in Turkey,' wrote Louis de Launay. 'The ostentatious display of their Christian faith is the best way in which they can express legally their most fervent desire . . . their future reunion into one vast and powerful Hellenic empire.'

As William Childs traipsed his way across the barren plains of central Anatolia – pausing each morning for his hearty cooked breakfast – he found the Greek revival in full swing. Some 2,000 high schools had been opened and he discovered that families who until recently had spoken only Turkish were now conversing freely in Greek. American mission schools were also playing an important role in educating the Greeks. They were run by a highly professional corporation in Massachusetts and their work was a multi-million-dollar enterprise. Many of the schools were equipped with the latest imported technology.

When Childs had set out on his extended hike, he had been filled with enthusiasm for a land that was home to scores of different nationalities. By the time he reached Anatolia's southern coastline, he was rather more sanguine. He had seen with his own eyes the tensions between these competing nationalities and had been told grim tales of ill-treatment and massacres.

Nor had his voyage been quite as comfortable as he had hoped. He finished his Cambridge sausages within a few weeks of setting out and had no option but to forgo the daily English breakfast he had promised himself.

His spirits were temporarily raised when he reached Adana and had the good fortune to be invited to a picnic hosted by the local British consul. In a delightfully bucolic setting, the consular servants 'spread a spotless table-cloth, set with table napkins, polished silver and bright glass'. As Childs regaled the consul with his experiences among the Greeks of Anatolia, a succession of platters were brought to the makeshift table. 'Roast quails, salad and wine were merely the surprises of this wayside meal.'

In spite of this end-of-voyage feast, Childs' long walk had left him with a lingering feeling of indigestion. He reported back to Whitehall that Turkey's different nationalities were close to being at loggerheads and he felt certain that any intervention by Greece in Turkey would drag the country towards catastrophe. 'You can have no idea of racial hatred,' he concluded, 'until you have seen it in this land.'

William Childs' warning of the troubles ahead fell on deaf ears. Although his footsore trudge was rewarded with a desk job in Whitehall, few seem to have heeded his call for caution. Ministers had little compunction about meddling in the internal affairs of another country and even less intention of listening to a member of their own security service. Most had made up their minds about the ailing Ottoman empire long before Childs returned from his travels.

At a dinner party held in Downing Street on 10 November 1912, Turkish affairs dominated the conversation for much of the evening. The guests at the meal table included some of the leading lights in Herbert Asquith's Liberal government, as well as the newly appointed Greek consul in London, John Stavridi. The host was Asquith's fiery Chancellor of the Exchequer, David Lloyd George.

Lloyd George's dinner-table discourse was as indiscreet as it was revealing and it would have remained secret had it not been for the fact that Stavridi was making a note of everything that was said that night. Lloyd George was to reveal a passion for Greece that would ultimately leave Smyrna a smouldering ruin.

At the time of the dinner party, he was still four years away from ousting Asquith from office and replacing him as prime minister, yet it was clear to everyone that his star was in the ascendant. 'My supreme idea is to get on,' he had written when still young. 'To this idea I shall sacrifice everything – except, I trust, my honesty.'

His time at the Treasury provided an inkling of what was to come. He had spent his time tearing apart discredited policies and injecting radical reform into Britain's antiquated tax system. He seemed to relish the constitutional crisis that was provoked by his People's Budget of 1909. He harangued his critics with searing clarity, making inflammatory speeches about the greed and rapacity of the landowning class. His National Insurance Act of 1911 was no less radical and provided the foundation stone of the welfare state.

His private life was even more tumultuous than his political one and could easily have brought an abrupt end to his political ambitions. He had enjoyed a string of lovers before marrying his wife, Margaret, and saw no reason to stop his infidelities while serving in government. While Margaret lived in Wales with the children, Lloyd George enjoyed the company of his lover-cum-secretary, Frances Stevenson. It was an arrangement that suited him perfectly. In the guise of a working relationship, Lloyd George was able to spend all his time with Frances.

Lloyd George would win the ultimate political prize in December 1916, seizing the post of prime minister in controversial circumstances. He would hold it until disaster struck in 1922, when his catastrophic policy towards Smyrna would abruptly terminate his political career.

On the evening of the dinner party, Stavridi arrived punctually at 7.30 p.m. and was ushered into the dining room of Number Eleven, Downing Street. He found Lloyd George in full flow, speaking with great animation about the ongoing Balkan conflict. For more than a month, Greece and her allies had been at war with Turkey and the Greek army had trounced Turkey in several major battles. Lloyd George had watched their progress with great interest and expressed his hope that Greece would emerge greatly strengthened from the war.

As the food was being served, he turned to the footman and called for champagne. Once everyone's glass had been charged, he proposed a toast. 'I drink to the success of the allies,' he said, 'the representative of one of whom we have here tonight, and may the Turk be turned out of Europe and sent to . . . where he came from.' The exact expletive he used has been lost to history. Even in his private diary, Stavridi declined to record Lloyd George's more scandalous turns of phrase.

As the champagne flowed, Lloyd George grew less and less guarded in his comments. '[He] said his one hope was that the Turk would now be cleared out of Europe entirely,' recalled Stavridi. 'Personally, I don't want him even to keep Constantinople.' He also praised the fighting qualities of the Greek army, whose battlefield victories had taken everyone by surprise.

The importance of Lloyd George's rhetoric was not lost on

the Greek consul; he sent a transcript of the entire conversation to the Greek prime minister. Stavridi was hopeful that Lloyd George's influence would bring about a reversal of British foreign policy, which had traditionally favoured the Turks.

Lloyd George's contemporaries were withering in their criticisms of his attachment to Greece. The historian, Arnold Toynbee, dismissed it as 'uninformed religious sentiment on behalf of Christians in conflict with non-Christians, and romantic sentiment towards the successors of the Ancient Greeks'.

There was more than a grain of truth in this and Lloyd George's 'sentiment' was made all the more reckless by the fact that he rarely listened to wiser counsel. '[He] has no respect for tradition or convention,' observed the newspaper magnate, George Riddell. 'He is always ready to examine, scrap or revise established theories and practices. These qualities give him unlimited confidence in himself . . . he is one of the craftiest of men.'

Riddell admired Lloyd George but was quick to point out his defects. 'Fondness for a grandiose scheme' was one of his habitual traits. He liked extravagant gestures and would always value boldness above caution. Another weakness was his dislike for small print: 'he is not a man of detail.' This was to have most unfortunate consequences when he came to formulate his policy regarding Smyrna.

Lloyd George was anxious to change government policy towards Greece while she had the upper hand in the Balkan War. He urged Stavridi to persuade Greece's prime minister to come to London in order that the two men could meet face to face. 'The future of Greece will be decided in London, not Athens,' he declared. 'It is a question of life or death for you.'

Lloyd George's persuasiveness soon wove its magic. Just four weeks after the Downing Street dinner party, he found himself hosting one of his famous breakfasts in honour of Greece's premier, the dazzlingly charismatic Eleftherios Venizelos.

It was to prove a most convivial meeting of minds, for there was an instant and magnetic attraction between both men. Like Lloyd George, Venizelos had a physical presence that commanded attention. He was imposing, broad-shouldered and handsome, and his wire-framed spectacles and pointed beard gave him the air of a bookish don. Lloyd George confessed that in all his years in politics he had never met anyone who left such a profound impression. 'He is a big man,' he confessed. 'A very big man.' He would later be even more exuberant in his praise, describing Venizelos as 'the greatest statesman Greece had thrown up since the days of Pericles'.

Lloyd George was fond of hyperbole, yet on this occasion his praise was shared by all who met Venizelos. Frances Stevenson was also bowled over by his charm. 'A magnificent type of Greek,' she wrote, 'cast in the classical mould, mentally and physically.' His traits were dynamism, extraordinary energy and a gift of oratory that enabled him to turn almost any argument on its head.

Venizelos's revolutionary youth provided colourful copy for the journalists of Fleet Street. He was born into a wealthy merchant family in Crete – then under Turkish rule – and had been christened Eleftherios or Liberator. The liberator spirit was certainly in his blood; his father had fought for Greece's independence and three of his uncles had died for their country.

Venizelos soon found himself following in their path, fighting with bravado for Crete's liberation from the Turk. Once this was accomplished, he turned his thoughts to the large number of Greeks scattered across Asia Minor. Their plight, which was to dominate his political career, had long troubled him. When training to be a lawyer in Athens, he startled his friends by outlining his vision for a Greater Greece. On a map of the Byzantine empire that hung on his wall, he drew the boundaries of the Greece that he hoped one day to create. It included large portions of Asia Minor, with the great city of Smyrna at its heart.

This, in a nutshell, was the so-called Megali Idea – the Great Idea – that had inspired Athens' intellectuals for decades. They, like Venizelos, looked forward to the day when all the Greek-speaking peoples of Asia Minor would be brought under the rule of a newly revived Greek empire. It was the stuff of dreams, a foolish fantasy – and a most dangerous one at that. The word 'megalomania' comes from the same Greek root.

The Downing Street breakfast meeting was one of several in which Venizelos spoke with great passion about his ideas of a new Greek empire. Lloyd George listened carefully and pondered how to make it a reality. He wanted a close union between the two countries and requested that ministers should keep 'in constant and intimate touch with each other'. More alarmingly, he suggested that each country should be able to 'call upon the other to assist in case of difficulties or war'.

For the next three weeks, Lloyd George, Winston Churchill and other ministers in Asquith's government thrashed out a dynamic new foreign policy. By mid-January, most of the key elements were in place. When John Stavridi went to meet Venizelos at the end of his stay, he found him in ebullient mood. Venizelos told him that 'Greece's future would be very different to her past, when she had to stand absolutely alone . . . with not a single friend to care what happened to her'. Now, with Lloyd George's backing, she 'would become a power in the East which no one could ignore'.

Venizelos was full of praise for Lloyd George, who had proved a most ingratiating host. 'He compared [Venizelos] with the old prophets of the Ancient Testament,' recalled Stavridi, 'and expressed his great admiration for his splendid capacities and clear insight of people and events.'

Venizelos's weeks in London, in which he wooed senior politi-cians and delighted the British press, were a triumphant success. *The Times* heaped praise upon 'the ablest of Greek statesmen', stating that his vision of creating a mighty Greek empire in Asia

Minor was breathtaking in scope and touched with genius. 'Large, bold and eminently practical, it pays homage to the exalted ideals and the glorious aspirations of Hellas, while it bears steadily in mind the most urgent and obvious of her material interests.'

No one seemed troubled by the fact that Venizelos was proposing a high-wire strategy of extreme danger – one that involved the complete dismemberment of the ailing Ottoman empire. Nor did anyone pause to consider how Smyrna's myriad nationalities would feel about being yoked to a new Greek heteronomy. The British press was far too blinkered to realise that it was the Ottoman system of government – with all its idiosyncrasies – that had allowed this great Levantine city to flourish. Instead, they chose to play on old stereotypes, reminding their readers of the cruelty and barbarism of the Turkish race.

Venizelos left London knowing that he had found a champion in Lloyd George. It is tempting to imagine him returning to Athens and unravelling the map of the Byzantine empire that had once adorned the walls of his student lodgings, gripped by the thought that his vision of the Great Idea now stood a chance of becoming a reality. He was prepared to invest everything in securing its success, vowing to create 'a great and powerful Greece, such as not even the boldest optimist could have imagined a few years back'.

It was the moment for which he had waited his entire life.

There was one central person missing from the Whittalls' Christmas feast of 1912. Magdalen Whittall had breathed her last earlier in the year and been buried in the little graveyard of Bournabat parish church. She had given her name to the church; now, her very flesh and bones were laid to rest in the shade of the tall plane trees.

For such a formidable woman, it is curious that no account of her passing has survived. Perhaps there was a feeling among family members that she had not really gone. After all, one of her great-grandchildren recalled that she continued to inspire fear for years after her death. Her flower-collecting son, Edward, felt her ghostly presence for the rest of his life, as did his wife, Mary. As Mary drifted in and out of senility in her final years, the terrifying spectre of Magdalen returned to haunt her. 'Daily life became shadowy and unreal,' recalled her granddaughter, 'but her early tussles with her mother-in-law remained clear in her mind.' She never forgave Magdalen for the public dressing down that she received in front of the entire congregation of Bournabat church. Her offence was to have worn a lilac bonnet that her mother-in-law considered 'too gay' for a married woman.

Magdalen's final injunctions to the family were revealed in her last will and testament. 'They are based on a long life's experience,' she wrote, 'and dictated by an earnest desire for your happiness.' Although she was no longer alive, she still demanded the deference of her sons and daughters.

Her commands read like the dictates of a Victorian ecclesiast: 'Never swerve from the truth, be honest and straightforward, fully exercise the gift of charity and try to live at peace with all men.' Most important of all was the survival of a dynasty that had, under her stentorian tutelage, risen to become the first family of Smyrna. 'I recommend to you union among all the members of our large family,' she wrote, 'forbearance towards each other, overlooking one another's failings [and] striving to further each other's welfare.'

The loss of Magdalen Whittall marked the end of an era. Her father-in-law, old Charlton Whittall, had founded the dynasty back in 1809 and Magdalen was the only surviving member of the family who could remember him as a young man. As a little girl, she had played in the grounds of the Big House, unaware that her marriage to Charlton's son was already being plotted by matchmaking aunts and uncles.

Although the family must have grieved for its loss, there was much that remained unchanged. Herbert Octavius remained the driving force in the family business, striking advantageous deals and enjoying the reward of even greater profits. Just a year earlier, the family had celebrated the centenary of the founding of C. Whittall and Co. It was an occasion for mutual congratulation: by 1911, the company had expanded to such an extent that it was the largest and most profitable of all Smyrna's foreign-run enterprises.

Increased profits from the company had enabled everyone to spend more time pursuing their hobbies. Herbert Octavius spent his weekends hunting big game on the Nymph Dagh mountains while his brother, Richard, found exciting new playthings to occupy his leisure hours. He particularly enjoyed tinkering with his motor car, one of the sights of Bournabat, although viewed with wonder and suspicion by the Whittalls' servants. 'The first time that our *kavass*, Iskender, saw Uncle Richard's Napier coming up from the station,' recalled Eldon Giraud, 'he rushed into the house yelling that the engine of the Bournabat train had come off the line and was heading for the square. He then dived under the kitchen table.'

Mary Whittall spent her fortune on keeping her children in check. 'With all the sea coast at her disposal she chose to build seven adjoining houses with a communal terrace in which her children and grandchildren lived during the summer months and were ruled with a rod of iron.'

The journey to these summer houses, which were situated on the coast to the north and south of Smyrna, was an exhilarating one for a young child. It took twelve hours in a horse-drawn carriage, 'with the risk of being set upon by brigands'. The Whittalls and Girauds were particularly enticing targets for the bandits, who had their hideouts in the lawless mountains behind Smyrna. Several members of the family were captured in this period, including James Whittall, a nephew of Herbert

Octavius. He was eventually released, but only after the payment of a significant ransom.

The brigands' success encouraged them to snatch another member of the extended family, Alfred von Lennap, who was seized while inspecting a newly imported tractor. They carried him to a secret hiding place and then sent an unambiguous message to the family. 'If we don't receive the ransom before the agreed day, we'll send you your son's ears, and then his nose . . .' Young Alfred was given right royal treatment while being held captive, for he was worth far more to the bandits alive than dead. 'He was always given the choicest pieces of chicken, lamb and other foods,' according to one of his relatives. The family eventually paid the ransom and Alfred was released with ears and nose intact. The brigands were not so fortunate. Tracked down by soldiers loyal to Smyrna's governor – and captured while arguing over the spoils – they were beheaded in the city centre and their heads stuck onto the spiked railings of the governor's palace.

Surviving childhood memoirs of Smyrna in the years prior to the Great War present a world that seemed timeless, secure (with the notable exception of the brigands) and filled with happy memories. There was Miss Florence's nursery school in Bournabat; the great Easter Monday family picnic; kite flying on the garden terraces. One girl recalled reading stories from dusty piles of *Strand Magazine* and *Household Words* that were stored in the Turkish bathhouse. Another had memories of dancing bears being brought down from the mountains by gypsy boys. And all remembered the great camel trains crossing Caravan Bridge before heading into the centre of Smyrna.

Although Bournabat seemed untouched by the cares of the world, there were underlying tensions in the great houses. Young Mary recalled the arrival of a new nurse – an eventful day for both her mother and her father. 'She arrived in Turkey, a beautiful young English girl . . . pretty, fair-haired [and] pink and white.'

Her roses-and-cream complexion proved an instant attraction, not only among the young men of Bournabat; Mary's father quickly made it his goal to have her as his mistress. '[He] was the sort of person who made a play for every servant girl around,' wrote Mary. In this case, he won the prize. The young girl became his long-term mistress, satisfying his physical needs while at the same time attending to the numerous children of the family. Edmund's wife knew of the affair and was most unhappy about it, but this did not seem to trouble him. Like so many of the wealthy Levantines, he had learned that he could behave exactly as he chose. 'He was an introverted autocrat,' wrote his daughter, 'flush with his own power . . . [and] very difficult to approach.'

It was a harsh judgement but an accurate one. Men like Edmund Giraud found it hard to believe otherwise. After all, they employed thousands of people whose lives were totally dependent on the success of the businesses that they owned. It was little wonder that they were objects of reverence, especially on Long Island where Edmund had his summer house. 'We were important people to those villagers in the same way that royalty is to the man in the street,' wrote Mary. 'If we ever went down to the village, people would run out of their houses to watch us go by.'

The Levantine families were extremely sociable and their coffee mornings and tea parties were the envy of the city. All the greatest dynasties also held an annual ball, usually in spring-time when the evenings were warm but not sultry. The local press was invited and would publish articles describing the ball gowns of the grandest ladies.

The most spectacular ball was hosted by the Paterson family; it was the social event of the year and all the city dignitaries were invited, including Smyrna's Ottoman governor, Rahmi Bey. He was always concerned that a gathering of all the richest notables would make the house an irresistible target for brigands.

'He placed troops on all the routes leading to the ball,' recalled Helena van der Zee, 'in order to protect the guests from any possible attack.'

The Paterson family lived in the largest mansion in Bournabat. It had thirty-eight rooms – more than the Big House – and was famous throughout Smyrna for its opulent interior. Two spectacular crystal chandeliers hung in the great atrium and the imported iron stair balustrade was one of the marvels of the colony. There were four grand pianos in the ballroom and each bedroom had a marble washbasin with running water. The mansion stood in grounds of more than 130 acres, half of which was given over to the family stud farm.

The Patersons had made their fortune in mining. Old John Paterson, founder of the clan, had been the first to discover chrome in Turkey. As the family coffers swelled, John's offspring found themselves eagerly pursued by the marriage-hungry aunts of the other Levantine clans. Old Magdalen Whittall ensured that at least one of her sons married a Paterson. The neighbouring Wood family also managed to strike a marriage alliance with the Patersons.

Among the regular visitors to the houses of the Levantine elite was Governor Rahmi Bey. In a land of powerful people, Rahmi was the most influential of them all – ruler of a city that generated a large slice of the wealth of the Ottoman empire. He cut a most imposing figure whenever he was seen in public. 'He was tall and very straight,' wrote George Horton, 'with piercing eyes and a high, thin-nostriled Turanian nose.' Fastidious in his dress, Rahmi liked to promenade through the streets of Smyrna dressed in his frock coat and clutching a silver-topped cane. He had spent his formative years in Salonica, a city that boasted almost as many nationalities as Smyrna, and was intelligent, cultivated and enlightened in his political views. When the Young Turk movement came to power in 1908, he was among the leading figures. He was soon given the governorship of Smyrna, a city that would become dear to his heart.

Rahmi managed the day-to-day affairs of his fiefdom with considerable aplomb, ruling with an iron fist, yet using his authoritarian streak for beneficent ends. '[He] was a shrewd despotic person,' wrote Horton, 'whose intellect was an equal blend of Oriental and European, the latter doubtless inherited from his Jewish ancestry.'

The governor felt a particular affinity for Smyrna's European and Levantine communities. 'He was especially friendly with the leading British citizens of Smyrna,' wrote Horton, 'who entertained him lavishly at their palatial homes.' They enjoyed his company, for he was a most diverting guest. 'He was a hearty eater and could carry any amount of European and Oriental liquor without losing his wits or power of locomotion.' Horton's admiration for Rahmi was shared by almost all who met him. Only the French consul, Jean-Marie Colomies, was critical of the manner in which he managed the affairs of the city, claiming that he seemed to view Smyrna as his personal satrapy.

If Rahmi Bey had a tendency to autocratic rule, it was because he had a well-nigh impossible job to perform. He was governor of a city whose population was majority Christian and not always in agreement with the decrees of the central government in Constantinople. Rahmi foresaw the potential problems that this might cause and wisely chose as his director of political affairs a wealthy Greek named Carabiber Bey. '[He] spoke perfect French without an accent,' wrote the Frenchman, Paul Jeancard, 'and used expressions which manifested his culture.' Carabiber was an important go-between – someone who could represent the Greek community within the framework of Ottoman rule.

In a metropolis of so many nationalities, the foreign consuls also had an important role to play. They were the figureheads of their communities, but also their representatives, and they provided another channel of communication with Rahmi Bey. There were scores of foreign consulates in Smyrna, each equipped with a large staff and a hospitality budget to match.

One of the most outgoing consuls was George Horton, custodian of the powerful American interests in the city. Cultivated, worldly and highly professional, he was a cut above the average American consul serving in the Levant. Horton's first posting had been to Greece, a country whose rich past had cast a spell over his undergraduate years. He taught himself ancient and modern Greek while studying at the University of Michigan, and he had translated Sappho's poems into English. He also wrote his own poetry, both in Greek and English. It was good enough to impress Walt Whitman; he preferred Horton's poetry to that of any other living American.

Horton married his Greek fiancée, Catherine Sacopoulo, in 1909. Then, after a brief stint as consul in Salonica, he was appointed to Smyrna in 1911. He was not the first to recognise that the city's prosperity and spirit had been created in large part by the great Levantine dynasties. The tensions that William Childs had found in the countryside of Anatolia were wholly absent from Smyrna. The Levantine factories employed all, regardless of race, and, in the dried-fruit warehouses and flour mills, Turks, Greeks, Jews and Armenians found themselves working alongside each other.

'We got on well with the Turks,' recalled a Greek lad named Ilias Kourkoulis, one of many refugees interviewed in the aftermath of 1922 about Smyrna's happier times. 'We visited them frequently and our homes neighboured theirs. We spent our leisure time together and all played in the same football team.'

By the early twentieth century, the lives of these groups were becomingly increasingly intertwined. Communities freely borrowed each other's customs, even helping themselves to bons mots and expressions as well. Two of Smyrna's champion wrestlers were thoroughbred Greeks who elsewhere in Turkey would have certainly vaunted their race and religion, yet to do so in Smyrna would have been frowned upon as unseemly. They chose the Turkish word *dana*, meaning 'bull', as their *nom de guerre*.

As neighbours became friends, so they were invited to each other's feasts and festivals. When the young Greek girl, Aglaia Kontou, got married, the couple received some fabulous presents from their Turkish neighbours. '[One] gave us a long clock with an eagle that announced the hours. On another occasion, we offered them a gramophone and seven records.'

In such a heterogeneous city, it was inevitable that there were occasional tensions, particularly among the poorly educated. The Jewish Passover was often a moment of stress between Greeks and Jews. There were those among the illiterate older generation who believed an ancient superstition that the Jews sacrificed a Christian child in order to mix its blood into their unleavened bread. When, in 1901, a young Greek boy went missing, a rabble flocked to the Jewish quarter and rang the bells of a nearby church as a call to arms. The Greek Orthodox archbishop and the city government were quick to condemn the mob. Its leaders were arrested, appearing in the dock in Smyrna's courtroom. Their humiliation was complete when the missing Greek boy was found alive and well. He had run away from home to escape a punishment from his parents.

Such disagreeable incidents were rare and quickly quashed by the city's governor. The rule of law always prevailed and for more than half a century – from the early 1860s until 1914 – Smyrna was one of the more enlightened cities on earth. Horton gave a great deal of thought to the reasons for this in his quest to identify the city's magic ingredient. It was not merely the fact that the city stood at the interchange of a dozen worlds. Smyrna's allure was more elusive and complex. Happiness was an emotion that defied measurement and yet it was the general sense of contentment that, time and again, struck foreign visitors to the metropolis. 'The lightheartedness of the Smyrniots was well-nigh irrepressible,' wrote Horton, 'and continued almost until the last days.'

Visiting European intellectuals were fascinated to observe such a racially mixed city at close quarters. When the Austrian savant, Charles de Scherzer, had visited Smyrna in 1874, he brought with him a most negative image of the Turks, yet he went away with all his preconceptions shattered. 'In matters of religion,' he wrote, 'they are – contrary to their reputation – the most tolerant people of the Orient.'

Scherzer concluded that the Levantines – torch-bearers of culture and learning – had created a truly remarkable environment. 'The philanthropist notes with satisfaction how the progress of western civilisation has swept through every layer and class of society and that Smyrna acts like a beacon to every other province of the Ottoman Empire.'

Smyrna's population continued to enjoy the gaiety of life throughout the spring of 1914. There were afternoon tea dances in the salons of the clubhouses and a season of Italian operettas in the Alhambra garden theatre. But as Easter approached, it became clear that the beautiful coastline to the north of Smyrna was in deep turmoil. Thousands of Muslim refugees had fled in panic from the continued fighting in the Balkans and they were now bent on revenge. Their target was the Greek community living on the Aegean coastline of Turkey.

The crisis began in May, when a large number of refugees arrived in the town of Adramyttium, some seventy miles to the north of Smyrna. They were accompanied by armed bands of *chettes*, or irregulars, equipped with clubs, knives and rifles. Surging into the centre of town, they began ransacking homes and shops owned by Greeks. The offices of the town's richest merchants, the Kazaxi family, were destroyed and the family was given twenty-four hours to leave Turkey. When they appealed to their Ottoman overlords for help, they were met with a wall of silence. The government in Constantinople was still smarting from a string of military defeats in the Balkans and in no mood to leap to the defence of the Greeks living in its midst.

'So far from discouraging them [the irregulars],' wrote Arnold Toynbee, who was to travel widely in Turkey over the coming years, 'the authorities armed them, organised them and gave them a free hand to accomplish results which they desired to see accomplished but preferred not to obtain openly for themselves.'

Faced with a complete absence of any protection, the Greeks of Adramyttium found that events quickly began to spiral out of control. 'What a night we passed you cannot imagine,' wrote the town's physician, Dr Charalampides. 'The sound of shots increased our agony . . . towards dawn, shrieks and lamentations filled the streets.' Hundreds of Greeks were forced from their houses and sought shelter in the town's church. 'The *bashibazouks* [irregulars] broke open the doors of the houses, attacked and stripped the men of their belongings, robbed the women of their trinkets, insulted the young maidens and drove them all out of the houses with clubs, and then proceeded to loot.'

Dr Charalampides was evicted from his home, getting badly wounded in the process. He made his way to the harbour, along with the other Greeks of the town, and sought passage to the nearby Greek island of Mytilene. When he finally reached safety, he asked himself why the great European powers – which he had long respected – had turned a blind eye to the crisis. 'I have often wondered how it is that Europe, and especially England, which is so famous for her love of liberty, allows the half-civilised Turks to perpetrate these atrocities and this destruction.' It was a question that was to be repeated many times over in the years to come.

The sack of Adramyttium was the start of a long summer of persecution for the Greek communities that had lived for centuries on Turkey's Aegean coastline. Scores of other villages were attacked and their Greek inhabitants massacred or ordered to leave Turkey. As spring turned into summer, the attacks drew ever closer to Smyrna. By June, there were reports that Muslim *chettes* had landed in Old Phocaea, a mere twenty-five miles to the north of the city. The French archaeologists, Félix Sartiaux and Monsieur Manciet, were working on an excavation at the time of their arrival. 'I shall never forget the day and night which followed,' wrote Sartiaux, 'the cries of the victims, the scream of the bullets, the torture and massacre of old men, women and children and the brutal expulsion of the population.'

The Levantine families in Bournabat read with consternation of the upheaval that was taking place to the north of Smyrna. Yet they remained surprisingly sanguine in the face of such violence. Although these events were occurring less than an hour's ride from the city, they were confident that they would be safe. It was unthinkable that Rahmi Bey would tolerate the arrival of *chettes* anywhere near the vicinity of Smyrna.

Their complacency was to be rudely shattered one Saturday morning in late June. Edmund Giraud was sailing the *Helen May* across to Long Island when he got the shock of his life. 'On entering the bay shortly before midday,' he wrote, 'a most astonishing sight came into view.' The little Greek village on the island had been overrun: '[It was] in the possession of a number of armed Turkish irregulars gathered in groups and loitering about the sea front.' On the other side of the bay – on land that he owned – there was an even more startling scene. 'I could see the entire population of the village, about four thousand souls, all herded together within the barbed-wire fences of my hillside.' When Edmund turned his gaze towards his house, he received the third unwelcome surprise of the morning. 'My wife, with our Albanian guard, Izzet, was down below at the gate by the sea, keeping a number of more venturesome Turks from entering the property.'

Edmund landed and – in true patrician style – demanded to meet the leaders of the irregular forces. When brought to him, they were suddenly cowed by his imposing presence. '[They] seemed anxious to make a plausible story of what had occurred,' informing him that they had been sent from the mainland to search for weapons. Edmund's wife told a rather different story. Fourteen men from the village had been shot in cold blood; everyone else was being menaced by the Turks and in fear of their lives. All links with the mainland had been cut and even the daily food supply had been prevented from landing.

Edmund acted with characteristic energy. He immediately despatched the *Helen May* to the nearest telegraph office on the mainland and relayed to his friends in Smyrna what had happened. 'As a result of this,' he wrote, 'the Greek Consular authorities sent several boatloads of bread the following day to feed the unfortunate villagers.' Edmund also ordered the Turkish irregulars off his property, informing them that they were trespassers and would be treated as such. They meekly complied, moving themselves over to the other side of the little bay.

As soon as Edmund realised that he had temporarily defused the volatile situation, he returned to Smyrna and paid a visit to Rahmi Bey. When he told the governor what had occurred, Rahmi was extremely concerned and decided to visit the island in person. 'He made arrangements to do so on a gunboat the following morning and invited two of my friends and me to accompany him.'

For such an event to have occurred in his fiefdom was indeed alarming. Rahmi had not sanctioned the landing of irregulars on Long Island and was furious at their intrusion. He resolved to calm the situation as quickly and efficiently as possible.

As his gunboat headed out across the bay, Rahmi Bey noticed a large steamer approaching the island from the other direction. It was flying the Greek flag '[and] had been despatched from Mytilene by the Greek government to relieve the islanders, at the suggestion of the Consular Authorities in Smyrna'. When the Greek captain realised that Smyrna's Turkish governor was about to land, he kept a discreet distance from the island.

As soon as Rahmi Bey was ashore, he was led up to the panoramic terrace in front of Edmund Giraud's house. He was shown exactly where the irregulars had landed and was able to see the difficulty of the situation in which he found himself. There were still scores of terrified villagers crowded around Edmund's property and they refused to leave until the irregulars had been sent away. 'They clung to the walls of my home,' wrote Edmund, 'as if there was some saving virtue in the very stones they touched.' Although Rahmi gave them his absolute assurance that they would not be molested and encouraged them all to go home, the fact that fourteen of their number had already been killed had caused them to lose all faith in the Turkish authorities.

In the end, Edmund himself managed to strike a deal that was acceptable to everyone. Those who wished to return to their homes would be able to do so with a guarantee of safety issued by Rahmi himself. He selected a guard of twelve gendarmes who were to be permanently based in the village. Those who wished to leave, meanwhile, would be allowed to board the Greek steamer and take all their possessions with them.

In the event, the villagers decided to leave en masse. Having heard dark stories of massacres up and down the coastline, they no longer felt safe and asked to be taken off that very day.

With no desire to witness the spectacle of their departure, Edmund and his wife set off into the bay on the *Helen May*. But later that evening, his little yacht passed quite close to the Greek steamer. 'I never expect to see such a sight again,' he wrote. 'Herded about the ship in every corner available were donkeys, goats, sheep, pigs, dogs and poultry mixed up with crowds of men, women and children of all ages.' The villagers had taken absolutely everything they possessed. 'Baggage and litter of every description were piled up in all sorts of ways, as even doors and shutters had been wrenched from the houses and carried away. Quite a lot of this was hanging on the rigging Christmas-tree like.' There were too many people to fit aboard the steamer so other craft had been requisitioned. 'The steamer had about fifteen or more small boats in tow, all likewise full of baggage and with one or more human beings in charge.'

When the Greek villagers caught sight of the *Helen May*, they let out a great cheer. 'The people must have been glad to get away and feel quite safe at last, for the shouts which greeted us as we passed afforded unmistakable evidence of this.'

Edmund had promised the villagers that he would continue to water their crops and harvest them when they were ready. This he duly did, selling them in Smyrna and then delivering the money to the islanders who had built new lives on Mytilene.

Although Edmund was glad that he had been able to evacuate the villagers in some semblance of order, he was desperately sorry to see them go. 'I do not think that I shall ever forget the awful loneliness which brooded over the village after its evacuation by the inhabitants, about four thousand souls. A few stray dogs and cats were the only living creatures left behind and it was pitiful to hear the dogs howl at night.'

The evacuation of Long Island was one of the last upheavals in the long months of unrest. A visit to Smyrna by the Minister of the Interior defused the tension and the *chettes'* reign of terror temporarily came to an end. But as the summer heat intensified, it became increasingly apparent that all was not well in the world of international politics. Turkey was about to become embroiled in the countdown to war − and the side that she would take in the forthcoming conflict would be decided not in Smyrna or in Constantinople, but in the English city of Newcastle, on the River Tyne.

Enemy Aliens

Newcastle was basking in a summer heatwave. The mercury had touched thirty degrees on the previous afternoon and it looked set to rise even higher during the course of the weekend. Local newspapers were predicting a rush of day-trippers to the seaside, although they warned that thunderous storms had been forecast for later in the weekend. If they had known about the extraordinary events taking place on Newcastle's wharves, they might also have predicted tempestuous times in the world of international politics.

There was much to keep the people of Newcastle entertained on that sweltering August weekend in 1914. At the Empire, the impresario, G. H. Elliot, was performing his much loved vaudeville act, 'the chocolate-coloured coon'. At the Tyne Theatre, the Antarctic explorer, Cecil Meares, was lecturing on Captain Scott's fateful expedition to the South Pole. But one attraction looked set to overshadow all of these. On Sunday, 3 August, just two days after Turkey and Germany had signed a secret alliance, a colourful military pageant was to be held in Newcastle docks. The largest dreadnought in the world – the mighty *Sultan Osman I*, which was being built in the shipyards – was to be handed over to a Turkish captain and crew.

The ceremony was to be performed with all the pomp and circumstance that Newcastle could muster – and with good reason. The *Sultan Osman I* was by far the biggest dreadnought ever built. She was 700 feet long and 90 feet wide, so big that it was feared she would not fit under the two bridges that spanned the river. She was also the most heavily armed fighting ship in the world; her fourteen guns could fire 23,000 pounds of high explosive each minute, enough to overwhelm any other dreadnought afloat.

For more than a year, this beast of a ship had been an object of wonder to the cityfolk of Newcastle. They had watched in awe as her giant twin funnels became an ever more impressive addition to the city skyline. The local dock workers returned to their families each evening with eye-stretching tales of the ship's interior. The officers' wardroom had polished teak decking, silk-shaded lamps and Turkish rugs to adorn the floors. It was furnished with mahogany gaming tables and cretonne-covered armchairs. In each corner there was a brass spittoon for the pious Muslim officers who did not like to swallow their saliva during the fast of Ramadan.

Ottoman ministers had been obliged to borrow more than £4 million – some £225 million in today's money – to buy the *Sultan Osman I*, along with a second ship named *Reshadieh*. Servicing the bank loans for these two dreadnoughts soon proved an impossible burden. Ministers found themselves facing a massive shortfall of money and were forced to appeal directly to the people. There were collections in villages across Turkey and patriotic fund-raising events were organised, even in the farthest-flung outposts. According to one observer, 'agents had gone from house to house, painfully collecting these small subscriptions . . . there had been entertainments and fairs and, in their eagerness for the cause, Turkish women had sold their hair for the benefit of the common fund.'

Now, after a long wait, the vessels were almost ready to be delivered. No one was looking forward to the Sunday handover ceremony more than Captain Raouf Bey, the much decorated

naval hero of Turkey. He had arrived in Newcastle just a few
days earlier, having been appointed commander of the dreadnought by the Turkish government. Such was his enthusiasm at
being aboard the ship that he had failed to notice that his Turkish
crew was being secretly monitored by Newcastle's dockyard
police. Nor had he realised that the Admiralty in London had
sent a top-secret telegram to the shipbuilders, requesting that
the final stages of construction be slowed down. There was good
reason for this delaying tactic. On 28 June, news had reached
London that Archduke Franz Ferdinand, heir to the Hapsburg
throne, had been assassinated. In the five weeks since, an event
that had seemed like a local crisis had escalated into something
of far greater significance. As rumours about general mobilisation in Central Europe reached London, ministers argued that
this was the worst possible time to be handing over the world's
largest dreadnought to a country whose loyalty in the event of
war was at best uncertain.

No one was more concerned than Winston Churchill, the
youthful First Lord of the Admiralty. He knew that Raouf Bey
and his crew had arrived in Newcastle and had been warned
that the Turkish captain had a reputation for acting precipitately.
Churchill feared that Raouf Bey would suspect that work on
the ship was being deliberately delayed and would attempt to
board her by force. 'There seemed to be a great danger of the
Turks coming on board,' he later wrote, '[and] brushing aside
Mssrs Armstrong's workmen and hoisting the Turkish flag.'

The prospect of such a scenario caused grave concern in
Whitehall, especially as the Turkish and German governments
were forging ever closer links. On the last day of July, just hours
before the German Kaiser ordered the mobilisation of his armies,
Churchill took a decision that was to have profound and far-
reaching consequences. The *Sultan Osman I* was to be
impounded.

Raouf Bey, unaware of this change of policy, was still looking forward to the handover ceremony, but as he gazed across the dockyard on the morning of the pageantry, he was greeted by a most unwelcome sight. A company of Sherwood Foresters was marching towards the *Sultan Osman I* and all of the men were carrying guns with fixed bayonets.

By the time he realised that the vessels were being impounded, it was too late for him to act. The dockside was ringed with troops and Raouf Bey was a captain without a ship.

Churchill was delighted when he learned of the successful seizure. 'The addition of the two Turkish dreadnoughts to the British fleet seemed vital to national safety,' he wrote. But in Turkey the requisitioning was viewed very differently. There was disgust at Britain's action and the tens of thousands of people who had donated money felt that Churchill had stolen what was rightfully theirs. In the days that followed, the Ottoman army was mobilised and Turkey put on a war footing.

Churchill thought this to be nothing but bluster and continued to act as if Turkey were a valued ally. He even offered the Turkish government £1,000 a day in compensation for the commandeered battleships. But he was about to be outsmarted by the German government, which had followed with great interest the saga of the *Sultan Osman I* and *Reshadieh*. Anxious to capitalise on the tensions between Britain and Turkey – and strengthen the bond with Constantinople – they hatched a plan to present their Oriental ally with the very prize that had been denied them by Britain.

The seizure of the dreadnoughts attracted little notice in Smyrna. Few people in the city had given money towards the purchase of the *Sultan Osman I* and *Reshadieh*. Indeed, the Greek population had been dismayed by the news that Turkey was to take delivery of the vessels. Now, there was a certain satisfaction to be gained from the news that the two ships had been impounded.

The reactions were more mixed among the elite of

Constantinople. Sultan Mehmet V, the head of a dynasty that had ruled the Ottoman empire for more than 450 years, was outraged by the turn of events, yet he had little appetite for war and certainly had no desire to fight Britain. Fearing that it would lead to the further disintegration of his formerly huge realm, he declared himself firmly in the peace camp.

This would certainly have been the wisest course for Turkey, but the sultan no longer wielded much power. The day-to-day running of the country had fallen into the hands of a small group of men who were attempting to halt the decline of the once-mighty Ottoman empire. In the years since the Young Turk revolution of 1908, which had deprived the sultan of much of his authority, decision-making had increasingly been concentrated in the hands of three men – Enver Pasha, Mehmet Talaat and Ahmed Cemal. Of this triumvirate, it was Enver Pasha who was the most energetic in banging the drums of war.

Enver Pasha aroused strong feelings in all who met him. The American ambassador to Constantinople, Henry Morgenthau, had initially been struck by Enver's youthful looks. 'He was an extremely neat and well-groomed object,' he wrote, 'with a pale, smooth face, made even more striking by his black hair, and with delicate white hands and long tapering fingers.' His most striking feature was his neatly clipped moustache, whose ends he waxed and twisted upwards in the German manner.

Enver was a charming host, yet there was a more disturbing side to his character. The ambassador found him to be extraordinarily egotistical and noted that his favourite armchair was positioned between portraits of Napoleon and Frederick the Great. 'This fact gives some notion of his vanity,' wrote Morgenthau. 'These two warriors and statesmen were his great heroes and I believe that Enver thought fate had a career in store for him not unlike theirs.'

Enver Pasha had first-hand experience of the crushing defeat suffered by the Ottoman army during the Balkan Wars of 1912 and 1913. These conflicts had robbed Turkey of much of her European territory and left the Ottoman army extremely demoralised. If it was ever again to be an efficient fighting machine, it would require root-and-branch reform.

Enver got some inkling as to how this might be achieved while serving as military attaché in Berlin. He found much to admire in the German army and felt that a military alliance represented Turkey's best hope of future military success. Soon after the end of the Balkan Wars, he negotiated the appointment of a German general named Liman von Sanders as inspector general of the Ottoman army.

Liman von Sanders was appalled by the state of decline into which the once-great army had fallen. The guard of honour that assembled to greet him was in a wretched condition: 'a considerable part wore torn boots or shoes,' he wrote, '[and] others were barefooted.' He and his team of seventy German officers set to work with clinical efficiency, retraining troops and acquiring new equipment. The effects of these reforms were rapid and startling. When Henry Morgenthau was invited to a public review of the troops in July 1914, he was astonished by the transformation. 'In the preceding six months,' he wrote, 'the Turkish army had been completely Prussianised. What in January had been an undisciplined, ragged rabble was now parading with the goose-step.'

It was by no means a foregone conclusion that Turkey would join Germany in the event of war. Enver Pasha was avowedly pro-German in his views but other members of the inner circle were looking elsewhere for military alliances. Mehmet Talaat favoured joining Russia while Ahmed Cemal, the third member of the ruling triumvirate, looked to France for military co-operation.

Germany had invested large sums of money in allying herself to Turkey and had no intention of losing that investment. Her secret weapon came in the form of a towering Thuringian aristocrat named Baron Hans von Wangenheim, Germany's ambassador to the country.

Wangenheim was a veritable giant, 'his huge, solid frame, his Gibraltar-like shoulders, erect and impregnable, his bold, defiant head, his piercing eyes, the whole physical structure constantly pulsating with life and activity'. So wrote Morgenthau, who so despised the man that he dispensed with all diplomatic niceties when describing him.

Wangenheim vowed to do everything in his power to win Turkish support, especially now that Britain and France were at war with Germany. He knew that with Turkey on board, the German navy could close the Dardanelles – the only practical line of communications between the Allied powers and Russia. Russia would no longer be able to export grain, her greatest source of revenue, nor receive any munitions.

On 11 August 1914, Morgenthau visited Wangenheim in order to discuss some matters of official business. He found his German counterpart behaving in a most unusual fashion. 'Never had I seen him so nervous and excited. He could not rest in his chair more than a few minutes at a time; he was constantly jumping up, rushing to the windows and looking anxiously out towards the Bosphorus.'

The reason for his excitement soon became apparent. After a final glance out of the window, he gave a joyous little skip and informed Morgenthau that two German battleships – the *Goeben* and *Breslau* – had just arrived in Constantinople. They were to be offered to the Turkish government by its German counterpart – a replacement for the two dreadnoughts that Britain was refusing to hand over.

'Wangenheim had more than patriotic reasons for this exultation,' wrote Morgenthau. 'The arrival of these ships was the greatest day in his diplomatic career.' When tidings of the offer reached news-stands across Turkey, Germany was presented as the country's only true friend.

Scenes of extraordinary jubilation marked the appearance of the ships. The German commander, Admiral Wilhelm Souchon, was lifted onto the shoulders of his crew and displayed to the crowd. The German sailors donned Turkish fezzes and the vessels were given Turkish names. Although not as big as the dreadnoughts in Newcastle, they had the advantage of being ready to put to sea immediately. They were to be crewed by German mariners sailing under the Ottoman flag and Admiral Souchon was made commander-in-chief of the fleet.

As the countdown to war with Turkey now began to gather pace, even the most optimistic politicians in Britain conceded that the country was certain to side with Germany. The decisive moment came on 29 October 1914. At 3.30 a.m., and without a declaration of war, Admiral Souchon's ships bombarded the Russian ports of Odessa and Sebastopol. Four days after this unprovoked attack, Britain, France and Russia declared war on Turkey. Enver Pasha had at last got his way. Although four Ottoman ministers resigned, there was no turning back.

The sultan was informed of these events in his Dolmabahçe Palace. 'To make war on Russia!' he exclaimed in horror. 'But its corpse alone would be enough to crush us.' The German community living in Constantinople agreed, believing Enver's actions to have been extraordinarily reckless. A German acquaintance of Sir Edwin Pears, a historian who lived in Constantinople, remarked: 'Sir Edwin, you have written *The Destruction of the Greek Empire*; I think you are going to live to write *The Destruction of the Turkish Empire* . . . they are committing suicide.'

House guests in Bournabat in the summer of 1914 noticed little outward change in the cool interiors of the Levantine villas. Life continued its unhurried pace, seemingly untouched by the outside world, yet the dinner-table conversations had lost the gaiety and sparkle of previous years. Families like the Whittalls and Girauds were deeply concerned. While they continued to fix one eye on their gardens and hothouses, they fixed the other on the deepening international crisis.

The Whittalls were kept informed of events by the British consul, Clifford Heathcote-Smith. He saw no immediate reason for the Levantines of Smyrna to panic although he did foresee difficulties for the British expatriate community. On the day after Britain's declaration of war against Germany, he summoned all of his country's nationals to an emergency meeting in the flower garden of the consulate. He warned everyone that they might have to leave Turkey at short notice, but reassured them that any evacuation would be orderly.

One who attended the meeting was Alexander MacLachlan, director of the American International College in Paradise, who held a British passport. 'There was great excitement,' he wrote. 'Our government had declared war on Germany and our patriotism was deeply stirred.' Unlike the Levantines, the British in Smyrna viewed with mounting enthusiasm the prospect of mounting an attack on Germany. Many thought that such a conflict was long overdue.

Clifford Heathcote-Smith asked MacLachlan to address the meeting and he readily agreed. '[I] made an appeal to the youth present to offer their services to their country. Calling for a show of hands, some eighteen British lads at once volunteered.' Among them were MacLachlan's two sons, who were to spend the next four years fighting with distinction in France, Egypt and Greece.

The offspring of the Levantine families displayed less willingness to volunteer immediately, preferring to bide their time and see how events evolved. The first dramatic warning bell came just a few weeks after the meeting at the consulate. In September, Ottoman ministers announced the abolition of the Capitulations – the trading privileges that had enabled the Levantines to amass such fortunes.

These privileges, negotiated between the Levantine and

European communities and the sultan, had given them significant advantages over local merchants. They included the right to transport and sell goods free of any excise duty. In return, the dynasties were expected to offer tacit political support to the sultan's government. Now, after more than 330 years – and in a single stroke – families like the Whittalls were deprived of the benefits they had enjoyed for so long.

The news provoked a strange reaction in Smyrna. For years, the Levantine cómmunity had been accorded the greatest respect by the different nationalities in the city. They were the city's biggest employers and thousands of families depended upon them for their continued prosperity. Yet the loss of these concessions was greeted with 'undisguised contentment' in the poorer Turkish quarters of Smyrna. Few paused to consider the fact that financially penalising the Levantine merchant princes in such a sudden fashion would have catastrophic consequences for Smyrna's booming economy. Nor did they consider the many benefits that the Levantines had brought to Smyrna. By the summer of 1914, the city's exports were more than double those of Constantinople and had increased in such dramatic fashion that even the Levantines themselves were beginning to marvel at their Midas touch.

The abolition of the Capitulations was a heavy blow that threatened to drain their very lifeblood. But there was even worse news on the way. On the orders of government ministers in Constantinople, the Turkish military authorities began requisitioning supplies 'in a manner that becomes increasingly thorough and increasingly objectionable'. Heathcote-Smith found himself facing a torrent of complaints from the Levantine magnates and factory owners – men who had always been scrupulous in adhering to Ottoman laws. Now, those very laws had been summarily swept away in a smash-and-grab raid on anything that could be considered useful for the future Ottoman war effort.

No one was taken by surprise when war on Turkey was finally declared, yet it was still a huge shock and had an electrifying effect on the city of Smyrna. Years later, people could still recall with absolute clarity where they were and what they were doing. Mary Giraud, then a young girl of just five or six years old, was with her mother in the family's summer house on Long Island. They first realised that something was seriously wrong when they observed the Turks closing the narrow entrance to Smyrna's harbour. Mary's mother, Ruth, guessed what must have happened and suddenly panicked. Her husband, on business in Smyrna, would now be unable to return to Long Island in the *Helen May*. The only possible way for them to leave was to use the little rowing boat pulled up on the beach below the house.

Ruth had no intention of remaining on the island. She gathered up all her children, seated them in the rowing boat and braced herself for a long and tiring journey of several miles across to the mainland. 'We must have rowed all that day,' recalled Mary many years later, 'reaching Vourla [the closest port] at night.' They then had to get back to Smyrna in order to rejoin the wider family and discuss what should be their next move. 'I have uncomfortable and claustrophobic memories of riding in an overflowing bus full of jostling hysterical people in the dead of night.' The family was eventually reunited with an anxious Edmund in the early hours; he confirmed to his wife that Turkey was now at war with Britain, France and Russia. The Giraud family – still French nationals after many decades in Turkey – suddenly learned that they were enemy aliens.

They were not the only ones to find themselves in a most delicate position. The Whittalls, Woods and Patersons, along with all the other Levantine dynasties, discovered that they had divided loyalties. Although they had clung to their original nationalities and were proud of their roots, they still considered Turkey to be their true home. To abandon their villas in Bournabat and return to England, France or Italy seemed unthinkable. Yet to remain on enemy soil appeared reckless and foolhardy, especially as they all had large numbers of young children.

Once war had been declared, the Levantines were seen as fair game by ministers in Constantinople. After raiding their offices and warehouses, the military authorities impounded their yachts, yawls and steam cruisers. Herbert Octavius's motor cruiser, *Nacoochie*, was seized and stripped of all her parts. So, too, was Edmund Giraud's beloved *Helen May*. Everything of value was removed and she was then left to rot on the foreshore.

The final insult was reserved for Edmund's father, Frédéric Giraud. A keen sportsman and friend of the sultan, he had long been granted the honour of shooting on the land surrounding Gellat Lake – territory that belonged to the Civil List. This was a great privilege, for Gellat was rich in duck, woodcock and partridge as well as wood pigeon and quail. Now that war had been declared, the honour was peremptorily withdrawn. Neither Frédéric, nor any of his friends, was allowed to shoot in the hills above Smyrna.

The awkward situation that had overtaken the Levantine families was mirrored by that of many others in Smyrna. This great city was a statistical anomaly: at least two-thirds of its population were either active supporters of the Allied cause or, at the very least, sympathisers. Among them was the city governor himself, Rahmi Bey. Ever since the Young Turk revolution of 1908 and his subsequent appointment as governor of Smyrna, he had found himself increasingly disenchanted with central government in Constantinople. The triumvirate in control had once been his confidants. Now, the relationship was severely undermined by their decision to enter the war on the German side.

'[Rahmi Bey] is one of those more intelligent Turks who thinks that war with France and England is a piece of folly in which Turkey is sure to lose,' noted George Horton. Rahmi mistrusted all the German military officers whom Enver Pasha had invited to Turkey, and he had a particular aversion to the pompous Liman von Sanders. Although Rahmi tried to remain impartial in public, Horton had no doubts as to what he really thought. 'In reality,' he wrote, 'he cordially detested the Germans, whose officers were often overbearing and rude to him.' In a country now swarming with the German military, Rahmi felt as uncomfortable as many of the inhabitants of Smyrna.

Edmund Giraud also mistrusted the German officers. He had come into contact with one of their fact-finding missions some months earlier and had noticed with alarm the thoroughness with which they were surveying the coastline that surrounded the city. They had made a particularly meticulous study of the non-Turkish communities living in and around the bay of Smyrna.

Now, as Edmund cast his mind back to the evacuation of Long Island, he became increasingly convinced that the German mission had deliberately provoked the violence. Indeed, he felt sure that the Germans had encouraged the Turkish irregulars to land on the island and so terrify its inhabitants that they were left with little option but to flee. 'There is not much doubt that the existence of so many Greek villages on the coast commanding the entrance of the gulf was not well looked upon,' he wrote. Although he never managed to find hard evidence to support his suspicions, they certainly seemed plausible in the light of Germany's active involvement in the Turkish war effort.

While the Giraud family agonised over their next move, the Greeks of Smyrna found themselves overtaken by events. The central government was fearful of this potential fifth column – an enemy within – and had no qualms about rekindling the hatred that had ignited the coastline just a few months earlier. The ruling Committee of Union and Progress began printing flyers that blamed the economically successful Greeks for all of

Turkey's woes. 'Greece is the enemy of our religion, our history, our honour, our patrimony and – above all – our very existence,' read one. 'You must buy nothing from a Greek or from anyone who looks Greek . . . it is in this way that we shall save the honour of our patrimony and our religion.'

These Turkish news-sheets, printed secretly in Smyrna, soon began to inflame an already tense situation. George Horton was appalled by the stream of vitriol being produced by the home-spun printing presses that were operating without licence from the governor's office. 'Cheap lithographs were got up,' he wrote, 'executed in the clumsiest and most primitive manner, evidently local productions. They represented Greeks cutting up Turkish babies or ripping open pregnant Moslem women and various purely imaginary scenes, founded on no actual events.'

Such propaganda quickly had an effect. 'A series of sporadic murders began at Smyrna . . . the list in each morning's papers numbering from twelve to twenty.' The situation was even worse in the rich farmland that surrounded the city. 'Peasants going into their vineyards to work were shot down from behind trees and rocks by the Turks.'

Rahmi Bey grew increasingly impatient with the policies being promoted by Constantinople and began preparations to regain his authority over a city that wished to have no part in Enver Pasha's war. His determination to remain aloof from the conflict, coupled with his friendship with the Levantine families, encouraged many of them to remain in the city. Herbert Octavius considered all his options before declaring his intention of staying in Smyrna. His brother, Edward, followed suit. He had no desire to close his factories and lay off his workers; he preferred to chance his luck in the only place he knew as home. One by one, the Levantine families of Bournabat and elsewhere elected to remain in Smyrna.

One of the reasons for their staying was highlighted by Henry Morgenthau. 'The great majority had never set foot in England,' he wrote. 'Their retention of their European citizenship is almost their only contact with the nation from which they have sprung.' They were also fearful of what might happen to their businesses in their absence. Besides, there seemed little reason to act precipitately. Many were already predicting that the war would be over by Christmas.

Smyrna's foreign consuls were given rather less freedom to decide their future. All of the consulates – with the exception of Germany, Austro-Hungary and America – were closed by order of the government. Their staffs were ordered to leave on the first available vessel.

It was a particularly heavy blow for Clifford Heathcote-Smith, who had grown to love the city that had been his home for six years. At the end of October, he took a last wistful stroll along Smyrna's quayside and said his private farewells. He felt as if the city had reached a milestone in its history and wondered whether he was witnessing the end of an era. The majority of the city's population was on the Allied side: 'it is probable that they, rather than the Turks, will suffer,' he wrote.

Heathcote-Smith believed that Smyrna would be unable to avoid becoming embroiled in a war that was not of her choosing. And in the process it was even more unlikely that this enchanting, glittering city would ever be quite the same again.

Rahmi's Double Game

A few days after the outbreak of war, Edward Whittall's neighbours in Bournabat awoke to a surprising new addition to the skyline. A large Union Jack fluttered proudly over the Whittall residency – an unambiguous declaration that Edward's sympathies lay wholeheartedly with the Allied cause.

It was a most provocative act, given that Britain was now at war with Turkey, yet one that Edward performed with customary relish. It was his own personal statement of defiance, his red rag to a bull. He was informing Turkey's rulers that although they were able to lead the country into an unpopular conflict, he had no intention of allowing them to impinge on the way he lived his life.

Bournabat's merchant princes were nevertheless concerned that the hostilities would bring about an irrevocable change to their lives. The closure of the harbour was a particular worry; they feared having to close their factories and lay off the tens of thousands of workers they employed. Such a course of action would cause real hardship throughout Smyrna, since most families had only one breadwinner whose salary had to support a large number of young children.

Edward Whittall, in common with all the Bournabat merchants, had always been an old-school philanthropist. He felt personally responsible for the men he employed in his factories and had no intention of allowing them to suffer because of a lack of work. Whenever his businesses went through a slack period – and the exigencies of war forced him to close his warehouse doors – he dug deep into his own pockets and paid his employees 'to scour the mountainside for new rarities of bulbs'.

It was a characteristically patrician approach to a crisis as well as being an extremely costly one, but it provided a lifeline to all the men who worked in his factories.

As the weeks drifted by, it became apparent that the Bournabat dynasties were able to shield Smyrna from many of the detrimental economic effects of the hostilities. The loss of trading privileges did not strike a mortal blow to their inherited fortunes and the heavy-handed requisitioning soon came to a halt. If it had not been for the minor alterations to their daily routines, they could easily have forgotten that they were living in a country at war. However, they no longer received daily newspapers from London and Paris – one of life's numerous little inconveniences – and had to rely on George Horton to bring them the latest intelligence from the outside world. The stories he recounted were so grim that it was hard to believe they were true. Europe was tearing itself apart in a struggle that appeared to be on an altogether more violent scale than the conflicts of old.

In the first battle of Ypres, 12 October – 11 November 1914, the British Expeditionary Force had come under sustained attack from the German army. The battle had rapidly turned into a slaughter, but one that led to stalemate rather than outright victory. As torrential rain turned Flanders into a soupy quagmire, experts were beginning to predict that the war would not in fact be over by Christmas. Horton informed the Whittalls that the troops had dug trenches in the waterlogged soil and were gazing forlornly over a landscape of mud, shattered trees and absolute desolation.

Such tales were greeted with despondency in Bournabat, whilst having about them an air of unreality. 'Isolated from the Kaiser's war and the changes it had brought to Europe, the family still lived in their own little private Raj.' So wrote Edward Whittall's granddaughter, Ray, in a poignant memoir set down on paper many years later.

Elsewhere, the world had erupted into violence and the social hierarchy of Europe was being shaken up as never before. Yet in the genteel colony of Bournabat, the Whittalls and Girauds stuck rigidly to the old rules and conventions. Their daily lives retained the Edwardian splendour that had left such a deep impression on Gertrude Bell. No one had noticed that twilight was rapidly approaching.

The children continued to attend Miss Florence's primary school, which was to remain open throughout the conflict, and spent their weekends flying kites and playing in the gardens of their family homes. Many of the Greek gardeners, maids and domestics had returned to their home country on the outbreak of war; their places were now filled by Turkish Smyrniots. It was the first time that the Whittalls had employed a Turkish cook 'and there was some feeling against her at first in the kitchen', recalled one member of the family. 'No one could pronounce her name and she was finally called Effet, which was something like it.' She provided considerable entertainment for those working 'below stairs' on account of her enormous, protruding belly.

In the two years since old Magdalen's death, Edward Whittall's wife, Mary, had slipped comfortably into the matriarchal role formerly occupied by her mother-in-law. She did her utmost to ensure that the familiar conventions remained unchanged. The older generation continued to gather each afternoon in their private loggias to discuss matters concerning the family, which seemed of far greater import than the terrible news coming from Europe. War or no war, there were still marriages to be arranged and dowries to be negotiated.

Aunt Blanche had also scaled the family hierarchy and was now the self-appointed custodian of the younger Whittalls, ruling over them with an iron fist and paying particular attention to their deportment in church. 'We hardly dared move in our seats,' recalled her great-niece, 'for she would later report our behaviour to our mothers and, in the process, she managed to censure nieces and great-nieces alike.'

The governor of Smyrna, Rahmi Bey, paid regular visits to his friends in Bournabat, despite the fact that they were enemy aliens. He was aware of the need to tread with care when dealing both with his Levantine acquaintances and with government ministers in Constantinople. His aim was to keep Smyrna out of the war and it was going to take all his guile to ensure that the unsettling incidents of the previous few months were not repeated.

'The governor-general had no faith in the final victory of the German-Turkish armies,' wrote George Horton, '[and] was extremely anxious to keep an anchor to windward. He was playing a double game; keeping in at the same time with the authorities in Constantinople and the prominent British, French and Italians at Smyrna.'

Rahmi viewed Liman von Sanders as the diabolical genius behind the government's every move. It was an opinion shared by Horton, who blamed German staff officers for many of the difficult situations that arose in the first months of the war. 'The Germans in the capital were continually pressing Enver and Talaat to be more severe with the Allied colonies at Smyrna,' he wrote. All were baffled by Rahmi Bey's behaviour and could not understand why he allowed families like the Whittalls and Girauds to remain in the city. 'Unpleasant orders were frequently received,' wrote Horton, 'which Rahmi evaded to the extent of his power. He told me frankly that such was his policy and [he] agreed to cooperate with me.'

As New Year approached, ministers' bafflement turned to frustration and anger. '[Rahmi] is . . . in considerable disfavour in German circles,' noted Horton, 'because of the marked partiality that he shows towards the English and French who are . . . receiving at present the utmost protection that can be desired.' Government officials found themselves caught between two stools. They did not dare to remove Rahmi Bey, for fear that they would plunge Turkey's most prosperous city into chaos at the very time when her industrial facilities were most likely to be needed. Yet they grew increasingly incensed at the manner in which Smyrna's governor flagrantly flaunted their orders.

Rahmi Bey did everything he could to shield all the city's different communities from the worst effects of the hostilities. The Jews and Armenians were encouraged to operate their businesses as normal, while the Greek community was told to keep open the city's shops and brasseries. Many of Smyrna's migrant labourers had left when war was declared, yet there were still some 45,000 Greek nationals living in the city at this time – men, women and children who called Smyrna their home but remained subjects of King Constantine of Greece. 'With reference to these . . .' wrote Horton, 'the vali [city governor] frequently told me that he intended to treat them well, as he considered King Constantine an ally of Turkey and Germany.'

But Rahmi's hands were tied when it came to the city's 110,000 *rayahs* – the Greeks who had been born in Smyrna and held Turkish nationality. As these young men were liable for national service, the government began conscripting them in earnest. They did not dare to provide them with arms; instead, they were drafted into labour battalions whose wartime role was to dig trenches and build roads, often in shocking conditions.

Smyrna's *rayahs* fared better than most, for the majority managed to avoid the draft, but the situation was very different in the countryside that lay beyond the perimeters of the city. '[They] were massacred, robbed, driven out of their homes, ravished or were drafted into the army,' wrote Horton, 'and set to digging trenches and other work of that nature, without food or clothing, until many of them died of starvation or exposure.'

The draft of the *rayahs* served as a reminder to everyone inside Smyrna that their future welfare was absolutely dependent upon Rahmi Bey being able to keep the city at arm's length from the war. This was to prove an increasingly difficult task as hopes of a rapid victory retreated into the distance. In the winter of 1914, Rahmi was brought the unwelcome news that an entire division of the Turkish army was on the move in eastern Anatolia. He was to find himself ensnared in a highly dangerous game of war and peace – and it was Enver Pasha's turn to throw the dice.

Some three weeks before the Whittalls sat down to enjoy their Christmas lunch, Enver Pasha had paid a visit to General Liman von Sanders at his offices in the War Ministry in Constantinople. The relationship between the two men had grown increasingly stormy since the general's arrival in Turkey. Enver disliked Liman's punctiliousness and was almost certainly jealous of him; Liman von Sanders was continually exasperated by Enver Pasha's vaunting pride.

Enver had brought with him a map of the Caucasus, which he proceeded to spread out on Liman von Sanders' desk. After pointing to the positions of the various battalions of the Turkish Third Army, he informed the German commander that he was heading to Anatolia in order to take personal command of that army. Furthermore, he intended to lead it into battle against the Russians.

Liman von Sanders was aghast when he heard this. He told Enver that such a campaign was 'wholly impracticable' and tantamount to suicide. He was familiar with the topography of the Caucasian mountains and considered such terrain to be totally unsuited to offensive operations.

Angered by Liman von Sanders' objections, Enver revealed his true colours. He harboured fantastical dreams of crushing the British empire and told von Sanders that, after annihilating the Russian army, 'he contemplated marching through Afghanistan to India.' He then made a hasty exit, thereby forestalling any more criticism from the German.

The Turkish commanders on the ground had a rather more pragmatic approach to warfare than Enver Pasha. The Third Army had its bases in the barren hinterland of eastern Anatolia and had yet to benefit from von Sanders' modernisation programme. 'The condition[s] there were absolutely indescribable,' wrote Clarence Ussher, an American missionary living in the garrison city of Van. 'Even the remembrance of the filth I witnessed seems to stifle me as I write.'

There was another obstacle to Enver's planned offensive – one that would destroy the lives of a million people and ultimately have profound repercussions for the doomed city of Smyrna. The six provinces of eastern Anatolia were home to a large population of Armenians, many of whom had an ambiguous relationship with the Ottoman government. They had long suffered from state-sponsored persecution: more than 200,000 Armenians had been massacred between 1894 and 1896. At the outbreak of the First World War, the Armenian patriarch in Constantinople had vowed to support the Ottoman government. But many of his flock living in Anatolia quietly prayed that Enver's offensive in the Caucasus would be snuffed out by their co-religionists in Russia.

The extent to which the Armenians actively undermined Enver's offensive is unclear. According to Ussher, the Third Army's Armenian regiments fought valiantly against the Russians, and despatches written by German military officers suggest that reports of an armed Armenian insurgency were wholly unfounded. It is certainly true that the scattered communities of Armenians living on the frontier threw in their lot with the advancing Russians, yet such a course of events should have been envisaged by Enver Pasha. 'After massacring hundreds of thousands of Armenians in the course of thirty years,' wrote the American ambassador, Henry Morgenthau, 'outraging their women and girls and robbing or maltreating them in every conceivable way, the Turks still apparently believed that they had the right to expect from them the most enthusiastic "loyalty".'

Enver Pasha arrived in Anatolia in mid-December and began planning his offensive. He had at his disposal some 95,000 men and he intended to drive his army northwards into Russia within ten days. Russian intelligence was quick to notice the Turkish troop movements but attached no great significance to them. They could not believe that Enver Pasha's army would attempt an offensive across the Caucasus in the middle of winter. It was only when the Russian commander, General Myshlaevsky, was almost killed by a Turkish sniper that he awoke to the extent of the attack.

Unwilling to fight Enver's army, Myshlaevsky ordered a general retreat. However, a second general in the Russian command, Nikolai Yudenich, was convinced that the Turkish winter offensive was doomed to failure, especially as the weather was on the turn. Thick banks of snow clouds had begun to roll in from the horizon and were now piling up over the mountains ahead.

The first few flakes began falling early on the morning of 24 December, the harbingers of a cruel and murderous storm. As the wind began screaming through the mountain defiles, the snowfall developed into a spectacular blizzard. The Turkish divisions were caught in an exposed position on a mountain ridge and bore the full force of the storm. Enver drove his men forwards, still hopeful of victory, but these frost-bitten troops were no longer in a position to fight. Over the days that followed, they were annihilated by General Yudenich's infantry.

Enver's great offensive had proved a spectacular rout. He had begun the campaign with 95,000 men — far more than on the

Russian side – and ended it with fewer than 20,000. Three weeks after embarking on its offensive, the Turkish Third Army had ceased to exist as a fighting force.

Enver left Anatolia in the second week of January. Although he congratulated the shattered remnants of his army and wrote bulletins comparing their 'success' to the glorious victories of the early Ottoman empire, the truth of the matter was very different. Enver had been crushed and the only way for him to salvage his reputation was to find a scapegoat for his defeat. He blamed the enemy within and vowed to liquidate that enemy before it could do any further damage.

Tidings of Enver Pasha's defeat was greeted with weary delight in England. It was a glimmer of good news after months of stalemate in France and Flanders, but it had to be balanced against the brutal treatment of the Greek communities of Anatolia. This, in many people's eyes, was confirmation that the Turks were every bit as barbaric as their German allies.

British ministers were quick to realise that the stories filtering out of Turkey could be exploited in the interests of realpolitik. As dark tales of forced labour began to circulate in British broadsheets and the scale of Enver's defeat became apparent, there was a feeling that it was time to persuade Greece to join the war on the side of the Allies. Britain's plans for an audacious attack on the Gallipoli peninsula were well advanced. It would be invaluable to have Greece on board as an ally.

On 23 January 1915, Britain's foreign secretary, Sir Edward Grey, wrote a highly secret memo to Greece's prime minister, Eleftherios Venizelos, offering him 'most important territorial compensation for Greece on the coast of Asia Minor' on condition that Greece joined the war on the side of the Allies. Smyrna, along with all the rich farmland that surrounded the city, was to be handed to him on a plate.

Venizelos rose to the bait, as the British knew he would. With

Smyrna in Greek hands, he would have achieved his dream of a lifetime. The Megali Idea – a Greek empire in Asia Minor – would be within a whisker of becoming a reality.

Venizelos would have set Greece on a war footing immediately but for one insurmountable obstacle in his path. King Constantine was the brother-in-law of the German Kaiser and had no desire to lead his country into a conflict against his own family. He turned down the Allies' offer of Smyrna and forbade Venizelos from contributing a division of Greek troops to the planned landings at Gallipoli.

Refusing to back down, Venizelos threw his energies into securing the backing of minister and generals, yet all his hard work came to nothing. The king steadfastly refused to sanction joining the Allies in a war against Germany, leaving Venizelos with very little option but to resign. Although he returned to power a few months later, his continual disagreement with the king made his position untenable and led to a second resignation in October. When he returned to power for a third and final time, it was to be in a most spectacular and surprising fashion.

While Venizelos was struggling to get Greece into the war, Rahmi Bey was doing his utmost to keep Smyrna out of it. He was appalled by reports of Enver Pasha's disastrous offensive in the Caucasus, fearing that it would have serious repercussions for his city.

He was in the midst of planning how best to keep his city at arm's length from the war when he was brought news that the British destroyer, *Euryalus*, had been sighted sailing into the bay of Smyrna. The ship's commander, Admiral Peirse, had been sent to the city by the British Admiralty with orders to destroy all the fortifications that lined the bay. The Admiralty was putting the finishing touches to its Gallipoli offensive and was concerned that Smyrna would be used as a base for German submarines.

Admiral Peirse set to work with gusto, launching a heavy bombardment on the two principal forts. His gunners excelled themselves in the hours before dusk, landing several dozen shells on target and twice hitting their magazines. Peirse was intending to continue his attack on the following morning, but was stopped in his tracks by a most unexpected telegram. Rahmi Bey — known in London to be sympathetic to the Allied cause — was keen to talk to the British admiral. He could not do so in person, for obvious reasons, so he offered to send his trusted deputy, Carabiber Bey, accompanied by the American consul, George Horton.

'We drove over a horrible road,' wrote Horton, 'which had been much cut up by shells from the British vessels.' All the bridges had been destroyed and it took the men several hours to reach the coastal village of Vourla. 'We could see the gray, dirty and businesslike cruisers sailing around in a semi-circle,' wrote Horton, 'dropping occasional shells on the hillsides and on the road.' When he and Carabiber Bey finally arrived at the port, they hired a caique and headed out towards the British fleet.

Although the battleships appeared not to notice them at first, the *Euryalus* eventually displayed a white ensign and sent a launch to meet the men. 'We were received on board by Admiral Peirse,' wrote Horton, 'a tall, thin, solemn old man, who took me to his cabin and questioned me minutely as to the official standing and character of Carabiber Bey.'

The discussions that followed left George Horton wide-eyed. 'I shall never forget sitting there on that dirty ship,' he wrote, 'drinking tea with the stern old British admiral and the Turkish representative, while I listened to words that could have come out of one of Sabatini's novels — or an unwritten page of British history.'

Rahmi's proposal was indeed most extraordinary. He wanted a private truce between Smyrna and the British government, offering to withdraw his city from the war in order to safe-guard its numerous different minorities. Such a course of action was, from the Turkish perspective, tantamount to treason. The Allied powers were about to launch a massive assault on the Gallipoli peninsula with the hope of capturing Constantinople and knocking Turkey out of the war. Yet just a few hours to the south, the country's most prosperous city was preparing to hand itself over to the enemy. The British could scarcely believe what they were hearing; it was akin to Manchester suddenly declaring itself on the side of the German Kaiser.

Rahmi Bey's negotiations with the British admiral took place in the greatest secrecy, yet the activity in the bay did not escape the notice of the spies and informers working in Smyrna on behalf of the central government. They immediately told the German consul of their suspicions and the consul, in turn, forwarded the news to Constantinople.

Government ministers were horrified at the prospect of losing control of Smyrna and responded with alacrity, lambasting Rahmi Bey for his conduct and ordering him to halt all negotiations with immediate effect. A few days later, Enver Pasha arrived unexpectedly in Smyrna, 'evidently to straighten things out and to impose the German will'.

His discussions with Rahmi Bey were held behind closed doors and their content will never be known. He must have been furious with Rahmi's treacherous overtures to the British, yet he was perhaps not unduly surprised. He had already convinced himself that the greatest threat to Turkey's future came from the enemy within. Now, his worst fears were begin-ning to come true – not just on the eastern frontier with Russia, but on Turkey's prosperous Aegean coastline.

Although Enver was received in Smyrna with an outward show of respect, there were few in the city who held him in much esteem. At a dinner held in his honour, Horton learned that many prominent Turks in Constantinople sympathised with

Rahmi's position. He was told that 'proposals similar to those made at Smyrna . . . were being favourably considered at the capital.' It was perhaps the knowledge of this that prevented Enver Pasha from removing Rahmi from office. Smyrna was one of a dozen or more tinderboxes. Rahmi's dismissal could have proved the spark to set the entire Aegean coastline ablaze.

Admiral Peirse resumed his bombardment of the city fortifications as soon as he realised that the negotiations with Rahmi were doomed. 'The guns were so loud,' recalled Horton, 'that they shook the windows of the houses of the city. They gave forth a deep yet spiteful, coughing sound, like nothing so much as the barking of great dogs.' At times, they created a spectacle of sinister beauty. 'When there was a mist, or at night, red streaks could be seen pouring out from the guns . . . [and] when the shells exploded in the sea, columns of water rose into the air to a great height.'

The city's inhabitants were fascinated by the constant bombardment of the coastline. Watching the evening cannonade from one of the harbourside bars replaced the evening promenade as the city's most popular pastime. 'The quay was crowded every night with spectators,' wrote Horton, 'and seats at the many cafés along the waterfront commanded a high price.' The terrace of the American consulate was one of the most popular venues, for it afforded a spectacular view across the bay of Smyrna. Horton's friends and colleagues would gather here in the evenings in order to drink gin slings and watch the shells raining down on the city's outer forts.

Rahmi Bey also enjoyed watching the bombardment; his favourite venue was the terrace of Costi's Café, which was also on the waterfront. On one occasion, he caught sight of Horton walking along the quay and summoned him over for a chat.

'It is now five minutes to five,' he observed. 'I have noticed that our British friends always cease firing on our works at five o'clock and devote half an hour to taking tea, which is their national beverage. Ouzo (a kind of white whisky) is the Turkish national drink and while they have their tea, I always take my ouzo'. At five, he shut his watch with a snap and, in fact, the firing ceased. 'Come in with me', he said, 'and we shall all drink together'.

The British bombardment was rather less welcomed by Liman von Sanders, who watched the events in the bay with mounting anger. He was even more alarmed to learn that British forces had taken possession of Long Island and installed gun batteries along the shoreline. This enabled them to blockade the city, preventing any supplies from entering the harbour. 'But the extreme richness and self-sufficiency of the region prevented its being entirely effective as a coercive measure,' wrote Horton. He added that enterprising Greek merchants managed to keep the flour mills working at full speed, thereby ensuring that the bread supply never faltered. And although sugar eventually became scarce, the inhabitants instead used *pelmez*, a locally produced grape syrup. Horton, the classical scholar, rather enjoyed the mild hardship. 'I consoled myself with the reflection that the ancients had no sugar at all and depended entirely on honey.'

More than nine decades after these events took place, two of the elderly survivors remember the war as a time when the well-ordered pattern of daily life changed very little. 'Of course there were a few things missing,' says Petros Brussalis with a nonchalant wave of his hand, 'but we continued to live very much as we had always done.'

Alfred Simes, who was five years old when the British seized Long Island, agrees. 'I don't recall any shortages of food during my childhood,' he said, 'and no one in our family ever went hungry.' But the British blockade did succeed in causing a temporary rupture in the supply of medicines to the city and it was to prove fatal for young Alfred's father. 'He went fishing in the torrential rain,' recalls Alfred, 'and fell ill with a fever soon after.' With no medication available, he died after an illness lasting just a few days.

One of Alfred's earliest memories is of their last Christmas together. 'It was 1915 and my father gave me a horse's whip. It was what I'd always wanted. I remember opening our presents around the Christmas tree and then singing carols together.'

The death of Alfred's father might have spelled disaster for the family, especially in wartime. Fortunately, one of Alfred's aunts was married to a wealthy Italian naval captain, who paid for Alfred and his sister to continue their education. Life was never as happy as before, but the family had escaped falling into penury.

The surviving memoirs of the Levantine community suggest that age has not distorted the memories of Petros Brussalis and Alfred Simes. During this period of conflict, the department stores remained open and the brasseries continued to do a roaring trade. In Bournabat, the Levantine families saw no reason to change the habits of a lifetime. For many, these were the happiest years of their lives. 'The village [of Bournabat] was at its best,' wrote Eldon Giraud of the mid-war years, 'with the large houses well kept and the various carriages and footmen wearing the liveries of their masters.'

It was hard for people to believe that the battlefront was actually just a few hours to the north of Smyrna. In the sand dunes of the Gallipoli peninsula, a titanic clash of arms was taking place between the Turkish army and its British and Anzac adversaries. The Allied forces had landed in April 1915 after an intense aerial bombardment designed to destroy the shoreline batteries. For the next eight months, they tried desperately to advance out of their narrow beachheads – a bloody and terrible struggle that was ultimately to leave tens of thousands of men dead. Such was the intensity of the fight that many were killed by the bayonet rather than the gun.

The local press continually heralded the military victories of

Turkey and Germany, yet few in Smyrna credited such stories. 'The populace, which was overwhelmingly pro-Entente, did not believe any of this,' wrote Horton, 'but lived on rumors, mostly unfounded and untrue, picked up in various ways.'

In the spring of 1915, a most disturbing rumour reached the American consulate in Smyrna. Horton received news from Walter Geddes, an employee of Smyrna's MacAndrews and Forbes liquorice company, that Armenian communities across Anatolia were being evicted from their homes and marched into the desert by Turkish soldiers. Most never even reached their destination; they were butchered by the roadside or left to die in the heat and dust.

Geddes was travelling in Anatolia at the time of the deportations and was appalled by what he saw. 'From Kadma to Aleppo, I witnessed the worst sights of the whole trip,' he wrote in his report. 'Here, the people began to play out in the intense heat and no water, and I passed several who were prostrate, actually dying of thirst.' He stopped to help one old woman who had collapsed, unconscious from dehydration and fatigue. 'Further on, I saw two young girls who had become so exhausted that they had fallen on the road and lay with their already swollen faces exposed to the sun.'

As Geddes made his way back to Smyrna, he passed thousands more people being forcibly marched towards the desert. '[They] walk throughout the whole day at a shuffling gait and for hours do not speak to one another.' The children were treated no better than the adults.

Many of these little tots are obliged to walk barefooted along the road and many of them carry little packs on their backs. They are all emaciated, their clothes are in rags and their hair in a filthy condition. The filth has given rise to millions of flies and I saw several babies' faces and eyes covered with these insects, their mothers being too exhausted to brush them away.

Horton listened to Geddes' stories with a sense of revulsion and alarm. So, too, did Henry Morgenthau, who was still serving as American ambassador in Constantinople. He interviewed many of the American missionaries and physicians working in eastern Anatolia and was disgusted by what they told him. 'For hours they would sit in my office,' he wrote, 'and with tears streaming down their faces, they would tell me of the horrors through which they had passed.'

The deportations followed a depressingly familiar pattern. Placards were posted in towns and villages, ordering the Armenian population to assemble at a given time. The Turkish gendarmes would then steal anything of value before sending them on their long march towards the desert. 'Before the caravans were started,' wrote Morgenthau, 'it became the regular practice to separate the young men from their families, tie them together in groups of four, lead them to the outskirts and shoot them.'

On at least three occasions, Morgenthau went to visit Mehmet Talaat Pasha, the Minister of the Interior, and demanded an explanation for what was taking place. Talaat did not mince his words. After denouncing the Armenians as traitors intent on undermining the Turkish state, he told Morgenthau that the government had no intention of changing its policy. 'I must not get the idea that the deportations had been decided upon hastily,' he said. 'In reality, they were the result of prolonged and careful deliberation.'

The American ambassador warned Talaat that he was making a terrible mistake, but the minister was unmoved. '"Yes, we may make mistakes", he replied, "but" – and he firmly closed his lips and shook his head – "we never regret."' He also told Morgenthau to keep his nose out of Turkish affairs. '"It is no use for you to argue . . ." he said. "We have already disposed of three quarters of the Armenians; there are none at all left in Bitlis, Van and Erzeroum." '

The deportations of hundreds of thousands of people continued throughout the spring and summer of 1915. News about their scale and brutality quickly spread through Constantinople, whose Armenian population had hitherto been spared. But now they, too, found themselves targeted. 'How many countless times,' wrote Harry Stuermer, correspondent for the *Kolnische Zeitung*, 'did I have to look on at that typical spectacle of little bands of Armenians belonging to the capital being escorted through the streets of Pera by two gendarmes . . . marching them off to the "Karakol" of Galata-Serai, the chief police station in Pera, where he delivered up his daily bag of Armenians.'

Smyrna alone remained untouched by Talaat's policy. He did not dare – yet – to meddle with Rahmi Bey's fiefdom, although George Horton feared that it would only be a matter of time before the deportations would be extended to Smyrna's prosperous Armenian community.

By the summer of 1915, the leaders of this community were feeling so jittery that they held a public religious ceremony to pray for the success of the Turkish army. One of Smyrna's leading Armenian lawyers, Nazareth Hilmi, gave a rousing speech in which he declared the absolute fidelity to Turkey of the city's Armenian population. According to the Austrian consul – one of the dignitaries invited to the service – it was 'a patriotic speech that stressed the complete loyalty and submission to the Ottoman empire of the Smyrniot Armenians'.

Such demonstrations had little effect on the ministers in Constantinople, who had every intention of extending their purge to Smyrna. They did their utmost to provoke Rahmi Bey into action, informing him that a court in Constantinople had ordered the death penalty for seven Armenian prisoners being held in Smyrna. The offence committed by these men was unclear and Rahmi Bey was dismayed by such a travesty of justice. Believing the men to be innocent, he wired Constantinople with the message that under Ottoman law the accused had the right to appeal for clemency. Soon afterwards, he received his answer: 'Technically, you are right. Hang them first, and send the petition for pardon afterward.'

The seven Armenians were eventually saved from the gallows by the intervention of Henry Morgenthau, who directly petitioned government ministers. This went some way to reassuring Smyrna's Armenian community. So long as Rahmi Bey remained in charge of the city, they knew that they would not be molested. However, if he was to be removed from office, they felt certain to meet the same fate as their fellow Armenians elsewhere in Turkey.

George Horton and Henry Morgenthau remained in regular contact with Turkish ministers throughout the autumn of 1915; they were never in any doubt that the Armenian deportations had been planned and orchestrated by senior figures in the government. But it was hard to find written proof of this in the years that followed the end of the First World War when there was talk of charging those responsible with crimes against humanity. Most of the Ottoman archives were shredded, burned or dispersed in an effort to efface all record of what had taken place. Nevertheless, a handful of documents escaped the destruction and one of these was brought to the attention of Clifford Heathcote-Smith, Smyrna's former consul.

'I was approached confidentially by someone who stated that there was still, in the Director of Public Security, Constantinople, an official who had been in the Minister of the Interior's Department during the whole of the war.' This individual had been in charge of all the material relating to the Armenians and the measures ordered by the government. 'He said that just before the Armistice, officials had been going to the archives' department at night and making a clean sweep of most of the documents, but that the original draft of the orders relating to the Armenian massacres had been saved.'

It was this draft document that Heathcote-Smith managed to acquire. It was entitled 'The Ten Commandments of the Comite Union and Progress [sic]' and was the minutes of a secret conference attended by the Minister of the Interior, Talaat Bey, and four of his senior officials in the winter of 1914.

Commandment One set the tone for the entire document. It called for the arrest of all Armenians who were working against the government and their ostensible deportation to Baghdad or Mosul. Once they were on the march, their Turkish guards were to 'wipe them out either on the road or there'. Commandment Three called on officials to excite Muslim opinion in Van, Erzeroum and Adana '[and] provoke organised massacres'. Commandment Five was to 'exterminate all males under 50, priests and teachers, [and] leave girls and children to be Islamised'. Commandment Eight called for the murder of any Armenians still serving in the army, while Commandment Nine ordered that 'all action . . . begin simultaneously, and thus leave no time for preparation of defensive measures'.

The document might have provided enough evidence to convict Talaat Bey of crimes against humanity, but by the time Clifford Heathcote-Smith handed it over to British ministers, events had moved on. The war was over and Talaat Bey had been killed by an Armenian assassin. Heathcote-Smith's document was quietly filed away in the Public Record Office, bound together with a sheaf of miscellaneous papers in box FO371/4172. It remains there to this day.

Saving the Enemy

George Horton and his wife had long been accustomed to spend the hour before dusk relaxing on the terrace of their apartment on Frank Street. From here, they had an alluring view of the bay of Smyrna, especially in the evening when the westerly sun dipped below the Aegean.

The Hortons were admiring this very scene on the evening of 23 May 1916 when they noticed two black specks in the sky, far out to sea. As they grew larger, Horton realised that two planes were speeding towards the city, 'low down and very near, glittering in the sun'. They dipped even lower as they approached the shoreline, then veered away from the European quarter, heading towards Mount Pagus and the Turkish part of town. As they flew over the souks, they dropped shells onto the buildings below.

Horton watched in a mixture of awe and fascination. 'They tipped slightly every time a bomb was dropped,' he wrote, 'as though to let it slide off.' The planes also dropped hundreds of printed proclamations, all bearing Britain's royal coat of arms. These declared that such bombing raids would continue for as long as German Coastal guns fired on the British vessel at anchor in the bay of Smyrna.

The damage caused by the raid provoked a serious escalation in tensions inside the city. Four Muslims were killed and part of the Turkish quarter was destroyed. The bombardment also created a crisis for Rahmi Bey. He was under mounting pressure to obey directives issued in Constantinople. Now, the British action had further inflamed Turkish indignation at the leniency he showed towards the Allied nationals still living in the city.

Horton sympathised with Rahmi Bey. He sent an urgent despatch to Constantinople, and thence to London, warning that families like the Whittalls and the Girauds – and therefore Smyrna itself – would face disastrous consequences if there was another raid. He pointed out that the bombardment had caused considerable destruction of life and property but had failed to hit a single military target.

Horton's undiplomatic language irked British Admiralty officials. They were especially riled by the consul's remarks on the inaccuracy of the targeting and responded by releasing a statement defending their actions. 'All reasonable efforts were made to confine the bombardment of Smyrna to railway stations, fortresses, harbours and other places of military importance.' Horton would later remark wryly that 'in those days, if an aeroplane bomb dropped within a mile of its objective, the pilot was commended for good marksmanship.'

The next few days passed peacefully, giving Horton confidence that his strongly worded telegram had been heeded by London. He was therefore astonished when he saw the same planes racing towards the city less than a week after the first raid. Thirty bombs were dropped on residential districts, killing fifteen people and wounding twice as many. Eleven houses were pulverised in the bombardment and many other buildings were seriously damaged. When Horton walked through the city once the raid was over, he was confronted by scenes of such horror that he was to remember them for years to come. 'A Greek mother . . . ran about the streets, screaming and stark mad, carrying in her arms the body of her headless babe.' All the victims were innocent civilians who had played no role in the war. Among the dead were an Armenian couple who had been married just hours earlier and had been killed in their nuptial bed. 'The whole front of their house had been torn off,' wrote Horton, 'so that they could be plainly seen.'

As this new raid looked certain to spark civil unrest, Rahmi Bey took the highly unusual step of addressing in person the city's inhabitants. 'The *vali* himself, splendidly mounted, rode through the city with a staff of aides and announced to various groups of people that they should be calm and have implicit confidence in the government.' He was helped in his task of assuaging Muslim passions by the fact that all of the dead were Christian. 'If those bombs had dropped also in the Turkish quarter,' wrote Horton, 'there would have been a massacre of Englishmen, Italian and French at Smyrna of which the world would have been talking yet.'

Yet this second raid left Rahmi Bey with little room for manoeuvre. Government ministers in Constantinople were threatening 'severe measures' unless he punished everyone of English, French and Italian origin. Rahmi had no option but to intern all the adult male nationals of the Allied powers.

It is strange that few of the surviving Levantine memoirs make any mention of an episode that must have been stressful, upsetting and undignified. Herbert Octavius, Edward Whittall and many of their neighbours must surely have been interned in the spring of 1916. But only Mary Giraud, Edmund's daughter, made anything more than a passing reference to the events that followed the second bombing raid. She recalled how the Turkish military arrived at their Bournabat mansion one evening and arrested her father. '[He] was put into [a] concentration [camp],' she wrote, 'and I remember visiting him at a hospital without exactly understanding the reason for his incarceration except that it had something to do with the war.'

Frightened by this rude intrusion into her idyllic childhood, Mary asked her family why her father had been taken away against his will. This, however, was still a time when the young-sters were excluded from the affairs of the adult world. 'No one saw fit to explain things to children,' she wrote, 'and obviously didn't understand their sense of fear.'

The wives left behind in Bournabat hoped that the intern-ment of their husbands and sons would force the British govern-ment into reconsidering its strategy towards Smyrna. But the Admiralty in London displayed a remarkably cavalier attitude towards their own nationals, despatching planes on a third bombing raid in mid-June. This proved even less successful than the previous two. The pilots managed to hit the American Girls' School and the Scottish Mission Hospital, severely wounding four French children.

When news of this third raid reached Clifford Heathcote-Smith, now serving as an intelligence officer in Athens, he wrote a highly charged letter to ministers, urging them to treat Smyrna as a case apart from the rest of Turkey. 'The all-powerful Governor-General, Rahmi Bey, has persistently adopted an atti-tude of benevolence towards British subjects,' he wrote, 'often against the wishes and instructions of other Turkish and German authorities.' He reminded Whitehall that the city's population 'is composed, in its large majority, of our friends – Entente subjects, neutrals, Greeks and Armenians'.

Heathcote-Smith's letter struck a chord with the foreign secre-tary, Sir Edward Grey. He had never been comfortable with the idea of bombing Smyrna and now called an immediate halt to the raids. The city was to be spared any future attack from the air. It was the best possible news for the Levantine families. The interned men were quietly released by Rahmi Bey and allowed to return to their homes in Bournabat, Cordelio and the other suburbs.

The bombing raids served as a reminder to Smyrna's inhabi-tants that they were living in a country at war. For a brief moment, their lives had been in real danger, but no sooner had the attacks been brought to a halt than the war once again receded into the distance. The only reminder of the conflict was the occasional dogfight that took place in the skies above the city.

One of these exhilarating battles was witnessed by Horton and two of his colleagues. They were chatting on the terrace of the consulate when they noticed two British aircraft swooping in from the sea. These were being chased by a third aircraft – a German one – approaching from the east.

It rose to a great height over Mount Pagus, hovered momentarily in the still spring air, then swooped down and opened fire on the two British planes. One was raked with shot, cutting the fuel supply to its engines. '[It] sank slowly and obliquely to earth,' wrote Horton, 'exactly like a wounded duck.' The German craft trailed its victim for a moment in order to survey the damage, then made a steep ascent and banked into the clouds. Horton later learned that the two English pilots managed to crash-land their plane in a vineyard, suffering only bruises and a broken ankle.

As the second British plane circled the city, the German fighter gave hot pursuit. Horton and his companions watched a life-and-death air battle played out before their eyes. 'The rapid fire of the machine guns, though very distinct, did not have a vicious sound,' he wrote. 'Tat! Tat! Tat! Tat! – such a noise as a boy might make by beating on a table with the flat side of a ruler.'

The two planes fought and feinted for what seemed like an eternity, dodging gunfire with deft manoeuvres in the air. To observers on the ground, the battle was curiously graceful – a display of lethal acrobatics that was watched with reverence and respect. Yet this was a fight to the death and the outcome was dependent on the skill of the respective airmen. After more fencing in the clear blue sky, the German pilot locked onto his adversary and peppered the craft with bullets. In seconds, the fight was over. The British plane flipped onto its belly, then went into a long nosedive.

The pilots managed to prise themselves from the cockpit, but they must have known that they were doomed. 'First fell the hapless bodies of the Englishmen like inanimate bundles,' reads one eyewitness account. 'Then came the slowly descending wings.' To Horton, it looked 'for all the world like a huge dragon-fly, falling, falling. On account of the great height and the distance from us, it appeared to be coming down slowly, which of course, was an illusion.'

When the plane finally hit the ground, it exploded into a fireball. The aircraft was 'smashed to a pulp and charred to cinders'. Nevertheless, the corpses of the airmen were recovered and put on display. 'The Turkish soldiers stripped the mangled corpses and sold the clothes as souvenirs . . . the bodies were exhibited to the crowd, a piaster being charged for the sight, and photographs were taken and sold.'

The German military authorities, however, were appalled by the behaviour of the Turks. 'They destroyed the plates and photographs and ordered a military funeral.' This was held on the day that followed the dogfight. The procession to the British church passed through the heart of the city and thousands of people lined the streets. The English pastor, Reverend Brett, gave the funeral address, 'and a sadder and more impressive one I have never heard', wrote Horton. As the men's scorched remains were interred, the German pilot, Buddecke, circled about the skies dropping flowers on the men's final resting place. It was a curiously civilised gesture in a time of dirty war.

The British were able to continue their dogfights over Smyrna for as long as they controlled the little airstrip on Long Island. Their continued presence infuriated Liman von Sanders, who vowed to recapture the island and rid the bay of Smyrna of British soldiers.

On the night of 4 June, he landed a sizeable Turkish force on the southern tip of Long Island. They were heavily armed and expected to have to fight for every inch of land, but as they crept gingerly up the beaches, they were met by absolute silence. The only signs of life came from nesting seabirds and a few goats.

Although the Turks feared some sort of trap, they soon found that they had the island to themselves. The British had left some days before, abandoning equipment and empty drums of kerosene. The failure of the Gallipoli offensive had ended all talk of any future military action on Turkish soil. The continued occupation of Long Island was no longer considered necessary.

The Turkish flag was soon flying over the island and news of the 'victory' was flashed back to Smyrna. The official celebrations that followed provided Horton with an opportunity to meet Liman von Sanders – 'my first contact', he was later to write, 'with German military pomposity'. The general had become a laughing stock among the Levantine community; his visit to Smyrna was preceded by tales of his behaviour at a formal dinner in Constantinople, at which he had fretted and fumed over his seating position at the high table.

Now, at a glittering party hosted by the Austrian consul, von Sanders refused to be introduced to anyone. 'His Excellency wished only to refresh himself from his labor by talking with young girls,' noted Horton with malicious relish. 'There was a pert young Levantine miss with whom he fell hopelessly in love and he took rooms on a narrow street directly opposite her house. Here he installed himself at a window and gazed across the way hour after hour.'

It was to no avail, as their relationship remained a platonic one. The girl had no desire to get entangled with a man old enough to be her father.

The German capture of Long Island was greeted with weary resignation by many in the city. All now knew that any hope of deliverance by British forces was at an end. 'People used to walk the quay and scan the horizon for the delivering vessels,' wrote Horton. But most knew that the Allies were far too preoccupied with the western front – and the aftermath of the disastrous Gallipoli campaign – to contemplate landing in the bay of Smyrna.

For the Allies, the war was indeed going from bad to worse. By the summer of 1916, senior generals were unclear about how to break the stalemate. The British government had introduced conscription in May, aware that a conflict of attrition could only be won by harnessing all the human lives they could find. Now, Allied military tacticians began planning a mighty thrust eastwards against German forces close to the River Somme.

'The wire has never been so well cut,' wrote General Haig on the eve of battle, 'nor artillery preparations so thorough.' Yet when the men went over the top in July 1916, they found themselves attacking heavily fortified positions that had survived the artillery barrage. By the end of the day, 21,000 men were dead or missing.

The situation on the home front was no less grim. There were shortages of food and fuel, and inflation was starting to hurt the moneyed classes. The time was fast approaching when the government would have to introduce rationing for essential supplies.

In Constantinople, the conflict brought changes that were more subtle but nevertheless had far-reaching consequences. The exigencies of war allowed Talaat Pasha and Enver Pasha to push forward and extend their programme of Turkification. The first stage of this had been to rid Turkish soil of its Armenian population. Now, the government passed laws insisting on the use of Turkish – rather than Ottoman Arabic – on all documents, even those in private offices.

Yet there remained one goal still to be accomplished. The country's Aegean coastline continued to be home to large numbers of Greeks whose sympathies with the Allied cause were undiminished by the depressing news coming from the western front. At some point in early 1916, it was decided to deport to the interior the Christian communities living along this coast.

Whether or not this was done with Liman von Sanders' approval is difficult to gauge; he later clamed to have been against the deportations. Yet they were certainly done with his knowledge and he raised no objections to the manner in which they were undertaken. 'The old men, the women and the children were grouped into convoys and were driven into the interior under the lash of the Turkish soldiery,' wrote the Frenchman, Félix Sartiaux, who compiled a report on the deportations at the end of the war. 'No transport, no provisions were provided and these pitiable convoys were forced to struggle across the sun-scorched and wind-swept plateaus of Anatolia.'

Few coastline villages were spared the terrifying ordeal of eviction and deportation. The Gallipoli province, Brussa, Buyuk-Dere, Isnik, Kyzicos, Merefte: all were cleansed of their Greek populations by the Turkish military. 'I can state from personal experience that the Greek communal buildings – churches, schools, hospitals, baths – were wantonly desecrated and defaced and mercilessly ransacked, even beams and window-frames being removed.' So wrote Arnold Toynbee, who added that once the families had been evicted, 'the private homes were thoroughly plundered and then occupied by Moslems.'

Eyewitness accounts of the deportations, later published by the Ecumenical Patriarchate in Constantinople, make for distressing reading. 'The sight is ghastly,' wrote one observer. 'Large and small living skeletons roam through the town . . . More than 180 died on the way; the women dropped their new-born babies to keep up with their companions.'

Another saw a mother collapse and die on the steps of

Baloukeser station. 'Her little hungry children who thought that their mother was asleep, were trying to wake her up and crying and begging for bread.'

More than 200,000 Greeks were to endure the horrors of deportation. Yet Smyrna itself was once again spared. All who lived within the confines of the city – and that included the bourgeois suburbs – remained untouched by the government decrees emanating from Constantinople.

Some Levantine families flaunted these decrees quite flagrantly, hiding conscripted Greeks in the cellars of their houses. One Whittall girl remembered her parents hiding a Greek deserter who had been drafted into the Turkish army, an act of treachery that could easily have cost them their lives. 'By day, our deserter remained hidden in the Turkish bath [while] the sofa in the cooling room was his bed at night.' She added that he only ever emerged from his hiding place after dark, when he was given a meal. 'He was very young, hardly more than a boy, and I remember my surprise when I first saw him, and being told not to say anything about his presence in the house.'

Ministers were deeply unhappy at the way in which Rahmi Bey's Levantine friends behaved as if they believed themselves to be untouchable. As the battlefront news became increasingly bleak, the government sent Rahmi an order to deport to the interior all the city's Levantines, including families like the Whittalls and the Girauds.

Rahmi Bey summoned George Horton to his office and explained his predicament. If he refused to obey the directive from Constantinople, he was told that he would be removed from office. But if he carried out the government order, then the Levantine deportees were unlikely to survive. He told Horton that he intended to play his 'double game' for as long as possible, undertaking a limited fulfilment of the government's orders so that he would be seen to be doing something. 'I will begin with the *vauriens*, the disreputables, and the poor devils who would be miserable anywhere,' he told Horton, 'and proceed slowly in the hopes that there may be a change before I reach the others.'

He asked Horton to send a telegram to Constantinople, protesting against the inhumanity of the measure. 'Say "deportation begun",' he told him, 'and that will throw sand in the eyes of the Germans.'

The deportations affected about one hundred people – a far cry from what Enver and Talaat had intended. Nor were any of the Levantines of Bournabat sent to the interior. But the military guards in charge of the operation were nevertheless rough and ruthless, evicting people from their houses in the early hours when they were least able to resist. '[They] were not even given time to put on their shoes,' wrote Horton. 'They were [then] locked in dirty prisons, without food, were beaten and were threatened that, if they did not raise large sums of money, they would be sent on foot to Sivas – a sentence equivalent to a lingering and painful death.'

As the winter of 1916 approached, Horton began to question how much longer he would be able to remain in Smyrna. America was still a neutral power but the geopolitical climate was changing fast. Relations between the United States and Germany had been fraught ever since the sinking of the *Lusitania* eighteen months earlier. Now, Germany informed Washington that she was commencing unrestricted submarine warfare on all vessels approaching the British Isles. It was also discovered that she had struck a secret alliance with Mexico, in which the two countries were to 'make war together [and] make peace together'. Mexico's reward for joining the war effort was to be large areas of Texas, New Mexico and Arizona.

American public opinion was appalled by this news and it enabled the federal government to justify inching ever closer to declaring war. In mid-February 1917, two months before the

99

rupture actually occurred, George Horton received a secret despatch from Washington, instructing him to destroy all consular documents that might compromise any American or Allied inhabitant of Smyrna.

Horton was also ordered to get as many Americans out of Smyrna as possible without betraying the fact that hostilities were impending. This he managed to achieve, smuggling all but sixty-five Americans out of Paradise and into safe places in Europe. When the rupture in relations finally came – on 20 April – Horton was able to conduct the remaining few nationals out of the country. He had become the only American left in the city.

But he, too, had to pack his bags. He was now an enemy alien and all diplomatic niceties had been superseded by war. He paid a final visit to his old friend Rahmi Bey and found the governor as charming as ever. 'He informed me that a private [train] compartment had been prepared for me as far as Constantinople, and that I could go ahead and pack my baggage, which would not be inspected by the local authorities.' Horton and his wife headed first to Berne and then to Rome. Just a few weeks later, Horton was posted to Salonica.

His departure from Smyrna brought to an end the daily chronicle of life in Smyrna during the blackest days of the First World War. There are few accounts describing the city in the final year of the conflict, although prints and letters suggest that life returned to near-normality after the difficult early period. One of the most extraordinary mementoes is a photograph taken in 1917. This was one of the darkest years of the First World War, the year of Passchendaele and stagnation in the mud of Flanders. Yet the photo suggests that a very different story was unfolding in Smyrna. It shows Greeks, Turks, Levantines and Jews assembled in the Smyrna Opera House – all in black tie and tails – for the première performance of Verdi's *Rigoletto*.

The Levantine diaries reveal that food was abundant in the

latter years of the war and no one went short of essential supplies. Many families supplemented their diet by shooting the little game birds that were found in the grounds of their houses. 'My mother often went round the gardens . . . carrying an air-gun or a "flaubert" – a very small gun – bringing home a string of *beccaficos*, which she cooked for us,' wrote one of the Whittalls. 'These most delicious of tiny birds were fried in a pan and almost eaten whole.'

The Levantine memoirs also suggest that life in Bournabat also continued at its unhurried pace. Families still gathered for afternoon tea; the social club remained open to fee-paying subscribers. And the family balls continued to be held in the grounds of the great houses. 'The balls used to be something unbelievable,' recalled Eldon Giraud many years later, 'especially in winter, when parts of the front gardens used to be covered by tents as was the case when Uncle Edward [Whittall] gave a ball and I was taken to see the preparations.' Young Eldon was amazed by the extravagance. 'The ponds in front of the house had all been enclosed and floodlit by candles and Chinese lanterns. I have never seen such a sight – or ever will again.'

That ball was to be Edward Whittall's last. In 1917, the flower-collecting brother of Herbert Octavius breathed his last. He was sixty-six years of age: a young man by Whittall standards, but one whose life had been enriched by his passion for horti-culture.

'I remember his funeral,' wrote his granddaughter, Mary, 'even though I was only seven. Not only was the church overflowing with people, but the whole yard was packed with crowds of Greeks, Turks and peasants.' All had come to pay their last respects to a man who had given them employment – and paid for it out of his own pocket – throughout the last three years of war.

The crowds of workers filed past Edward's coffin with heavy heart, aware that life was certain to be much more difficult in the future. All had enjoyed working for a man who was in every respect larger than life. Now, they watched in silence as his coffin was interred in the churchyard of St Mary Magdeleine, close to the grave of his mother. His memory was to be kept alive in the exquisite gardens that had entranced Gertrude Bell many years earlier and continued to flower throughout the final months of the war.

'I am lucky enough to remember such things,' wrote his granddaughter towards the end of her life, 'and the sweet smell of the tiny clusters of mauve flowers on Libya grass, newly watered, still lingers nostalgically.'

George Horton was saddened by his departure from Smyrna. It had been his home for six years and he was extremely attached to its cosmopolitan social life. Now that he had left, he could only pray that Rahmi Bey – and the city's spirit of independence – would survive the outcome of the First World War.

That outcome was by no means certain in the spring of 1917. Although the United States had entered the war, the Allied powers knew that it would be many months before the American army was fully mobilised. Russia was meanwhile spiralling into chaos – Tsar Nicholas II had abdicated in March – and there was stagnation on the battlefields of northern France. At a series of secret meetings in London and Paris, generals began asking themselves whether a new front, centred on the strategic Greek port of Salonica, might hold the key to the future of the war.

Horton arrived in Salonica after a roundabout voyage that took him first to Berne and then to Rome. By the time he reached the city he was mentally and physically drained. For months he had been sustained by adrenaline alone and he now suffered a mild breakdown. The British doctor who examined him was alarmed by his condition. '[He] informed me that I was overcome by fatigue and would probably never be able to work any more.'

This diagnosis brought Horton sharply back to reality. After a week in bed, he got dressed, discharged himself from the infirmary and headed straight to the consulate. Within a few hours, he was back at his desk.

His recovery was well timed. Greece was in the process of undergoing a momentous political earthquake and it was to have the most serious repercussions for Smyrna. The turmoil had been sparked by the failure of the Gallipoli campaign in the winter of 1915. Once the scale of the disaster became apparent, its architects – among them Winston Churchill – ordered a full-scale evacuation. The shell-shocked survivors were plucked from the sand dunes and transported to Salonica in the hope that they would be able to strike inland in order to protect Serbia from a three-pronged attack by Bulgaria, Germany and Austria.

There was one drawback to this strategy. Greece was still a neutral power and King Constantine remained implacably opposed to joining the Allied war effort. In the face of his intransigence, the British and French followed a time-honoured tradition and simply chose to ignore him. They sailed their battleships into Salonica's harbour and began landing the first battalions of a force that would eventually number more than 300,000 men. King Constantine fumed and stamped his feet. 'I will not be treated as if I were a native chieftain,' he told the British and the French. But he was – and there was very little he could do about it.

By the time the troops were ready for action, it was too late to help Serbia. Austrian and German forces had already swept into Belgrade. Allied commanders in Salonica scratched their heads and wondered what to do with the men under their command. 'Damn. What the devil have they sent us here for?' asked the commander of the British Salonica Force. 'Here I am – and not a word of instructions. What the devil do they want me to do?'

The answer was provided by Venizelos. After harnessing

support in Crete and the Greek islands that flanked the coast of Asia Minor, he staged a *coup d'état* and made a triumphant entry into Salonica in October 1916. His first act was to establish a provisional government and a new national army. Within six weeks, Greek battalions were serving under British command.

The British and French bent over backwards to help their new Greek ally, unaware that they were creating terrible problems for the future. It fell to the French intelligence officer, Antoine Scheikevitch, to warn that Venizelos had joined the war for one reason alone: '[it would] permit the servants of the Great Idea to count in the decisions of the arbiters of the peace'.

Scheikevitch's warning fell on deaf ears although hindsight was to prove him right. Venizelos was prepared to commit his forces to fight alongside the Allies, but his gaze was once again turned towards Smyrna and the East.

By the time Horton arrived in Salonica, Greece was in the unhappy position of having two governments: one in Athens, presided over by King Constantine, and the other in Salonica, headed by his arch-rival Venizelos. However, this woeful state of affairs was soon brought to an end by Allied forces. In the summer of 1917, French troops landed at Corinth, prompting the flight of King Constantine. He headed to Switzerland, where he was to spend the rest of the war in exile.

Within days of his departure, the French occupied Athens in the name of the Allied powers. Shortly afterwards, Venizelos made his entrance into the city amidst scenes of unprecedented enthusiasm. One of his first acts was to officially enter the conflict on the side of the Allies.

The arrival of American troops on European soil at long last tipped the military balance in favour of the Allied powers. In London, Paris and Washington, there was a feeling that Germany and her allies could now be defeated.

The first glimmer of hope came from an unexpected quarter.

In October 1917, General Allenby launched his lightning offensive against Ottoman forces in Gaza, scored a swift victory and pressed on towards Jerusalem. This he also captured, delivering Lloyd George – Britain's prime minister since 1916 – the 'Christmas present' that he had fondly requested. Allenby spent the following spring and summer completing the conquest of Palestine, ably aided by Colonel T. E. Lawrence 'of Arabia', until the Ottoman forces were driven back towards Damascus and Aleppo.

The war on the western front was also reaching its denouement. In the summer of 1918, General Ludendorff launched his much vaunted *friedenssturm* [peace offensive] against the British and French forces, hoping to annihilate them before the bulk of the American army was ready for action. His failure to achieve this breakthrough – though it cost many Allied lives – was to spell the end for Germany. The armies of Britain, France and America were quick to launch a counter-attack and at long last penetrated the German front. As Ludendorff's troops retreated to the Hindenburg Line, the general realised that Germany was a spent force. He informed the Kaiser that he would soon have to seek an armistice.

Events now began moving with extraordinary rapidity. The Italian army had already brought about the disintegration of the Austrian front. Now, the forces at Salonica were also put into action. They had won a victory of sorts a few months earlier when Venizelos's new Greek army triumphed over the feared Bulgarian 49th Regiment on the Skra di Legen, a wind-blown summit on the frontier of Serbia. By the summer of 1918, the Salonica army was driving northwards with remarkable speed, capturing scores of hitherto impregnable Bulgarian positions.

On 30 September, the war-weary Bulgarians finally capitulated, the first of the Central Powers to do so. It was the news that Lloyd George had long been waiting to hear. At last he knew that his forces could head east towards Turkey, with the hope of knocking out one of Germany's staunchest allies.

What Lloyd George did not know – and neither did any of his fellow Allied leaders – was that there was a very real possibility of Turkey knocking herself out of the war. Rahmi Bey had known for some time that his country's defeat was inevitable. Now, he decided to take control of Turkey's woes – and save the great trading dynasties of Smyrna – by staging a *coup d'état*.

The details of his plot might have remained a secret, had it not been for the fact that a handful of Rahmi's private papers have survived in the archives of the Foreign Office. They reveal that he hoped to replace the discredited wartime government with one that was fully in accord with the Allied powers.

'I've just returned from Constantinople,' wrote Rahmi in a private letter at the beginning of October. 'After having made contact with all the most influential political players, I have worked out all the different ways to bring down the government.'

Rahmi's most loyal supporters were in Smyrna. They included his deputy, Carabiber Bey, and senior members of the Whittall family. Rahmi intended to give the Whittalls ministerial positions in his post-war government.

As the British cavalry made their final advance towards the Turkish frontier-post at Dedeagatch, Rahmi Bey realised that there was not a moment to lose. His *coup d'état* was set for 10 October and he told his supporters that he was 'confident of complete success'. All he needed to do was ensure the backing of the British government.

The British first grasped that something extraordinary was afoot on 5 October when Whitehall received a 'secret and urgent' telegram from Rahmi Bey. A few days later, government ministers received a second telegram, informing them that Charles Giraud and Carabiber Bey had arrived in Mytilene. They told the British commander that they had been entrusted with a 'very important mission to [the] Imperial British Minister'.

This news caused a stir in Whitehall. Senior officials wrongly surmised that the delegation had been sent by the Ottoman government with the intention of suing for peace. Giraud and Carabiber were whisked to Athens on a British warship for a meeting with the British minister, Lord Granville, who was expecting news of Turkey's unconditional surrender. Instead, he found himself discussing Rahmi Bey's plan to overthrow the Ottoman government. He was handed a letter from Rahmi – written in elegant French – in which the governor reminded the British of his long-standing sympathy for the Allied cause. The letter set out a seven-point peace plan that his government would adhere to as soon as it held power. It included the principal British demand: the freedom of the Straits.

Although Lord Granville himself was intrigued by Rahmi's proposal, British ministers in London remained sceptical. 'It hinges on the possibility of Rahmi Bey overthrowing Enver and the military party now in power,' they wrote. 'We have no guarantee that his operations . . . are even likely to succeed.' Besides, they were all too aware that Turkey was in its final death throes and they wanted nothing less than total surrender. After much discussion, they decided against backing Smyrna's mercurial governor.

Rahmi's proposed *coup d'état* was perhaps doomed from the outset, yet it is tempting to imagine how different Turkey's future might have been had it succeeded. A government with Rahmi Bey at the helm might have negotiated far more favourable peace terms with the Allies. His urbane charm would have been a most useful counterfoil to Venizelos, and his protection of Turkey's minorities would have seriously undermined the arguments of all who supported Venizelos's vision for Asia Minor. Smyrna would certainly have been saved the horrors of 1922; Rahmi cared too much for his adoptive city to allow her to be reduced to rubble.

Allied troops were within striking distance of Constantinople when Rahmi received his negative reply from the British government. The soldiers pressed ahead with their march to the frontier – a long and weary one for men who had been at war for more than four years. The October rain tipped down with monotonous regularity, turning the eastern Balkans into a vast swamp. 'The track was literally the bed of a stream,' wrote one soldier of the Royal Field Artillery, 'with deviations through bushes and scrub. The wear and tear on men, animals and wagons was severe; horses would jib, poles or traces or axles would break and vehicles would turn over . . . Everyone was tired or angry or both.'

By 30 October 1918, the advance units had reached Dedeagatch, a bleak frontier town less than ten miles from the Turkish border. In the distance, the men could glimpse the pencil-thin peninsula of Gallipoli, where so many of their comrades-in-arms had lost their lives three years earlier.

By the time they pitched camp, the Ottoman empire was in meltdown. Talaat Bey had already resigned two weeks earlier – a clear sign that the end was near. Now, a newly convened Turkish cabinet opened the peace negotiations with the British commander in the Aegean, the splendidly named Admiral Sir Somerset Gough Calthorpe. On the very day that British troops at the border prepared themselves for action, the Ottoman government signed an armistice. Turkey was out of the war.

PART TWO

Serpents in Paradise

Peace and War

Five days after the Ottoman government signed the armistice, the inhabitants of Bournabat awoke to a most unusual sight. Hundreds of freed prisoners of war – all British – could be seen marching through the village square. They were gaunt and malnourished, and their clothes were decidedly the worse for wear, but every one of them was delighted to be a free man after more than two years of internment.

They numbered 1,350 – the fortunate survivors – and many of them were taken to the European quarter of Smyrna, where they were given temporary lodgings in the empty seafront hotels. Among them was Lieutenant Colonel John Barker, who had been captured at the infamous siege of Kut-el-Amara almost two and a half years earlier. As he explored the city's streets and department stores, he had to pinch himself to believe that it was true. The place was untouched by war and everyone he met was in the best possible humour. The women in particular caught his eye; their hemlines were alluringly revealing and their thin blouses were a far cry from the dowdy worsteds so popular in England.

'Heavens, what a place this is!' he wrote in a letter to his wife. 'The feminine element from the age of about thirteen overdresses like a professional. Hardly any of any age have dresses more than two inches below the knee.'

The newly released prisoners of war found Smyrna prohib-
itively expensive, even though their backdated salaries had been
paid by the army. Barker decided to spend his last savings on a
room in the Bey Hotel – not the best in Smyrna, but clean
and comfortable nevertheless. 'I could not pig it any more,' he
wrote, 'sleeping on the ground [and] feeding off the ground.'

The lively nightlife also ate into his precious resources, especially the ragtime bars that stayed open until the early hours.
In a letter to his wife, Barker admitted that he was having a
wonderful time after his terrible years in captivity. 'The Greeks
and Armenians want to pet us,' he wrote, 'and as for the girls
– oh lord! Imagine how they walk when their foot-gear is like
this.' He followed this with a helpful sketch of an elegant, high-
heeled boot.

Poor Mrs Barker must have been wondering whether her
husband would prove capable of resisting the charms of the
local females, but Barker assured her that he had no intentions
of eloping with a Levantine maiden. He found them too eccentric and foreign for his taste. '[They] are terribly chee-chee,' he
wrote, 'and some are very dusky – including the sister of an
awfully nice fellow, Routh, who is our consul.'

Barker was disconcerted to discover that even the Anglican
vicar, the Reverend Brett, had adopted the chichi habits of the
Levantines, especially in the way he spoke. 'His "h"'s wander
about his speech in the oddest way.' He got an even greater
surprise when he heard Brett's eccentric organ compositions at
the Sunday church eucharist. 'Such a noise I have never heard
before,' he wrote, 'and hope never to do so again.'

Not all the British ex-prisoners took lodgings in the city.
Many were housed in the American International College of
Paradise, which had lain empty since America's entry into the
war. The college was not as comfortable as the Bey Hotel, but
it had its own generator that provided them with hot running
water. It was served by a team of volunteers from the local

Levantine community, led by Herbert Octavius, who had used his considerable financial resources to establish a Relief Committee to help the English prisoners.

'He was the life and soul of every undertaking in our behalf,' recalled one of those lodged in Paradise. 'I think that every British officer at Smyrna will agree with me in considering this gentleman's work above all praise.'

The Reverend Brett also worked tirelessly to help the prisoners. 'Every day saw him bringing clothing, medical supplies and other articles we were much in need of,' wrote one. 'He tended our sick and buried our dead and did everything possible for our welfare.'

A third group of ex-prisoners – the most fortunate – were given lodgings in the Bournabat villa of one of the French Levantines who had left at the outset of the war.

'After months in prison camps,' wrote Eldon Giraud, 'these chaps were received by the residents in Bournabat with open arms. One party at my father's house I still remember, when my sister, Joyce . . . entertained five British officers.' The sight of fresh fruit and meat proved even more enticing than the lovely Joyce Giraud. '[They] fell on the food like a chap falls on a bucket of water after crossing the Sahara with empty water bottles.'

A few of these men also had the chance to meet Rahmi Bey, whose days as governor of Smyrna were fast running out. Enver Pasha and Talaat Bey had fled Turkey several weeks earlier, along with the governors of the country's most important cities. Rahmi saw no reason to flee his post, yet at the beginning of October he received a telegram from Constantinople informing him that he was being deprived of office. The newly installed Turkish government led by Izzet Pasha wanted to wash its hands of everyone who had served under the wartime regime – even those who had defied its dictates. Rahmi was one of their first victims.

News of his departure quickly found its way onto the front pages of the Turkish newspapers. But in Smyrna itself, those pages were made available for Rahmi Bey, in order that he could have the last word. '[There] appeared a touching letter of farewell to his dear Smyrniots from Rahmi Bey,' wrote Annie Marshall, a newly arrived British national who had been interned during four long years of war. '[He] left that day for Constantinople to give place to his successor.'

He had done everything he could for his beloved city. Now, its future well-being would rest in other people's hands.

In the chaotic weeks that followed the armistice, the Allied powers were preoccupied with taking control of Constantinople and the Straits. Not a single vessel could be spared for Smyrna and neither could anyone agree who should land troops there. The Greeks assumed that the city would soon be theirs and devoted their energies to reinforcing the garrison on the nearby island of Mytilene. Italy's foreign secretary was meanwhile acting under the mistaken assumption that Smyrna had been promised to the Italians. While the Greeks and Italians bickered – and the French staked their own claim to the city – the British seized the initiative, landing a small group of soldiers in the heart of the city.

Rumours of their arrival were greeted with great enthusiasm by the Greek community. 'In preparation for the event, the Greeks made hundreds, perhaps thousands of flags,' wrote Annie Marshall. 'A Greek friend told me that a Greek church had spent £300 in making a large silk flag embroidered with gold, and that Greek families were expending from £20 to £30 in preparing flags.'

For once, the speculation turned out to be true. At 1.30 p.m. on 6 November, a British vessel bearing the prosaic name *Monitor No. 29* entered the port of Smyrna. The ship's commander, Allen Dixon, was overwhelmed by the scale of the welcome. Thousands of Greeks had congregated on the quayside to hail him as the liberator of their city.

'The whole population went wild with excitement and enthusiasm,' wrote Marshall. 'The streets were thronged with crowds of men, women and children, wearing their national colours and waving little flags. Overhead fluttered the gay coloured flags of many nations – British, American, French, Italian, a few Turkish, one or two Armenian, and a multitude of blue and white Greek flags.'

Among those celebrating Dixon's arrival were the former prisoners of war, who were overjoyed to see a British vessel sail into the bay. Lieutenant Colonel John Barker had never witnessed such scenes of jubilation. 'The town is mad,' he wrote, 'quite Mafeking mad.' He was so overwhelmed with emotion that he plunged into the sea and swam out to greet Commander Dixon. He was hauled aboard to great cheers from the mariners.

'The latest news, the grip once more of the hand of a free man . . . the taste of a whisky and soda and the feeling of being on British ground again was grand,' he wrote.

The reception granted to the British troops was even more raucous when they finally came ashore. '[Commander Dixon] was mounted shoulder high and carried in triumph through the streets, while the people shouted, "Vive l'Angleterre, Vive l'Entente".'

For Annie Marshall, it was a moment to be savoured for years to come. 'It was like the reception of a relieving army by a beleaguered city,' she wrote. 'The enthusiasm continued all evening. From the crowded cafés on the quays echoed the strains of "God Save the King" and the Marseillaise. The searchlight from the ship played along the seafront, illuminating the happy and excited faces of the multitudes. It was touching to see the reception accorded to this small British warship – so insignificant in itself, but the people hailed it as a symbol of British justice and protection.'

Dixon and his troops made a tour of the city, accompanied by the prisoners of war. 'We were mobbed on our return by cheering crowds,' wrote Barker. 'Two were carried off their feet and shoulder high to the Bey Hotel.'

Only one community in Smyrna did not fully participate in the festivities. Many Turks were still smarting from their defeat at the hands of the Allies and were deeply offended by the sight of thousands of Greek and Allied flags. Commander Dixon was quick to realise the sensitivity of the situation and posted a proclamation in the newspapers, published in English, French, Italian and Greek.

'Although the demonstrations in honour of the Allied men-of-war are much appreciated,' he wrote, 'the population must not lose sight that peace has not yet been arranged . . . All demonstrations must cease.'

Smyrna's newly appointed governor, Edhem Bey, differed from Rahmi in almost every respect. '[He is] slow [and] well meaning towards the Allies,' wrote Dixon after his first meeting, 'but lacking sufficient vim to enforce his ideas.'

He also proved incapable of enforcing law and order in the countryside around Smyrna. Brigands began raiding nearby villages, terrifying their Greek inhabitants and forcing them to remain indoors. 'Murders take place every day,' wrote David Forbes, a Levantine merchant living in one of the outlying suburbs. 'Some ten days ago, four Greeks, each working in his vineyard, were shot by a band of armed men and their throats cut, all within sight of my house.'

Two days after this distressing incident, Forbes was startled by the sound of gunfire. 'I got on the roof of my house and saw Turkish gendarmes advancing down the hill close to my house . . . [They] started shooting indiscriminately at every Greek they saw, whilst over the hillsides you could see Greeks scurrying like rabbits in all directions.'

Brigands also attacked the small watermill that lay just a stone's throw from his house and seized two of the men who worked there. '[They] trussed them like fowls, carried them outside, hacked them to pieces and threw them in the mill race.'

Emboldened by their success, the brigands lit upon a more enticing target: prosperous Bournabat. They did not dare approach any of the great houses, preferring instead their old practice of seizing hostages who could then be ransomed. Their first target was Alp Arslan – Rahmi Bey's young son – who was being cared for in Bournabat while his father sought employment with the new government.

Alp was returning home from Miss Florence's school with two friends, Eldon Giraud and Stefa Caligah, when the boys noticed a strange-looking carriage parked outside the cemetery. Eldon hung back, for he was suspicious, but the other two continued walking.

'As Alp and Stefa reached the carriage, I heard a shout and looked round. I saw two men grab Alp, push him into the carriage and drive off at a furious pace up towards the Magnesia road,' wrote Eldon.

The men were indeed brigands – and they were led by the feared bandit, Çerkez Ethem. They took Arslan to the remote slopes of the Nymph Dagh and then sent a message back to Bournabat, demanding a large ransom.

Many years later, Alp Arslan gave an interview to a Turkish newspaper about his abduction. He could still recall the terror of being seized and remembered sobbing uncontrollably when he heard the voices of search parties combing the wild mountainside. The bandits warned him to keep quiet, informing him that they had slit the throat of their previous victim.

Alp remained in captivity for twenty-three days. The bandits were demanding an exorbitant sum – 53,000 gold coins – and it took time to raise the money. However, the Whittalls and the Girauds were eventually successful in buying back Arslan's freedom. When he returned, he was carrying the dagger and jewel-encrusted girdle of Çerkez Ethem – gifts of the bandit. They remain in the family's possession to this day.

There were many who criticised the tactic of paying off the bandits, but James La Fontaine, a neighbour of the Whittalls, explained why the Levantine community of Bournabat had been prepared to dig deep into their pockets. He said that everyone owed a debt of gratitude to Rahmi Bey, 'whose extraordinary generous and considerate treatment of enemy subjects will ever be remembered by those who lived, during the war, in Smyrna'.

Many of Smyrna's inhabitants were appalled by the return of brigandage and shocked by the dramatic deterioration in relations between the different communities. Everyone had appreciated that the months that followed the armistice would be difficult. But now, for the first time in years, the city's spirit seemed to have been broken.

At this critical moment in her history, Smyrna was adrift. All eyes turned to Constantinople in the vain hope that Turkey's capital might have an answer to their woes.

The view from the imperial Palace of the Star was always at its most spectacular in the few minutes before dusk, when the minarets of Stamboul were sharpened by the evening sun and the water was veiled in autumn mist. When palace retainers gazed out of the windows on the evening of 12 November 1918, however, the sight chilled them. A huge squadron of vessels could be seen approaching the city. No fewer than thirty-two Allied ships were sailing up the Bosphorus – a combined fleet of British, French and Italian vessels.

Sultan Mehmet VI Vadhattin, only recently installed on the throne, was immediately told of the extraordinary events taking place just below the palace. He was so distraught that he could not bring himself to be a witness. 'I can't look out of the window,' he said. 'I hate to see them.'

There was a tense atmosphere on most of the Allied ships, because of the great uncertainty as to how they would be received by the Turks. Nevertheless, on the single Greek vessel, an armoured carrier, a riotous party was under way. 'The Greeks are very jubilant at going as conquerors to Constantinople,' wrote an English captain sailing with the fleet. 'I expect the Turk will turn round and scupper some of them if they don't keep quiet.'

But the Turk was not given the chance. On the following morning, Lieutenant General Sir Henry Maitland Wilson landed in Constantinople, accompanied by 3,000 soldiers of the Middlesex battalion. They marched up the steep hill into Pera – the European quarter of the city – and set up a military head-quarters in the English Girls' School. When the Ottoman government protested, claiming that occupation was not part of the armistice terms, Wilson curtly informed them that the soldiers were merely members of his staff.

He was being disingenuous, for the city very soon fell under Allied control. Although the sultan remained on his throne, his puppet government was powerless to act. Real power lay with the three Allied High Commissioners – British, French and Italian – who dictated their terms to the subservient grand vizier.

As Christmas 1918 approached, the Allied powers found that they held in their hands the fate of Constantinople, Smyrna – and even Turkey itself. The vanquished Ottoman army had disintegrated and the country was fast imploding. When a young army officer named Harold Armstrong arrived in Constantinople, he was shocked by the demoralised state of the people. 'I found the Ottoman Empire utterly smashed, her vast territories stripped into pieces and her conquered populations blinded and bewildered.' He noted that the Turkish people accepted their defeat with weary resignation: 'any terms of peace could have been imposed without resistance.'

The Allies should have acted immediately, dictating their terms and forestalling trouble. But instead of taking decisions, the victorious governments vacillated and played for time.

The large numbers of Greeks in Turkey were convinced that their hour had come. Those in Smyrna had already manifested their joy at the Allied victory. Now, their compatriots in Constantinople followed suit. Blue-and-white Greek flags were strung from churches and a gigantic portrait of Venizelos was erected in Taksim Square. The Greek community's greatest moment of triumph came in February 1919 when the French war hero, Marshal Franchet d'Espérey, landed on the quay at Galata. He assumed the role of Christian conqueror, riding to the French embassy on a white horse – the gift of a Greek – in mocking imitation of Sultan Mehmet the Conqueror's entry into the city in 1453.

The heady optimism of the Greeks was not without reason. There was a growing feeling among British ministers that Turkey should lose control of both Constantinople and Smyrna – a policy that struck a chord with the British electorate. There had been widespread revulsion at the treatment of British prisoners of war at the hands of the Turks. When the government published its report into their sufferings, the British press allowed itself free rein to attack all things Turkish.

The Times was outspoken in its criticism; the *Morning Post* was well-nigh hysterical: 'All the crimes committed by Nero, Caligula, Attila and Abdul Hamid, sink into insignificance beside the millions wantonly murdered in Turkey during the last few years.' It concluded that the offences of the Turks 'could not have been worse unless actual devils had had the work in hand'.

It was one thing for newspapers to express such sentiments; quite another when they came from the mouths of British ministers, yet many in the government agreed with the leader-writers of Fleet Street. Lord Curzon, the foreign secretary, wrote a document entitled 'The Future of Constantinople', into which he poured his loathing of all things Turkish. 'For more than five centuries, the presence of the Turk in Europe has been a source of distraction, intrigue and corruption . . . of oppression and misrule . . . It has been an equal obstacle to the proper or good government of his own people, whose resources have been squandered in the polluted *coulisses* of Constantinople.'

Curzon believed that the defeat of Turkey presented the Allied powers with a unique opportunity to punish the Turks with the utmost severity. 'Let not this occasion . . . be missed of purging the earth of one of its most pestilent roots of evil.' He wanted the Turks out of Constantinople.

But if Turkey was not to govern its own capital, it raised the question of who would. Nor was it clear who was going to govern all the rest of Turkey's majority-Christian areas. Lord Curzon was adamantly against awarding Constantinople to Greece, arguing that her army would be incapable of brokering a peace. France was the next to be rejected, on the grounds that she was Britain's principal rival. So, indeed, was America. And Britain herself was already overburdened with global respon-sibilities. Curzon felt that only an International Commission could be trusted to rule a city that was home to so many rival and competing nationalities. It was a solution that would have suited Smyrna, whose non-Turkish population was proportion-ately far larger than that of Constantinople.

Curzon intended his commission to be overtly biased towards Christianity. He wanted to expel the sultan-caliph from Constantinople and reconsecrate the great Byzantine basilica of St Sophia, converted into a mosque in 1453. This proposal found support among his senior colleagues. Many viewed such a move as Britain's moral obligation, incumbent upon her status as a Christian world power.

'The Empire,' wrote Arthur Hirtzel of the India Office, 'has been given to us as a means to that great end for which Christ came into the world, the redemption of the human race. That is to say, it has been given to us to make it Christian.'

British ministers seemed clear as to their goal but unsure as to how it should be implemented. Their indecisiveness was to prove disastrous in a country that was in desperate need of direction. The brigandage already taking place around Smyrna rapidly spread across the country with the result that great tracts of land were completely out of control, ruled by bandits and local warlords. In the absence of any intervention on the part of the Allies, the hitherto impotent Turkish government finally decided to act. It proposed sending a senior military figure to central Anatolia in order to quell the unrest. One candidate was favoured above all others: Mustafa Kemal – later to be known as Ataturk – who had come through the First World War with an unblemished record.

Kemal had fought with stubborn determination against Anzac forces in Gallipoli and worked hard to halt the British advance in the Middle East. At the war's end, he had travelled to Constantinople – an out-of-work commander who was humiliated by the Allied occupation of Turkey's capital. On one occasion, jovial British officers in the Pera Palace Hotel asked the waiter to invite him over for a drink. Kemal replied sniffily: 'We are the hosts here. They are the guests. It is fitting for them to come to my table.'

A few days later, he asked the *Daily Mail*'s correspondent, George Ward Price, to take coffee with him in the same hotel. Ward Price found Kemal sober in both his manners and dress. 'He was wearing a civilian frock-coat and fez,' he wrote. 'A handsome and virile figure, restrained in his gestures [and] with a low, deliberate voice'.

Kemal was sanguine about Turkey's defeat. 'We took the wrong side in this war,' he told Ward Price. 'We should never have quarrelled with our old friends, the British. That we did so was a result of the pressure exercised by pro-Germans like Enver

Pasha. Well, we have lost and we must now be prepared to pay heavily for our misguided policy.'

He expected the Allied powers to divide Turkey between them and hoped that the British, not the French, would hold the lion's share. 'If the British are going to assume responsibility for Anatolia,' he continued, 'they will need the cooperation of experienced Turkish governors to work under them. What I want to know,' he concluded, 'is the proper quarter to which I can offer my services in the capacity.'

Ward Price duly passed on his offer to British intelligence but it was treated with scorn. 'There will be a lot of these Turkish generals looking for jobs before long,' was their answer. They would live to regret their rejection of Kemal's advances.

Kemal soon found offers coming from other quarters. An underground resistance movement called Karakol had been founded in Constantinople with the aim of smuggling arms and officers to the Anatolian heartlands. Allied forces had yet to reach the easternmost parts of the country and Karakol's leaders urged Kemal to head to the countryside where he would provide a rallying cry for the fledgling resistance. Kemal vacillated for months in the hope of being appointed Minister of War. He was granted three audiences with the sultan in the months that followed the arrival of the British forces, but was given no assurances of a post in the government. Demoralised by their attitude, he renewed contact with nationalist officers who were trying to stop the demobilisation of the Turkish army in Anatolia.

It was not until April – by which time Kemal had abandoned all hope of serving in the government – that he was finally given the post of inspector-general of Turkish forces in northern Anatolia, with special responsibility for bringing order to the region. Kemal immediately accepted, aware that he was presented with a unique opportunity to save Turkey from humiliation. Just before leaving Constantinople, he was summoned to an audience at the imperial palace. It was at this meeting that the sultan uttered his famously ambiguous words: 'My pasha, my pasha, you may be able to save the nation.' That is precisely what Kemal intended to do, but in a very different fashion from that envisaged by the sultan.

His campaign was to be given an unexpected kick-start by the Allied peacemakers who were assembled in Paris. The fate of Smyrna was the subject of heated discussions – and those entrusted with safeguarding the city's future were about to take a decision that would plunge Turkey into another war.

When talks began in the French capital in the early days of 1919, scores of nations, would-be nations and pressure groups sent delegations to the world's largest peace conference. Jostling for position alongside presidents and prime ministers were brigands, princesses, deposed kings and Albanian warlords, all hoping to gain something from the spoils of war.

The four most important players were those who represented the victorious Allies: the American president, Woodrow Wilson; Britain's Lloyd George; France's Georges Clemenceau; and the prime minister and foreign secretary of Italy, Vittorio Orlando and Sidney Sonnino. For almost six months, this inner circle discussed proposals, listened to petitions and attempted to create a new world order that would secure a lasting peace.

They met twice a day, usually in Wilson's study: four men from very different backgrounds and with strikingly different temperaments. Wilson was stiff and formal, 'like a college professor criticising a thesis'. Several British diplomats found him physically disgusting. 'One does not see the teeth except when he smiles,' wrote one, 'which is an awful gesture.'

Clemenceau was more passionate and irascible; he did not suffer fools gladly. At the official opening of the conference, Britain's foreign secretary, Arthur Balfour, wore a top hat whereas Clemenceau wore a bowler.

'[Balfour] apologised for his top hat,' wrote Harold Nicolson, one of those present at the ceremony.

'I was told,' Balfour said, 'that it was obligatory to wear one.'

'So,' Clemenceau answered, 'was I.'

Clemenceau was impatient with Wilson and his fourteen-point peace plan. 'God himself was content with ten commandments,' he said. 'Wilson modestly inflicted fourteen points on us.'

The French president found Lloyd George no less infuriating, although he could not help but succumb to his charms. The two men occasionally took tea in Lloyd George's private apartment where Britain's prime minister was at his most congenial: 'Wrapped in the utmost indifference to technical arguments, irresistibly attracted to unlooked-for solutions, but dazzling with eloquence and wit.'

Orlando, the fourth member of the inner circle, was highly strung and had a habit of shedding tears when decisions went against him. The stiff-upper-lipped British contingent found such displays of emotion distasteful. One said he would have spanked his son if he caught him weeping like Orlando.

President Wilson's contribution to the peace conference was the principle of self-determination. This suggested that oppressed smaller nations would finally be allowed to rule themselves. It also brought the hope of self-government for minorities and the potential creation of many new states. Yet few attending the conference understood exactly what the president meant by the phrase 'self-determination'. Did it mean that Armenia should be a nation state? That the Greeks of Anatolia should be allowed to rule themselves? And where did it leave Smyrna? If ever there was a case for self-government, then it was to be found in Turkey's only majority-Christian city.

By the end of 1919, Wilson wearily admitted that his choice of phrase – which had brought hope to so many oppressed peoples – had been most unfortunate. 'When I gave utterance to those words,' he said, 'I said them without the knowledge that nationalities existed which are coming to us day after day.'

By the time he admitted his mistake, the damage had been done. His principle of self-determination had been seized on by many as the means to an end and none had used it more effectively than Eleftherios Venizelos, Greece's prime minister.

Venizelos had come to Paris with the hope of at long last achieving a revived Greek empire carved out of the vanquished Ottoman state. He worked around the clock to this end, courting supporters with his customary charm and eloquence. He had long ago won the unstinting support of Lloyd George. Now, he wooed the rest of the conference, inviting the key players to restaurant lunches and hosting intimate soirées in his private quarters at the Hotel Mercedes. A great raconteur, he regaled his guests with stories of his escapades in the mountains of Crete.

> He tells us stories of King Constantine [wrote Harold Nicolson], his lies and equivocations. He tells us stories of the old days of the Cretan insurrection, when he escaped to the mountains and taught himself English by reading *The Times* with a rifle across his knee. He talks of Greek culture, of modern Greek and its relation to the classical and we induce him to recite Homer. An odd effect, rather moving.

Venizelos's initial appearance before the Supreme Council was on 3 February 1919. This was his first opportunity to present Greek claims to Smyrna and the coastline of Anatolia. He had worked with indefatigable energy in the weeks prior to his primary performance and now had absolute mastery over his subject.

He fully exploited the underlying weakness of Wilson's principle of self-determination. Urging his classically educated audience to cast their minds back to the noble age of antiquity, he argued that the Greeks of Asia Minor 'have been established there uninterruptedly for three thousand years [and] constitute the purest part of the Hellenic race'.

Armed with facts and figures, he read excerpts from books by eminent geographers and historians. He even brought along photo albums, which showed happy Greek sponge fishermen on the islands that he now wished to claim for Greece. Nicolson was impressed by Venizelos's panache; no other leader would have dared to bring along his holiday snaps. 'He talks gaily and simply,' he wrote, 'and they look at his photograph albums which puts them in a good temper.'

In a letter to his father, Nicolson added: 'I can't tell you the position that Venizelos has here. He and Lenin are the only two really great men in Europe.'

Venizelos had a ready line in flattery, inverting his own argument if it gave him the chance to produce a compliment. He admitted that many Greeks in Turkey could not speak Greek, but said that this made them no less Greek. Indeed, he told his audience that some of his closest Greek friends spoke Albanian at home, 'even as Mr Lloyd George would speak Welsh to his children'. Such flattery was pure Venizelos; Britain's prime minister was deeply touched by this nod to his Welsh ancestry.

Venizelos was careful to compliment President Wilson in the very next breath. He explained that the reason so many Greek children were well educated was because they had been taught in American mission schools. 'Wilson beams delight,' wrote Nicolson in his diary.

The American delegation was beguiled by Venizelos's charm. 'I can see how he got his reputation for great statesmanship,' wrote one. '[He] realised that his strongest asset would be our belief in his honesty . . . This policy was almost Bismarckian in its cleverness.'

Venizelos pitched his claims high. Smyrna was his principal

goal, but he also wanted the Turkish islands in the Aegean, the Italian-controlled Dodecanese, northern Epirus and all of Thrace. He shrewdly dropped all claims to Constantinople, joking that he was 'the only Greek in the world who could turn down Constantinople'. He made no mention of British-controlled Cyprus.

Yet his projected empire was on a grand scale. He hoped to gain a huge slice of land around Smyrna; 200 miles wide, it stretched from Kastellorizo in the south to Panderma in the north and included all of Turkey's most fertile farmland.

Venizelos contended that the area around Smyrna contained 800,000 Greeks, who formed the economic and intellectual backbone of the country. There was much truth in this, but the Turks were nevertheless in the majority in three of the four *sandjaks* (districts) that Venizelos hoped to acquire. When the Americans raised this point, the Greek prime minister argued that they had neglected to include the 370,000-strong population of the coastal islands, which would fall under the same administration. In so doing, he managed to boost the Greek population sufficiently to make it constitute a slim majority.

Venizelos was helped in his claims by hundreds of petitions that arrived daily at the peace conference, sent by Greek towns and villages across Asia Minor. All of them demanded self-determination, aware that this would then enable them to seek union with Greece.

The hierarchs of the Orthodox Church played their hand with skill. Instead of reminding the conference of Anatolia's Byzantine Orthodox heritage – which held little appeal to the classically minded peacemakers – they instead focused on Turkey's pre-Christian Hellenic traditions.

'It was in this region that Hellenism was born,' they wrote. 'All the towns which are to be found here, large or small, without a single exception, were founded by our ancestors some three thousand years ago.'

No mention whatsoever was made of the great patristic fathers of the Byzantine Church. Instead, the hierarchs told the peace-makers that 'this is where the Hellenic civilisation flourished in all its splendour and where, for the first time, the idea of liberty was born.'

Venizelos urged the leaders in Paris to heed the call. 'After the tragic experience of a whole century,' he told them, 'it is impossible to entrust the future of the Christian populations of the Ottoman Empire to fresh attempts at reform.' He was the first to admire the Turks as 'good workers [and] honest', but as rulers 'they were insupportable and a disgrace to civilisation'.

Venizelos presented his claims in two long hearings. At the end of the second day, he was warmly congratulated by all four of the leading peacemakers. Clemenceau, bowled over by his masterful performance, turned to his secretary, Jean Martet, and lectured him on the achievements of the classical world. 'Immerse yourself in Greece, Martet,' he said. 'It is something which has kept me going. Whenever I was fed up with all the stupidities and emptiness of politics, I turned to Greece. Others go fishing. To each his own.'

The peacemakers were sympathetic to Venizelos's vision and established a special committee to thrash out the details. It quickly became apparent that fixing a border between Greek and Turkish territories was fraught with difficulties. It made no sense to separate Smyrna from the rich hinterland that provided so much of its trade, yet the hinterland was overwhelmingly Turkish.

The committee's work was further complicated by the fact that the Italians pressed ahead with their claim to Smyrna, based on a secret agreement that they had signed with the Allied leaders in 1917. They countered Venizelos's claim that western Turkey had been the birthplace of classical Hellenism, arguing that it had also been an integral part of the Roman empire.

The Italian argument was not without logic, but neither

Orlando nor Sonnino possessed Venizelos's persuasive powers and their stance won them few friends at the conference. 'I can't understand the Italian attitude,' wrote Nicolson. 'They are behaving like children, and sulking children at that. They obstruct and delay everything – and evidently think that by making themselves disagreeable on every single point they will force the conference to give them fat plums to keep them quiet.'

The delicate negotiations were not helped by the ignorance of the principal players, whose grasp of detail was comically lamentable. Nicolson was present at a meeting between Lloyd George and the Italian delegation, all of whom were seated around a large map of western Turkey.

> Lloyd George shows them what he suggests [wrote Nicolson]. But the Italians only frowned and asked for the Turkish town of Scala Nova as well.
>
> 'Oh no!', says Lloyd George. 'You can't have that – it's full of Greeks!'
>
> He goes on to point out that there are further Greeks at Makri and a whole wedge of them along the coast towards Alexandretta.
>
> 'Oh no,' I whisper to him, 'there are not many Greeks there.'
>
> 'But yes,' he answers, 'don't you see, it's coloured green?'
>
> I then realise that he mistakes my map for an ethnological map and thinks that green means Greeks instead of valleys and the brown means Turks instead of mountains.

The British and French peace negotiators were prepared to overlook the serious problems that would be caused by awarding a great slice of Turkey to Greece. So too, after much persuasion, were the Americans. By March, it looked as if Venizelos was on the point of pulling off his cherished dream.

This news caused great anxiety among the Levantine

merchants living in Smyrna. Many believed the Greeks to be incapable of administering a multinational city and argued that rule from Athens would create even greater tension between the different communities.

As the pleasure gardens of Bournabat began to bud and blossom, the Whittalls, the Girauds and the Allied officers stationed in Smyrna had regular meetings to discuss whether and how they could influence the policy being thrashed out in Paris.

'Every Sunday, there was a line of cars outside our house,' wrote Eldon Giraud, 'and tea was served beside the tennis court, under the umbrella tree.' He recalled that their discussions lasted from teatime until dusk. Then, 'when it got dark, everyone used to come in and the gramophone would get going and dancing would ensue until late at night.'

By the end of February, Herbert Octavius was sufficiently alarmed to offer the peacemakers some advice. He wrote a seven-page report on the future of Smyrna, pleading with the politicians in Paris not to be hoodwinked by 'the clever advocacy of that most eminent statesman, Mr Venizelos'. He argued that Venizelos's facts and figures should be treated with extreme caution and he poured scorn on the notion that Smyrna was a Greek city. 'The population . . . is very cosmopolitan [and] made up of about one third Greeks and two thirds Turks, Jews, Armenians and Europeans.'

He pointed out that all of these nationalities had lived side by side in peace and friendship for many decades. And although the policies of Turkey's wartime government had done much to destroy the city's unique spirit, this did not justify handing the reins of power to the Greeks. Many were hankering for revenge and 'certain to trample on their Turkish neighbours' if placed in a position of power.

Herbert Octavius believed that Turkey had forfeited the right to govern Smyrna, even though he acknowledged that Rahmi

Bey had peacefully steered the city through the First World War. But Rahmi was an exception to the rule. 'The Turks,' he wrote, '. . . have proved themselves utterly incapable of governing Christians.'

In Herbert Octavius's eyes, there was only one possible solution to this crisis. '[It] is the unanimous opinion of all – Armenians, Jews, Turks, Europeans and not a few unprejudiced and foresighted Greeks – that the province be administered under a system of local government.'

Herbert Octavius realised that this would need outside support. He recommended that England, France or America should act as guarantors of the peace. His personal preference was England, 'who alone and single-handed has defeated Turkey and brought her to her knees in a manner which no other nation could have done'.

Herbert Octavius's document – together with letters from the other leading Levantines – began to have an effect on the peacemakers. By mid-April, the specialist committee was no longer convinced that Greek rule was a good idea. When Harold Nicolson and Arnold Toynbee sat down to draft an agreement over the division of spoils in western Anatolia, they suggested a U-turn on policy. '[We] propose to cut the Gordian knot,' wrote Nicolson. 'Let the Turks have Anatolia as their own. Give the Greeks European Turkey only.'

But at the very moment when Greece seemed to have lost the argument over Smyrna, the Italians unwittingly handed Venizelos his trump card. On 24 April, Orlando and his team – furious over the Allies' refusal to grant them the Adriatic port of Fiume – stormed out of the conference. Just a few hours later, they packed their bags and left Paris. Lloyd George drew a renewed burst of energy from the crisis. 'Well,' he said, 'the fat is in the fire at last.'

Never were truer words spoken. Italy now took matters into her own hands, landing small bands of troops at various points on Turkey's Aegean coastline in order to create an Italian sphere of influence around Smyrna. The first group of marines were sent ashore at Adalia. These were followed by more landings – at Makri and Marmaris – and this time the troops pushed inland. It was reported that Italian agents on the ground were collaborating with the Turks and encouraging them to resist any attempted Greek landing.

Soon, the conference received even worse news. President Wilson informed Lloyd George and Clemenceau that the Italians were sending warships to Smyrna itself. 'The attitude of Italy is indubitably aggressive,' he warned. 'She is a menace to the peace.' Clemenceau could not help making a sideswipe at the American president. 'A fine start to the League of Nations!' he chortled.

Later that evening, Harold Nicolson and Lloyd George discussed the growing crisis. Nicolson was aghast at the manoeuvring of the Italians. 'By trying to steal a march on the Asia Minor coast,' he wrote, '[they] have helped the Greeks more than they know.'

The crisis only deepened in the days that followed. On 5 May, Lloyd George was warned that the Italians would soon be fully installed in Anatolia. He proposed immediate action. 'We should let the Greeks occupy Smyrna,' he said. 'There are massacres starting there and no-one to protect the Greek population.'

Clemenceau seemed inclined to agree. 'Do you know how many ships Italy has off Smyrna at the moment?' he asked. 'She has seven.'

The crisis was discussed yet again on the following day and this time there was a real urgency to their deliberations. Orlando and Sonnino had announced their return to the peace conference, adding that they would be in Paris in time for the next day's proceedings. If the three principal players were to take a quick decision about Smyrna, this would be their last opportunity.

They were in the middle of a lengthy discussion about the behaviour of Italy when an impatient Lloyd George broke into the conversation. For six long years he had supported Venizelos's goal of a Greek empire in Asia Minor. Now, at last, he saw his chance to act.

'My opinion,' he announced, 'is that we should tell Mr Venizelos to send troops to Smyrna. We will instruct our admirals to let the Greeks land wherever there is a threat of trouble or massacre.'

President Wilson thought for a moment before signalling his agreement. 'Why not tell them to land as of now?' he said. 'Have you any objection to that?'

'None,' said Lloyd George.

'Nor have I,' added Clemenceau. 'But should we warn the Italians?'

'In my opinion,' responded Lloyd George, 'no.'

As soon as the three men had finished their luncheon, Lloyd George telephoned Venizelos and summoned him to the Quai d'Orsay. The British prime minister was concise. According to Venizelos's diary entry, the exchange went as follows:

'Do you have troops available?'

'We do. For what purpose?'

'President Wilson, M. Clemenceau and I decided today that you should occupy Smyrna.'

'We are ready.'

When this news was taken to Britain's Chief of Imperial Staff, Field Marshal Sir Henry Wilson, he was horrified. 'I asked Lloyd George if he realised that this was starting another war.'

The prime minister paused for a moment before brushing him aside. He had no time for self-doubt.

Blood on the Quayside

Donald Whittall's day began with a ritual that was familiar to all the Levantine men of Bournabat. As soon as it was light, he would wash, dress himself in suit and starched shirt and walk the 200 yards from his *fin-de-siècle* villa to the little railway station. Here, he would find a highly polished steam train awaiting him, as well as his uncle Herbert Octavius and all the other merchant princes of Bournabat.

'The train was like a private club on wheels,' wrote Eldon Giraud, one of Donald's numerous cousins. 'The guard ... Ali Çavas, knew all his passengers intimately. The train would never leave in the morning unless all were present.'

Five minutes before the scheduled departure, Ali Çavas would give a series of blasts on the train's whistle. 'And you would see a sort of marathon headed by the Keyser family, most of whom were still dressing as they ran, and as soon as the last one entered the station, Ali Çavas would wave his green flag and the train would move off.'

Such slovenliness on the part of the Keyser family was frowned upon by Herbert Octavius. Indeed, even Donald, in his youth, had behaved in a manner that was unbefitting a Whittall. One day, he had secretly unhitched the last carriage of the train – the one that carried all the Whittalls – leaving them stranded in Bournabat station. He was subsequently known as Mad Donald.

There was a pleasing familiarity to the morning routine that even the high-spirited Donald came to appreciate. 'Every one had his own private seat in his particular carriage,' recalled Eldon. 'This seat was sacred and God help any stranger who was unaware that he had taken Uncle Richard's, Uncle Edward's or Dr Denotowitz's place.' If such an outrage should occur, the Levantine grandees would summon Ali Çavas, 'and the offender was ejected immediately in such a way that he often left the train at the first station'.

On 15 May 1919, Donald boarded the train as usual. It left punctually and arrived exactly on time at its destination. As he strolled down Boulevard Aliotti towards his offices on the water-front, he noticed a large crowd assembling on the quayside. Something momentous was about to take place – and Donald Whittall was to become an eyewitness to everything that followed.

The countdown to trouble had begun on the previous morning, when the British flagship, *Iron Duke*, had sailed into the harbour. On board was the British admiral, Sir Somerset Gough Calthorpe, who had come to meet Smyrna's governor. He landed and, accompanied by his senior officers, made his way to the governor's residence. After the customary courtesies, he informed Governor Izzet Bey that Allied forces were about to officially occupy his city.

Izzet Bey's first question was to ask whether the Greek army would be taking part in the landings. He and his advisors blanched when they were informed that this would indeed be the case. 'Though they must have realised before that this landing was contemplated,' wrote Ian Smith, one of the British intelligence officers at the meeting, 'the official communication of it was a severe shock.' The governor felt betrayed by Britain and expressed his deep anxieties about his city being 'handed over unprotected to the rule of a race whom they feared [and] who nourished a feeling of hatred for the Turks'.

George Horton, who had just returned to Smyrna after an absence of two years, was in agreement with Izzet Bey. He would later argue that this one bad decision set in motion a chain of events that would eventually lead to catastrophe. '[It] ultimately caused the Greek disaster and the destruction of Smyrna,' he wrote.

News that the city was to be occupied spread rapidly through the different quarters, causing patriotic delirium among Greeks and Armenians, and corresponding despair among Turks. The Levantine population was equally unhappy about the turn of events, fearing that the Greeks would be unable to keep the peace.

Having listened to the concerns of families like the Whittalls, Admiral Calthorpe ordered small detachments of Allied troops to enter the city and guard the European consulates, as well as the banks, post offices and shoreline forts. By early that afternoon, the operation was complete and the British congratulated themselves on their success. It boded well for the landing of the Greek army on the following morning.

Admiral Calthorpe was unaware that news of the intended Greek occupation had been met with such fury in the Turkish quarters of Smyrna. A group of Turkish agitators immediately established a Committee Against [Greek] Annexation, which called for protest meetings throughout the city. It also made use of Turkish-owned printing presses to spread the word throughout the Turkish quarter. Angry proclamations were posted on public buildings, urging people to demonstrate against the Greek occupation.

The city's Turkish inhabitants were enjoined to assemble that evening on the steep hillside above the Jewish cemetery. 'Flock there in your thousands,' read one of the proclamations, 'and show to the whole world your crushing superiority of numbers . . . On this occasion, there is no distinction between rich and poor, educated and illiterate – only an overwhelming mass repudiating Greek domination.'

This was to be the public side of the protest; there was also a secret side. Unbeknown to the Allies, the committee began transporting weapons and ammunition into the countryside around Smyrna. It was an ominous portent of things to come.

As dusk fell on the evening of 14 May, more and more Turks heeded the call to demonstrate against the imminent Greek landing. According to some eyewitnesses, as many as 50,000 men, women and children made their way onto the heights of Bachri-Baba. There was something of a carnival atmosphere surrounding their demonstration. They lit bonfires and banged drums in protest.

In the city itself, there were rather more sinister developments. At some point during the evening, several hundred convicts were allowed to escape from the Turkish Central Prison. This was a troubling development, particularly as the fugitive prisoners seemed to have had help from outside. Their escape almost certainly took place with the complicity of Major Carossini, the Italian head of Allied Prison Control, who was implacably opposed to the Greek annexation.

There was even more alarming news in the early hours of the morning. A Turkish military depot was looted and large numbers of Turks were reported to have been supplied with arms and ammunition. Allied intelligence agents picked up rumours of a planned resistance at the Quarantine, a building close to one of the intended debarkation points for Greek troops. There was even talk of Italians being actively involved in organising the resistance.

The Greek troops, who numbered some 13,000 men, spent the night in nervous excitement. The Smyrna-bound fleet had dropped anchor at nearby Mytilene island so that the soldiers could be briefed about the planned landings. The operation had been deemed so secret that most men had been told that they were being transported to Bessarabia in order to take part in military operations in the Ukraine. Only at the last minute did they learn that their goal was infinitely more exciting.

One of the senior Greek commanders, Colonel Nikolaos Zafiriou, was all too aware of the delicacy of the operation that he was about to lead. In his eve-of-battle address, he warned his men to temper their patriotism. 'The enthusiasm filling our hearts is fully justified,' he said, 'but any improper manifestation of this enthusiasm will be entirely out of place.' He informed them that Smyrna was by no means an exclusively Greek city – a surprise to many of the troops – and urged them to consider everyone as equals. 'We must not forget that when we reach our destination, we shall meet Turks, Jews and Europeans of other denominations. Everybody should be treated in the same way.'

The Greek troops were awakened at dawn and told that the time for action was fast approaching. Much planning had gone into how to take control of the city without any blood being spilled. There were to be three separate landings: one regiment was to encircle the southern part of the city; another was to surround the north-eastern quarters; while a third regiment was to drive a wedge between the Greek and Turkish areas in order to prevent any ethnic clashes. It was a sensible plan that had every prospect of success. The shoreside forts were already in Allied hands and the Turkish troops were confined to their barracks.

In the city itself, the excitement was palpable. As Donald Whittall made his way to the family offices that morning, he saw thousands of Greeks spilling onto the seafront in order to welcome the Greek troops. Blue-and-white flags fluttered from every building on the quayside and the crowds were starting to shout, 'Long live Venizelos!' All were longing for the moment of liberation.

Shortly before 7 a.m., there was an excited gasp from the crowds closest to the water. Thin wisps of smoke could be seen in the far distance, heralding the arrival of the Greek vessels. A few minutes later, the first transport ships could be seen entering the bay of Smyrna.

One of those at the water's edge was a nine-year-old Greek boy named Alexis Alexiou. His parents had taken him to witness the arrival of the troops, aware that history was in the making. 'The whole of Smyrna was celebrating as if it was Easter,' he later recalled. 'You could hear cannon-shots from the ships and the blue and white flags flew everywhere.'

At 7.30 a.m., the great liner, *Patris*, drew alongside the waterfront, followed by the *Averoff*, *Atromitos* and *Leonidas*. Within minutes of the vessels docking, the first troops were stepping ashore.

One of the witnesses to the unfolding chain of events was Robert Berry, the commanding officer of the USS *Manley*. He was dismayed by the ill-disciplined manner in which the troops disembarked. 'Their arrival was accompanied by violent outbursts of enthusiasm and rejoicing on the part of the Greek civilian population,' he later recalled. Nor did he like the fact that the ships kept blowing their whistles in response to the cheers of the crowds.

Berry was even more disturbed when he saw the troops stacking their weaponry in a great pile on the quayside and then performing Greek dances around it. 'Little or no tact and discretion were shown by the Greeks in handling a people the occupation of whose territory by them was the bitterest pill that could be administered.' It took two hours to land the first batch of troops and for the whole of that time the crowd kept up their frenzied cheering.

In spite of the tactlessness on the part of the Greek soldiers, everything seemed to be going like clockwork. One regiment marched north and sealed off the European quarters of the city. Another fanned out towards the eastern areas.

But when it came to landing the 1/38 Evzones regiment, the meticulously planned operation spectacularly broke down. The Evzones were meant to have disembarked at the Quarantine, at the southern tip of the quay. They were then charged with driving a wedge through the Greek and Turkish quarters of the city in order to forestall any sectarian trouble. But their orders were either misunderstood or misinterpreted for they were landed in the middle of the quayside where the crowd was at its thickest and most jubilant. Metropolitan Chrysostom, robed in full church vestments, stepped forward to bless the troops and wish them success. 'With tears in his eyes,' wrote the Greek author, Phanis Kleanthis, 'Chrysostom kneeled down, embraced the glorious flag of the regiment and gave it his blessing.' For the metropolitan, it was the happiest moment of his life.

Overcome with emotion, he greeted the regimental commander, Colonel Stavrianopoulos, and then beckoned the troops to follow him along the quayside. He intended to lead them through the city that Greece had coveted for generations.

'Everyone's eyes were filled with tears,' wrote Kleanthis. 'The army advanced as if it was on a parade and, as it passed, was showered with flowers. The clock towers filled the air with the clanging of bells, adding to the welcome given to the army of liberation.'

The action of Chrysostom and the Evzones regiment was not just insensitive, but also extremely foolhardy. If all had gone according to plan, the soldiers should have been sealing off Prophet Elias Street, which bordered the Turkish quarter. Instead, they proceeded to march southwards along the quayside – a route that passed the shoreside barracks that housed the city's Turkish troops.

Many of the Levantine merchants had offices that lined the quayside. As the crowd marched along with the troops, these merchants spilled out onto their balconies to watch the procession. Among the spectators was Donald Whittall, whose office had a magnificent view of the quayside. Another was George Perry, the secretary of the American YMCA in Smyrna.

It was as the Evzones regiment passed the Turkish barracks that someone fired a shot. There would later be much argument over who actually pulled the trigger. Some claimed it was a Greek; others swore it was a Turk. A more sinister possibility is that it was fired by an Italian – Major Carossini – who was giving the signal for a Turkish attack. Turkish witnesses later claimed that the Italian steam launch came alongside the barracks at the very moment when the shot was fired; Italian sources confirm that Carossini was on board.

In the confusion of the moment, it was difficult to be certain about the precise sequence of events. Donald Whittall claimed to have heard several shots coming from the nearby coffee houses. George Perry heard a single shot fired from the crowd. The only certainty is that it unleashed a devastating riposte from the Greek troops passing the barracks. '[They] lined the edges of the square,' wrote Whittall, 'and commenced a terrible fusillade at the barracks, the coffee houses and Government House.' For twenty-five minutes – perhaps more – they kept up a sustained barrage of fire.

One of those caught in the crossfire was Ahmed Feizi, a prosperous Turk from the Levantine suburb of Boudja. He dived for cover, taking shelter in the pleasure gardens that were next to the barracks, although he soon realised that he was still in danger of being hit. 'So I jumped from the garden into the central barracks and tried to avoid the firing by hiding in the above-said building, but I was not long there before I heard machine guns going off and bullets going through the windows.'

The Greek troops had by now trained all their guns onto the building and were systematically shooting out all the windows. Other soldiers began firing at buildings all along the quayside.

Some of the wilder elements began smashing windows and

kicking down doors. '[They] broke into the houses and dragged out all Turks whom they found,' wrote an English businessman named Forbes, 'and looted everything they found in them.'

The commanding officer of the USS *Arizona* watched in horror as one group of Greek soldiers 'fired promiscuously on the surrounding populace'. The exact number killed by their action was estimated at between fifty and a hundred civilians. The Evzones meanwhile kept up their fusillade on the barracks, while the soldiers inside returned fire for as long as they had ammunition. Only then did they drape a makeshift white flag out of one of the shattered windows.

Once all the gunfire had ceased, the Turkish soldiers tentatively emerged from the building, holding their hands above their heads in token of their surrender. The first action of the Greek troops was to separate the Turks from the Jews, Armenians and other Christians who had taken refuge in the barracks. For Ahmed Feizi, it was a terrifying experience. He removed his fez and threw it away but he was spotted by one of the Greek soldiers and told to stand with the other Turks. 'They were made to go through no end of humiliation and received a good deal of knocking about,' wrote Donald Whittall, who at this point locked up his offices and descended into the streets.

The captured Turkish soldiers were lined up and marched along the quayside towards the Greek ship, *Patris*, where they were to be held prisoner. As they passed through the crowds of jeering Greeks, they were punched or struck with pieces of wood. '[They] all had their fezzes torn off and were hurried along with their hands in the air,' wrote Ian Smith, Britain's acting chief officer in Smyrna, 'being compelled by blows from the butts and bayonets of the escorting troops to keep up a cry of "Zito, Zito"' (an abbreviation of 'Long live Venizelos').

Ahmed Feizi feared for his life, but he was about to be saved by a stroke of good luck. 'Some American and English subjects recognised me and delivered me from the clutches of this barbarous crew.'

Others were not so fortunate. As Donald Whittall followed the procession along the quayside, he was appalled to see Greek soldiers beating the Turks with their guns and prodding them with their bayonets. 'As far as the custom-house, I only saw one Turkish porter shot and then bayoneted,' wrote Whittall. 'From there up to the Kraemer Palace Hotel, I was the unwilling witness of the massacre of some thirty unarmed men.'

As the prisoners passed the main entrance to the Kraemer Palace, the violence increased in intensity. Several were killed in cold blood, with the worst of the treatment reserved for the senior ranks. 'A fat Turkish officer, shot in the stomach, tried in his agony to sit up,' wrote Whittall. 'A Greek soldier at once rushed at him and struck him with the butt end of his rifle.'

The surviving Turkish prisoners were eventually taken aboard the *Patris*, yet this did not bring the unrest to an end. Discipline among the troops now broke down completely and they went on the rampage.

'Led on by the roughs of the town, the Greek soldiers [were] firing recklessly to right and left at every head that protruded from window or balcony,' wrote Alfred van der Zee, the Swedish consul. '[They] forced open houses and stores, dragged out the wretched Turks who had sought shelter therein, and, after robbing them of all they possessed, marched them to the transports.'

The violence looked set to rage for the rest of the afternoon, but it was brought to a sudden halt by the elements. Just after 4 p.m., the breeze whipped into a fierce squall and the bank of thunder clouds, which had been steadily rolling in off the Aegean, suddenly emptied themselves over Smyrna. The rain was so torrential that even hardened criminals sought refuge.

As soon as the storm came to an end, Greek troops and civilians poured back onto the streets and began to ransack the Turkish quarter. Corpses – which numbered between 300 and

500, according to different eyewitnesses – were also stripped of anything of value and left naked in the street. 'Paper money, sometimes in very large quantities, also gold coins, jewels, watches and all kinds of valuables, are seized and carried off,' wrote the commanding officer of the USS *Arizona*. 'In some cases, and on the main streets, homes are forcibly entered by the mob.'

The breakdown of law and order encouraged gangs of criminals to head to the prosperous suburbs – Paradise, Bournabat, Boudja and Cordelio – and to ransack the larger Turkish-owned villas. In Bournabat, nine men were shot and livestock stolen. In Cordelio, twenty-three people were killed. When Ahmed Feizi returned to his villa in Boudja, he found that all his belongings had been pilfered. 'Clothes, boots, bedding, jewels, money &c., everything gone, and several other Turkish houses had undergone the same treatment.' Feizi was appalled by the behaviour of the Greek troops. 'Such things,' he wrote, 'we never expected from a European nation.'

As the disorder continued into the evening, the commander of the Italian dreadnought stationed in the harbour made contact with Admiral Calthorpe, suggesting that Allied forces should land immediately and restore order to the city's streets.

Calthorpe refused, fearing that the Italians would use the opportunity to seize the city for themselves. Nevertheless, he realised that something had to be done and sent his chief officer, Ian Smith, to meet Colonel Zafiriou and demand that the Greek army restore order immediately.

Smith was taken aback by the Greek colonel's nonchalance. '[He was] under a complete misapprehension as to the situation,' he wrote. 'He appeared to have taken no measures to restore order, nor to realise that there was any necessity to do so.'

As dusk fell and some semblance of normality returned to the city, people began to count the cost of the day's violence. The quayside had been the worst-affected area. Although the heavy rain had washed away the blood, there were still dozens of corpses strewn on the ground. 'Bodies of the murdered Turks were found in every place,' wrote one English eyewitness, 'in the sea, where some of the severely wounded had been thrown to drown, in lighters which were moored alongside the quay; even in the grounds of the British gasworks.'

The lull in the fighting encouraged people to emerge from their houses and pick over the wreckage. There was a general fear that the violence would flare up again that evening and many of the British sailors were glad to be spending the night on their ships. 'Suppose tonight will be a pretty sticky one ashore,' wrote Lycett Gardner, a lieutenant on the *Iron Duke*. 'Glad I'm not a Turk or a Greek.'

Any commander worth his salt would have imposed a curfew during the hours of darkness, but Colonel Zafiriou seemed not to understand the seriousness of what had happened. Two senior British officers visited him once again that evening and spoke to him in the strongest possible terms. 'We both felt, however, that this officer failed to appreciate the gravity of the situation.' His intransigence baffled the British and it ensured that sporadic looting continued throughout the night.

The following morning dawned bright and sunny and the violence seemed to have come to an end. At 11 a.m., George Perry of the American YMCA considered it safe enough to make a tour of the city in order to inspect the damage.

'I went to the Turkish quarter by way of the quay,' he wrote, 'where all along I saw pieces of torn fezzes.' At the Konak (the governor's palace), he noticed two dead Turks still floating in the water. He also observed that groups of Greek troops and civilians were gathered at every corner. Farther along the quay, he noted 'two cafés, a barber's shop and a small home which had been looted — windows, chairs and tables were completely broken. In one café, there was a large amount of blood on the floor.'

As he made his way into the Turkish quarter, he observed that the looted shops had become objects of interest for the local Greeks. 'All during the afternoon, morbidly curious Greek people were passing through the Turkish quarter, gloating and priding themselves over their efficiency in pillaging and looting.'

Perry next visited one of the city's morgues, driven by some compulsion to view the corpses that had been brought there. He counted twenty-two dead, all Turks; most of them had been stripped of clothing and valuables. 'There was one spare leg which appeared to have been hacked off by an axe just below the knee.' With ghoulish inquisitiveness, he sorted through the corpses with some care before concluding that 'the rest of that particular body was not there.'

The exact death toll remains unknown to this day, but most witnesses agree that the Turkish dead and wounded numbered between 300 and 400 while the Greeks lost about a hundred. These were just the victims of the unrest in Smyrna itself. Many more were killed in the villages that surrounded the city.

The violence had been entirely sectarian, pitting Greeks against Turks in a manner that seemed certain to preclude any peaceful coexistence in the future. Yet in all the chaos and carnage, there were a few instances of the rival nationalities helping each other. One Turkish merchant told Commander Berry of the USS *Manley* that his life had been saved by his Greek neighbours. Another Greek family, the Frangoulises, went out of their way to protect their Turkish-Albanian friends. But such acts of kindness were the exception to the rule; there were very few uplifting stories to salvage from the bloodshed and brutality.

Three days after the landing of Greek troops, Smyrna was finally at peace. The killings had stopped and the looting was at an end, but the behaviour of Venizelos's soldiers had caused irreparable damage to the Greek cause and had poisoned for ever the relationship between Smyrna's different nationalities.

'I well remember the bewilderment and alarm with which I heard on a lovely afternoon in Paris of this fatal event,' wrote Winston Churchill. 'It was impossible to excuse the imprudence of this violent act, which opened so many new perils when our resources were shrivelling.'

The Greek occupation provided the Turkish nationalists with a powerful rallying cry: Smyrna must be liberated. 'The result of this [violence] was like breaking open an ants' nest,' wrote Sir John de Robeck. 'Temporary stupefaction, much running about and a few hardy souls spitting acid at the invaders.'

The Greeks suddenly found themselves in a race against the clock. Their most urgent task was to restore some semblance of harmony to Smyrna's competing national groups, aware that this alone would prove them worthy custodians of the great city.

News of the occupation of Smyrna sent shock waves through the streets of Constantinople. There had already been protests about the Allied powers' seeming intention of carving up Turkey. Now, the realisation that this had become a reality − and that Greek troops were patrolling the streets of Smyrna − was the last straw.

One of the leading activists was Halide Edib, a highly educated member of the Constantinople bourgeoisie who had connections with several of the fledgling resistance movements. These organisations were attracting a growing number of former officers from the Turkish army, officers who devoted their energies to smuggling military hardware to distant towns in Anatolia.

Yet they were acutely aware that the time was not yet right for military action. The public needed to be galvanised and the occupation of Smyrna gave the resistance the rallying cry it so desperately needed.

'I hardly opened my mouth on any subject except when it concerned the sacred struggle which was to be,' wrote Edib. 'Turkey was to be cleared of murderers, the so-called civilising Greek army . . . Every detail of the coming struggle was of the utmost importance and worth any sacrifice we were willing to make.'

Edib's greatest talent was public oratory. She knew how to inflame the passions of a crowd and cajole it into action. Shortly after the landing of the Greek army, she was provided with the opportunity to perform her first service on behalf of the resistance. A huge outdoor protest meeting was organised at the Sultan Ahmed mosque in Constantinople and she was to address the crowd.

Edib was unusually nervous on the morning of the meeting and she grew even more anxious as she made her way through the streets. 'I could hardly stand on my feet,' she wrote, 'so fast and loud was my heart thumping: it was only when I entered the huge square that this violent thumping was stopped by the surprise of the spectacle.'

The minarets of the Sultan Ahmed mosque had been draped in black, as if in mourning for the Greek occupation. In front of the mosque, inscribed in huge letters, was a banner bearing the words, 'Wilson's Twelfth Point' – a reference to the American president's statement that the Turkish territories should be guaranteed their own sovereignty.

More than 200,000 people had gathered to hear Edib speak – a crowd so large that the British and French military authorities were seriously alarmed. 'Allied aeroplanes fled in and out of the minarets, policing the crowd,' she wrote. 'They buzzed like mighty bees and came down as low as they could in order, I believe, to intimidate the crowds.' Edib spoke with all the passion and force she could muster, in defiance of the Allied aircraft.

'From the tops of the minarets nigh against the heavens,' she

began, 'seven hundred years of glory are watching this new
tragedy of Ottoman history.' She informed the crowd that the
occupation of Smyrna was nothing short of a religious war –
a battle between Islam and Christianity. 'The European powers
would have found a way to send armies of conquest to the stars
and the moon had they known that Moslems and Turks inhabited those heavenly bodies. At last they have found a pretext,
an opportunity to break to pieces the last empire ruled by the
crescent.'

She reserved her greatest contempt for the peacemakers in
Paris – Wilson, Lloyd George and Clemenceau – who had
allowed the Greek army into Smyrna. 'They were all sitting at
a court whose ostensible object was the defence of human and
national rights, yet all that court did was to sanctify the spoli-
ation of the defeated peoples.'

Her words had an electrifying effect on the throng. Some
cried; some broke down completely. One woman repeatedly
screamed in a hysterical voice, 'My nation, my poor nation.'
Even representatives of the Allied powers were visibly moved
by her passion. One French general was spotted standing amidst
a group of Turkish youth with tears streaming down his cheeks.

Edib's speech had a particularly powerful effect on her own
countrymen: it brought home to people the critical situation
in which Turkey now found itself.

It also sent shock waves through the Greek districts of the
city, where the occupation of Smyrna was still being celebrated
with dancing and festivities. On the day of her speech, all the
celebrations came to an abrupt end. 'While we were crying
and talking and behaving peacefully in Sultan Ahmed,' she
wrote, 'a great panic was going on in Pera, the Christian quarter
of the town. People were running about the streets with a cry
of terror on their lips; "The Turks are coming, the Turks are
coming!"'

They were not coming yet; indeed, it would be two years

before the Turks felt confident enough to tackle the Greek military. But momentous events were starting to unfold in the wilds of Anatolia that were sparked – and fuelled – by the landing of the Greek army in Smyrna.

Ex Oriente Lux

It had been a gruelling twenty-four hours for Colonel Toby Rawlinson and his men. They had hoped to reach the eastern city of Erzurum in a matter of days, unaware that the mountain road they were following was only passable in midsummer. Long before they had crossed the first range of peaks, they were forced to bivouac on an exposed ridge in the teeth of a blizzard. 'The winds blow with terrific force,' he wrote in his diary, 'and a piercing cold defies all furs.' As he shivered in his canvas tent, Rawlinson had a very real fear that they would all die of exposure.

He had been sent to Anatolia in the spring of 1919, charged with enforcing the terms of the armistice signed six months previously. He was to supervise the surrender of armaments and oversee the demobilisation of the numerous battalions and units that were still under arms in Anatolia.

'In order to ensure these conditions [were] being carried out,' he wrote, 'it was, of course, necessary to inspect and, in fact, to supervise the measures taken by the Turks for the purpose, and this was the duty now officially allotted to me.'

He gathered a team of a dozen men, bought three antiquated cars in the Black Sea port of Trebizond and set out on a 200-mile journey towards Erzurum, the headquarters of the Turkish Ninth Army. After days stuck in deep snow, he and his men eventually dug themselves out and struggled towards Erzurum, where they hoped to find hot baths and comfortable beds. They were quickly disabused of this notion. Like so many of Turkey's cities, Erzurum had suffered enormous damage during the war and was now devastated by disease and famine. Rawlinson was told that more than 90 per cent of the population had died or fled.

Rawlinson's first task was to visit the local army commander, Kiazim Karabekir, with whom he hoped to forge a constructive working relationship. He was pleasantly surprised when he was introduced: 'The most genuine example of a first class Turkish officer that it has ever been my good fortune to meet.' Karabekir seemed willing to help Rawlinson collect and destroy the stockpiles of weaponry that were scattered across the countryside. He led him to a cache of 500 guns, which he immediately surrendered, and then proceeded to hand over more than 200,000 rounds of ammunition. Rawlinson was delighted to have such support from Karabekir, but when he looked more carefully at the weaponry he discovered that the guns were 'of antiquated pattern' and that the ammunition was 'in an absolutely dangerous condition'.

He soon began to suspect that the Turks – who seemed so accommodating and helpful – were surrendering only old and broken weaponry. These suspicions were confirmed when he chanced upon forty big field guns in perfect working order. 'These, the Turks assured me, had been "overlooked" by them.' He added sardonically: 'but thanks to our enterprise, they had not been overlooked by us'.

Kiazim Karabekir and his men were indeed concealing weaponry, reasoning that events in Smyrna left them with no option but to break the terms of the armistice. 'The landing of the Greeks in Smyrna, and the disastrous events which resulted thereupon, entirely changed the situation,' wrote Clifford Heathcote-Smith, who was working for the British High

Commission in Constantinople. 'The country was flooded with accounts of what had occurred. These accounts, which naturally were exaggerated, came as a great shock to the Turks, and had an unifying effect on the various factions into which the country was at that time split.'

George Horton explained the situation succinctly for his American audience. He said that the Turks were more insulted by the landing of the Greek army in Smyrna 'than the white citizens of Mobil would be if it were given over to a mandate of negro troops'.

The behaviour of officers such as Kiazim Karabekir was one cause for alarm; that of Mustafa Kemal was another. Kemal had landed in the Black Sea port of Samsun just four days after the Greek occupation of Smyrna. He had ostensibly come to commence his work as army inspector, charged with bringing order to the war-ravaged countryside, but the news from Smyrna galvanised him into action. He now saw his task as twofold: to awaken the Muslim population to the threat posed by Greece; and to unite the dispirited army officers into a cohesive fighting force.

Kemal travelled first to the town of Havza, where his visit coincided with a public demonstration about the events in Smyrna. At Kemal's instigation, a local notable delivered a rousing speech in which the town's inhabitants were told that their destiny was hanging in the balance. They were to 'hold themselves ready to sacrifice their lives and property if necessary to recover Smyrna'.

A British intelligence officer named Captain Hurst was in Havza at the time and described the mood of the people as extremely volatile. 'The air was heavy with rumours and menaces, the population was being deliberately excited and a spark would have sufficed to bring an outbreak [of violence].'

Hurst attributed the sudden change of mood to the arrival of Kemal, who spent his waking hours energising the local population and contacting army commanders. 'He had been carrying on a large telegraphic correspondence with the surrounding towns and beyond,' wrote Hurst, 'so much as to have practically monopolised the telegraph, and his officers have been seen in several, or most, of the villages of the neighbourhood, where their influence had certainly not made for conciliation.'

Captain Hurst's anxieties were reflected by the British High Commissioner in Constantinople, who informed the Foreign Office that dozens of Turkish officers had headed to eastern Turkey in order to organise resistance to the Greeks. 'The movement is so natural, and I feel it is so universal, that it seems to me hopeless to endeavour to stop it.'

There was still much uncertainty as to the strategy of Mustafa Kemal, who remained an unknown quantity to the British military. Many character assessments were written about him by Whitehall civil servants but they read more like wishful thinking than actual fact. According to one intelligence dossier, he was said to have indulged in 'dissipation' in his early years and contracted venereal disease. This had given him a 'contempt and disgust for life' and driven him to 'homosexual vice'. He was charged with having disobeyed Liman von Sanders during his spirited defence of Gallipoli. Strangest of all, he was reported to have lost an eye in the fighting against the British. Although Sir John de Robeck studied all the available information on Kemal, he failed to get any measure of the man. 'He is,' he wrote despairingly, 'a good deal of an enigma.' Lloyd George was more dismissive: 'a carpet seller in a bazaar' was his opinion of Mustafa Kemal.

Yet it soon became clear that the carpet seller was proving an effective force in uniting the disparate elements in central Turkey. After several weeks in Havza, he made his way to the conservative Muslim town of Amasya, where he met his comrades-in-arms: Ali Fuat, Rauf Orbay and Refet Bele.

Together, they plotted resistance, discussed tactics and wrote the famous Amasya Circular. This asserted that the sultan's administration in Constantinople was incapable of governing, since the city was under Allied control. It called upon the numerous defence organisations established in the wake of the Smyrna occupation to be co-ordinated into one central body. And it convoked a congress to be held in the eastern city of Sivas, preceded by a smaller gathering at Erzurum.

Emboldened by this document, Kemal delivered a rousing speech to the citizens of Amasya. 'We must pull on our peasant shoes,' he told them. 'We must withdraw to the mountains, we must defend the country to the last rock. If it is the will of God that we be defeated, we must set fire to all our homes, to all our property; we must lay the country in ruins and leave it an empty desert.'

Kemal next made his way to Erzurum, where Colonel Rawlinson was still engaged in his forlorn search for weaponry. When the English colonel sought an early interview with Kemal, he was struck by the Turk's professionalism. 'He has read much and travelled widely,' he wrote, 'and is thoroughly competent to give a considered opinion on all subjects of general interest.'

Rawlinson warned his superiors in London that Kemal was a Turkish thoroughbred who was fired by patriotism. He also did his best to counter the received wisdom that Kemal was dissolute. 'Many scurrilous reports have been circulated from time to time with regard to his private life,' he wrote, 'but I have never observed the slightest foundation for them.'

Rawlinson was correct in highlighting Kemal's dynamism, yet his portrait once again failed to capture the essence of the man. A more insightful sketch comes from the pen of Halide Edib, who was soon to become one of Kemal's closest associates. She found much to admire in him while also recognising that he had serious defects of character. 'He was by turns cynical, suspicious, unscrupulous and satanically shrewd,' she wrote. 'He bullied, he indulged in cheap, street corner heroics.' He was, she said, a master at adapting his tone to his audience. 'One moment he could pass as the perfect demagogue – a second George Washington – and the next moment fall into some Napoleonic attitude.'

She added that whilst he was often surrounded by men who were his superior in intellect 'and far above him in both culture and refinement', yet Kemal had one unique quality that set him apart from his peers. 'Though he excelled them in neither refinement nor originality,' she wrote, 'not one of them could possibly cope with his vitality. Whatever their qualities, they were made on a more or less normal scale. In terms of vitality, he wasn't. And it was this alone that made him the dominant figure.'

Within six weeks of the Greek army landing in Smyrna, Kemal's activities in central Anatolia were causing serious alarm in Constantinople. Matters came to a head when the British High Commission decided to strip him of his position as army inspector and recall him to the capital. To this end, they sent a telegram, demanding his immediate return.

Kemal's reply was unambiguous. He refused to obey the order, declaring that he was now serving 'the forces of the nation'. At the same time, he instructed all Turkish military officials to stop co-operating with the British arms inspectors and proposed co-ordinated action against any further actions on the part of the 'enemy'. This was a direct challenge to the British, who sent a second telegram, repeating their demand that he return to Constantinople.

Kemal's close associates urged him to resign his post in order to avoid the stigma of being stripped of his command. Kemal uncharacteristically hesitated. 'It is a fool's belief that people like their leaders only with ideals,' he told them. 'They want them dressed in the pomp of power and invested with the insignia of their office.' This was true enough, but by the second week of July his dismissal from the army had become an inevitability.

Kemal reluctantly took heed of his colleagues and sent a telegram to Constantinople, submitting his resignation. It crossed with an incoming telegram that stripped him of his rank.

He remained deeply concerned that his authority would be fatally undermined by his resignation, especially in the wilds of Anatolia where military rank counted for so much. But his doubts were soon quelled by his powerful comrade-in-arms, Kiazim Karabekir, who offered to serve under Kemal's leadership. 'I've come to pay my respects on behalf of all the officers and men under my command,' he said. 'You remain our respected commander just as you've been until now. I've brought a car and an escort of cavalry, as befits a corps commander. Pasha, we're all at your service.'

With these words, the nationalist movement was born.

Five days after the landing of Greek troops in Smyrna, an imposing and austere-looking gentleman could be seen alighting on the quayside. He was dressed in a grey suit, wore gold-rimmed spectacles and carried a long cane. At first glance, he might easily have been mistaken for a wealthy doctor or lawyer. Aristeidis Stergiadis was indeed a lawyer by training, but he had come to Smyrna as the newly appointed Greek governor.

Ahead of him lay an unenviable task. He was charged with restoring harmony to this shattered city and rebuilding links between the different nationalities. More than that, he had to prove to the Allies that Greece was capable of ruling the richest part of Asia Minor.

From the moment that people met Stergiadis, they realised that they were in the presence of someone extraordinary. He was a man of conviction and principle, whose underlying sense of fairness was underpinned by an adamantine core. He had been hand-picked for the job by Venizelos, a friend from the days when they were both revolutionaries in the mountains of Crete.

Stergiadis had specialised in Muslim law and gone on to make his name as an enlightened governor of Epirus. Here, he had achieved the remarkable success of shattering the power of the local brigands. At his first meeting with a particularly notorious group of outlaws, he was seized by one of them and held at gunpoint. His response was pure Stergiadis. Unfazed by the men's threats to kill him, he launched a blistering verbal offensive that left the bandit quaking in his boots. '[He] over-whelmed the trickster with such a torrent of invective that between shame and astonishment, he lost his head and was immediately rushed into satisfactory terms of capitulation.' So wrote the historian Arnold Toynbee, who met Stergiadis on many occasions and had an opportunity to study his leader-ship at close quarters.

Toynbee was initially startled by his odd mannerisms and method of governing. 'He is highly strung – resourceful and courageous but capricious and hot-tempered,' he wrote, 'and his method of administration was to strike unexpectedly and hard, as if he were pleading a weak case or fighting a desperate duel.' Yet he was most impressed by the way in which Stergiadis brought order to a city wracked by internecine strife. 'He could hardly have had a worse start or performed a more brilliant acrobatic feat than to keep afloat as he did in such a sea of troubles.'

Stergiadis was a man who always imposed his will, whether dealing with brigands, generals or church hierarchs. His aloof manner raised people's hackles within hours of arriving in the city. He declined all invitations to the tea dances and soirées in the Levantine villas of Bournabat, preferring the solitude of the governor's palace. '[He] lived as a hermit,' wrote Horton, 'accepting no invitations and never appearing in society.' Stergiadis told Horton that he intended 'to accept no favours and to form no ties, so that he might administer equal justice to all, high and low alike'. The Levantines and Americans found him dour; he was very different from the genial, gin-drinking Rahmi Bey.

His idiosyncrasies caused particular offence to the Greeks serving under him. He always carried a cane, which he would use to beat subordinates who disagreed with his decisions. He liked to boast about how he intended to govern by the stick; he certainly had no intention of also offering a carrot.

Stergiadis had limited means and a perennial shortage of manpower, yet he quickly wrested control of a very precarious situation. A large part of his success was due to his unshakeable belief in his own ability. 'The task we have undertaken in Asia Minor is not beyond our capabilities,' he wrote, 'and I am convinced that it will be completed.' Yet he warned that it was unlikely 'that we will complete it impeccably'.

The reason for this caveat was staring him in the face. The local Greek population was behaving in abominable fashion, lording it over the Turks as if they were triumphant conquerors. They displayed an equal hostility to Stergiadis and his team, whom they quickly learned to despise.

Stergiadis won few friends in the Greek community by ensuring that all involved in the bloodbath that followed the army's landing were roundly punished. A court-martial was established, which began hearing cases against Greeks who had looted Turkish property. The first sentences were handed down almost immediately: three Greeks were given the death penalty for their part in the violence. '[They] were taken out to a square beside the railroad connecting Boudja and Smyrna,' wrote George Horton, 'and publicly shot and buried where their graves could be seen by all the people passing between that popular summer resort and the main city.'

Horton added that the fact that the overwhelming majority of those convicted were Greeks 'contributed no little to the unpopularity of the governor-general among the native Christian population'.

The new governor was determined to establish courts of law that were scrupulously fair. At times, he even appeared to favour the Turks. Toynbee was witness to several occasions when Stergiadis showed 'spectacular acts of partiality towards Turks, when Turks and Greeks were in conflict'. And when the Allied commissioners sent an inspector to investigate complaints about biased Greek government, he concluded that the Turks under Stergiardis 'enjoyed such good care and protection which they could have never dreamed of'.

One of the governor's master strokes was to retain all the Turkish functionaries who had served before the Greek landing, raising their salaries as an inducement for them to remain at their posts. He also informed the Armenian and Jewish communities that he expected them to play a significant role in the governing of Smyrna, since his aim was to create a multiracial administration that reflected the city's demographic.

Among the many thorns in his side were the local church leaders, whose fiery and uncompromising sermons helped to fan the flames of resentment. Few irritated him more than Metropolitan Chrysostom, who had greeted and blessed the Greek soldiers on their arrival at Smyrna. Stergiadis found his rousing nationalism most distasteful and vowed to rein him in. An opportunity soon presented itself. He was attending a church service at which Chrysostom gave a sermon that quickly strayed into political territory. George Horton, who was also at the service, recalled how Stergiadis stood up in front of the entire congregation and stopped the metropolitan in mid-flow. He shouted out, 'But I told you I didn't want any of this.'

Chrysostom was stunned; no one had ever spoken to him before in such a fashion. '[He] flushed, choked and breaking off his discourse abruptly, ended with, "In the name of the Father, Son and Holy Ghost, Amen."'

On another occasion, Stergiadis visited a country village in which the local priest had refused to say prayers over the body of a dead child because the mother could not afford the fee. When Stergiadis was presented to the mayor and priest, '[he] slapped the latter soundly in the face, saying: "Wretch! I don't want to know you. You are a disgrace to the Greek nation."'

The local villagers were aghast. 'But this isn't the same priest, Excellency,' they told him. 'This is a good man. We sent the other away.'

Many men would have blushed with embarrassment, but not Stergiadis. '"Give him a hundred drachmas for his poor," said His Excellency to his secretary, and thus the incident was closed.'

His treatment of the church leaders, coupled with his absolute impartiality, earned Stergiadis the undying hatred of many local Greeks. They had thought their hour had come, yet they now found themselves ruled by a governor whose sympathies seemed to lie with the Turks. One Greek businessman made the extraordinary assertion that Stergiadis's goal was to 'terrorise the Greeks of Smyrna and Anatolia, persecute them, martyr them, do them harm and turn every circumstance to the profit of the Turks, Levantines, foreigners and Jews'.

Such sentiments must have brought a rare smile to Stergiadis's face; they sent a signal to the outside world that he was ruling his fiefdom with complete justice. This, after all, was what Venizelos had ordered him to do, aware that the Megali Idea itself was on trial. 'The territorial extent of our rule will depend on the impartiality of our administration and our strong defence of the rights of the minorities,' he wrote. Venizelos, who was in the process of negotiating a far larger empire in Asia Minor, knew that he would succeed only '[if] we are not even subconsciously inclined to avenge our sufferings at the hands of the Turks . . . and that we know how to treat them because we are the carriers of a higher civilisation'.

The stability brought about by Stergiadis's administration encouraged a flood of Europeans to return to Smyrna. Merchants, consuls, intelligence officers and prominent locals – people who had exiled themselves during the war – now poured back into the city.

As Smyrna's foreign population swelled to its pre-war level, the *grands magasins* found themselves achieving unprecedented profits. Traders hastily restocked their shelves with imported foreign goods, aware that there were a large number of Europeans with a great deal of money to spend. Elsewhere in Anatolia, brigandage and unrest were causing absolute chaos, but in Smyrna, Stergiadis had reversed a desperate situation. As the economy began to boom, so the city's clubs and brasseries found themselves doing a lively trade.

One of the British officers posted to Smyrna was Sir Tom Bridges, whose working hours were spent keeping a watchful eye on the Greek army. Nevertheless, he found plenty of time to relax and socialise, quickly striking up friendships with several of the Levantine dynasties living on the outskirts of the city. 'Most of our friends belonged to the old Levantine families – English, French and Greek, who lived *en prince* in the beautiful suburbs of Boudja and Bournabat,' he wrote.

These houses were fully staffed within weeks of the armistice and soon recovered the gaiety of the pre-war years. 'One of them I remember naming "The House of the Fruitful Vine" for its procreative atmosphere,' wrote Bridges. 'There was a large family of charming people and always a new baby, new puppies, kittens or perhaps the ancient parrot would lay an egg.'

Eldon Giraud, a lad of nine at the time, remembered the months that followed the end of the war as a time of endless tea parties for the adults, followed by uproarious evenings involving alcohol, music and extravagant dancing. Among the regular visitors to Bournabat was the Allied commander, General Hanbury, whose magnificent car was a source of constant fascination to young Eldon. 'I was especially impressed with [this],' he later recalled, 'a dark green Sunbeam, with carbide headlights that used to stink like hell. I always used to sit and admire the cars and get pieces of rubber tubing from the drivers to make catapults.'

Another source of amusement was the activity in the skies above Bournabat. Eldon's sister, Joyce, was an attractive nineteen-year-old at the time and quickly gained the notice of the newly arrived Greek troops. One of them – a young lad named Skouze – took a particular fancy to her and demonstrated it in extravagant fashion. '[He] used to fly over our garden and drop sweets for my sister,' wrote Eldon. 'These never managed to land in our garden, however, but he provided me and my pals with great sport.' The young lads used to get out their airguns 'and try to shoot him down . . . it was lucky for him that we did not hit our target as he would have ended up on one of the cypress trees.'

Helena van der Zee, daughter of one of the largest and wealth-iest Levantine families, also remembered the Greek occupation as a time of heady excitement. 'At our house in Cordelio, the doors were always open to all. There were tennis parties, bathing expeditions and outings by moonlight, and the tradition of sere-nading began once again,' she wrote. 'Often the little landing craft of the warships, both Greek and Allied, came to collect us so that we could spend the rest of the evening in the city. The house was full of marine officers of every nationality.'

The van der Zees' mansion was spectacularly large and required a veritable army of servants to keep it in order. As more and more people returned to Smyrna, the van der Zees were once again able to employ a full complement of Greek domestics: several maids, a chef, sous-chef, dressmaker and ironer, as well as a German governess and two English nurses. In addition, they took on a new team of gardeners and boatmen.

These servants enabled life to resume its unhurried rhythm, even when there were visitors constantly coming and going. Sunday breakfast was one of the high points of the week and all fifteen members of the immediate family were expected to attend. 'We would assemble around a large table laid out in the shade for breakfast,' recalled Helena. 'A famous Greek baker in Cordelio, Adami, was particularly renowned for its *katimeria* (large pastries dusted with sugar and cinnamon) and for its *loucoumades* (honeyed doughnuts) which he only made on Sunday mornings.'

The table was presided over by the family's attendant body-guard, an Albanian by origin, who cut a most resplendent figure. 'He was magnificently attired in puffed breeches, fez, a bolero specked with gold and a huge belt coiled around his belly, into which he stuck daggers and pistols.'

When breakfast was finished, the older members of the family would retire to hammocks and chaises longues, while the children headed to the jetty in order to swim in the bay. It was an idyllic time for the younger van der Zees. 'The house was always exciting . . . all the children were allowed to invite friends for meals without first having to ask permission. There was always enough food for everyone.'

For the older children, the post-war years saw a revival of tennis parties on the family courts. Helena and her brothers would challenge young officers of the Dutch, Italian, English and French marines to games of doubles; bottles of iced lemonade would be provided by the family's maids.

The van der Zees were particularly friendly with the many Greeks who lived in Cordelio and everyone in the family was brought up speaking fluent Greek, as well as English, French, Dutch and German. Helena was a particular favourite with the local Greek lads, who spent their evenings serenading local beauties under the windows of their houses. She recalled being wooed one night by a group of boys from Cordelio. 'It was wonderful to be woken at night by the sound of the songs drifting in through the open windows. One of my best memories was being suddenly woken by the soft music of these songs.'

If life was benign for the Levantines of Smyrna, it was even better for the Greeks. During the war years, they had lived in fear of persecution, deportation and worse. Now they were masters of their own domain. Petros Brussalis, a seven-year-old boy at the time of the Greek landing, still has clear memories of the first Easter under Greek rule. 'The Greek army invited thousands of people to a field near to Cordelio and they cooked large numbers of lambs.' Everyone partied until late into the night, 'and I remember some soldiers giving me sweet wine to drink'.

The speed with which Smyrna recovered its vitality was entirely due to the ever-energetic Stergiadis, who overcame numerous hurdles in the first weeks of his administration. Some 250,000 Greek refugees wanted to return to the city and surrounding countryside. Stergiadis ensured that this was managed with military precision. Makeshift camps were set up to provide accommodation for the 41,000 families whose houses had been destroyed and a judicious deployment of police officers prevented any clashes between Turks and Greeks.

Stergiadis also imported scores of tractors and ploughs from America as he wished to introduce mechanical farming to the rich land around Smyrna. He established an experimental farm at the village of Tepe Keui, which was to provide instruction in the use of this new machinery. The farm was one of Stergiadis's pet projects. Another, on an altogether grander scale, was the foundation of the Ionian University of Smyrna. Its aim was to provide education for all – irrespective of race or nationality – and demonstrate that 'Greece did not go to Asia Minor to conquer alien populations but to bring them to her superior civilisation.'

Stergiadis had no doubt as to whom he wished to run the university. He hired Professor Karatheodoris, the modern-minded professor of mathematics at Göttingen University. The professor launched himself into the project with great gusto, putting into practice all of Stergiadis's ideas. The university's motto was 'Ex Oriente Lux' and it was to offer an impressive range of disciplines. Among the languages to be taught were Turkish, Arabic, Farsi, Hebrew, Greek and Armenian. Stergiadis hoped that it would open its doors to the first year's students in September 1922.

The American consul, George Horton, had nothing but praise for the work of Stergiadis and his advisors. In a report to the American Secretary of State, he described the Greek administration as 'the only civilised and beneficient regime which that country has seen since historic times'. He added, 'I was in close touch with Mr Sterghiades [sic] through it all, I have travelled widely through the country, I have talked with scores of native-born Americans who have travelled over the region and I absolutely know of what I am talking.' He was particularly impressed by the impartial judicial system that had been established and the fact that Stergiadis had managed to restore law and order to the streets of Smyrna.

'Brigandage was practically suppressed, security very generally reigned and, insofar as the means of the Greek government permitted, Mr Stergiadis supported and originated civilised institutions and progress and promoted agriculture and industry.'

But while Smyrna was prospering under Stergiadis's governorship, the countryside around the city was increasingly troubled by unrest. 'The dark side to this seemingly idyllic picture,' wrote Horton, 'is that quite frequently the two or three Greek officials [of an outlying village] would be found some morning with their throats cut.'

It was even more dangerous in the villages farther along the coast. The return of refugees within the Greek-controlled zone had been orderly and well managed. The same could not be said for the thousands of Greek refugees pouring into towns still under Turkish control. Furious to find their family homes occupied by Turks, they began taking the law into their own hands.

This tense situation was made even more volatile by the fact that the Turkish resistance was growing stronger by the day. One of those helping the irregulars in the countryside around Smyrna was Colonel Bekir Sami, commander of the 17th Army Corps. Unable to dislodge the Greeks from the centre of the city, these forces vowed to harass and kill any Greek soldier who was foolish enough to stray into the countryside. 'With technical help from the regular officers who kept themselves behind the scenes,' wrote one, 'they made the region too hot for the Greeks.'

Stergiadis found himself in a terrible dilemma. He had to decide whether to stand back and watch his compatriots being attacked by Turkish brigands, or risk sending his own troops into former Greek villages, which were now riven with sectarian violence. The danger of the first option was to risk alienating still further the Greek population of Smyrna; the danger of the latter was to provoke all-out war.

Stergiadis weighed up the pros and cons before deciding to despatch troops into dozens of towns and villages, including Aidin and Aivali. He hoped that the drive outwards into the countryside would bring order and stability with little loss of life. This quickly proved to be wishful thinking. Turkish regulars and irregulars were waiting for the Greek army and forced them to fight their way into many of the towns and villages.

The town of Aidin was a case in point. It had survived the First World War almost intact and was little changed from how it had been in 1914. 'It had its finely placed church, its well equipped hospital, its school, its theatre, its cinema, its electric light, its flour mills, its factories for crushing olives and making soap.' So wrote Toynbee, who had visited Aidin before the war. Now, as the Greek army forced its path into Aidin, it was met by a scene of devastation. The Turkish irregulars had gone on the rampage and their slaughter was total and indiscriminate.

'Women and children were hunted down like rats from house to house and civilians caught alive were slaughtered in batches – shot or knived or hurled over a cliff.'

The Greek quarter had been razed to the ground. 'The houses and public buildings were plundered, the machinery in the factories wrecked, safes blown or burst open and the whole quarter finally burned.'

Witnesses to the massacre disagree as to why the Turks behaved with such brutality. Some blamed the conduct of the Greek troops as they advanced up the Maeander Valley, claiming that they torched Turkish villages en route. Others assert that the Greeks advanced in an orderly fashion in the face of extreme provocation. Whatever the truth of the matter, the episode in Aidin only served to inflame a very tense situation. One unnamed English eyewitness reported that the recapture of the town was followed by a new outbreak of patriotic fervour on the part of the Greeks.

'One cannot help remarking that the Greeks are doing their level best to make themselves obnoxious, unpopular and hated by the Turks . . . Their continual processions with flags, portraits of Venizelos in all the houses, shops and cafés, their ridiculous patriotic songs, sung all day long by the street scum and by the soldiers under the very nose of the Turks cannot but create ill-feeling and a wider breach between these two races.'

This same witness went on to report that a new batch of Greek troops had recently arrived in Smyrna. 'Whilst marching through the town . . . [they] were singing as follows: "Now that the *foustanella* [Greek kilt] has come to Smyrna, the fez will disappear and the blood of the Turks will flow. Now that we have taken Smyrna, let us fly to Aghia Sophia. The mosques will be razed to the ground and the Cross will be erected thereon."'

By the end of the summer, Stergiadis had a whole new crisis on his hands. He had dramatically increased the amount of territory controlled by the Greek army but in doing so he had further inflamed tensions between the two communities. As he attempted to seize control of the situation, he was brought news that Allied leaders were having serious doubts about the wisdom of sending the Greek army into Smyrna. They were also dramatically rethinking their own position in Constantinople. In the eyes of many in the Allied senior command, it was time to be far more bullish in their attitude towards the vanquished Turkish nation.

The Shattered Vase

As darkness enveloped Constantinople on the evening of 15 March 1920, just ten months after the landing of the Greek army in Smyrna, two figures could be seen flitting through the city's unlit backstreets. They glanced over their shoulders nervously, fearful that they were being followed. There was good reason for their anxiety. Halide Edib and her husband, Dr Adivar Adnan, a prominent politician, had learned that the British were going to take control of Constantinople that very night. Parliament was to be disbanded, nationalist sympathisers arrested and the city placed under military occupation.

Halide Edib and Dr Adnan knew that there was no time to lose. They had to flee from Constantinople and join Mustafa Kemal in Anatolia before it was too late. Both of them were already known to be activists and would certainly be arrested – and quite possibly imprisoned – if caught. They disguised themselves as pious Muslims and crossed the Bosphorus to the Scutari district of the city, where nationalist sympathisers were running an underground safe house.

Dr Adnan and his wife soon found they were not alone. Four parliamentary deputies were also hiding here and another group had already set off to join Mustafa Kemal. It was imperative that all of the new arrivals should head east as soon as possible, for the British were redoubling their efforts to round up nationalist sympathisers. 'That very day,' wrote Edib, 'posters had been put up all over the city in English and Turkish, threatening death to any one who gave refuge to a Nationalist. I remember one of the posters at the station, with "DEATH" in enormous letters.'

Their flight to eastern Anatolia came in the nick of time. The British formally occupied Constantinople on 16 March, a devastating blow to the nationalist cause. Ministers, city governors and officials were arrested and subsequently deported to Malta, where they were held without trial in a military prison. Among those seized by the British was Rahmi Bey, who was living in Constantinople at the time of the military occupation. He protested his innocence of any wrongdoing and found ready support from his Levantine friends in Smyrna, but the British military officials refused to listen to his pleas. In their eyes, Rahmi was tainted by his association with the old regime. He was incarcerated in Malta – prisoner number 2691 – and his only consolation was that his case would soon become a cause célèbre.

The British were anxious to prevent activists from joining Mustafa Kemal in Anatolia and began patrolling all the roads leading out of the capital. The first stage of Dr Adnan and Halide Edib's flight took them to the village of Samandra, twenty miles from the capital. The area had just been occupied by the British military but the nationalists were able to keep ahead of the game by intercepting the British wires. They travelled at night, aided by nationalist sympathisers who were busily smuggling arms to Angora in defiance of the British-imposed armistice. 'Cartloads of arms had to be hidden in sacks of coal or loads of hay, transported by night, and buried before dawn,' wrote Edib. 'Simple as it sounds, it really required bravery, intelligence and resourcefulness – and a minute knowledge of the country and the character of its inhabitants.'

For night after night, Edib and her husband travelled across mountain passes, pausing in villages where safe houses had been

arranged. At each place they encountered nationalists like themselves, some of whom would soon assume senior roles in the
drive to liberate Smyrna.

After more than a week on the road, they received a telegram
from Mustafa Kemal, informing them that the English garrison
in Eski Shehir had been driven out by nationalist soldiers. This
meant that they could continue their journey to Angora by rail,
since that stretch of line was now in the hands of Kemal's
supporters.

'It was wonderful not to be hunted any more,' wrote Edib,
'to feel that here was a bit of our country really our own.' The
countryside was still dangerous, but the towns alongside the
railway were relatively safe. Edib and her husband boarded a
train at Eski Shehir and within a few hours arrived in Angora.

The door of our compartment opened suddenly and
Mustafa Kemal Pasha's hand reached up to help me down
the step [she wrote]. In that light, his hand was the only
part of him I could see distinctly, and it is that part of him
which is physically most characteristic of the whole man.
It is a narrow and faultlessly shaped hand, with very slender
fingers and a skin which nothing darkens or wrinkles . . .
It differed from the large broad hand of the fighting Turk
in its highly strung nervous tension, its readiness to spring
and grip its oppressor by the throat.

Edib found Mustafa Kemal in ebullient mood. A large number
of nationalist supporters had made it safely to Angora and all
were determined to prevent the Greeks and their allies from
further carving up the remnants of the disintegrating Ottoman
empire. However, they knew that before this could be accomplished, they needed to drive the Greek army out of Smyrna.

Although Mustafa Kemal was surrounded by an increasing

number of nationalist supporters, his position remained far from secure. While Angora itself was safely under his control, great swathes of Anatolia were fast descending into civil war. Circassian and Abkhaze brigands infested many rural areas and each town seemed to have spawned bands of criminals who preyed on anyone, regardless of nationality. By the spring of 1920, there were few areas of the countryside that were not wracked with civil unrest.

The situation became even more precarious when the sultan – who was by now nothing more than a British puppet – appointed his brother-in-law, Damad Ferid, as grand vizier. Ferid was bitterly opposed to the nationalists and vowed, as he said, to place his trust in God and Great Britain. To this end, he leaned on the Seyhulislam, the body that governed religious affairs of state, to issue a fatwa against the most prominent nationalists in Angora. This stated that it was the duty of every Muslim to kill Mustafa Kemal and his senior advisors, including Halide Edib and her husband.

'[I] was accused of inciting the Turkish people to revolt against the government of the sultan, and of stirring up civil strife and bloodshed throughout the whole country,' wrote Edib. 'For some reason, they honoured me with the longest and most picturesque description of misdeeds.'

A few days after the fatwa, Damad Ferid established a disciplinary force whose task was to hunt down and defeat nationalist forces. To Kemal's supporters in Angora, it seemed as if their enemies were increasing with every week that passed: Greeks in the west, the British in Constantinople and now forces loyal to the sultan and his government.

'Trouble and difficulty were gathering like an avalanche,' wrote Edib, 'and threatening to wreck the movement at its onset.' Yet Mustafa Kemal functioned best under trying circumstances. He persuaded the nationalist mufti of Angora to publish a counter-fatwa – signed by hundreds of fellow muftis – declaring that the sultanate was being held hostage by the infidel British and that its fatwa was therefore invalid. Kemal then turned his attentions to the two most pressing problems that beset his nationalist movement: the lack of an effective army; and the need for some sort of political assembly that could be seen to be acting on behalf of the Turkish nation.

His inner circle of politicians, advisors and military commanders met daily in a sequestered farm school on the outskirts of the town. They spent much of their time planning a Grand National Assembly that was intended to represent the voice of the nation. This took effect at electrifying speed. Nationalist organisations across Anatolia were instructed to elect and send delegates to Angora with all possible haste. On 23 April, just five weeks after the British occupied Constantinople, the assembly met for its opening session. Kemal did not mince his words when he spoke to the delegates: 'We call on the whole nation to come together in unity and rise against the Greeks in total determination. The jihad, once it is properly preached, will, with God's help, result quickly in the rout of the Greeks.'

While the politicians got to work in the assembly, Halide Edib was busy setting up her news and propaganda agency. She knew that the effective dissemination of information would be a key to the future success of the nationalists. 'Both the outside world and our own people knew very little about our movement,' she wrote, 'and all the people I had seen on the way [from Constantinople] seemed to be suffering from lack of news.'

Her idea was to wire news to every town and village that had a telegraph office; it could then be printed and pasted to the walls of the central mosque. She also began ordering English and French newspapers in order to monitor the prevailing wind of opinion. 'We decided to take the Daily Chronicle,' she wrote, 'because it was said to be the mouthpiece of Mr Lloyd George.'

When she was not working at the agency, Edib was busily chronicling the historic events that were taking place around her. Like many of the new arrivals from Constantinople, she had never been to Angora and found herself in a small rural town that offered none of the bourgeois comforts of the capital. The low houses were roughly built and the streets were choked with dung. According to one American visitor, the few hotels were 'as primitive in comfort as appearance, built of mud in which large holes can be seen and full of danger to the unwary on their rickety staircases'. The houses were not much better: 'Weather-beaten mud and thatch dwellings [that] are mostly heated by mangals [braziers] of burning charcoal that give out poisonous fumes.'

Life among the nationalists was communal, with all the key members of Kemal's team sharing lodgings and eating under the same roof. 'We lived like members of a newly founded religious order in all the exaggerated puritanism of its inception,' wrote Edib. 'Mustafa Kemal Pasha shared our life and while among us was strictly pure as a sincere Catholic priest. But some evenings he disappeared and we knew that some feast had been prepared in one of the summer-houses round about Angora . . .'

These were occasions when Kemal and a few of his closest friends would indulge in heavy drinking. He had a voracious liking for alcohol, although he was careful not to indulge in public. But he would admit to Halide Edib that he had spent the night drinking, often with the *hodjas* and holy men of Angora. 'Don't you believe in the holiness and purity of the hodjas,' he told her. 'In public they're against drink, aren't they? But they can outdrink anyone.'

At the two congresses organised by Kemal – at Erzurum and Sivas – delegates had agreed that the Greek occupation of Smyrna was to be resisted by force of arms. They now had to work out how to bring about the destruction of the Greek forces.

Kemal had already given this much thought. He intended to

make use of the remnants of the Ottoman army, even though the soldiers were demoralised, poorly equipped and lacking leadership. He also intended to co-opt as many irregular forces as possible, aware that their lack of discipline was compensated by their bravado. Principal among the irregulars was Ethem the Circassian – a veritable giant of a man whose 2,000-strong cavalry column had repeatedly proved its mettle on the field of battle.

Edib penned a vivid portrait of Ethem at the height of his power, when he travelled to Angora to visit Kemal. 'His figure was more like that of a powerful skeleton than like that of a body of flesh and blood,' she wrote. 'It was built on the best Circassian model – very wide shoulders, a slim waist, long arms and legs and a large fair head with a short nose and eyes whose gaze was even paler and colder than that of Mustafa Kemal Pasha.'

Ethem placed his forces at Kemal's disposal, leading them into battle against Abkhaze rebels in north-western Anatolia. His cavalry drubbed these rebels and then went on to destroy several other bands of troublemakers. They were so effective as a fighting force that Colonel Ismet, Kemal's chief of staff, grew seriously alarmed. 'They are armed to the teeth, each one of them,' he warned. 'They look down on everyone else in their confident pride. Who controls the country today? They or us?'

'We do,' replied Kemal, 'because we have the brains.'

Ethem nevertheless gave the appearance of being the dominant force. He returned to Angora after his triumphant campaign in order to enjoy the fruits of victory. 'When he came, the streets were thronged with his men,' recalled Edib, 'all of them beautifully equipped in wild irregular fashion . . . Ethem himself was the most picturesque of all. He was received with great honours. Mustafa Kemal Pasha lent him his car, the only car we had in Angora then.'

It was not long before Ethem's cavalry, with the support of

Colonel Ismet's regular forces, came into direct conflict with the British military. The catalyst was a clash between Kemal's fighters and the sultan's forces on the outskirts of Izmit, an important town that lay just a hundred miles from the capital. Kemal's ragtag army attacked with such bravado that many of the sultan's troops immediately switched sides. The nationalists, flushed with success, then ventured to attack a British battalion, which brought swift retribution. The British returned fire with all the weaponry at their disposal, including bombing the nationalists from the air. Kemal's forces were eventually beaten back, but the British commander was so alarmed by the attack that he demanded more British troops to defend his forward positions. Yet herein lay a problem: there were none available. The only soldiers that could be deployed with immediate effect were Greek.

Britain's senior military advisors were adamant that to call upon the Greeks for help would be courting disaster. Lloyd George saw matters rather differently. Believing that he had been presented with a unique opportunity to deal a knockout blow to the Turkish nationalists, he had no qualms about allowing Venizelos's forces to deliver the *coup de grâce*.

'[He] is persuaded that the Greeks are the coming power in the Mediterranean both on land and on the sea and wants to befriend them,' wrote Britain's senior field marshal, Sir Henry Wilson, in his diary. 'The whole of Lloyd George's foreign policy is chaotic and based on totally fallacious values of men and affairs.'

It may have been chaotic but at least it was also consistent. Lloyd George contacted Venizelos and asked him to spare a division of troops for the protection of Constantinople. In return, he gave his Greek compatriot the green light to deploy his forces out from Smyrna.

The Greek advance was rapid, decisive and brilliantly executed. One corps pushed due east and halted only when it reached the town of Alashehir, more than a hundred miles from the city. A parallel advance up the Maeander Valley extended Greek control far to the south. A third corps drove northwards, crossing tortuous mountain paths until it reached the Sea of Marmara. The Greek cavalry penetrated even further east and scored the notable success of capturing Bursa, the first capital of the Ottoman state. By the time that military operations were brought to a halt, the army had created a buffer zone that extended some 200 miles around Smyrna.

The Greek army had excelled itself, defeating the nationalist forces in every encounter. There was horror and outrage when news of their offensive reached Angora. The platform of the Grand National Assembly was draped in black as a token of mourning.

There was a similar despondency among Turks in Constantinople. The efficiency of the Greek advance convinced the sultan and his grand vizier that they had no option but to agree to unconditional terms for a conclusive peace. The treaty that they signed was based on the draconian terms drafted by the Allies at the Italian town of San Remo four months earlier. Smyrna and all of its extended hinterland was officially awarded to Greece. Although Turkey was to retain nominal sovereignty of this zone, there was to be a plebiscite after five years that would decide whether or not it should be permanently annexed to Greece. Few doubted the results of such a vote.

Smyrna was not the only loss. Kurdistan in the east was to become autonomous and Armenia an independent state. The Straits were internationalised, and the French and Italians divided up the whole of southern Turkey into spheres of influence. Thrace was awarded to Greece. So, too, were most of the islands of the Aegean. Although Constantinople was to remain the country's capital, the rump of the nation was now far away in the hinterlands of Anatolia.

The grand vizier appended his signature to the treaty in

August 1920, signalling his government's consent to its terms, but the nationalists in Angora refused to recognise its validity. '[It] was,' wrote Halide Edib, 'like fresh fuel thrown onto the smouldering fire of hatred which the Western world had provoked by its conduct in Turkey.'

The French president, Raymond Poincaré, noted wryly that it was apposite for the treaty to be signed in Sèvres, home to fragile porcelain. 'It, too, is a fragile object,' he said. 'Perhaps a shattered vase.'

But one man was jubilant with the signing of the treaty. Venizelos was experiencing his finest hour. After a few weeks of military action, he had achieved his long-cherished goal of reconquering the lands of Ancient Greece and Byzantium. The Megali Idea had become a reality and Smyrna's status was enshrined in international law.

Lloyd George also felt vindicated, reminding his colleagues that, under his leadership, Britain had backed a winning horse. Alone among senior politicians in London, Winston Churchill foresaw that war was now an inevitability. 'At last, peace with Turkey,' he wrote. 'And to ratify it, war with Turkey. However, so far as the Great Allies were concerned, the war was to be fought by proxy. Wars when fought by great nations are often very dangerous for the proxy.'

They were to prove very dangerous for Smyrna as well.

The dramatic events unfolding in eastern Anatolia seemed a far remove from Bournabat. Life had returned to the careless pleasures of the pre-war years and the Levantine merchant princes – most of whom had been implacably opposed to the Greek occupation – were forced to concede that Stergiadis had performed a miracle.

Herbert Octavius swallowed his pride and made a very public U-turn, offering the Greek governor his full and public endorsement. In a letter to *The Times*, he wrote: 'I feel it impossible

. . . as one of the oldest British residents in Smyrna . . . not to bear testimony from my own personal knowledge, to the correct and impartial behaviour of the present Greek civil authorities and especially of Mr Stergiades.' He added that the most tangible sign of Stergiadis's even-handedness was the fact that he was despised by the local Greeks. '[They] are furious with him,' he wrote, 'for what they call his unbearable partiality for the Turks.'

Bournabat was particularly lively in the months that followed the Greek occupation. The Bournabat Club had always been popular with young bachelors. Now, an influx of Greek offi-cers led to long nights of revelry and high jinks. 'There are many tales about the "doings" in that club,' wrote Eldon Giraud, almost all of which involved lashings of alcohol and girls with loose morals. Eldon recalled one particularly drunken night when old John Wood 'had to be taken home in the Greek weekly paper . . . minus his trousers'. Exactly how he lost them remains a mystery, but no one censured him for his conduct. After the uncertainty of the war years, there was a feeling among the younger men that outlandish behaviour was acceptable, even though it was frowned upon by the elderly great-aunts.

The Greeks established their own Officers' Club in a spec-tacular eighteenth-century mansion in Bournabat. It had once been the home of an American consul serving in Smyrna; now, the club began serving sumptuous dinners to the Levantines living in the vicinity and became a centre for many social activ-ities.

'Balls and parties were [held there] for adults,' wrote one of the Whittalls. She also recalled that the club served high tea to children to the accompaniment of a string quartet.

There were parties and balls once more in the villas of Bournabat. Herbert Octavius hosted one memorable soirée in the Big House for the sailors of the British squadron that lay at anchor in Smyrna harbour. The Royal Navy reciprocated by inviting all the Levantine merchants and their families to an evening aboard their ships.

The Greek soldiers based in Bournabat participated in the partying with as much enthusiasm as their Levantine friends, seeking out the company of the local Greek girls who were far more coquettish than those at home in Greece.

'By our doorstep,' recalled Herbert Octavius's niece,

> on warm afternoons, our young and pretty housemaid sat on a chair in the street, holding some roses in her lap. She had no need of roses for attracting the passing Greek soldiers to her side: one and all they stopped to chat and she would offer them a rose. As the lucky soldier stretched out a hand, she would pause as if considering the question, and ask: 'Are you for Constantine or Venizelos?' [a reference to the ongoing dispute between Greece's exiled king and prime minister].
>
> If the soldier said 'Constantine', she tossed her head and replied, 'Well, I am for Venizelos, so I can't give you a rose.' If the answer was Venizelos, she of course backed Constantine. It was a daily game which provided her with much entertainment as she dismissed each soldier in turn.

Writing many years later, she noted that, 'though treated as a joke at the time, these divided loyalties were, later on in the campaign, to cause disunity in the Greek army.' Yet the idea that there were troubles on the horizon seemed unthinkable to the inhabitants of Smyrna. 'The export season was just beginning,' she wrote, 'warehouses were filling up, figs and raisins were being packed for the European markets. All was well.'

The stability brought about by Stergiadis's administration enabled many of the popular leisure activities – curtailed by war – to begin again. There was horse racing at the Boudja racetrack and shooting once again took place on the Nymph

Dagh. The Levantine families were also informed that their yachts and yawls were being released by the authorities.

For Edmund Giraud, this was the moment he had awaited for six long years. His beloved motor cruiser, *Helen May*, had been confiscated by the Turkish government in the winter of 1914. Now, at long last, she was handed back to him. Having been allowed to rot during the war years, she was in a terrible state. '[She] was returned to me stripped of her motor and every article of metal,' wrote Edmund. 'She was just a bit of wood without motor, tanks, parts, propeller shaft, skeg or metal anywhere about her.'

He was dismayed at her unseaworthy condition. 'I loved this little ship and her return to me in such a state greatly pained me. I was dismayed to find, on enquiry, that her replacement would have amounted to well over three times her original cost.' After seeking advice from the local boatbuilders, Thornycrofts, he decided to pay for her to be restored.

It was money well spent, for Edmund was once again able to spend the weekends at his Long Island summer house, which he had not visited since 1914. '[The island] was quite deserted,' he wrote, 'my house being much the worse for five years of neglect.' He sent over a team of builders and cleaners to repair damage caused by storms and rain. Edmund was pleased to note that several of the Greek villagers, who had left after the violent events of 1914, were encouraged by his presence and began to trickle home.

The restoration of his property took time and it was not until the summer of 1921 that the work was at last complete. New furniture was despatched from Bournabat and the family headed to Long Island for the long summer vacation in July of that year.

Long before the work was complete, Edmund and his chums were once again undertaking yachting expeditions in the bay of Smyrna, with occasional forays up and down the Aegean coastline. The Greek coastal villages had sprung back to life with the return of the refugees and now became a popular destination for the Levantine yachting parties. Many of the Levantines who were not fortunate enough to possess their own summer houses rented shoreside villas in which to spend the long weekends.

The fact that eastern Anatolia had erupted into violence did not impinge on the way in which they lived their lives. Neither did the news that Mustafa Kemal's nationalist resistance movement was growing in strength with every day that passed. Everyone in Smyrna was looking west, towards Greece, and to the Allied warships at anchor in the bay. They turned a blind eye to everything that was happening in the hinterlands of the country.

Besides, families like the Whittalls were adamant that they had nothing to fear. Constantinople was in British hands, Smyrna was controlled by the Greeks and Turkey itself was now being carved up by the victorious Allied powers. Few were in any doubt that Kemal's nationalists would soon be snuffed out, either by Allied forces, the Greek army or whilst fighting among themselves.

Mid-morning on Monday, 15 November 1920, Lloyd George was handed a telegram that brought the worst possible news. The unthinkable had happened – a political earthquake so unexpected that the implications had not yet been fully understood. In the previous day's Greek general election, Venizelos had been trounced at the polls.

It was an upset that no one, not even Venizelos's critics, had ever imagined. His supporters had spent much of the previous day traipsing from party to party in anticipation of a victorious landslide. They had woken up to discover that there had indeed been a landslide – but that they had been on the wrong end of it.

The cause of the upset was a tall, fair-haired figure with soft blue eyes and a quizzical smile. King Constantine, living in exile since 1917, had become the rallying cry for the opposition. Aware that they had no hope of defeating Venizelos on his foreign policy – for the Megali Idea was extremely popular – opposition politicians championed the cause of the king. He was held up as the embodiment of liberalism and democracy, both of which had suffered under the towering and often tyrannical personality of Venizelos.

In backing Constantine, they also had one eye on the history books. A Constantine had founded Constantinople and a Constantine had lost the city to the Turks in 1453. Popular ballads and folk songs had long prophesied that a third Constantine would re-enter the city at the head of a re-conquering Christian army.

Much to the surprise of the opposition, their election strategy struck a chord with the electorate. They turned out in droves to vote for the return of Constantine, ousting Venizelos and his government from office. When the election result became known, these same people poured into the streets to celebrate their unexpected victory. 'From morning to night, enormous crowds paraded the streets and organised demonstrations in favour of Constantine,' wrote Chivers Davis, an expatriate Englishman living in Athens. 'In the Rue du Stade and Place de la Concorde, every shop that could produce photographs of the ex-King and ex-Queen Sophie did a roaring trade, and in front of practically every shop the pictures of Venizelos, which had adorned it for the past week, were replaced by that of Constantine.'

Chivers Davis was one of the first to realise the scale and consequences of the defeat. 'It was a disaster,' he wrote, 'absolute, complete and practically incredible. Even the opposition was amazed.' Not only was it a personal catastrophe for Venizelos, it also had serious consequences for the future of the Big Idea.

Greece was dependent on Britain to guarantee its empire in Anatolia, but Britain was unlikely to continue supplying Greece with arms and loans once King Constantine, a reviled figure in England, returned to claim his throne.

The fall of Venizelos left senior politicians in London reeling, none more so than Lloyd George. 'I happened to be with Mr Lloyd George in the Cabinet Room at the time the telegram announcing the results of the Greek election . . . arrived,' wrote Winston Churchill. 'He was very much shocked and still more puzzled. But with his natural buoyancy, and hardened by the experiences we had all passed through in the Great War, he contented himself with remarking, "Now I am the only one [of the war leaders] left." '

Many of Lloyd George's generals hoped that the return of King Constantine would spell an end to his pro-Greek policy. '[He] will find that he has backed the wrong horse,' scribbled Field Marshal Sir Henry Wilson into his diary. 'The fall of Venizelos is a great defeat for Lloyd George, as he had put his shirt on the old Greek.'

Churchill agreed wholeheartedly and could not imagine how Lloyd George could continue to back Constantine. 'Here was a potentate who, as we saw it, against the wishes and the interests of his people, had for personal and family reasons thrown his country, or tried to throw it, on the enemy side, which had also turned out to be the losing side.'

Churchill added that 'the return of Constantine therefore dissolved all Allied loyalties to Greece . . . just at the moment when her needs were greatest and her commitments were becoming most embarrassing to herself and to others, she had of her own free will sponged the slate.'

News of King Constantine's return might have been expected to unsettle the Levantines of Smyrna. Although they had mistrusted Venizelos, they could at least be sure that he had the full backing of the British government. Yet they received the news from Athens with their customary insouciance, seeing no reason to fear any change of policy towards Greek-administered Smyrna.

As 1920 drew to a close, the Giraud family decided to throw a New Year's ball that was to be more colourful and extravagant than any Bournabat had witnessed for many a year. It was to be held in the mansion of Charlton Giraud, proprietor of the mighty Giraud trading empire, which stood in the heart of Bournabat.

To ten-year-old Eldon Giraud, Charlton's son, the preparations left him spellbound. A veritable army of workmen were busily transforming the family's botanical garden into a fairy-tale landscape of marquees and magic lanterns. Ponds, lakes and flower-beds had all been enclosed in tents of silk. It looked like the setting for a medieval jousting tournament.

Inside the house, the human activity was even more intense. For three weeks or more, dozens of chefs, butlers and liveried footmen had been hard at work. In the kitchens, the famous Greek pastry chef, Madame Dimitroula, was putting the finishing touches to her celebrated game pies. In the pantry, a team of waiters were mixing gin slings in preparation for the evening's festivities. To young Eldon, it was clear that this was to be a party that would be remembered for many years to come.

All the Levantine dynasties received invitations and Charlton also invited every British, French and other Allied officer who was stationed in Smyrna. General Hanbury was included on the guest list, along with the senior Greek officials serving in the administration that governed the city. The only person not in attendance was Stergiadis; he did not have time for such frivolity.

As the long-case clock struck six, Eldon was summoned to his room by the family governess in order to get changed into his fancy-dress costume. 'I wore a blue blouse, red trousers and a white sash,' he later recalled, 'and was presumably supposed to represent the French flag.' His sister, Joyce, ten years older than Eldon, was dressed as a seductive Columbine.

Elsewhere in the city, the great and the good were dusting down Victorian frock coats and polishing swordsticks. Wives and mistresses were looking forward to wearing ball gowns that had not seen the light of day since before the First World War.

As the first of the cocktails were poured – and the orchestra struck up a polka – the young bachelors began flirting with the unattached women. Eldon Giraud watched in amusement as Olivia Rees was chased by Major Johnston (she later married him) and Helen Xenopoulo was courted by Monsieur Destribat (his declaration of undying love was not reciprocated). Eldon's sister, Joyce, was meanwhile being tailed by Major Philgate, one of the British officers in Smyrna, who proposed marriage to her (an offer she accepted but later declined). And all the while, two Greek male diplomats, Messrs Kamara and Romano, were casting loving glances at each other. 'They went every-where together,' wrote Eldon, '[and] I think they were pansies.'

As the evening wore on, the tempo increased and the dancing grew more extravagant. When the clock struck midnight, the assembled guests toasted Joyce Giraud, who was going to be twenty-one in the New Year. They then toasted the New Year itself and saluted the fact that their charmed lives were seemingly unassailable. Neither war nor civil strife was able to touch them.

No one present paused to consider the reality of what was taking place in eastern Anatolia. No one foresaw that menacing forces threatened to destroy their fragile world. As they danced through the night in Charlton Giraud's candlelit villa, no one realised that this was the ball to end all balls; that Smyrna would never see its like again.

'It was a brilliant affair,' wrote Eldon Giraud towards the end of his life. 'And even to this day, it is still talked of by the older generation.'

★   ★   ★

In the months that followed the return of King Constantine, there was intense diplomatic activity as the Allied powers wrestled with the thorny issue of how to bring peace to Turkey. It was a well-nigh impossible challenge. The Turkish nationalists had no intention of allowing a single Greek soldier to remain in Turkey, while the Greeks refused to contemplate the abandonment of Smyrna and its hinterland.

At the London Conference in February 1921, British, French, Greeks and nationalists attempted to thrash out some sort of compromise, but the talks were fatally undermined by Lloyd George, president of the conference. He continued to back Greece, even though King Constantine was now at the helm. Indeed, his attitude towards the Greek delegation was so favourable that they were left with the impression that he wanted them to make further inroads into Anatolia.

Lloyd George's relations with the Turkish nationalists, never good, swiftly deteriorated during their time in London. He harboured an intense dislike for Bekir Sami Bey, the leading representative of Mustafa Kemal. In an aside to King George V, Lloyd George said; 'A little while ago I had to shake hands with Sami Bey, a ruffian who was missing for the whole of one day, and finally traced to a sodomy house in the East End.'

Lloyd George added for the king's edification that Bekir Sami 'was the representative of Mustafa Kemal, a man who I understand has grown tired of affairs with women and has lately taken up unnatural sexual intercourse'.

Lloyd George soon lost interest in attempting to broker any compromise at the London Conference. At a private meeting with the Greek delegation, he effectively gave them the green light for a new military offensive. His only fear was that the Greek forces might be beaten by the Turks. 'If the Greek army sustained a reverse,' he told them, 'it would make the Angora Government impossible to deal with.'

A reverse was the very thing the Greeks were determined to avoid. Having purged the army of Venizelos-backed commanders, they prepared themselves for action. Just five days after their meeting with Lloyd George, Greek forces prepared to push even deeper into Anatolia and deliver what it hoped would be a knockout blow to Mustafa Kemal's troops.

The Greek generals in charge of the operation might have been wise to consider more carefully the ultimate goal of their military adventure. They were faced with two alternatives, each of which had as many drawbacks as advantages.

Their first option was to establish an impregnable frontier between themselves and the Turks – a mined and fortified, barbed-wire border that would safeguard the Megali Idea from Kemal's ramshackle but increasingly effective army. Although costly in financial terms, this would bring safety and security to the Greek-administered zone.

The second option was to penetrate far inland in order to hunt down and annihilate the nationalist forces. Whilst having the advantage of taking the fight to the enemy, this also brought the corresponding risk of their over-extended supply lines being ambushed.

The Greek General Staff's preferred option had long been the first – a secure frontier – but each time they seemed to have achieved it, they found themselves confronting newly emboldened Turkish forces that kept up relentless attacks on their forward positions.

The problem was compounded by the topography of Anatolia. The Greek army had occupied much of the flat pastureland that stretched inland from Smyrna. They had 'liberated' village after village before coming to a halt at the foot of the escarpment that swept dramatically upwards to the great Anatolian plateau. This lowland position afforded them a most unsatisfactory frontier. Their border guards were continually harassed by Turkish irregulars, and communications with

Smyrna were threatened by bands of guerrillas. The only possibility of preventing such attacks was to neutralise the Turkish
forces dug in on the top of the escarpment and then create
a new frontier on the plateau itself. But it did not take a military genius to realise that the only practicable line for such a
frontier lay a further 150 miles to the east – on the edge of
the desert-like land in the heart of Anatolia.

A frontier so far from Smyrna was sure to bring many more
problems. 'It vastly increases the area which the invader has to
occupy,' wrote Toynbee, 'lengthens his communications, leaves
mountains hospitable to guerrillas in his rear, brings him up on
to the inclement plateau, and yet does not present him with a
physically strong frontier which he can hold without effort.'

The Greek General Staff plumped for the worst of all options.
They decided to scale the escarpment, capture the Turkish positions and then create a new frontier right there, on the edge
of the plateau.

It was a high-risk enterprise. The two armies were almost
evenly matched, with some 35,000 men apiece, but the Greeks
were far better equipped, with machine-guns, motor transport
and air cover. As a result, the Greek generals remained optimistic about capturing the commanding heights above them.

Arnold Toynbee, reporting on the offensive for the *Manchester
Guardian*, wrote a series of vivid eyewitness despatches from the
battlefield. He arrived at Greek battle headquarters at the end
of March 1921, just in time to join the troops as they prepared
for battle. The Greek strategy was to scale the escarpment in
two separate advances. A northern group was to drive up and
over the broken ridges towards the town of Eski Shehir; the
southern group, meanwhile, was to assault the town of Afyon
Karahisar.

Toynbee joined the northern offensive, hitching a lift in a
motor ambulance over the rough tracks that led up to the
escarpment. 'As we climbed painfully up the heights,' he wrote,

'. . . I began to realise on how narrow a margin the Greeks had gambled for a military decision in Anatolia.'

The craggy landscape was littered with weapons' dumps and artillery stockpiles that would supply the 7th Division when it led the Greek right flank into battle.

> The place was infested with the atmosphere of war which makes inanimate hills and valleys seem malevolent and adds something sinister to the most ordinary landscape [wrote Toynbee]. But this place was haunted by history as well. That railway, with its magnificent embankment and culverts and bridges intact, and even its telegraph wires uncut, but with neither rolling-stock nor staff, was the Anatolian Railway – the first section of the Baghdad line. In its derelict condition it seemed symbolic of a great nation's frustrated ambitions. The giant had fallen, and smaller people were fighting for this fragment of the heritage.

Greek military headquarters soon received good news from the southern group. After encountering stiff resistance from Kemal's forces, they managed to overrun the Turkish defences and were steadily fighting their way into the town of Afyon Karahisar. The northern group faced a much tougher challenge. They were no longer fighting bands of poorly disciplined irregulars. The great escarpment was defended by forces belonging to the new nationalist army, under the capable command of Colonel Ismet. He had thrown all his energies into planning the defence of the escarpment, aware of its strategic importance.

'A good deal of the ammunition and the arms were brought from Erzerum, Diarbekir and Sivas,' wrote Colonel Arif, who was organising the defence of the high ground, 'on camels and in ox-carts under the worst possible weather conditions, across roadless deserts and over mountains.' The Turks were caught in a race against time to bring weaponry and ammunition to the front line. Much of it had been smuggled out of Constantinople and taken to the east. Now, it was hauled back overland to the battlefront. 'Workshops were improvised so that every single weapon might be examined and repaired,' wrote Colonel Arif. 'Men walked on foot from the East under the same hard conditions. Women undertook the hardest part of the transport – when ox-carts were broken or stuck in the mire, they carried the heavy loads on their backs.'

The Greek 7th Division made slow progress up the escarpment. Toynbee, at the rear, picked up only rumours of the murderous hand-to-hand fighting that was taking place on the hills above. 'As we approached the southern end of the defile,' he wrote, 'the guns began to be heard. That afternoon, it was too late to visit the front line and I sat there discerning nothing but the extreme tension in the air.'

As darkness fell, an eerie silence descended over the landscape, broken by the occasional low boom of heavy artillery. 'A column of smoke began to rise sluggishly from behind the hill to our left rear . . . As it grew dusk, this smoke caught the reflection of the unseen fire below, and stretchers came down slowly from over the hill to our left front, where the artillery observers were standing on the sky-line. Then, as the light vanished, it grew suddenly very cold.'

On 29 March, after an intense battle that was fought largely in hand-to-hand combat with knives and bayonets, the Greek 7th Division began to sense that the Turkish resistance was in trouble. The men in the vanguard clawed up the slopes of the upper escarpment with renewed confidence, fighting for every inch of land. After many hours of combat, they at long last caught a glimpse of the top. They were within sight of their goal.

The battle for the ridge was murderous and fraught with danger. 'All along the northern rim of the crest, there was a tilted outcrop of limestone scrag,' wrote Toynbee, 'turning the

193

slope for a few yards into a precipice and here, where the nullahs met the scrag, lay most of the Greek dead.'

After one final push, the Greeks found themselves in possession of the heights of Kovalitsa. They had fought without a break for almost two days and now controlled the highest area of the escarpment. Toynbee hung back while the last few pockets of Turkish resistance was snuffed out. Then, when the all-clear sign was flashed down the slopes, he made his way up through the splintered forest of mangy scrub oak until he reached the highest area of land.

As the sun rose and the mist cleared away, it became evident how magnificent the position was. The Turkish trenches facing north commanded the southern exits of the defile, through which I had come the day before. From the crown of the hill a rift in the mist suddenly revealed a corridor of plain stretching away toward Eski Shehir, with nothing between us and it except a low ridge, a mile or so off, on which a few Turks were still visible through the periscope.

The situation on the ground inspired rather less romantic sentiments. A thick pall of smoke hung over the summit and its uppermost edges were tinged golden yellow by the light reflecting off the fires burning in the valley below. The heights were littered with the corpses of Greek soldiers who had been slaughtered by bullets and bayonets. Many of their Turkish opponents had been shredded by shellfire and shrapnel. The spring sunshine provided a little warmth in the daytime, but as soon as dusk fell a frosty chill enveloped the heights. The wounded faced an agonising stretcher ride down from the escarpment, jolted over the rocks, paths and river beds.

'I wondered how anyone could think the military possession of those summits worth the price,' wrote Toynbee, 'and then I looked down the plain of Eski Shehir and thought of the historical consequences which the capture of those summits might involve.'

The Greek victory was a stunning achievement that looked set to guarantee the future of Smyrna. In just six days – and against all the odds – they had managed to wrest control of the entire western escarpment of the Anatolian plateau.

They did not have long to celebrate. The Turks, smarting from their defeat, were preparing to launch a lightning counter-attack before the Greeks had a chance to consolidate their positions. On 31 March, less than forty-eight hours after being evicted from the escarpment, Colonel Ismet led a daring assault against the Greek positions. His timing was brilliant. The inaccessibility of the escarpment had delayed Greek reinforcements and the soldiers holding the ridge were still exhausted after the tough battle. They were in no position to withstand a fresh onslaught.

The 10th Division was the first to crack. After a tremendous firefight, they were pushed back over the escarpment. The 7th Division, too, found itself in extreme difficulty. The men fought like tigers throughout the night before realising the hopelessness of their situation. As dawn broke on 2 April they abandoned their hard-won positions and fled down the mountainside. They tried to salvage as much weaponry as possible but this proved difficult under stiff Turkish gunfire.

'It was a weird march,' wrote Toynbee, who was fleeing with the retreating division, '. . . in choking dust transfused with moonlight, and reeking with the odour of animals and men.' As the defeated troops passed through the defile, confusion reigned. It quickly became apparent that this was no localised defeat; the entire Greek army was pouring off the escarpment.

'The men were angry,' wrote Toynbee, 'angry at spending so much blood and labour in vain, but even more humiliated at a defeat which broke a long record of victory of which they had been intensely proud.'

The courage and hardiness of these defeated comrades left a deep impression on him. Toughened by years of warfare, they helped each other off the slopes of the ridge.

The descent was not much easier than the terrible ascent.

The single road along which we were moving was badly broken up by the constant passage of heavy traffic and ox-carts and motor transport seemed equally apt to break down. But the break-downs were repaired, the stream of wheeled traffic was kept constantly moving in single file, the mules were passed along in parallel columns across the fields and officers were detailed to direct the movement at bridges and fords.

After twenty-three hours on the march – and a hitched lift in a motor vehicle – Toynbee finally made it back to Bursa in order to file his despatches.

Colonel Ismet was jubilant when he was brought news that his forces, newly trained and fresh to battle, had evicted the Greeks from their forward positions. He immediately sent a telegram to Kemal, informing him that 'the enemy has abandoned the battlefield to our arms, leaving thousands of dead behind.'

Kemal's response was extravagant in style and lavish in praise. 'Few commanders in the whole history of the world have faced a task as difficult as that which you undertook . . . The independent life of our nation was entrusted to the heart-felt care of your commanders and comrades-in-arms, who have honourably discharged their duty under your brilliant direction.'

Colonel Ismet almost trumped his battlefield victory by cutting off the retreat of the army. Only after a desperate fight did the southern group manage to reach its base at Ushak. Although they eventually got back safely to their barracks, they were left in no doubt that they were no longer battling it out against a ragtag army of bandits and irregulars. Kemal's forces had been transformed into an efficient fighting machine that was led by men experienced in modern warfare.

In Smyrna, far from the battlefront, life continued as normal, but for the soldiers on the front line, everything had changed. They had suffered their first major reverse and it put into question the entire strategy of the Greek army. The Megali Idea was suddenly in peril.

The Greeks were in control of a vast area of Anatolia, yet the population of this zone, with the notable exception of Smyrna, was principally Turkish. There were some in the army who began arguing, with chilling clarity, that it was time to alter the demographics in the Greek-administered area.

Into the Desert

On a blustery day in May 1921, a lightly armed British warship named *Bryony* steered into the little port of Kapakli on the southern shores of the Sea of Marmara. Kapakli lay almost 200 miles from Smyrna, yet it fell well within the Greek-controlled zone of Anatolia. It was an area of startling natural beauty – a rolling landscape of olive groves, orchards and villages inhabited by both Christians and Muslims. But all was not well in this once-peaceful peninsula. It was rumoured that Greece's self-declared mission to bring civilisation to Turks – Venizelos's long-cherished aspiration – had gone desperately awry.

The British immediately despatched an inter-allied commission to find out whether there was any truth to the tales of looting and massacres. The commission consisted of three senior officers, their Greek and Turkish interpreters and Maurice Gehri, a trusted senior delegate of the International Committee of the Red Cross. Also present was Arnold Toynbee, just back from the front line and anxious to witness how the Greek army was behaving in the wake of its first defeat.

No sooner had the *Bryony* docked at Kapakli than the investigating commission realised that something was wrong. A thick pall of smoke hung over the village and many of the buildings were still smouldering. As Gehri picked his way over the deserted ruins, his fears of a massacre were soon enough confirmed. He found eight bodies of people who had clearly been killed just a few hours earlier. 'In the case of one woman, the blood was still flowing,' he wrote. 'Another woman had been killed on a mattress.' The few survivors found cowering among the ruins declared that Greek soldiers had descended on their village and slaughtered everyone they could find.

It was a similar story at nearby Kutchuk Kumlar, where hundreds of terror-stricken inhabitants emerged from hiding places when they saw the commissioners arrive. 'It was difficult to obtain exact information, so great was the panic among the population,' reads the official report that the international observers later compiled, 'but it was gathered that a detachment of Greek soldiers and brigands had gone through the village a few days before.' When the commissioners turned to leave, the surviving villagers declared their intention of leaving with them. They followed them back to the *Bryony* '[and] refused to leave the beach, imploring us to take them to quiet and safety'. The commissioners felt it was their duty to offer some sort of protec-tion until such time as the local Greek commander could be confronted. 'The Bryony remained at anchor beyond the landing-place, throwing her searchlights over the beach and the adjoining hills all night long, in order to reassure the refugees.'

On the following morning, Toynbee decided to ride inland and visit some of the villages not accessible by ship. At Samanly, he was met by terrified Turkish inhabitants and 'several ruffianly-looking fellows, armed to the teeth but not in uniform, standing guard over them. These, we were told, were Greek "rural guards".' Toynbee managed to speak to a few of the Turks out of earshot of the Greeks. 'We want to go!' they told him. 'Take us with you; take us! We are afraid.' Toynbee said that 'they loved the homes they would be leaving, but they would abandon every-thing if they could save their wives and children's lives and their own'.

He rode on towards Akkeui, where he was greeted by an

even more lamentable tale. The village *hodja* told him that, just a week before, Greek brigands had passed through and slaughtered sixty people in cold blood. 'Some are buried in the open square through which you have just come,' he told Toynbee, 'others on a little hill between the two mahallas [quarters] of the village.'

While Toynbee collected information about the killings, Maurice Gehri took practical steps to contact the local Greek commander. He wished to request that the Red Cross be allowed to evacuate the growing number of refugees who had flocked to the harbour where the *Bryony* lay at anchor.

The local Greek captain, Dimitri Papagrigoriu, reluctantly signalled his consent to the embarkation of the refugees, but then did everything in his power to obstruct the process, fearful that the villagers would denounce him and his men to the authorities in Constantinople.

'We had to wrestle for their lives,' wrote Toynbee, 'not only family by family but person by person.' The Greek captain argued over each refugee. 'He struggled to retain in his power every individual, however feeble or defenceless or old. He separated (I have instances vividly in my mind) wives from husbands and mothers from children.'

The final embarkation was chaotic and there was absolute terror among the Turkish refugees. Their anxieties were not eased by the Greek onlookers who told them that they would all be thrown into the sea once the ship had weighed anchor. 'The Christian women looked on and gloated,' recorded Toynbee. 'We took a photograph of them laughing at the scene.'

The *Bryony* finally set sail with more than 1,000 men, women and children; a further 333 were rescued in a second mission spearheaded by the Red Crescent.

The commissioners soon discovered that excesses committed by the Greek military – in tandem with irregulars – were not confined to this peninsula. When the army had withdrawn from

Ismid in the wake of its defeat, it left behind a scene of carnage. Toynbee arrived some thirty-five hours after the departure of the troops and was appalled by what he saw. 'The streets leading to the jetties were heaped with the wrecks of these carts and the water littered with the offal of the oxen which had been slaughtered on the quay ... Corpses of Turkish carters – murdered in return for their services – were floating among the offal, and one or two corpses of Turkish women.'

Toynbee looked over the bodies before heading into the town centre, where the scene was one of desolation. 'The Turkish shops had been systematically looted – the Christian shops being protected against the destroying angel by the sign of the cross, chalked up on their shutters with the owner's name.'

The report compiled by the inter-allied commission was damning in its conclusion. The massacres committed by the Greek army and irregulars were not isolated incidents but had been orchestrated by the military with the aim of changing the demographics in the Greek-administered zone. It concluded that the Greek army was engaged 'in a systematic plan of destruction of Turkish villages and extinction of the Muslim population'. Although many of the atrocities had been carried out by irregulars – both Greek and Armenian – these forces had every appearance of operating 'under Greek instructions and sometimes even with the assistance of detachments of regular troops'.

Maurice Gehri wrote a separate report for the International Committee of the Red Cross, which drew a very similar conclusion. He had been particularly shocked by the callousness of many in the Greek military. When he asked one local lieutenant, John Costas, why he had allowed his men to kill Turks, the officer had shrugged his shoulders and replied, 'Because it gave me pleasure.'

The two reports did not mince their words when criticising the Greek military. Neither did they make comfortable reading for the Turks. Areas outside Greek control were entirely at the

mercy of Turkish irregulars, who were attacking, looting and
burning Greek villages with just as much enthusiasm. The Greek
administration compiled its own report on these Turkish atrocities, claiming that dozens of villages had been torched in the
preceding weeks and 12,000 Greeks massacred. The inter-allied
commission made its own investigation and declared that the
Greek report 'should be accepted as fundamentally true, notwith-
standing a certain amount of exaggeration in the figures'.

The inescapable conclusion was that both Greeks and Turks
were behaving with absolute disregard for law and order. The
cycle of violence had become so ingrained and widespread that
it was no longer possible to point the finger of blame at specific
individuals. 'The atrocities reported against Christians on the
one hand, and Moslems on the other,' concluded the report,
'are unworthy of a civilised government.'

Toynbee told his readers that the current carnage should act
as 'a warning of what might happen on a much larger scale if
the statesmen whose policy was responsible for this war of extermination in Anatolia' – Venizelos and Lloyd George – 'should
altogether fail to retrieve the mischief which they had made'.

Toynbee feared that if the Greek army did not defeat the
nationalists – and was therefore forced to flee from Turkey –
the entire country would be plunged into a bloodbath. 'The
horror which I have deliberately described was almost bound
to be repeated through the length and breadth of the occupied
territory,' he wrote, 'from Brusa to Aidin and from Eski-Shehir
to Smyrna.'

The troubles afflicting the Greek-controlled zone around Smyrna
came as no surprise to British prisoner 2691, also known as
Rahmi Bey. He had predicted such a turn of events many years
earlier. Now, kept under lock and key in Malta, he was powerless to do anything to save the city he cherished.

The great Levantine families of Smyrna were appalled by the

incarceration of their wartime ally and protector. They were even more shocked to discover that he was being held without any prospect of a trial. To their eyes, it seemed a gross travesty of justice, yet the British no longer displayed any interest in the international rule of law. Admiral Calthorpe had announced at the time of the arrests that the prisoners were 'to be tried and punished in such a manner as the Allies may subsequently decide upon'.

The Levantines petitioned the British authorities in Constantinople, begging them to release the man who had guaranteed their lives and fortunes during the Great War, although their pleas fell on deaf ears. 'I consider it most undesirable that a man of his character and importance should be set at liberty,' wrote the acting High Commissioner in Constantinople. 'There seems to me no justification for his release solely on the grounds that he did not actually order the massacre of the foreign population in Smyrna.'

This was a gross misrepresentation of Rahmi Bey's wartime role. He had protected not only the Levantine community, but had also done his best to shield the Greeks and Armenians from the appalling excesses of the central government.

Nevertheless, there was growing unease in the Foreign Office about the decision to imprison Rahmi Bey. It was he, after all, who had attempted to negotiate a peace with the British government. And he had furthermore been prepared to stage a *coup d'état* against the discredited wartime administration of Enver Pasha.

The Foreign Office was also concerned about the increasingly vociferous campaign being waged by the Levantines of Smyrna. They wanted Rahmi released and made no secret of the fact that they were prepared to pull all possible strings in order to achieve it. Their campaign soon had an effect in Whitehall: several senior civil servants added their voices to the growing chorus of disapproval at the incarceration of Rahmi

Bey. Even Venizelos seemed surprised by the British government's decision. When the diplomat, Harold Nicolson, asked him what he thought about Rahmi's imprisonment, Venizelos mumbled something about Greek deportations before changing the subject. He told Nicolson that 'he would really prefer not to talk up the case'.

The more the Levantines of Bournabat protested, the louder was the chorus of disapproval. Nevile Henderson, a senior diplomat living in Constantinople, declared himself appalled by the actions of his government, even going so far as to describe the establishment of the prison camp in Malta as 'the one action of ours since 1918 which I am absolutely incapable of defending'.

In the end, it was Charlton Whittall, one of Herbert Octavius's younger brothers, who secured Rahmi's release. He leaned so hard on the British government – and quite possibly threatened to use his extensive media contacts to ensure damaging publicity in *The Times* and elsewhere – that prisoner 2691 was eventually set free in October 1921. There were no apologies for having held him without trial and no question of compensation. Rahmi never spoke out publicly about his incarceration so it is impossible to know whether his feelings had changed towards the country he had admired for so long. He certainly had no desire to return to Constantinople now that it was in the hands of the British. He headed to Morocco in order to enjoy the comforts and sunshine of Casablanca. It was infinitely preferable to facing an uncertain future in war-torn Turkey.

The future had indeed become uncertain. The inherent gaiety of the Levantine families continued to suggest that all was well. When the Girauds had toasted the New Year at their spectacular fancy-dress ball, they seemed oblivious to the fact that Smyrna was teetering on the edge of financial catastrophe. Nor did they realise that the continued fighting in central Anatolia was taking its toll on people's morale. So long as the troops met

In the early 20th century, Smyrna's imposing quayside – lined with hotels, brasseries and banks – was famous throughout the Levantine world.

The Greek waterfront at the time of the fig harvest. Smyrna's prosperous Greek population was more than double that of Athens.

Smyrna's European quarter was rich and on a grand scale. The Sporting Club, above, was frequented by Herbert Whittall and his circle.

Smyrna's American quarter: the suburb of Paradise. The American Collegiate Institute, above, was one of numerous charitable organisations.

Frank Street, home to the city's biggest department stores, was narrow, noisy and bustling. It led to the wealthy Armenian quarter.

Petros Brussalis, aged 4 and 93. As a young boy, his aunts took him shopping in Frank Street.

The Turkish quarter was dilapidated and picturesque. Tourists came here in order to glimpse the fabled Orient.

The richest Levantine dynasties lived in fin-de-siècle palaces. They required an army of servants and dozens of gardeners.

The Levantines of Bournabat enjoyed frivolity. 'They walk in and out of one another's houses,' wrote Gertrude Bell, 'gossiping and laughing.'

Eleftherios Venizelos, Greece's charismatic prime minister, was the principal architect of the 'Big Idea'.

Rahmi Bey – Ottoman governor of Smyrna – was rich and cultivated. He socialised with the Levantines and protected them throughout the Great War.

Magdalen Whittall, matriarch of the dynasty, was a formidable figure. She had 13 children and 91 grandchildren.

Edmund Giraud, a grandson of Magdalen, spent much of his leisure time yachting. The Giraud businesses employed 150,000 people.

Edward Whittall was a favourite with the youngsters of the family. He cultivated rare plants in his vast botanical garden.

Herbert Octavius Whittall – Magdalen's eighth son – was as ruthless and terrifying as his mother.

Smyrna's American Consulate. Consul George Horton lived here for many years and was a key eyewitness to events of 1922.

Hundreds of thousands of Christians – Armenians and Greeks –were deported into the interior of Turkey. Most died of exhaustion or starvation.

Armenians and Greeks were targeted by the Turkish regime and hanged for trifling offences. In the First World War, they were viewed as the enemy within.

In 1917 – one of the darkest years of the war – Verdi's Rigoletto was performed in Smyrna. Note the audience dressed in black tie finery.

The British army landed in Constantinople in 1918. The Allied powers held
Turkey's fate in their hands, yet seemed unable to reach decisions.

The Big Four at the Paris Peace Conference in 1919. From left to right:
Britain's David Lloyd George, Italy's Vittorio Orlando, France's Georges Clemenceau,
America's Woodrow Wilson.

The architect of modern Turkey.
Mustafa Kemal, later known as
Ataturk, circa 1922.

Nationalist activist, Halide Edib,
addressing the protest rally against the
occupation of Smyrna in May, 1919.

The same rally; it was attended by thousands of Turks. The occupation of Smyrna
galvanised Turkey's nationalists and gave them a rallying cry.

The Greek army landed in Smyrna in May 1919. Twenty minutes after this picture was taken, the city erupted into violence.

The landing of the Greek army in Smyrna was chaotic. Metropolitan Chrysostom was allowed to lead them in triumph along the quayside.

Metropolitan Chrysostom – martyr to the Greeks, villain to the Turks. A staunch nationalist, he was hacked to death by a mob.

The Greek army pushed ever deeper into Anatolia. Crossing the salt desert was a tactical error that cost Greece her new empire.

Towards Smyrna, 1922. Once the Turks had broken the Greek front line, they advanced at a lightning pace.

Wednesday 13 September, 1922. Fire breaks out in the Armenian
quarter shortly after noon.

By late afternoon, the fire – fanned by a strong wind –
had reached the waterfront.

By Thursday morning, the entire city was ablaze and up to half a million people were trapped on the quayside.

Thursday evening: the inferno was devouring everything in its path.
'One of the biggest fires in the world's history,' wrote *Daily Mail* reporter, George Ward Price.

Smyrna's fire brigade was hopelessly ill equipped
to deal with the conflagration.

Asa Jennings set up the
American Relief Committee
and saved hundreds of
thousands of lives.

Scenes on the quayside. All Christian men of military age
were deported into the interior.

A rescue boat capsizes as desperate refugees surge aboard. Seconds after this photo was taken, it flipped upside down and sank. Note the American flag on the rescue boat in the foreground.

The refugees on the quayside were trapped between the fire and the sea. Allied commanders refused to rescue them.

The American Consulate after the fire. George Horton remained at
his desk until the flames grew dangerously close.

The city after the fire. 'Smyrna Wiped Out' was the headline
in the *New York Times*.

with success on the battlefield, Smyrniots felt that they had nothing to fear, but when news of the Greek army's reversals reached them, there was widespread despondency. For the first time, Smyrna's inhabitants began to question the wisdom of the army pushing deeper into Anatolia.

James Morgan, the British vice-consul in Smyrna, was the first to predict that the city was heading for serious trouble. In January 1921, he noted that the annual caravans from the interior of the country had failed to arrive. 'There is practically no commerce between Smyrna and the parts outside the Greek occupation,' he wrote. He also observed that a significant number of Jewish merchants had sold their warehouses and left the metropolis – a sure sign of lean times ahead.

Yet neither he, nor anyone else, could have foreseen the speed with which the city would fall into decline. The economy went into sudden meltdown in the spring of 1921. There was no trade, no exports, no goods to be bought and sold. For the first time in living memory, silence reigned over the normally bustling port of Smyrna. The only naval activity in the bay was the coming and going of Greek destroyers and landing craft.

In April, Courthope Monroe, the British commercial secretary in Constantinople, visited Smyrna in order to see for himself the sorry state of affairs. He had been forewarned of the crisis facing the city, yet nothing prepared him for the reality of the situation. 'The condition of the town itself beggars description,' he wrote in his report to London, 'and the inhabitants, both European and native, seem completely apathetic.'

He was shocked to discover that the Turkish municipality – which had remained open for business during the first months of Stergiadis's governorship – had now ceased to function. Even the Ottoman Gas Company, which supplied all of the city's lighting, had shut up shop. 'After nightfall,' wrote Monroe, 'with the exception of one or two hotels and the larger shops, the town is in complete darkness.'

Street cleaning, public maintenance and the city's sewage disposal had likewise stopped functioning. 'The streets have large holes in them' – the consequence of too many armoured vehicles rumbling through the city – 'and where they have fallen in, [they] communicate with underground cesspools and the smell and filth is indescribable.'

This woeful situation was starting to have a profound psychological effect on all who lived in Smyrna. The Levantine and European merchants had always enjoyed hearty working lunches to the accompaniment of liberal quantities of wine and spirits, but now they seemed to do very little else with their days. 'The English club fills at noon with the majority of the European businessmen,' wrote Monroe, 'who apparently do not leave it again until six o'clock, which fact alone proves the complete stagnation of business.' It was a similar story in the city's bars and brasseries. '[They] are filled with Greek officers, who appear to spend most of their day in drinking and discussing politics.'

In the summer of 1921, the Greek community at long last got the lift that it so sorely needed. King Constantine landed in Smyrna and was given a hero's welcome. He was the first Christian king to tread on Anatolian soil since the time of the Crusades and the symbolism of his visit was not lost on the local Greeks. They poured onto the streets to hail a man whom they viewed as their saviour and conqueror.

A few people in Smyrna were surprised by the king's blond hair and blue eyes, and passed comment on the fact that he did not look very Greek. The king – whose father was Danish – was infuriated by such remarks. 'It is not true,' he wrote in a letter to the princess of Saxe-Weimar. 'I cannot bear the cold; I hate the fog; I am a Greek and was born in Greece.'

His tour of duty had been suggested by government ministers in the hope that it would raise morale in the army. The king himself saw his visit rather differently. To the alarm of many, he expressed his desire to lead the Greek army into battle just like the medieval kings of old. 'A king and a prince should be soldiers,' he wrote. '[And] in a country like mine, the king must really be the chief of his army.' More worrying still was the fact that he had come to believe the myth that he – a Constantine – was predestined to reclaim the throne of a newly triumphant Byzantine empire.

After the initial euphoria that greeted the king's arrival, the Greek generals in Smyrna settled down to discuss the grim business of war. They had been unnerved by their forced retreat from the Anatolian escarpment and were concerned that military self-confidence would take a further knock. In order to retain the initiative, they conceived a spectacular offensive that would drive the Greek army into the very heart of Anatolia.

By the first week of July, the soldiers were champing at the bit. The generals held a final meeting at the king's temporary residence in Cordelio and agreed a course of action. The Greek army would begin its offensive within days, pushing eastwards out of the Smyrna-administered zone towards the towns of Kutahya and Eski Shehir. The king himself was full of enthusiasm. 'The morale of the army, its spirit and its certainty of success are extremely high,' he wrote. 'God grant that we may not suffer disappointment! It will be a very hard struggle, which will cost us enormous sacrifices; but what a triumph if we win!'

When news of this offensive reached London, it was greeted with dismay. Cabinet ministers were overwhelmingly hostile and tried to impress their views on Lloyd George. Churchill was one of the most outspoken. 'If the Greeks go off on another half-cock offensive,' he told the prime minister, '[then] the last card will have been played and lost and we shall neither have a Turkish peace nor a Greek army.' He proposed an immediate blockade of Smyrna harbour in order to prevent the Greeks delivering any more supplies to their troops.

Lloyd George was having none of it. He remained convinced that he had aligned his country with the winning side and believed that a victorious Greece would serve Britain well. 'He is perfectly convinced he is right over this,' wrote his lover-cum-secretary, Frances Stevenson, 'and is willing to stake everything on it.'

The opening shots of the Greek offensive seemed to vindicate Lloyd George. The military swept everything from its path as it advanced out of the Smyrna-administered zone. Kemal's soldiers fought valiantly but in vain. As the Turkish defences crumbled around the town of Kutahya, a flood of wounded nationalists were rushed to the hospital at nearby Karaja Bey. Halide Edib, who had come to the front line to witness events at close range, had no illusions as to the scale of the Turkish defeat. 'From the stairs leading to the large landing there was literally a throng of stretchers, and crammed between them were men with bandaged heads and arms and supporting each other.' She said that the horror of the scene was such that everyone worked in complete silence. 'The doctors with blood-smeared aprons came in and out of the operating theatre, where lacerated masses of human flesh lay on the tables.'

When she visited Colonel Ismet, commander of the nationalist forces, she saw defeat written on his face. '[It] was haggard and his eyes feverish, and the lines about his mouth and eyes had multiplied,' she wrote. 'He had to face the incalculable result of the retreat which he himself had to order.'

The Greek army had swept all before it. In the third week of July, the first troops entered the town of Kutahya. Once all the principal buildings were safely in their hands, advance columns began moving out towards Eski Shehir. Quick to see the way the wind was blowing, the inhabitants of this town packed their bags and fled.

Their flight took place in a matter of hours, for the Greek army was now advancing at a cracking pace. Eski Shehir's population escaped by train or horse and cart, carrying with them a few clothes and a little food. 'Among the military transports were a large number of ox-carts laden with household goods,' wrote Edib, 'on which children sat looking at the movement in the street with frightened eyes. The women bending coaxed the oxen to make them go faster, and the whole human stream moved on and on.'

The garrison of nationalist troops also left in a hurry, abandoning weaponry and military hardware. Less than two days after the Greek army had captured Kutahya, it found itself in possession of Eski Shehir as well. The first part of the Greek offensive had ended in spectacular triumph.

Mustafa Kemal had no illusions as to the scale of the defeat. 'His face . . . was discomposed and sullen,' wrote Edib. 'He looked as he did during the worst days of the civil war [and] the trouble on his face was even deeper.' News of the nationalists' woes was greeted with elation on the part of Lloyd George, who now felt vindicated in his decision to back the Greeks. In a letter to his Minister for War, he poured scorn on the War Office, which had repeatedly insisted that the Greeks would be defeated by the Turks. 'The staff have displayed the most amazing slovenliness in this matter,' he wrote. 'Their information about the respective strength and quality of the two armies turned out to be hopelessly wrong.'

Yet the Greek victory was not as complete as Lloyd George wished to believe. Two major towns had fallen into their hands and yet more territory was now under their control. Even so, the nationalist forces had not been defeated – they had made a tactical retreat – and they still possessed a large quantity of weaponry. The Greek generals found themselves facing a familiar question: what to do next?

The Greek War Council gathered in Kutahya to settle this very question. There were two options open to them: to dig in around Eski Shehir and defend their newly won territory; or to drive on eastwards in pursuit of the Kemalist forces.

The wisest course would have been to sit tight and consol-

idate their territorial gains, but the Greek high command could
sniff victory in the air. With the complete annihilation of Kemal's
army now seeming tantalisingly close, they plumped for an
offensive that would carry them ever deeper into Anatolia.

Toynbee was appalled when he learned of their decision. 'It
was a crazy enterprise,' he wrote, 'for every rational objective
had disappeared.' He tried to work out what the generals hoped
to achieve by yet another offensive. 'The annihiliation of the
enemy? Three times already that stroke had missed its aim. The
occupation of his temporary capital? As if the loss of Angora
would break a Turkish morale that had survived the loss of
Constantinople.'

Toynbee's fears that the new campaign was misguided were
confirmed by the incoherent battle plan now drawn up by the
General Staff. In one sentence, it called for hit-and-run raids
on Angora; in the next it insisted that Angora must be occupied. It asserted that Kemal's forces would be crushed in a set
battle, yet conceded that they might retreat intact to the far east
of the country.

King Constantine's brother, Prince Andrew, agreed with
Toynbee's assessment of the Greek military strategy and lambasted
the generals for producing such a half-baked battle plan. 'That
which characterizes or ought to characterize a military document – ie: clearness and accuracy – are conspicuous by their
absence.' He repeatedly asked the General Staff to clarify their
aims, yet remained unclear as to whether they were ordering a
knockout blow to the nationalists or a series of raids that would
push Kemal ever farther from Smyrna.

'How far would we be able to pursue him?' he asked himself.
'Could we follow him through the immense expanses of Asia
Minor to Kurdistan and the frontiers of Persia?'

There was another, more tangible reason why Prince Andrew
urged caution. The proposed battle plan would require the Greek
army to cross a terrain more inhospitable than anything they

had so far encountered. The army would have to traverse a barren salt desert – the Axylos desert of the Ancients – where there was no water whatsoever. Prince Andrew repeatedly warned the generals of this formidable obstacle, but his words fell on deaf ears. 'No serious measures were taken to enable the army to cross this waterless tract of land, hundreds of kilometres in extent, though it was obvious that an area of such vast expanse, entirely lacking in means of communication or transport, presented the greatest obstacle to an advancing army.'

While the prince expressed his misgivings about the forth-coming campaign, his brother was busy inspecting the newly conquered territory in Turkey. It was his first foray out of Smyrna and he was most impressed by what he saw. 'The country round [Smyrna] is magnificent,' he wrote, '. . . [and] the cornfields are splendid.' However, when he visited the Turkish towns and villages, he was rather less enthused. 'They are filthy, badly paved, the streets being very narrow and winding, through which a large motor car cannot pass.'

The more he saw of his new fiefdom, the more King Constantine believed that the Turks were incapable of making progress. 'Today they are almost in the same state in which they were in the year 1500,' he wrote. He believed that the Greek army was doing a great service by defeating them on the battle-field. 'It is high time they disappeared once more and went back into the interior of Asia, whence they came.' It was a senti-ment that was shared wholeheartedly by Lloyd George.

The king made his way to Eski Shehir, which was now firmly in the hands of the Greek army. He enjoyed military pageantry and was delighted to officiate at a parade of his triumphant troops. 'It was one of the most magnificent and touching mili-tary ceremonies that I have ever witnessed,' he wrote. 'When you think that this took place near the battlefield, with troops that had only just returned, and when I saw the twenty-four standards, tattered and riddled with bullets, lowered in front of me for the salute, I felt a big lump in my throat.' The king's presence had an electrifying effect on the battle-hardened troops. 'Even the wounded get out of their ambulances and follow me when I pass by, dragging their bandages along [in] the dust.'

The Greek advance into the hinterlands of Anatolia began in the middle of August – a cruel month in which to under-take a long march across waterless countryside. The Second Army Corps faced the most challenging task; it had to traverse the heart of the Anatolian salt desert in order to outflank the Turkish forces defending the road to Angora. It soon proved to be a punishing march for men who had so recently been in the heat of battle. There were no wells in the desert and the cavalry created clouds of choking dust. Worse still, the men were forced to cover thirty miles a day 'on sandy soil with no vegetation – for one could not call the dry, khaki-coloured grass of the district, which no animal would touch, vegetation'.

It was not long before the troops were suffering from acute shortages of food and water. Malignant malaria affected many of the men, further debilitating those who were already weak-ened by extreme fatigue. There was no fuel for cooking – the men had to eat their rations raw – and the horses were so weak that they could carry only light loads. Surviving photographs of the campaign depict hot and footsore men hauling heavy artillery through a bleak landscape of sand and scrub.

Prince Andrew, who was leading one of the army divisions, said that conditions deteriorated still further as they neared the Turkish front line. 'Added to the usual trials were the flames and smoke of burning grass, which poisoned the already stifling atmosphere. These were days of horror.'

There was no hope of a surprise attack on Kemal's army. The dust clouds betrayed the movement and disposition of the advancing Greeks. By the time they approached the chain of low hills that formed the easternmost fringe of the desert, the Turks had correctly divined the Greek strategy and changed positions accordingly.

Mustafa Kemal had by now moved his headquarters to the battlefront and spent much of his time plotting troop movements on his large-scale maps. Halide Edib visited him when he was in the middle of planning his defence of the River Sakaria – one of the many natural obstacles facing the Greeks. 'There was the Sakaria traced out like a magic coil on the paper,' she wrote, 'there were the blue slips of paper on pins which were the Greek forces, and the red slips of paper which were the Turkish: they stood like blue and red butterflies sprinkling the map.'

Although superior in numbers, the Greek army faced a formidable challenge. The undulating landscape favoured the defenders and there were Turkish soldiers dug in on every rocky hilltop and ridge. Edib climbed one of the highest hills in order to get a panorama of the battlefield and was haunted by the barrenness of the landscape. 'It was primeval, on a grand scale – endless valleys walled in by semi-circular hills . . . in fantastic shapes, dark and sombre.' The highest point – and the most heavily defended – was Mount Tchal, 'a giant hill of ink-black earth seen through a silver haze'. From the top of Mount Tchal, the battlefield below seemed distant and unreal. 'The air was shaken with distant booms, and wreaths of smoke arose, sometimes a thick black mass, sometimes in bluer tapering shapes, and were lost in the many coloured void.' If the Greek army was ever to reach Kemal's capital, some eighty miles to the east, they would have to defeat the Turkish forces dug into the flanks of the summit.

Kemal was well aware of its strategic importance. 'Until they occupy the Mount of Tchal,' he would tell his generals, 'there is nothing serious to worry about; but if they do that, we had better look out . . . they [will] have us in a trap.'

The attack began on 26 August. As the Greeks splashed through the shallow waters of the River Gok they were in no doubt that the future of the Megali Idea would be decided in the opening days of the campaign. It quickly became apparent that they had a very real struggle on their hands. Under the blistering August sun, these thirsty and malnourished men had to fight their way up a succession of ridges in order to dislodge the enemy from its commanding positions. They gained ground 'very slowly and with infinite difficulty', according to one report, sustaining heavy losses as they advanced.

The horses and donkeys were by now in such a wretched condition that they no longer had the strength to pull the weaponry. Another serious problem was an acute shortage of petrol, which meant that the motor ambulances were rendered unserviceable. '[The] wounded men were transported by means of mules, springless carts and camels,' wrote Prince Andrew, 'by long marches . . . exposed to the dust, the almost unbearable heat, and the constant danger of capture by enemy cavalry who butchered our wounded when they found them.'

Yet the Greek army fought on, inching their way up to the ridges that overlooked Angora to the east. After five days of intense fighting, the Greeks had dislodged the Turks from many of their forward positions and seemed to be getting the upper hand. Their cautious optimism was given a dramatic boost when one group of battle-hardened Greeks trumped the success of their comrades by fighting their way, with bayonet and dagger, up to the summit of Mount Tchal. News of its capture was met with absolute despondency in the Turkish camp. 'There was a grim silence everywhere,' recalled Halide Edib, 'and the ugliest sort of fate seemed to hang over everyone in the headquarters.' Kemal himself was most affected. 'He fumed, swore, walked up and down, talked loudly . . . and tormented himself with inde-cision as to whether he should order the retreat or not.' In both camps, there was a very real feeling that the Turks stood on the brink of total defeat.

Yet the situation on the ground remained extremely precarious for the Greeks. Although they had made significant gains on the battlefield, the troops were by now in desperate straits. They were almost without ammunition and their bread ration had been slashed to an absolute minimum. The promise of fresh food and water remained elusive, for the Turkish irregulars were doing sterling work in attacking the vulnerable Greek supply lines that now stretched right across the desert. 'Greek transports were continually harassed and captured,' wrote Prince Andrew, 'their ammunition depots exploded, stations raided and railways destroyed.'

The harsh climate brought additional discomfort. At dusk, the heat of the day quickly subsided and was replaced by a piercing chill that prevented anyone from sleeping. It further weakened men who had already suffered from weeks of deprivation.

The Turkish cavalry increased its attacks on the Greek supply lines, aware that this was the surest way to defeat the enemy. By the beginning of September, it became clear that the Greek offensive had spectacularly run out of steam. Little by little, the Turks started to claw back the ground they had lost.

On 9 September 1921, they managed to regain control of Dua-Tepe, one of the higher peaks. 'My last vision of it,' wrote Halide Edib, 'was with a single Turk standing all alone against the setting sun, his water bottle glistening against the blue-gold sky.'

Just a few days after this success, the Turks sensed that their hour had come. Mustafa Kemal regrouped his army and ordered a dramatic counter-offensive, hoping to inflict a crushing defeat on his demoralised enemy.

It is testimony to the resilience of the Greek troops that they stood their ground for so long, as wave after wave of Turks attempted to dislodge them from their hilltop positions. But the commanders on the ground knew that continued resistance was pointless. The men were sick, hungry and lacking the will to fight. On 11 September, the army was ordered to retreat from its hard-won positions and take shelter on the west bank of the River Sakaria, where it would be reasonably safe from further Turkish attacks.

The retreat took place under the cover of darkness. It was disorderly, poorly planned and led by men with little knowl-edge of the terrain. The banks of the River Sakaria were marshy and treacherous, and the Greek army could have been easily annihilated if only Kemal had known how close his forces were to achieving total victory. 'If he had realised this,' wrote Prince Andrew, 'and brought down . . . a few machine guns to his own side of the river, our departure would have been turned into a flight, if not a panic, and the destruction would have been utter and complete.'

Although surprisingly few Greek lives were lost in the retreat, the depressing news from the battlefield so shocked King Constantine that he suffered a mental and physical collapse. 'I remained unconscious for an hour and a half,' he later wrote, 'and when I came to, I did not know at all where I was or what had happened to me. I was bled and put to bed; they said it was a case of auto-intoxication.' This may have indeed been the case, but he was also suffering from acute depression. In one of his last letters written from Asia Minor, he admitted that Greece was a spent force – especially as several European powers were now secretly supplying Kemal with weaponry. 'I am not merely fighting against Turkey,' he wrote, 'but against Turkey, Germany and France . . . The struggle is beyond our strength; we shall be unable to continue.'

The king had every reason to be depressed, for his army was now stranded on the edge of a desolate desert in the heart of Anatolia. The troops were in no condition to continue with their offensive, but neither were they able to retreat from their positions on the River Sakaria, aware that withdrawal would be tantamount to defeat. Their only option was to dig in and hope that their fortunes would take an upward turn in the months to come.

As autumn turned into winter, this looked increasingly unlikely. Churchill hit the nail on the head in his analysis of the Greek military campaign. 'The Greeks had involved themselves in a politico-strategic situation where anything short of decisive victory was defeat,' he wrote, 'and the Turks were in a position where anything short of overwhelming defeat was victory.'

What neither side had contemplated was the scale of the Greek defeat, nor the consequences of the Turkish victory.

PART THREE
Paradise Lost

Wednesday, 6 September 1922

Shortly after breakfast on Wednesday, 6 September, Hortense Wood – a venerable spinster who lived in the heart of Bournabat – was witness to a most alarming sight. From the window of her drawing room, she noticed a great column of soldiers shuffling through the village square. Intrigued by the spectacle, and curious to know where they were going, she made her way down the long drive towards the main gate of her property.

It did not take her long to realise that something catastrophic had happened to the Greek army in central Anatolia. '[I saw] endless streams of disbanded Greek soldiers,' she wrote in a letter to her niece. 'A miserable rabble, ragged, weary and wan; and with them were hundreds of refugees, both Greek and Turkish, plodding their way under a burning sun, through clouds of hot dust swirling in the air.'

Just a few moments earlier, Hortense had checked the thermometer hanging on the balcony outside her house. It was already thirty degrees in the shade and uncomfortably humid. She felt desperately sorry for these downtrodden and exhausted refugees.

'It was a most pitiable sight,' she wrote. 'They looked like so many hopeless mendicants, not knowing whither they were going or what was to become of them: poor women dragging along small children – strangers with none to help or guide them. I can't forget the sight of one of these women, sobbing as she went along, with three little children holding onto her torn skirts and looking frightened and bewildered at the scene around them.'

Hortense Wood was one of the first eyewitnesses to the fallout from the crushing defeat that had befallen the 200,000-strong Greek army in central Anatolia. For much of the previous year, these battle-hardened troops had clung to their perilous posi- tions on the western bank of the River Sakaria. Desperately short of supplies – and subject to constant attacks by Kemal's nationalists – they had nevertheless stood guard for almost twelve months over the eastern frontier of Greece's empire in Turkey. Most knew that their situation was hopeless. Greece was almost bankrupt and the army's guns and munitions were in an advanced state of decay. King Constantine had long since packed up his bags and headed back to Athens. In his place was a recently appointed chief of staff, General Hatzianestis, who was widely held to be mentally unhinged. There were days when he refused to get to his feet, believing them to be made of fragile glass. George Horton's considered opinion was that he should be locked up 'in a lunatic asylum'.

By August 1922, Greece's only hope of an honourable exit from the crisis lay in the diplomatic negotiations taking place in London and Paris. Yet no resolution was forthcoming. The Turks wanted the Greeks off their soil; the Greeks could not bring themselves to abandon the Megali Idea. Kemal's nation- alists meanwhile bided their time. Their army was well trained and newly equipped with weaponry secretly supplied by the French and Italians. By late summer, the soldiers were restless and impatient.

The order for battle was finally given by Mustafa Kemal on 26 August. 'Soldiers,' he told them, 'your goal is the Mediterranean!' The Turkish army struck at dawn and swept all before it. Five Greek divisions were destroyed in the opening wave of battle. More than 50,000 men were taken prisoner. Those who escaped fled from the field in absolute disarray.

The same story was repeated again and again, wherever Greek forces were stationed. Divisions were crushed; battalions were left with scarcely a man alive. Outgunned and outmanned, they turned and fled, pausing just long enough to torch every town and village that lay between them and the sea. If the Megali Idea was to be cast aside, then the Greeks wished to leave behind a charred and devastated wasteland.

The still-smouldering city of Afyon Karahisar fell back into Turkish hands within forty-eight hours of the beginning of the Turkish offensive. Ushak was the next big town to be captured. By the beginning of September, Kemal's forces seemed unstoppable. The Greek army had disintegrated and was fleeing to the coast with all possible speed.

The Turkish forces were stunned by the magnitude of their victory. Their good fortunes were further increased when they captured Greece's battlefield commander-in-chief, General Tricoupis. When Kemal asked the general whether he had anything to say for himself, he meekly asked whether he could send a message to his wife.

The first wave of rumours about the Greek army's dramatic collapse reached Smyrna within hours. They were dismissed as idle gossip in the city's brasseries and clubhouses, for no one could believe that such a large army could be put to flight with such apparent ease. Besides, the city's inhabitants were too busy enjoying the autumn sunshine to worry about events taking place many miles to the east. 'Arriving at Smyrna on Tuesday morning, August 29th, we found it bathed in sunshine and blissfully ignorant of the terrible fate overhanging it and many of its people.' So wrote a Manchester businessman who was enjoying a few days' sightseeing in the city. Trade had picked up since the dark days of 1921 and the port was once again busy. 'It was a scene of abounding life and vitality, with files of porters trucking raisins and figs to the labourers loading the barges waiting to be filled and towed alongside the steamers bound for Europe and America.'

The city's bourgeoisie were taking renewed pleasure in the customs of old, spilling onto the quayside for their evening promenade. 'The open air and indoor cafés, with their orchestras or singers . . . [were] busy and crowded, while the Opera House was filled with an enthusiastic audience showing their appreciation of the artistic efforts of an Italian opera company.'

The Greek military continued to offer an upbeat assessment of its strategic situation. In its first communiqué, it stated that the army was engaged in a tactical withdrawal. In its second, it claimed that Greek forces had scored a great victory.

Grace Williamson, a nurse working in the English Nursing Home in Smyrna, watched the scenes of daily life taking place in the streets below her window in those last days of August and concluded that rumours of an impending catastrophe were nonsense. Like most people, she felt there was nothing to worry about. 'The day was a bright fine one with a hint of autumn in it,' she wrote, 'and the quay was very gay with the different processions and their flags and banners.' She noted that 'the women were all out in their gayest and finest clothes [and] the bright parasols made the whole scene most picturesque and bright.'

Yet she had a niggling suspicion, one that she could not pinpoint, that something was awry. 'I remember saying to my friends that people were not as gay as they seemed and there was something at the back of their minds.' She was sufficiently disconcerted by their distracted manner – and by ugly rumours filtering into Smyrna – that she decided to recommence the diary that she had kept throughout the duration of the First World War. She thought it would be diverting to chronicle the rumours and tall tales that were spreading through the city.

George Horton was also disquieted by the dramatic reversals said to have been suffered by the Greek army, although he saw no reason to cancel his holiday in a Greek village to the south of the city. But his anxiety turned to alarm on 6 September when he was brought news that the first battalions of defeated troops were just a few hours from Smyrna. He rushed back to the city and arrived just in time to see the first regiments – those seen by Hortense Wood from her drawing room – make their entry.

'In a never-ending stream they poured through the town towards the point on the coast,' wrote Horton, '. . . silently as ghosts they went, looking neither to the right nor left. From time to time some soldier, his strength entirely spent, collapsed on the sidewalk or by a door.'

The sight of thousands of ragged Greek troops passing along the quayside sent the first ripple of alarm through the city, especially when it became apparent that there were large numbers of refugees in their wake. When Garabed Hatcherian, a senior physician of the Armenian National Hospital, strolled back to his home in Chalgidji Bashi Street that afternoon, he found his path blocked by many thousands of homeless people. '[They] are pouring into the courtyards of the churches, into hotels, asylums, houses, gardens,' he wrote, 'and, finally, wherever they can find a spot to sit down.'

Hatcherian felt a weary sense of déjà vu at seeing all these displaced people. In the First World War, the entire Armenian population of his village had been deported or massacred and their houses destroyed. Concerned that the influx of refugees was the prelude to something of wider significance, he decided to write a daily chronicle of these unsettling times.

It was not long before he had news to record in his diary. Within hours of the first defeated troops arriving in Smyrna, the Hatcherians' house had become home to several members of the extended family. Among the refugees fleeing from the interior of the country was Garabed's nephew, Costan, who brought confirmation that the defeated Greek troops had committed many atrocities. He also informed his uncle that the Greek government had secretly decided to abandon the interior of Anatolia and that it was contemplating withdrawing its troops from Smyrna as well.

Hatcherian refused to believe such stories. 'This last piece of information seems improbable,' he wrote, 'since the Greek army, under the protection of its fleet, could create around Smyrna a strategic barricade in order to make it possible for the Christian population to be evacuated to the Greek islands.'

In the absence of any certain news, people began to display the first signs of panic. Housewives stocked up on bread and pulses while their husbands attempted to contact relatives living in the countryside. Yet there remained a general feeling that the city itself would be safe. 'It seems very unlikely that brutalities would take place in Smyrna,' wrote Hatcherian, 'where so many Europeans live.'

There was a more tangible reason why people remained confident that Kemal's army would not enter Smyrna. There were twenty-one foreign warships in the harbour – including eleven British, five French and one Italian. Many of these vessels – previously stationed in the Mediterranean – had headed to Smyrna on receiving intelligence of the Greek army's defeat. Two American destroyers, the USS *Litchfield* and *Simpson*, had also recently arrived and it was rumoured that the mighty USS *Lawrence* was also en route to the port. Such a formidable presence in the bay reassured a population that was betraying signs of jumpiness. Few doubted that these vessels would act as a deterrent, if ever Mustafa Kemal should contemplate entering Smyrna by force.

By late afternoon on 6 September, thousands of troops and refugees had poured into the city and it was clear to everyone that the interior of the country was in complete turmoil. Grace

Williamson found herself caught up in the rapidly growing disaster, for many of the sick, pregnant and exhausted refugees had knocked on the doors of her nursing home, begging for help. 'Crowds and crowds of every sort and description of Greeks,' she wrote. 'Women with trousers and weird costumes carrying babies wrapped in gay colours and caps.'

Grace noted that the Greek ships in the bay were taking away the soldiers as quickly as they could be embarked; she assumed that they would soon take off the refugees as well. 'But where will they put them?' she asked herself. 'This is a huge country and there must be 40, 50 or 60 thousand, perhaps more.' There were, in fact, many more. At least ten times that number were making their way to Smyrna, carrying nothing more than their children, a bottle or two of water and perhaps a few provisions.

The scale of the impending disaster had not escaped the notice of senior diplomats in Europe and America. Several days previously, Henry Morgenthau – America's former ambassador to Constantinople – had warned that Kemal's nationalists were likely to follow their military victory with a massacre. 'Unless Britain asserts herself by showing that she, and somebody else, has an interest in protecting these Christians, the Turks will be as merciless as they were with the Armenians.'

Although his warning fell on deaf ears in London and Washington, in Smyrna, one man had already realised that the city was facing an altogether more serious crisis than anything it had endured during the Great War. Herbert Octavius Whittall had read between the lines of the Greek military despatches and concluded that the occupying forces had been absolutely and convincingly routed. His concern was not that the Turks would cause havoc if and when they entered the metropolis. Rather, he feared that the vanquished Greeks would indulge in gratuitous acts of pillage and vandalism as they passed through the bourgeois suburbs of Smyrna.

In the first days of September – at least seventy-two hours

227

before Hortense Wood sighted the first column of retreating soldiers – Herbert Octavius decreed to his family that it was time to depart – at least for the time being. They should escape while they still had the chance to save themselves and their most treasured belongings. He hoped that they would be able to return within a few weeks – if not days – but he was not prepared to take any risks. As effective head of the dynasty, he had a duty to protect everyone's lives.

His decision was unprecedented. Never before – not in all the 113 years that the Whittall family had lived in Turkey – had they felt in such imminent danger. Never had they fled in the face of danger. Even at the outbreak of the First World War, when they were specifically targeted by the government, they had remained at their posts. Now, they were taking their temporary leave.

Not everyone agreed with Herbert Octavius. His younger brother, Charlton, was on holiday in nearby Phocaea when he learned the news of his decision. Charlton refused to countenance the idea of abandoning Bournabat; indeed, he did not even see any reason to break off his holiday. As far as he was concerned, Herbert Octavius was making a fuss about nothing.

The Giraud family was also inclined to stay put. Edmund Giraud was in England on business and out of contact but his wife, Ruth, one of Herbert Octavius's many nieces, felt that the crisis was being overblown. She was spending a few days with her children at the family's newly restored villa on Long Island when she heard what had happened to the Greek army. She determined to remain on the island for a few more weeks until the panic blew over.

Other scions of the extended family took the decision to move temporarily from their Bournabat country villas into the heart of Smyrna. Jessie Turrell, another of Herbert Octavius's nieces, opened the doors of her town house to scores of relatives. 'Granny Mary, Aunt Blanche, my mother's eldest brother,

Edgar, his wife, son and Greek maid had come away from Bournabat . . .' wrote Jessie's daughter. 'The whole house became a dormitory but, somehow, there was a bed for everyone.' The family remained there for just two days. As news from the interior grew increasingly menacing, they accepted the offer of sanctuary aboard the *Thalia*, a British hospital ship at anchor in the bay.

The British consul, Sir Harry Lamb, was so alarmed by the incoming intelligence reports that he encouraged everyone with British nationality to follow suit. Hortense Wood could not see what all the fuss was about. 'All Bournabat has fled,' she wrote, 'fearing all sorts of dangers threatening them. I am sure nothing will happen.' She resolved to remain in her house come what may, along with a handful of other stalwarts. Nevertheless, the evening of 6 September was a melancholy one. Hortense's closest friends, the Charnauds and Reeses, had left earlier that afternoon and several of the great houses of Bournabat lay dark and silent. The only noise came from the constant shuffle of soldiers and refugees, passing outside the gates.

In the American colony of Paradise, there was also growing unease. Alexander MacLachlan, director of the American International College, had spent the day musing on how he should respond to the crisis. He was less concerned about the retreating Greeks than the advancing Turks, especially the *chettes* or irregular forces. Students of the college brought 'disturbing rumours' that a 5,000-strong band of *chettes* were approaching Smyrna from the south and would quite probably pass the college campus on their way into the city.

This particularly unsettled MacLachlan as the college was well known for its large population of Greek and Armenian students. He discussed the situation with a colleague and together they agreed a plan of action. The two men decided to meet the *chettes* if and when they approached, to 'warn them that the college was an American institution and that any interference with it would not only be resisted, but would create serious complications for the Turkish government and also themselves'.

Pleased to have established some sort of contingency plan – although one that depended on bluff – MacLachlan then instructed his college students to head to Paradise station and hand out water to the thousands of newly arrived refugees.

Smyrna's bishops and priests also spent much of Wednesday afternoon trying to work out how best to advise their flocks. The Reverend Charles Dobson, the Anglican vicar of Smyrna, paid a visit on Metropolitan Chrysostom – still the spiritual leader of the city's Greek Orthodox population – 'and found him in a state bordering on despair concerning the fate of his people'.

Metropolitan Chrysostom was one of the few people who thought that Kemal's army would enter the city and massacre its Christian inhabitants. He asked the Reverend Dobson to send a telegram to the archbishop of Canterbury, begging him to inform Lloyd George of the gravity of the situation. 'For Christ's sake,' read the last line of his message, 'hasten to avoid the calamity which we feel is approaching.'

The metropolitan's fears were temporarily mitigated by a meeting with consuls of two of the great powers. The French representative, Michel Grillet, told him that troops from France were due to arrive within days. The Italian consul gave similar assurances, adding that 'as he had to defend 15,000 Italian citizens, he would be the defender of all Christians as the citizens of his country lived in all quarters of the city'.

But when Chrysostom went to see Sir Harry Lamb, he found that Britain's consul was singing from a very different hymn sheet. He told the Greek metropolitan: 'Why have you come to ask me to defend you and to provide military intervention? ... How can British soldiers or the British Army be brought here for immediate defence when Greek soldiers are retreating in a disorganised manner? What army can resist an enemy that is advancing swiftly without hindrance with all the energy it can command?'

As dusk fell on the evening of 6 September, still the soldiers and refugees poured into the city. Charles Howes, a young British naval officer stationed in the bay of Smyrna, was shocked by the condition of the 50,000 Greek troops that had by now congregated on the quayside. 'I do not hesitate in saying that they were the most dilapidated, filthy, untidy, slouching lot of humans I have ever witnessed wearing uniform.'

He learned that most had received no supplies of food for twelve days and were 'haggard, hungry looking, some barefoot . . . no officers, no regulations, no marching, just sloughing along in twos and threes as fast as their stumbling legs permitted'.

As the inhabitants of Smyrna went to bed that night, there was a growing sense of unease. It was clear to everyone that a crisis – and perhaps a catastrophe – was just around the corner.

Thursday, 7 September 1922

When Hortense Wood awoke on the following morning, refugees were still streaming past her gates. 'They went on and on,' she wrote, 'and when asked where they were going, they invariably answered, "We don't know."' Hungry for more information, she quizzed them about the Greek army's defeat, but it was impossible to get any clear idea of the scale of the disaster. 'All sorts of rumours are afloat,' she wrote. 'Those who come from the interior, from Alascheir, Magnesia and other towns, give different versions of what has happened.'

One group of refugees told her that Ushak had been reduced to ashes. Others told her that only the oil and benzine depots had been torched. 'And so the days go by, enlivened with fanciful rumours or unreliable telegrams and newspapers. We must wait for some really authentic news.'

In the absence of any definite information, Hortense concerned herself with domestic matters. She was extremely worried about Cecil − one of her numerous nephews − who had just undergone an emergency operation on his foot. 'Blood poisoning had set in,' she wrote in a letter to her niece, 'and things may have turned very badly for him if [Doctor] Denotowitz had not been called in time.'

Yet even this seemed of trifling importance when compared to the scenes taking place outside her window. She stepped onto her balcony several times before lunch and at one point noticed that the first storm clouds of autumn were billowing up behind the bulky flanks of the Nymph Dagh. 'Rain would be a disaster now that so many thousands of refugees are homeless,' she wrote. One of her neighbours brought her news that the number of people camping out on the streets of Smyrna now exceeded 100,000.

There was by this time considerable disquiet among the Levantine families who had decided to remain in their homes. Just a few days earlier, Charlton Whittall had poured scorn on his brother's decision to leave the country. However, hearing more and more rumours of atrocities committed by the Greek army, he hastily cut short his holiday and returned to Bournabat.

'We arrived to find the roads choked with refugees trudging along,' recalled his son, Willem, many years later. 'With difficulty, we penetrated to Bournabat to find that practically everybody had already left.' Charlton still had no intention of joining the fugitives. He wanted to protect his property in the event of trouble.

Others displayed rather more caution in the light of the rapidly changing situation. Most members of the extended Whittall and Giraud families had already left Bournabat and moved into their Smyrna town houses. Now, they loaded their yachts with provisions and joined Ruth Giraud at her house on Long Island.

'The descent of relatives and friends upon our island solitude was spectacular,' wrote Mary Giraud, a young girl at the time. 'Boats kept rolling into harbour and aunts and cousins arrived up at the house to take temporary refuge.'

Not all the Levantine families had the luxury of second homes in Smyrna or on Long Island. In the absence of anywhere else to go, many sought lodgings at the English Nursing Home. By Thursday morning, Grace Williamson was beginning to feel the strain of caring not just for Greeks and Armenians but for local friends as well. '[At] eight o'clock, the whole Pengelly family arrived,' she wrote in her diary. 'Next came Louisa Langdon and three babies, nurses and granny; bundles galore, baskets, boxes, etc. – crying children, distracted mothers . . . Fortunately, there is an eating house quite close and we did not have to provide meals, but the confusion was awful.'

The Pengellys soon decided to board the British hospital ship in the bay, even though Grace urged them to remain in Smyrna. 'Oh! What they will suffer in that horrid little steamer, packed full. Of course, all the penniless – and people with very little brains – were on board.'

Grace was angered by the attitude of the British consulate, whose staff were urging people to leave. 'Why should they scare the English so?' she asked herself. 'French and Italians are calm and not one [is] leaving.'

She certainly had no intention of abandoning the nursing home. 'With us there is no choice, I am thankful to say. We have to stick by the clinic and our patients.' Her principal concern was the lack of space to lodge the incoming tide of people; even the flower garden of the Anglican church was by now cluttered with tents and bedding. 'Every mortal place is packed with refugees,' she wrote. 'We have given all we can.'

At some point on that Thursday morning, Grace surveyed the scene from her upstairs window and was suddenly struck by the scale of what was taking place. 'It is very pitiful,' she concluded, 'and they will suffer more and more.'

Many families camping in the streets were pinning their hopes on the American and European warships in the bay. There was a general assumption that the American and other Allied powers would intervene if and when the Turkish cavalry decided to enter the city.

People might have thought differently had they known more about the personality of the man who was directing American policy towards Smyrna. Admiral Mark Bristol, the High Commissioner in Constantinople, was a patriotic American who had always believed in placing his country's interests above any other consideration. 'I am,' he said, 'for the US, first, last and always.'

His policy towards the disintegrating Ottoman empire had long been one of ruthless pragmatism, exploiting any path that would bring profit to America. He had been implacably opposed to his country taking a mandate over Armenia at the end of the First World War, arguing that it was a land that was 'practically desolate [and] without natural resources . . . to use a slang expression, "we would be given the lemon"'.

Nor did he wish American investors to join forces with European and Levantine businessmen already working in Turkey. 'It is a task worthy of America to stand up for the big idea of clearing up the whole of the Ottoman Empire by once and forever destroying all European influences and concessions.'

Admiral Bristol believed that the Greek occupation of Smyrna had been nothing more than a British plot to extend her sphere of influence into the richest area of Turkey. In one of his more controversial statements, he declared. 'We fought to destroy the Prussian power; we may still have to fight to destroy the British power.'

His outspoken comments raised eyebrows in both Turkey and America. 'I am even accused of being pro-Turk,' he wrote to the president with more than a hint of indignation, 'but such things do not bother me fortunately because I believe there is only one correct road to follow and that is the right road.'

Admiral Bristol felt that American business interests would be best served by pursuing a resolutely pro-Turkish policy in this troubled land, caring little for the fact that Greeks were being massacred in their thousands in and around the Black Sea port of Trebizond. Indeed, he scandalised many in Constantinople by dismissing the reports of European eyewitnesses as 'propaganda from unreliable sources'. He knew that America would never win concessions to the region's rich oil supplies if it harped on about the persecution of minorities. And since he had the final say on where American journalists were allowed to travel – they needed passes for assignments in Anatolia – he was able to censor reports before they were even written.

He certainly had no intention of aiding the 150,000 destitute refugees that were, by noon on Thursday, camping out in the streets of Smyrna. The two destroyers already sent to the city – the *Litchfield* and *Simpson* – were under strict orders not to intervene in what he regarded as a Turkish internal affair. On 7 September, under pressure from Washington, Bristol ordered the USS *Lawrence* to head for the city also, but the crews were told 'to assist in care of American lives and property, it being clearly understood that sending war vessels is solely for such protection of Americans'.

The liberal elite in America was troubled by the government's approach to what was fast developing into a humanitarian crisis. A *New York Times* editorial lambasted senators for their refusal to help the persecuted. 'The Administration doubtless expects popular approvement of the view that Greek Christians may be shot down, so long as Americans are not knocked over by stray bullets.'

Admiral Bristol found himself under increasing pressure to allow journalists to sail with the USS *Lawrence*, especially as news from Smyrna was starting to find its way onto the front pages of the American dailies. When deciding to issue a couple of press passes, he took great care when selecting the journalists he felt he could trust. He eventually chose John Clayton of the *Chicago Tribune* and Constantine Brown of the *Chicago Daily News*. Clayton's reports were to reach a wide international audience, for they were syndicated to many newspapers, including Britain's *Daily Telegraph*. Brown's despatches were also widely read and did much 'to shape public opinion.

Bristol made it quite clear what was expected of these journalists before he allowed them to board the USS *Lawrence*. 'I
told them they must remember that going on my permission
and on one of our destroyers they must always keep in mind
that they were not free to report in the same way as if they
went on their own resources. I would trust them to protect my
interests along this line. They both stated that they understood
exactly what I meant and I could count on them.'

The only other journalist reporting from Smyrna was George
Ward Price, correspondent of the pro-Turkish *Daily Mail*. He
had hitched a ride down on the *Ajax* just a few days earlier
and was in the process of filing his first despatch to London.
Ward Price had a prejudice against the Greeks that was almost
as vehement as that of Admiral Bristol. The American High
Commissioner had not been aware of Ward Price's departure
from Constantinople but he could not have wished for more.
The only three Western journalists reporting from Smyrna were
all 'on message'.

As the USS *Litchfield* steamed its way southwards across the
Aegean, the Greek administration in the city was doing everything in its power to embark its defeated army before the arrival
of the Turks. Thousands of soldiers were taken off by the warships
at anchor in the bay. Once these were full, the troops were
directed to nearby Chesme, where there were more ships awaiting
them. The embarkation took place in a state of unnatural calm.
When Edwyn Hole, the British vice-consul, jostled his way
through the refugee-packed streets that afternoon, he was
surprised by the discipline of the defeated army. 'As fast as the
Greek soldiers reached the town they were put on transports
and removed,' he wrote. 'It had been feared that on their arrival
they would do a great deal of damage, but they were in such
a state of depression and exhaustion that their one desire was
to get away.'

The refugees were equally desperate to get away, but they

found this almost impossible, as the Greek transport ships refused to take them. Only those wealthy enough to buy passage on one of the local fishing boats were able to leave Smyrna.

The city's administration, still headed by Aristides Stergiadis, was also preparing its departure. Throughout the morning and afternoon of 7 September, officials, clerks and secretaries packed their belongings and arranged passage to the motherland.

By late afternoon, most of the city's Greek administrators had left their posts. General Hatzianestis had embarked on a transport ship a few hours earlier, having taken a last wistful look at the quayside palace that he had been in the middle of restoring. George Horton wryly suggested that the Greek army might not have been in such utter disarray if the general had devoted as much energy to his military campaign as he had to choosing his wallpaper and furnishings.

As dusk fell, the city's gendarmes also packed their bags and left, leaving Smyrna with neither a police force nor a civil guard. The last Greek official to depart was Stergiadis himself. '[He] had but a few steps to go from his house to the sea, where a ship was awaiting him,' wrote Horton, 'but he was hooted by the population.'

Horton was sorry to see him go, for he had come to respect this dour and humourless individual, feeling that Stergiadis could be justifiably proud of his achievements. Public health had been transformed; farm machinery had been imported from America; and the Ionian University, open to all races and nationalities, promised to be one of the most enlightened centres of learning in the Islamic world. 'He had done his best to make good in an impossible situation,' wrote Horton. 'He had tried by every means in his power to make friends of the implacable Turks, and he had punished severely, sometimes with death, Greeks guilty of crimes against Turks.'

The Armenian physician, Garabed Hatcherian, spent that evening at the house of his friends, the Verkines, discussing the fact that Smyrna was now without a government or a police force, although they were reassured to see that the refugees were calm. 'Nothing unruly happens,' wrote Hatcherian in his diary. 'The port looks solemn.' A few people tried to smuggle themselves away with the departing Greek soldiers but most wished to remain in the city, 'believing that these events will be short-lived, since fleets from every nation are in the harbour, filling the people with trust and reassurance'. Hatcherian's nephew, Costan, did not share his uncle's confidence. That very evening he managed to secure passage aboard a vessel bound for Cyprus.

'Everything is perfectly quiet here,' wrote Hortense Wood shortly before retiring to bed on the evening of 7 September. 'Not the slightest cause for alarm. We sat at the gate this evening watching the soldiers and refugees still coming on . . . Not one untoward incident has happened; no quarrels; no threats. They marched passed in silence. So did the poor refugees.'

Friday, 8 September 1922

News that the Greek administration had left Smyrna unsettled the Bournabat families who had remained in their own homes. Even Hortense Wood succumbed to a moment of panic when she awoke on Friday morning to discover that Smyrna was now minus a government or a police force.

'Things have come to a head!' she wrote. 'All our gendarmes have bolted. We are without protection and the fighting . . . is quite near. Nymphia, Afyon Karahisar, Cassaba, Alascheir and Magnesia are blazing! . . . The British authorities in town are still deliberating whether it is proper to send marines to Bournabat for the protection of ourselves and [our] properties.'

British naval officers were extremely reluctant to land troops in Smyrna, fearing they would get caught in skirmishes with the approaching Turkish army. They were also concerned that sending soldiers into the city – if only to protect British property – would be seen as an overtly provocative act. The last thing they wanted was to provide Mustafa Kemal with an excuse for advancing on Constantinople, where Allied troops were stationed in large numbers.

Hortense was outraged by the attitude of the British officers. 'Are [our houses] to be left to the mercy of infuriated Greek rebels and burnt to the ground?' she wrote. 'And when these have devastated Bournabat, we are told to expect the wild hordes of Circassians who will destroy everything that may have escaped the attention of the Greeks.'

Most of the remaining Levantines in Bournabat decided to depart when they realised that no protection would be forthcoming. 'Our people are leaving for town and taking with them small valises with a few things, all that the carriage can carry,' reported a disappointed Hortense on that Friday morning. She still had no intention of going with them. 'I remain here, come what may. I'd rather be killed than losing all my belongings [and] remain[ing] destitute for the rest of my life, a burden to all.'

Her sisters and their families had previously vowed to stay in Bournabat, but now, after a long discussion about the deepening crisis, they changed their minds and decided to follow their neighbours' example. 'Lucy left reluctantly,' wrote Hortense, 'and very much worried with Fernand staying here . . . She looked pale and had her [heart] pain. Louisa was excited and insisted on Ernest going with her to town.' Only Fernand de Cramer, Hortense's forty-seven-year-old nephew, elected to remain behind in order to look after his aunt.

The rest of the family spent the day packing their jewellery and other valuables. Confident that even military catastrophe would not interfere with the running of the suburban rail line, they intended to leave Bournabat on the 7.30 p.m. train to Smyrna.

The Greek newspapers continued to print upbeat stories about the tactical retreat of the Greek army, insisting that the soldiers were planning to defend Smyrna from the advancing Turks and that the city would be safe. However, when one of Hortense's Greek friends called at her villa that Friday morning, he warned her and Fernand not to believe a word of what was written.

'What the papers say is not true, he told us. It is merely to calm people. The truth would cause a revolution in Greece. The Greek army is not going to make a stand, he said. It is absolutely incapable of doing so. They have no officers, no food, nothing.'

This assessment was shared by the numerous British Levantines who had sought safety at the English Nursing Home in Smyrna. Grace Williamson was wondering how she would cope with the arrival of yet more refugees. 'This morning, early, Lilla [a helper] went down and found our sitting [room] full of sleeping men! . . . They turned out to be Englishmen! Some from Aidin and who had been travelling all night and day; among them was Leslie Stephenson, Jessie's husband!'

Grace was unsure where to house them all. 'Well, we have got to a pass and no mistake – more and more people crowding into the clinic. I don't feed them, they have to provide their own food and bedding – but what a fuss it creates.'

Once Grace had completed her morning round, she made her way across the city in order to visit the Dutch hospital. As she pushed her way through the crowds, she was surprised to discover that thousands of Greek soldiers were still on the quayside, waiting to embark. 'What we fear is the rabble and the crowd lest the Turks arrive before the army has cleared out,' she wrote. 'There are dozens and dozens of ships taking them as hard as they can, and the soldier, in his hurry to get off, pushes and scrambles and drops his rifle and everything he can so that the town is strewn with things and guns.'

Grace's sympathies lay entirely with the Turks and she had long held that Britain's pro-Greek policy was doomed to failure. 'I wish Lloyd George could have been here to witness all that has gone on,' she wrote in her diary that Friday morning. A little later she added: 'I rather hope Kemal will come soon.'

Although Grace's views were not shared by the majority of Smyrna's inhabitants, there remained nevertheless an overwhelming air of calm. Department stores remained open for business; butchers and bakers opened their doors as usual. Even the brasseries and beer houses continued to serve their regular customers as if nothing untoward was afoot. And at the Théâtre de Smyrne, a small queue of people were waiting to buy tickets for the evening motion picture – *The Tango of Death*.

George Ward Price of the *Daily Mail* disembarked from the *Ajax* on Friday afternoon and checked into the Grand Hotel Kraemer Palace. That done, he paid a visit on Sir Harry Lamb and his consular staff, whom he found making extraneous efforts to get all British nationals out of the country. '[They were] working day and night to issue passports for all inhabitants who could claim British nationality. Many of these were British in name only.'

The lack of any civil authorities in a city the size of Smyrna was causing as much concern to George Horton as it was to Sir Harry Lamb. A large number of Americans were still living in the city, as well as a sizeable population of Greeks and Armenians who held American nationality. Horton did not wish to create panic by advising all Americans to leave, yet he was acutely aware of his responsibilities as consul if and when trouble arose. Many American wives had already taken refuge aboard one of the ships at anchor in the bay and Horton advised his own wife to do likewise. 'But she refused, thinking that her staying might give comfort to those who remained.'

Horton was in regular contact with the French and Italian consuls who repeatedly assured him that Kemal's troops would behave in exemplary fashion if they decided to enter the city. However, Horton remained 'very uneasy' and decided to arrange a central meeting point for American nationals if there happened to be any disturbances. 'I picked out the American Theater, a large and suitable building on the quay, for the purpose – and called the leading members of the American colony, native and naturalised, to a meeting in my office and advised them of the measures taken.'

All agreed that this was a sensible course of action, but many also felt that they should be doing more to help the refugees in need. One American businessman, Rufus Lane, gave a passionate address to those who had assembled in the consulate. 'We did not come here solely to save our own skins,' he told them. 'The refugees ... are pouring by thousands and thousands into the city and dying of starvation and [have] nobody to help them.'

His words had an electrifying effect. A Provisional Relief Committee was immediately established and people donated money and equipment. 'All the leading American firms offered their lorries and automobiles and their personal services. Bakers were hired and set to work, stacks of flour found and purchased and in a few hours this organisation was feeding the helpless and bewildered refugees who were crowding into the city.'

Horton contacted the American authorities in Constantinople and Washington, requesting more warships to be sent with immediate effect. Although there were already two US destroyers in the bay – and the USS *Lawrence* was on its way – he felt that this was nowhere near enough. 'Our business interests and property holdings were very considerable indeed,' he later wrote, 'to say nothing of our large schools with the staffs of teachers and professors.'

His request, sent directly to Admiral Bristol, fell on deaf ears. '[He] had perfect confidence in the good intentions and administrative abilities of the Turks,' wrote Horton, 'and believed that the latter would bring a kind and benevolent administration to Smyrna.'

Bristol's convictions were not shared by Metropolitan Chrysostom, who paid a visit on Horton that Friday to ask what could be done to protect the city's Greek community. Horton could give no answer. Instead, he urged Chrysostom to escape while he had the chance. The archbishop – wan and ill – refused to countenance such an idea. 'As he sat there in the consular office, the shadow of approaching death lay upon his features,' wrote Horton. 'At least twice in my life I have seen that shadow upon a human visage and known that the person was soon to die.'

The archbishop's anxieties about the arrival of the Turks was shared by many of the city's Armenians. A little after midday, a young Armenian student, Hovakim Uregian, was witness to a surprising sight. Hundreds of his fellow nationals were locking up their homes and congregating at the Armenian church of St Stephen, reasoning that it was safer to be part of a crowd. By the time Uregian reached the building, 'the courtyard, the church, the adjoining rooms, the entire Prelacy was filled with people.'

In eavesdropping on their conversations, he learned that everyone was trying to convince themselves that the crisis would soon blow over. 'Everything was superficially the same,' wrote Uregian, 'the people, the buildings, the city, everything as it had been perhaps for the last 100 years. Where was the danger?'

The feeling that life would soon return to normal was echoed by Garabed Hatcherian, who had spent the day seeking out senior officials who might have access to more detailed information. In the middle of the afternoon, he chanced upon a senior attorney who worked for the French consulate. The attorney assured Hatcherian that there was nothing to fear. 'The Turkish army will enter the city in a most orderly way,' he said, 'to demonstrate to the whole world that the Turks are a civilised nation.'

He strongly advised Garabed not to leave Smyrna. 'In his opinion, it would be very unwise to leave behind one's house, occupation and position and head for unknown horizons.' Hatcherian was inclined to agree, especially when he noticed that yet more warships had entered the bay over the previous few hours. 'The proud presence of fleets from all nations continues to inspire confidence.'

As the afternoon wore on, Hortense Wood's extended family made their way to Bournabat station in order to catch the evening train into the city. 'Each of us with a bag in hand took the train at 7.30 p.m.,' wrote Lucy de Cramer, Hortense's older sister. Not everyone was convinced that they were making the right decision. 'Mrs Candall arrived saying what a shame that the English should get so frightened when all the other people kept so quiet in their homes.'

But as the train pulled into Smyrna, Mrs Candall was forced to eat her words. '[The station] was filled with soldiers and suddenly a sound of firing was heard. They barricaded the doors and the frightened crowd did not know where to take refuge!'

It was unclear who was shooting at whom, for the gunfire was coming from outside in the street. 'I sank into a chair exhausted,' wrote Lucy de Cramer, 'with a strong pain in my heart. Louise and the cook remained with me and the rest of our party, taking advantage of a moment of calm, went to search for a carriage.'

This search was interrupted by yet more gunfire and it was several hours before the family managed to hire a horse and cart that would take them to their town house. 'All the drivers refused to go into the firing and to arrive it was necessary to go through a street full of soldiers with menacing faces. At each moment, we thought they would strike us [but] finally we found ourselves safe and sound at our house.'

The gunfire, it transpired, had come from Greek royalists shooting at troops still loyal to Venizelos. As the last remnants of the Greek army stumbled into the city, some men saw it as the perfect opportunity to settle old scores.

Alexander MacLachlan was sufficiently alarmed by the deteriorating security situation to call for American troops to be landed. 'I sent to Captain Piper, who was in command of an American destroyer in Smyrna, requesting a number of guards to protect the college property.' Piper acceded to this request and landed twenty soldiers with himself at their head.

These were not the only troops to be sent ashore. As dusk fell, the captain of the newly arrived USS *Lawrence*, Lieutenant Commander Rhodes, ordered a second contingent to land. He warned these men to tread with care: Admiral Bristol had issued orders that American troops must 'not be in the position in any way to be operating with the Allies, the enemies of the Turks'.

Rhodes' thirty-five men were posted in small groups at the principal American institutions in the city: the consulate, schools, the YMCA and the YWCA, the Standard Oil terminal and the quayside theatre that was to be the refuge for American nationals in the event of trouble.

The British also took the decision to land troops that Friday evening. Some 200 marines were sent ashore with orders to guard the consulate, the fire station and the telegraph company. All requests to protect private property in Bournabat and Smyrna were turned down.

As dusk fell, the situation became increasingly alarming. Hortense, isolated in Bournabat and with only her nephew, Fernand, for company, was brought news of impending trouble. 'Half an hour ago,' she wrote, 'a young Turk, Rushdi, rushed into the hall where we were sitting and told us excitedly that Yemanlav, a village close by, had been destroyed by Circassians and Armenians and that these intended setting fire to Bournabat this evening.'

Rushdi strongly advised Fernand to take steps to protect his aunt's property, since it was clear that any unguarded house would be at risk. Fernand took heed of this advice. 'To save Bournabat from the fate of all the other villages of the interior, some gentlemen conceived the idea of organising strong patrols of villagers to prevent the Greeks from annihilating us,' he wrote. By 10 p.m. that Friday evening, armed civilian patrols were pacing the streets of Bournabat 'and all the Greek soldiers who passed by the Club were disarmed'.

Similar groups of lightly armed militia were being established in the other bourgeois suburbs. In Cordelio, Carel van der Zee raised a home guard to protect the prestigious villas that lined the coast. And in Boudja, the remaining Levantine families were boarding up their windows and dusting down their shotguns.

Fernand went to bed that night with a heavy heart. Unable to sleep, he decided to get dressed again and offer help to the refugees who continued to pour through Bournabat. 'The procession of ragged, foot-sore refugees and soldiers, of starved horses, cattle and sheep continues . . . Carts with rusty wheels, loaded with pathetic looking shabby bundles, pass by before our gate continually, silently, wearily!'

As the clock struck midnight, the only noise to be heard was the constant shuffle of refugees making their way towards the quayside of Smyrna. Fernand finally returned to bed and drifted into a fitful sleep, dimly aware of the commotion taking place below his bedroom window. Every other quarter of the city was eerily silent. The whole of Smyrna was waiting in anticipation – waiting to see what the dawn would bring.

It was an unsettling night for the American and British sentries. The moon had been swallowed by the clouds and the city was plunged into darkness. 'Everything quiet,' recorded Lieutenant Merrill, one of the American troops who had been landed a few hours earlier. He found the absolute silence of the streets unnerving. 'I thought the hollow sound of my foot falls on the paved streets could be heard all the way to Constantinople.'

Saturday, 9 September 1922

When Grace Williamson stepped out of the English Nursing Home on Saturday morning, the street was crowded with people laden with crates of food. It did not take her long to realise what was happening. With no one to guard the city's warehouses, Smyrniots had taken the law into their own hands and started helping themselves to supplies intended for the Greek army.

> This is the day of looting [she wrote]. Nothing can describe the sight past our windows, every miserable animal and every sort of cart was used to carry big sacks of flour, barrels of oil were rolled along, cases of sugar on every imaginable little cart or pram or barrow. Men, women and children carrying every mortal thing!! I wish I were an artist and could paint, it was a marvellous picture. I would not have missed the sight for the world.

The looting was carried out not just by petty criminals. Everyone – rich and poor – was helping themselves to the warehouse supplies. They justified their actions by arguing that it was better for them to have the food than for it to fall into the hands of the Turkish army.

Grace found the pillaging most diverting and decided to

acquire a few provisions for the nursing home. Yet her strict sense of right and wrong suddenly got the better of her and she insisted on paying for the stolen goods. 'We bought a case of sugar, a bag of coffee and a sack of soap for next to nothing,' she wrote.

Grace was not alone in witnessing the first signs of a breakdown in law and order. Early that morning, Alexander MacLachlan had driven into the city in order to meet senior American naval officers at the consulate building. 'Abandoned horses, oxen and mules wander about the streets . . .' he wrote. 'Here and there, street *gamins* [urchins] were unwinding their *koushaks* [girdles] and lassoing these animals and either riding them about the streets or hurrying them away into side streets to their houses.'

MacLachlan was surprised to discover that large numbers of Greek soldiers had not yet managed to embark. 'The remnant of the retreating army, in every degree of exhaustion and abandon, were also wending their way by different streets to the waterfront.'

He hoped these stragglers would find passage on a Greek vessel, as he had been reliably informed that the Turkish army would make its triumphant entry into the city on Monday, less than forty-eight hours away.

Five miles away in Bournabat, Fernand de Cramer was stirred from his sleep by an altogether more alarming event taking place outside his window. 'At a quarter to eight, I was awakened by such a fusillade and such a horrible din that I was led to believe in a battle in the square itself.' He leaped out of bed in order to find out what was happening. 'I see from my window a crowd pouring out from the street and running with horrible cries toward Smyrna. What a spectacle!' The gunfire was once again caused by retreating Greek soldiers who were taking advantage of the chaos to settle old scores.

Fernand was even more surprised to see Aunt Hortense in the thick of the crowd, gesticulating wildly but seemingly oblivious to the danger in which she found herself. He threw on some clothes and rushed outside in order to persuade her to take cover. Once both of them were back inside the house, he did his utmost to talk her into leaving Bournabat and joining the rest of the family in Smyrna. But this was easier said than done: 'Impossible to persuade her to make a decision,' he wrote.

Fernand found himself in an invidious position. Although he had no wish to abandon Hortense, especially as the gunfire was getting heavier with every hour that passed, he was most anxious about his mother, Lucy, who had a weak heart. In the end, he placed the health of his mother over the safety of his aunt and headed to Bournabat station, where the morning train was about to depart. 'I had just time to jump on the running board . . .' he wrote. 'The train had not made one hundred metres when a terrible fire of machine guns descends on Bournabat!!'

Fernand felt guilty about abandoning his aunt, but Hortense herself seemed to be relishing the events taking place below her bedroom window. 'The shots all round now fell thick and fast,' she wrote. 'Many people killed, they say. I don't quite believe it.'

Charlton Whittall – Herbert Octavius's brother – had hitherto displayed just as much sang-froid as Hortense, but the rattle of machine-guns caused him a sudden loss of nerve. He called to his wife and young son, Willem, and led them out through the back doors of the house. They pushed their way through shrubs and bushes before hiding themselves in a large underground flood drain that passed underneath the centre of Bournabat.

'It emerged into the garden of the old Whittall family house,' wrote Willem many years later, 'just near our own, and into its black cavity we crawled on hands and knees. There we lay for several hours until the sound of firing died down.'

While the Whittalls were in hiding, Hortense ventured back outside and walked down to the little kiosk at the edge of the village square. As she approached the decorated iron railings that surrounded the kiosk, the gunfire came to an abrupt halt and the air fell completely silent. It was as if someone had turned off a switch. Everyone found themselves looking eastwards, at the road that led from the interior of the country. Something dramatic was happening in the far distance. The first battalion of Mustafa Kemal's army was approaching Bournabat.

'I was glad to witness the entry of the Kemalist cavalry from the *kanghelakias* [railings] of the kiosk,' wrote Hortense. 'Splendid men wearing new, spotless uniforms and Circassian caps. Perfect discipline and perfect quiet. Their horses were in a very good condition.'

Three days earlier than anticipated – and in a manner that no one had expected – the advance columns of Kemal's army had reached the suburbs of Smyrna.

'I wonder what impression they made as they entered Smyrna . . .' wrote Hortense a few hours later. 'They must have enlisted everybody's admiration and surprise.'

This, it turned out, was the understatement of the day. George Horton was comfortably seated in his office at the American consulate when the air was pierced by the sound of screaming coming from the street below.

'Stepping to the door of my office, I found that a crowd of refugees, mostly women, were rushing in terror upon the consulate and trying to seek refuge within.' They would have succeeded in forcing the doors had it not been for the American marines standing guard at the entrance. Horton did not have to wait long to discover why they wanted sanctuary. 'One glance from the terrace which overlooked the quay made evident the cause of their terror. The Turkish cavalry were filing along the quay.'

Horton had been in the middle of a meeting with MacLachlan when the turmoil began. Both men were aware that they were witnessing a scene of historic importance and pushed their way out into the street.

> It was with difficulty that we were able to stem the tide of the frightened populace rushing up the Consulate street from the waterfront [wrote MacLachlan]. But before we had passed more than half of the sixty yards that separates the Consulate from the quay, we had the whole of the comparatively wide street to ourselves. Just as we reached the broad waterfront, the leading files of Turkish cavalry, with banners flying . . . were passing before the end of the street.

The sight of the mounted cavalry riding into the city made an indelible impression on all who witnessed it. One of those standing on the quay that Saturday morning was Anna Birge, the wife of an American missionary stationed in Smyrna. 'The first that entered were dressed in black, with black fezzes with their red crescents and red star, riding magnificent horses [and] carrying long curved swords,' she wrote. 'With one hand raised they called out to the terrified inhabitants, "Fear not! Fear not!" but the inhabitants of Smyrna, knowing the reputation of the Turk, were filled with terror.'

Among the terrified was the Armenian student, Hovakim Uregian, who had taken refuge in a quayside store as soon as he heard rumours that the Turkish army was about to enter the city. He was joined by many other Greeks and Armenians who had no desire to be out on the streets when the Turkish troops arrived. 'After a while, holding our breath and listening in terror, we heard the sounds of approaching cavalry. The trotting of horses continued. They passed by the shop in which we were hiding and we drew a breath of relief . . . as we opened the shutters, we saw them advancing in the direction of the Konak [the governor's palace] in the Turkish quarter of Smyrna.'

Uregian was reassured by the high level of discipline among the cavalry. So, too, was George Horton. 'Anyone who saw those mounted troops passing along the quay of Smyrna would testify, if he knew anything at all of military matters, that they were not only soldiers, but very good soldiers indeed, thoroughly trained and under perfect control of admirable officers.'

As the cavalry approached the central section of the quay-side, it found a most unexpected obstacle blocking its way. Captain Thesiger of HMS *King George V* stepped into their path and held up his hand. 'He looked for all the world,' wrote one, 'like a London policeman.'

There was a tense moment of silence. Thesiger's crew watched nervously from the deck of their warship, fearing that their impulsive captain would be trampled underfoot. Suddenly, and with military precision, the cavalry column came to an abrupt halt. 'The leader gave a blast on his whistle commanding silence,' wrote Charles Howes, one of the sailors on the *King George V*, 'and, dismounting, held out his hand.'

The Turkish officer addressed Thesiger in French, asking him why he was preventing the cavalry from riding along the quay. 'I am a captain in His Majesty's navy,' replied Thesiger with all the pomp and bravado he could muster, 'and have been commissioned to assist in the surrender of this town to you.' He added that the city was calm and that no one had the slightest intention of resisting the victorious Turks. 'But if you enter yelling and brandishing your scimitars, you will undoubtedly be asking for trouble.'

It was as the two men were talking that Horton and MacLachlan suddenly became aware of an even more extraordinary scene. 'Between the long line of cavalry that was close to the curb and the edge of the water, there straggled along the last remnant of the Greek army moving along in the same direction as the victorious Turks, but with a very different objective, namely, Chesme . . . their port of embarkation for Greece and home.' Victor and vanquished were within spitting distance of each other.

MacLachlan had little sympathy for the Greeks, yet he could not help but feel sorry for these footsore soldiers, many of whom had been fighting continuously since the Balkan War of 1912.

It was while he was watching this ragged procession that someone hurled a grenade at the officer leading the Turkish cavalry. It failed to explode but struck the soldier on his cheek, inflicting a nasty gash. Seconds later, a shot was fired by a man hiding behind a pile of sacks. This, too, missed its target.

One British mariner, observing the unfolding events from his warship in the bay, recalled what happened next. The Turkish officer, with admirable calmness, 'got off his horse, walked over to the Greek, took his rifle, broke it across his knee, and sent him on his way without even touching him'. The Turks were later to claim that both the grenade and shot were fired by Armenians, thereby justifying many of the terrible events that were to follow. But that same British witness, Lieutenant Charles Howes, was adamant that the men responsible were Greeks.

It quickly became apparent that these were isolated incidents. The procession was soon able to continue along the length of the quayside and, for the next hour or more, Turkish troops poured into the city.

To Grace Williamson, busily doing her round at the English Nursing Home, the morning's events came as something of an anticlimax. She, like most people, had been expecting trouble, but the arrival of the Turks had passed off with scarcely an incident.

'What a week we have spent!!' she wrote. 'I believe there was hardly a bit of trouble, only one silly fellow fired at the officers . . . No shooting in the streets! Thank God. Such a relief; everyone is inwardly delighted to have the Turks back again.'

Alexander MacLachlan remained on the waterfront until 12.30 p.m., when he started back for Paradise in the college car. On the way, he paid a visit on his optician who lived in the Armenian quarter of the city. 'As we passed along,' he wrote, 'the streets were completely deserted, apart from groups of mounted Turkish patriots who were moving about here and there calling out as they rode through the streets, "*Korkma! Korkma! Bir shay olmayajack!*" [Don't be afraid! Nothing will happen!]'

By the time MacLachlan reached the southern edge of the city, he had passed some sixty mounted patrols. 'As we approached with the car bearing an American flag,' he wrote, 'a way was opened for us to pass through their ranks.'

The crowds were out in force in the city's Turkish quarter, which 'presented one solid mass of fezzes, as far as the eye could reach'. There was a rather different scene in the outer suburbs, which were predominantly Greek. 'The shops were all closed, as were also the houses, with their shutters fastened and with no sign of life anywhere. We passed one dead body some distance along this road, but whether it was Greek or Turk I am unable to say.'

As MacLachlan approached Paradise, the roads were littered with the detritus of war – guns, carts and armoured vehicles. There was no one walking the streets and it was not until he reached Paradise that he saw the first sign of life – 'a mother and her little girl, who were apparently quite ignorant of the cause of all these strange conditions'.

MacLachlan parked his car outside the American International College and was pleased to note that US marines had placed a row of machine-guns outside the porter's lodge. Once he was safely inside the campus, he ordered the American flag to be raised over the building. Almost immediately, large numbers of Greeks and Armenians who lived in the neighbourhood began to converge on the college. All were given sanctuary on the condition that they turned in any weapons before entering the premises. Many were laden with their most precious belongings.

'Some of them brought their bedding and a sewing machine on their shoulders; others, a loaded cart piled high with their household equipment.'

A few families arrived with all their livestock. The animals were denied entrance, for the college was rapidly filling up with people. By 3 p.m., some 1,500 local inhabitants had taken refuge in the building.

At this same hour, Sir Harry Lamb took the decision to enforce the departure of all British citizens remaining in the city. Although the Turkish troops had so far behaved impeccably, Lamb was fearful of what might happen after dark. Hortense Wood's sister, Louise, left the city that afternoon, along with her husband and other members of the family, but many refused to follow Sir Harry's instructions. Hortense's other sister, Lucy, held dual nationality and used this as an excuse to stay in the city. 'I promised to remain and guard the house as an Austrian subject and friend of the Turks!'

Hortense herself was still in Bournabat and had no intention of leaving. Indeed, she was delighted to discover that the Turks had reopened the local gendarmerie and assigned guards to each of the Levantine mansions. 'All is quiet,' she noted in her diary.

Hortense's conviction that all would be well was not shared by the Armenian community. Garabed Hatcherian had watched the arrival of the Turkish army with alarm and instinctively mistrusted their declaration that no one in the city had anything to fear. Concerned that the Armenian quarter would be the first target if trouble arose, he resolved to move his family into the house of his friends, the Verkines. Mrs Verkine was more than happy to provide them with beds: she was due to give birth in a few days and Garabed was her family doctor.

The Hatcherians made their way on foot to the Verkines' quayside house. Garabed, worried about being stopped by Turkish troops, disguised himself as a Turk. 'I have left my hat at home,' he wrote, 'and I am wearing a fez. I have also pinned the Ottoman military medal of honour and the gold-coloured crescent on my waistcoat.'

The Hatcherians were not the only Armenians to have taken refuge from potential trouble. Krikor Baghdjian, a twenty-one-year-old teacher, had headed to the Armenian Club on Rechidie Street, where he found fifty of his compatriots already gathered. That afternoon, they took the decision to bolt the door against any possible incursion. 'Our suspicions proved to be correct,' wrote Baghdjian, 'because a short while later, while looking through the window and iron shutters onto the street, I saw groups of Turkish soldiers stopping civilians and taking money and valuables from them.' It was not just the troops who were beginning to cause mischief. Edwyn Hole, the British vice-consul, witnessed armed civilians harassing the few Greeks and Armenians who were still out and about.

By the time dusk fell, the Turkish army was approaching the city from all sides. In the prosperous suburb of Cordelio – home to many wealthy Armenians, Greeks and Levantines – their arrival caused panic. Petros Brussalis, who was then nine years old, still has vivid memories of his first glimpse of the Turkish mounted infantry. 'At their head rode a Turkish officer and he was dragging a Greek flag along the ground behind him. I remember looking at my parents and seeing the terror on their faces. The Turkish forces were not a normal army . . . there were many chettes, irregulars, and my parents feared there would be atrocities.'

The Greek servants working for the neighbouring van der Zee family were also frightened. One of their gardeners was carrying a large trunk to the waterside jetty when he caught sight of the Turkish cavalry. The shock was such that he suffered a heart attack and died on the spot. 'He was buried secretly in our garden,' recalled Helena van der Zee. 'A priest among the refugees performed the last rites.'

The arrival of many more irregular forces later that day further unsettled the homeless Greeks sheltering in the outhouses of the van der Zee family. 'Each time there was a noise, an explosion, a strange noise, they panicked,' wrote Helena.

The tension increased as dusk fell and the behaviour of the Turkish irregulars became increasingly menacing. The Pittakis family of Cordelio were about to sit down to their evening dinner when they heard the sound of breaking glass, followed by distant screams of women and children. A few minutes later, the same noises were repeated, only this time much closer. 'My wife fainted,' wrote Pittakis senior, 'my children clung to me in tears and the peasant families I had taken in . . . knelt down and invoked the protection of God.' They spent the rest of the night listening to the neighbouring houses being broken into and pillaged.

The only explanation as to why they escaped the same fate was that the quick-thinking Pittakis, aware that Italy had been supplying weapons to Mustafa Kemal's army, hung a large Italian tricolour outside his house.

Violence was by now beginning to break out in the centre of the city as well. The Reverend Abraham Hartunian, an Armenian priest, was about to eat his evening meal when the trouble began. 'My wife was preparing lentil soup for supper. The table was set. I offered the blessing and we were about to sup. Suddenly, there was a scream in the house next to ours, Our neighbours had been attacked. The chettes were threatening them with death unless they gave money. Our neighbours were pleading, saying, "We have none!"'

The Hartunians decided not to await the arrival of the *chettes*. Slipping out of their house, they headed straight to the American Collegiate Institute, where they were given sanctuary.

On board the USS *Lawrence*, Captain Arthur Hepburn was writing up his diary for the day. 'Funny thing,' he wrote, 'the terror is in the air and quite palpable when it begins to grow.'

He snapped shut his notebook and turned to write a report of the day's proceedings for his boss, Admiral Mark Bristol. The admiral was given a very different version of events. 'At this hour, 11.50 p.m., everything is quiet [and] peaceful . . .' he wrote. 'I must say that the Turks deserve a high mark for their efficiency, good discipline and high military standards.'

It was just what Bristol wanted to hear.

Sunday, 10 September 1922

The Christian population of Smyrna was accustomed to being awoken on Sunday morning by the ringing of church bells. But on this particular Sunday – for the first time in centuries – the dawn was eerily silent. It was an ominous sign for the thousands of Armenians who had taken refuge in the prelacy building. They feared that the day of reckoning was nigh.

Hovekim Uregian was one of many who had passed a sleepless night. Throughout the early hours, Turkish soldiers had been heard taking up positions around the prelacy compound, 'shouting threats and firing guns, running around like packs of wolves, stopping every Christian passer-by, asking for his money and valuables'. Uregian also heard screams at regular intervals during the night, 'and the soul-tearing quality of these screams left little doubt as to the fate of the victims'.

As first light approached, he placed a mirror against the corner windows of the building in order to get a clearer view of what was taking place outside. 'And we watched in horror what I can only describe as a real picture of hell.' Turkish troops could be seen rampaging through the Armenian quarter, breaking into private homes, looting, raping and killing. 'Groups of regular or irregular Turkish troops would knock on a door and proceed to break it down. Any young girls found inside would be brought out and taken to some shop nearby or across the street by two or three soldiers. Screams would follow and occasionally a gunshot.'

Other eyewitnesses would later confirm that the violence in the streets around the Armenian prelacy had been every bit as ugly as Uregian claimed, yet it had remained confined to the Armenian quarter. Elsewhere in the city the night had passed relatively peacefully. Garabed Hatcherian and his family had spent the evening with the Verkines at their house on the seafront and been unaware of any disturbances. After eating breakfast on Sunday morning, Hatcherian and two other guests set off on foot to check on their homes. It was only when they met a group of Armenian youths that they learned that the Armenian quarter had been badly looted.

Hatcherian's companions chose to go on farther, but Garabed himself – still dressed as a Turk – was keen to discover the extent of the damage and decided to continue alone. At one point he was stopped by Turkish soldiers and asked for directions to the city barracks. Hatcherian pointed the men towards Armenian Boulevard Reshidiyah, only to be told that the area around this street was 'a bloody hell'.

He pressed on towards his house, fearing that he would find it looted. Yet although the lock was jammed due to repeated attempts to break it down during the night, the building had not been entered. Unable to get inside, Garabed continued down the street in order to make contact with his neighbours. 'I knock a few times at the door of Levon Arakelian; there is no answer. The Illuminator Street is deserted. In front of Miss D. Kasparian's house, I see a large amount of dried blood.'

Hatcherian noted that the streets were empty, eerily silent and scattered with broken glass. 'Without flinching, I proceed to the Armenian Grand Boulevard. First, I see the house of the Balikjians, where the doors are broken and the furniture is a jumbled mess in the courtyard. The doors of the houses on the Grand Boulevard have been broken one by one and there are traces of blood all over. The stores, too, have been broken into and looted.'

As he turned a corner and made his way deeper into the Armenian quarter, he was stopped in his tracks by Turkish troops in the process of ransacking a house. They looked him up and down and, assuming him to be Turkish, continued with their looting. Deciding not to chance his luck by remaining any longer, Hatcherian headed straight back to the safety of the Verkines' house.

The Armenian families who had taken refuge inside the prelacy feared that sooner or later they were likely to meet with the same fate as those who had chosen to remain in their houses. As the morning wore on and there was no sign of the violence abating, the men began discussing how best to defend the building if and when it came under attack.

'We counted all the males and singled out all those who had some experience in using a gun,' wrote Uregian. Many had come to the prelacy equipped with old rifles and pistols. These were now distributed, along with all the available ammunition. There were also a few old hand grenades to be used as a last resort. 'We took positions in the nearest room above the door,' '. . . and agreed that we would fire only if necessary; only if the Turks tried to break down the door.'

At about 11 a.m. there was a loud rap on the side door of the prelacy. It was a group of regular Turkish soldiers who shouted in English: 'We have come to liberate and defend you; open the door.'

The men inside knew they had little option but to obey. While one of them went to find the key, the rest prepared their weapons 'in case the game turned foul'.

It took some time to locate the key and Uregian could see that the troops outside were getting jumpy. Yet even he was not prepared for what happened next. Suddenly – and quite without warning – the Turkish officer barked an order and each of the soldiers hurled a hand grenade over the prelacy walls. There was a blinding flash of light as they detonated, followed by a deafening roar. 'A grenade exploded somewhere near me and for a second I thought I was seeing stars,' wrote Uregian. 'A horse standing near me seemed to jump into the air and then fall flat on all fours. I touched my limbs to make sure I had not been hurt and [then] I jumped to run towards a corner to be safer.'

Uregian was one of the lucky ones. A comrade-in-arms who had been crouching down next to him had been hit by shrapnel and was bleeding, groaning in pain.

The Turks who had thrown the grenades took cover in the backstreets while other troops fired on the building. 'A machine gun somewhere outside the walls was shattering all the high windows and hitting quite a number of my compatriots.'

After half an hour of constant gunfire, the shooting came to an abrupt end, although the women and children inside continued to scream and moan in the aftermath of the attack. Many had been maimed by flying debris and it took time to clean and dress the wounds of the injured. When this was finally done, the rubble was swept away and the building checked for any signs of structural damage. For the rest of the day, the prelacy was quiet. 'Silence fell and people huddled together waiting for hostilities to start anew.'

The Turkish army had by now been in the city for more than twenty-four hours, yet there had been no sign of Mustafa Kemal. He was still at the town of Nif, some twenty-five miles from Smyrna, preparing to make his triumphal entry. Five cars, newly polished and decked with olive branches, were waiting to convey him and his entourage to the city.

At noon, Kemal left his battlefield headquarters, brushed down his uniform and stepped into the first car. This was the moment he had been awaiting for three long years.

The cortège entered Smyrna through the Turkish quarter, where the cavalry was awaiting Kemal's arrival. 'In a single lightning flash, two long lines of horsemen drew their swords,' wrote Halide Edib, 'and the sun gleamed on their steel as they galloped past us on either side.' It was a magnificent spectacle. 'The clash of steel and the beat of iron hoofs became deafening as we crossed the closed bazaars . . . Along the smooth marble pavement reeled the moving walls of men and steel, horses sliding and rising, and the steel curving like swift flashes of lightning in the sombre air of the arches.'

After stopping to acknowledge the exultant crowds, Kemal's entourage headed straight to the Konak in order to discuss how to bring order to Smyrna. Kemal's first act was to appoint General Noureddin as military governor of the city. It was a strange choice that would alarm many inhabitants. Noureddin was known to be a cruel and ruthlessly ambitious individual who harboured an intense hatred of foreigners.

Halide Edib joined Kemal's generals shortly after their arrival at the Konak.

On the table lay a sword sent by an Eastern country to be given to whoever should first enter Smyrna [she wrote]. Several units had entered the city simultaneously from different parts, so there were several claimants. But there was the commander of a cavalry unit, Lieutenant Sheraffedine, who had reached the quay first. He was standing in the middle of the hall, a little dapper figure: legs of a cowboy, head and one arm in bandages, but tingling all over with adventure, and telling his story with a boyish lisp.

One of the first people to learn of Kemal's arrival was the *Daily Mail* journalist, George Ward Price. He had already met the Turkish leader two years earlier at the Pera Palace Hotel in

Constantinople; now, he hoped to get the scoop of his life. But Kemal refused to see anyone. After lengthy discussion with his advisors, he was whisked away to a house in Cordelio where he was due to spend the night. Several witnesses record that a Greek flag had been laid in front of the entrance to the house; Kemal refused to tread on it.

By mid-afternoon, the Turkish army was in control of both the streets and government of the city. General Noureddin's first order was that everybody should go peacefully about his business. This went some way to calming people's nerves and many prayed that the violence would now come to an end. They were unaware that Kemal had sent a telegram to the League of Nations, informing them that he took no responsibility for any breakdown in law and order. He warned that 'on account of the excited spirit of the Turkish population, the Angora government would not be responsible for massacres.'

In the suburb of Paradise, many of the American residents had been shaken by the sight of several corpses lying in the road close to the American International College. This had also disturbed Dr MacLachlan and he asked one of the Greek priests taking refuge at the institute to bury them. Once this was promptly done, MacLachlan looked forward to a quiet lunch with his colleagues. His hopes were rudely shattered by a burst of gunfire. 'Shortly after 12.30pm,' he wrote, 'and just as we were about to sit down to lunch, we were startled by the rattle of machine guns in our immediate neighbourhood.'

Everyone dived for cover under the tables and it was some time before MacLachlan dared to venture to the window in order to discover who was responsible for the shooting. He saw that a bank of Turkish machine-guns had been positioned some one hundred yards to the north-west of the institute. To the south – and the target of their guns – was a 6,000-strong battalion of Greek troops who were trying to reach the coast. 'In the direction of Sevdekeui, great dust clouds betrayed the approach, along the main road leading from that village to Paradise, [of] a considerable body of troops.'

The Greek forces realised that the Turks had cut off their route to the sea and that they had little option but to fight their way out of the impasse. The Turks – scenting victory – were determined to stop them. For the next three hours, Dr MacLachlan and his staff were caught in a ferocious cross-fire between the rival armies.

'For the first time in my life and, I trust, also the last, I was able not only to watch a battle in progress, but also with the aid of a good pair of field glasses, to study its developing phases from an exceptionally good point of vantage, viz: from the gallery windows of the College Chapel.'

The battle looked set to overwhelm the American International College. The Turkish cavalry attacked from the eastern and western sides of the campus, while their infantry attempted to pass to the south. The Greeks meanwhile pounded the advancing Turks with shells and high explosives with the aim of halting their advance.

'The whole of the campus and all our homes were directly between the opposing forces,' wrote MacLachlan, 'and consequently in the direct line of their fire. We realised this rather unpleasant and yet excitingly interesting situation, as the shells whistled over our heads and when the rifle fire was cutting the leaves from the trees before our doors.'

The college was in the firing line of bullets and shells for the duration of the battle, 'making our position on the campus an exceedingly uncomfortable one; for although no shells fell on our premises, many fell within a few yards of them, while hundreds of rifle bullets fell short of their mark and within our boundaries'.

At 3.30 p.m., the firing suddenly stopped. Dr MacLachlan and his colleagues surmised – correctly, as it transpired – that this last vestige of the vanquished Greek army had surrendered. The troops had realised that they were hopelessly outnumbered and would never reach the coast. Unwilling to fight to the death, they chose to lay down their arms. All were taken prisoners of war.

Less than half an hour after the battle at Paradise had come to an end, a Turkish military patrol drew up outside the offices of Metropolitan Chrysostom. Three men jumped out of the vehicle, entered the building and informed the church hierarch that he had been called to a meeting with General Noureddin. He was to be taken to the general's headquarters immediately.

The Greek metropolitan was not unduly surprised by such a summons. He was Smyrna's most senior cleric and – under the Ottoman system – recognised as the effective head of the city's Greek population. He was expecting to be given instructions from the city's new governor.

It so happened that a French military patrol was passing at the very moment when Chrysostom stepped into the awaiting Turkish vehicle. Among the French troops was a civilian visitor to the city who persuaded his comrades-in-arms to follow the Greek metropolitan to the Konak. In doing so, they became eyewitnesses to the momentous events that followed.

Several other witnesses were also at the scene. They were later interviewed by the Armenian bishop of Smyrna, Ghevont Tourian, who wrote a report on the proceedings of that Sunday afternoon.

According to the French observers, Chrysostom was driven to the Konak and led into General Noureddin's office. The content of the two men's conversation remains unknown; the only certainty is that the Greek metropolitan was dismissed after a meeting that lasted just a few minutes. As Chrysostom descended the steps of the Konak, the Turkish general is said to have appeared on the balcony and shouted to the mob: 'If he has done good to you, do good to him. If he has done harm to you, do harm to him.'

Bishop Tourian recorded events somewhat differently. He said that General Noureddin had decided to imprison Chrysostom and assigned guards to escort him to the city's jail. But as this group left the Konak, the crowd surged forward and physically assaulted the metropolitan.

Whatever the truth of Noureddin's actions, the end result was the same. 'The mob took possession of Metropolitan Chrysostom and carried him away,' recorded the Frenchmen. 'A little further on, in front of an Italian hairdresser named Ismail . . . they stopped and the Metropolitan was slipped into a white hairdresser's overall. They began to beat him with their fists and sticks and to spit on his face. They riddled him with stabs. They tore his beard off, they gouged his eyes out, they cut off his nose and ears.'

The French soldiers were disgusted by what they saw and wished to intervene, but their commanding officer was under orders to remain strictly neutral. At the point of a revolver, he forbade his men from saving the metropolitan's life. Chrysostom was dragged into a backstreet in the Iki Cheshmeli district, where he eventually died from his terrible wounds.

He was not the only senior figure to lose his life on that Sunday afternoon. As the French patrol made its way back to the European quarter of the city, the men were witness to another gruesome spectacle. Monsieur Jurukdoglou, the well-known director of the *Réforme* newspaper, was seen being dragged behind a car, his head dashed to pieces on the cobblestones. And when the French patrol passed close to the Armenian church of St Stephen, they saw the headless corpses of three young children.

At around 5 p.m. on that Sunday, it occurred to Alexander MacLachlan that he had received no word from Ray Moreman, one of his colleagues at the college. Moreman had gone to the suburb of Boujda more than forty-eight hours earlier in order to raise the American flag over the Greek orphanage. Since then, there had been no communication between the two men.

MacLachlan was so concerned that he took the college car and, accompanied by two friends, decided to drive over to Boudja. 'As we entered the village, a place of some thirteen to fourteen thousand inhabitants, a strange feeling took possession of us that serious events were either expected or had just taken place,' he wrote. 'We could see no sign of human life anywhere in town. Doors, windows and shutters were everywhere closed.'

It soon became apparent that all was not well. As MacLachlan and his friends approached the orphanage, they found two corpses lying by the roadside, 'and at once recognised the faces of Mr and Mrs Oscar de Jongh ... whom I had known for more than thirty years'.

The sight of their lifeless bodies came as a great shock. Oscar and Cleo de Jongh were the first Levantine fatalities. The Turks later claimed that they had been killed by accident, trampled underfoot by the advancing cavalry, but a friend of the de Jongh family had examined their corpses within an hour or so of them being killed and came to a different conclusion. 'The blood was still oozing from their gun-shot wounds,' he wrote. The de Jonghs were buried shortly afterwards since there was a concern that the cadavers would be eaten by wild dogs. 'They were buried in one grave, just as they were, without any further service, no clergyman being available.'

While this hastily arranged internment was taking place, Dr MacLachlan made his way to the Greek orphanage where Moreman recounted a woeful story of fighting and violence. The trouble had started when the Turkish infantry entered the main boulevard and were fired upon by Greek civilians. It was the signal for an all-out attack. 'At once the troops took the law into their own hands and rushing about shot down anyone who happened to be in the street at the time.'

Dr MacLachlan tried to persuade Moreman to return to the American International College. 'He refused, saying that he would rather take his chances with those who now looked to him as their protector.'

The news of the troubles in Boujda further unsettled the Levantine families who remained in nearby Bournabat, yet most of them still refused to abandon their homes. Charlton Whittall certainly had no intention of leaving his villa to the mercy of the Turkish army. He hung a large Union Jack from his gatepost – a most unwise thing to do – and then locked himself and his family inside the house. For the next hour or more, he stood guard inside the drawing room of his home, 'his trusty shotgun across his knees . . . peering from behind drawn curtains'.

At first the Turkish soldiers were friendly and waved at the Whittalls cowering inside their house, but by midday, the mood was beginning to change. 'An armed Turkish rabble passed, ugly looking, they stopped at our garden gate, tore down the Union Jack, spat on it in the dust.' So wrote Charlton's son, Willem, then a young boy. 'One lot approached our gate. [They] tried to open it [but] it was locked and they commenced to break open the gate.'

The behaviour of these Turkish irregulars so frightened Charlton that he decided to move his family back into the safety of the covered flood drain, knowing that it was one place where they were most unlikely to be discovered.

Hortense Wood too had remained in Bournabat and was trying to put a brave face on the spiralling downturn of events. At some point in the afternoon, Dr Denotowitz called at her house to warn that Turkish soldiers had broken into at least one Levantine villa. He also brought rumours that several other houses – those owned by the Pagy and Lawson families – had been sacked.

271

Hortense did not have to wait long for confirmation of the fact that Bournabat was now gripped by violence. As daylight began to fade, she saw a huge fire take hold of a nearby mansion belonging to the Mancolo family, who had fled some days earlier to the relative safety of Smyrna.

'Tremendous clouds of smoke,' wrote Hortense, 'in the midst of which flames lept [sic] sky-high and millions of sparks flew over tiles and fell into the garden.' She had a very real fear that these cinders would set her own house alight. 'At one time, it seemed as if the stables had caught fire,' she wrote, adding that 'the horses had been stolen that very morning by bashibouzouks [irregulars].'

One of Hortense's neighbours, Dr Murphy, had also decided to remain in his home. It was to prove a fateful decision. Eighty-seven years of age, the doctor was seated in his drawing room with his wife and daughters when Turkish troops forcibly entered the house. Having wrecked furniture and valuables in the front rooms, they surged into the drawing room and attacked Dr Murphy. 'Several vases were broken on the unfortunate man's head, his wife was badly injured and the two daughters only saved from brutal molestation by their persecutors turning their attentions to the servants, all of whom were brutally outraged.'

Dr Murphy was shot, then stabbed several times and Mrs Murphy was also severely injured. The intruders then smashed the piano – along with all the remaining objets d'art – before leaving.

'Dr Murphy . . . is dying,' wrote Hortense Wood in her diary. 'Mrs Murphy was horribly ill treated, beaten and her face covered with wounds. The girls were also ill treated. Everything has been stolen from them – their money, their silver, all they possessed.'

Dr Murphy and his wife were eventually taken to the English Nursing Home where Grace Williamson did all she could to keep the elderly doctor alive, although she did not hold out much hope of nursing him back to health. 'Both had their heads banged by the butt end of a rifle and he was shot in the shoulders,' she wrote. 'I don't expect the old doctor will live.' She was right. He died the next day – the third Levantine casualty of the disaster.

Monday, 11 September 1922

Charlton Whittall and his family spent Sunday night in hiding, concealed once again in the large flood drain at the bottom of their garden. They were unable to sleep, for intermittent gunfire continued throughout the early hours. During one lull in the fighting, Charlton crept back to the house and returned with a hunk of dry bread, the only food he could find. He wished he had heeded Herbert Octavius's advice and left Bournabat while it had still been possible. Now, there was no chance of escape because the whole area was swarming with Turkish irregulars. The family spent a fitful few hours waiting for dawn, hoping that the soldiers would eventually tire of their pillaging and move elsewhere.

Hortense Wood had also spent a troubled night. She was defiant to the last, remaining in her house even though all her neighbours had fled. But the sound of shooting troubled her sleep and the flicker of burning buildings cast a sickening glow into her bedroom. It was not until dawn that the irregulars finally left Bournabat and Hortense managed to catch a few hours' rest.

She was woken during the morning by a knock at the front door. At considerable personal risk, her ever-loyal nephew, Fernand, had ridden all the way from Smyrna in order to check on her well-being. He brought with him a dismal tale of looting and destruction. For much of the night, Turkish irregulars had occupied themselves with ransacking the great villas of Bournabat. Any item that could not be carried off had been destroyed and many of the houses had then been torched. It was a miracle that Hortense's own house had been left untouched.

> You would not believe your eyes [he told his aunt] if you saw the houses of Sidney Lafontaine, Keyser, Richard Whittall, Molinari, Frank Wilkerson, Ed Lafontaine, H[erbert] W[hittall], Pagy, Clarlaki, W Charnaud (only partially destroyed, fortunately), Mathezis (completely, alas!), Sunoman, Fritz, Mme Turrell-Murphy . . .
>
> In short, all the houses as far as the station [have been sacked]; and in most of them, without taking into account the total pillaging, a vandalism without name. All the Greek houses large and small as far as La Havousa are but a ruin.

As he had ridden through the ruins of the Levantine colony, Fernand counted just seven houses that remained untouched.

He was even more shocked when he passed the various churches and graveyards that were dotted throughout Bournabat. The little Anglican church of St Mary Magdaleine built by the Whittall family − had been one of the first targets. The graveyard housing the tombs of old Magdalen Whittall and her flower-loving son, Edward, had been torn apart; the church had then been ransacked. 'All the monuments and crosses are in rags,' wrote Fernand, 'broken in fits of rage (the dirty [Turkish] Cretans of this place are largely to blame!).' The church itself had also been violated. 'Its coloured panels [were] broken [and] all the upholstered benches opened.'

This was not the only Christian place of worship to be targeted. 'As for the Catholic and Greek cemeteries,' wrote

Fernand, 'many of the vaults and coffins have been rifled and a mass of buried, known to us all, lamentably exposed.'

As he surveyed the smouldering ruins of Bournabat from the upper windows of his aunt's mansion, he felt a deep and terrible sense of loss. For more than a century, the Levantines of Bournabat had lived a charmed existence. Here, in the richest corner of the Ottoman empire, they had built their own financial kingdoms that had enriched everyone. Their factories had employed thousands of local Smyrniots – Greeks, Armenians, Turks and Jews – and the charitable institutions they directed had supported hospitals, nursing homes and orphanages. And in their palatial villas they had courted grand viziers, Ottoman *valis* and even the sultan himself. Now, those same villas lay in ruins.

'Finished, finished is Bournabat for us,' wrote Fernand.

The violence had spread to other areas of the city during the night. When Alexander MacLachlan drove from Paradise to Smyrna on Monday morning, he noted many dead bodies by the roadside, as well as abandoned loot that had been stolen from ransacked factories. 'Among many articles of household equipment, I noticed a number of sewing machines in the ditch at one point,' he wrote.

MacLachlan was on his way to a meeting with General Noureddin. He wished to ask the new city governor for an increased level of protection for the American International College. While he was waiting outside the general's bureau, he struck up a conversation with Noureddin's aide-de-camp. This individual was free of tongue, informing MacLachlan that the Turks had uncovered an Armenian plot to resist Kemal's newly victorious army.

MacLachlan was as surprised by this news as he was sceptical. He was well connected with the Armenian community and yet he had heard no such rumours. He knew of the existence of a small band of fanatics who had declared their opposition to the Turkish army, but this organisation did not elicit any support from the local Armenian population. 'I must add,' wrote MacLachlan, '. . . that in so far as the existence and purpose of this organisation were known to the Armenians of Smyrna, not only did they withhold their sympathy and support from it, but they utterly disapproved [of] and condemned it.' They believed that counter-violence would only serve to increase the danger in which they found themselves.

The two men's conversation was interrupted by the sounds of a commotion in the street outside. MacLachlan and the aide stepped onto the balcony and watched as yet another procession of Greek prisoners of war were led along the quayside. All were being forced to shout, 'Long live Mustafa Kemal.' The aide explained to MacLachlan that they were being thus treated in retaliation for the manner in which the Greeks had behaved towards the Turks in May 1919.

'I confess it was a sickening sight,' wrote MacLachlan in his memoirs, '. . . yet it is fairly indicative of the spirit of vindictive reprisal that has always characterised the relations of these two races.'

MacLachlan was eventually ushered into Noureddin's study and given a cordial welcome. The general was the epitome of charm and immediately acceded to MacLachlan's request for troops to guard the American compound. He suggested that the Americans make direct contact with the district commander.

MacLachlan promised to do this as soon as he returned to Paradise, but he was to find himself delayed by circumstances that put him in peril of his life.

The brutalities that had rocked Bournabat, Paradise and the Armenian quarter of Smyrna had not yet spread to the rest of the city. The great boulevards of the European district were still untouched and – to the amazement of many –

several of the bars and brasseries on the quayside remained open for business. When Grace Williamson walked to the British consulate that Monday morning, she was pleased to note that all the principal thoroughfares were being patrolled by Turkish police. She had been concerned by the sound of gunfire during the night but her enthusiasm for the Turks remained undiminished.

'This is a rather celebrated day,' she wrote, 'the taking over of the whole town by the Kemalists. No end of blue funk . . . Houses on the quay that were occupied by the G.H.G [Greek head of government] left wide open and a Turkish flag stuck on the door.'

Grace gave the Armenian quarter a wide berth, having heard stories of atrocities, and she thought it imprudent to remain outside for too long. After having secured some provisions from the consulate, she returned to the nursing home.

The Armenian doctor, Garabed Hatcherian, also ventured out that Monday morning. He was heartened by the fact that the trams were still running and that women were out and about, 'which inspires some kind of hope to our troubled souls'. An eternal optimist, Hatcherian believed that the worst of the ordeal was now over.

Yet signs of the previous night's violence were everywhere in evidence. In the marketplace, he noticed a twelve-year-old girl with terrible bruises on her head. When he enquired as to how she had acquired her injuries, he was informed that she had been beaten and raped by Turkish soldiers during the night.

Hatcherian, still wearing his Turkish military medals, found himself being treated with uncustomary respect. When he entered the butcher's shop, he was addressed as 'Bey effendi', offered a chair and told to wait while the butcher fetched better meat. As he did so, he looked out of the window and noted that the street was strewn with official papers from the former Greek headquarters. All the filing cabinets there had been broken open and their contents thrown out of the windows.

George Horton spent much of Monday morning collating all the intelligence reports that he was receiving from different areas of the city. He had no reason to mistrust them. Most were from people he knew personally – men and women who worked for American charitable institutions 'whose duties took them into the interior of the town [and who] reported an increasing number of dead and dying in the streets'.

When he finally ventured outside to see for himself what was taking place, he was shocked by the scenes that greeted him. 'I saw a number of miserable refugees with their children, bundles and sick, being herded toward the quay . . . One grey-haired old woman was stumbling along behind, so weak that she could not keep up, and a Turkish soldier was prodding her in the back with the butt of his musket. At last, he struck her such a violent blow between the shoulder-blades that she fell sprawling upon her face on the stony street.'

Horton was under strict instructions from Admiral Mark Bristol that no American official should be seen to be helping the Greek or Armenian communities. Yet many Americans living in the city were no longer prepared to turn a blind eye to the terrible events that they were witnessing. Horton encouraged them in their humanitarian work, proud that his fellow compatriots were so courageous in offering shelter to the wounded and needy.

'There was not one who showed the least indication of fear or nervousness under the most trying circumstances,' he would later write.

Not one who flinched or wobbled for an instant throughout a situation which had scarcely a parallel in the history of the world for hideousness and danger. They endured fatigue

279

almost beyond human endurance that they might do all in their power to save their charges and give comfort and courage to the frightened hunted creatures who had thrown themselves on their protection.

Among the hunted were the Berberians – a family with three children who lived in the heart of the Armenian quarter. Mr Berberian owned a barber's shop in the suburb of Karatash and had headed there on the previous Friday in order to protect his business. He did not return on the Saturday or Sunday; indeed, he was never seen again. He was almost certainly killed in the massacre at Karatash that took place on Monday night. British officers on the *Iron Duke* watched it through their field glasses.

By Monday morning, Mrs Berberian was desperately anxious about her husband and increasingly fearful for the safety of the rest of her family. All night long, her sleep had been punctuated by the sound of screams and gunshots. Many years later, Rose Berberian – then just sixteen years old – recalled Turkish soldiers in the streets outside taunting all those who had remained in their houses. 'Come out!' they would shout. 'Why are you hiding like mice? Come out or we will come in and kill you!'

Two doors away from the Berberians lived a wealthy Armenian merchant named Mr Aram, who had provided Kemal's army with much needed supplies and equipment. In return, he had been given an official letter, requesting that he and his family should be left unmolested in the event of trouble. Knowing this, Mrs Berberian was therefore delighted when Mr Aram offered to shelter the Berberians over the next few days. The two families spent a tense Monday morning together in the Arams' salon, listening to gangs of Turkish soldiers forcing their way into nearby houses and looting anything of value.

'We were frightened,' recalled Rose, 'but Mr Aram kept waving his letter and telling us to relax. He was a fat man, normally jolly and easygoing, but he was perspiring and pacing the floor and fingering his letter. He couldn't sit still. Once, he was on the verge of running outside and offering it to a Turkish officer supervising a gang of looters across the street.'

After lunch the young women tried to get some rest in an upstairs room but their repose was brutally cut short by the stampede of feet on the stairs. Mr Aram had finally lost his nerve, opened the front door to his house and proffered his precious letter to a Turkish sentry. The soldier snatched it, scrunched it into a ball and — after throwing it in the gutter — forcibly entered the property, followed by three comrades-in-arms. After a cursory inspection of the ground floor, they went upstairs to the room where the women were resting.

Young Rose presented a most enticing prize for the soldiers and they lunged at her, but she was too quick for them. She ran out through the french doors and onto the terrace, hoping to scale the wall and jump down into the adjoining garden. 'Lift my feet, my feet,' she screamed to Mr Aram's fourteen-year-old daughter, a burly girl who was far taller than Rose. With help, Rose managed to scale the wall and throw herself over into the neighbouring garden. As she did so, she heard Mr Aram's daughter scream as the soldiers grabbed her and pulled her away.

Rose was in a blind panic, yet she kept her head. She noticed that the terrace doors to the adjoining house were open and thought this a good sign, indicating that the house had already been sacked and looted. Making her way down into the concealed cellar, she hid there for the rest of the day.

'I had the feeling that I was the only Armenian alive on the street,' she later recollected, 'that soon I would be the only one in the entire city.'

It would be nightfall before she was to discover what had happened to the rest of her family.

★   ★   ★

While the Armenian quarter was systematically being ransacked, Alexander MacLachlan found himself caught up in a most desperate predicament in Paradise. He had returned to the American International College after his meeting with General Noureddin, arriving shortly after noon. He was hoping to snatch a few minutes' rest after lunch, but was disturbed by news that one of the settlement houses was being ransacked by Turkish soldiers. Furious about this intrusion on American property, he asked Sergeant Crocker and a few others to accompany him to the far side of the campus in order to scare away the looters.

They drove over in one of the college cars and parked some one hundred yards from the house. As they walked towards the building, they saw that all the windows had been smashed and that there were Turkish irregulars moving around inside.

'I shouted in Turkish, "What are you doing here, this is an American house; this is American property! Get out of here!"' The Turks immediately raised their rifles and pointed them at MacLachlan.

MacLachlan shouted a warning to Sergeant Crocker and his men, who had fanned out in front of the house, but it was too late. The irregulars emerged from the building in considerable force; Crocker, realising that he was dangerously outnumbered, decided to hold fire. 'He took his revolver from his holster and threw it on the ground before him, holding out his empty hand as a sign that we do not wish to fight,' wrote MacLachlan.

In the intervening stand-off, the American troops were able to retire to a distance of fifty yards. MacLachlan and Crocker, however, were not given the chance to escape. Unarmed and defenceless, they were at the mercy of the *chettes*. 'One man . . . came up to me and said, "Give me that watch,"' wrote MacLachlan. 'I started to give it to him but he snatched it from

282

my hand and tore it loose from my coat.' He then helped himself to all of MacLachlan's money before taking the coat itself.

'By this time, I was almost completely surrounded by the Turks and then I noticed that two men about twelve feet distant were levelling their rifles to shoot me.' At this critical moment, a Turkish college student arrived on the scene and pleaded with the irregulars not to fire.

In the pause that followed, MacLachlan displayed a bravado that bordered on foolhardiness. 'This building belongs to the American college over there,' he shouted, 'and I am the head of that college.' He warned the Turks not to shoot him, informing them that it would have serious consequences.

As he parleyed, the looters relived MacLachlan of yet more clothing and continued to harass him. They stole his shoes and stockings '[and] knocked me down three times with the blows of their rifles'.

Sergeant Crocker grasped that the soldiers were preparing to kill MacLachlan. One of the Turks had fitted a bayonet to his rifle and was moving menacingly towards the American principal. 'I jumped forwards,' wrote MacLachlan, 'and caught it [the rifle] with both hands.' As the soldier reeled backwards, the bayonet detached itself and clattered to the ground.

MacLachlan was now deprived of his last possessions – a gold ring and his trousers – before being severely beaten with the soldiers' rifles. He was still being assaulted when a Turkish officer rode up and, disgusted by the lack of discipline among the irregulars, ordered them to stop.

'When he saw that they obeyed him,' wrote MacLachlan, 'he came forward and pulled my arm over the horse's neck so that I could support myself, for I was completely exhausted.'

The arrival of the officer in full military uniform had an extraordinary effect on the *chettes*. They melted away, enabling the American soldiers to come to the rescue of MacLachlan and Crocker. The two men were carried back to the American

International College, where their wounds were dressed by the college doctor. Both men knew they had had an extremely lucky escape.

As the afternoon wore on, the owners of the city's smaller bars and brasseries began to close their doors, although the larger establishments remained open – among them the Grand Hotel Kraemer Palace. At some point that afternoon, the hotel found itself receiving a most distinguished guest. Mustafa Kemal entered the foyer and asked for a table. No one recognised him at first and he was told that the bars and restaurants were full. But when hotel staff were informed of the identity of their guest, a table was quickly made available. Kemal ordered a raki – a Turkish liquor – and asked the staff: 'Did King Constantine ever come here to drink a glass of raki?' When he was informed that the Greek king had never set foot in the hotel, he replied: 'In that case, why did he bother to take Izmir [the Turkish name for Smyrna]?'

Although the Grand Hotel Kraemer Palace continued to do business for the rest of the day, all of the other establishments now decided to close. Shutters were securely fastened and all external doors double-locked. The wide boulevards – which had hitherto remained lively – suddenly emptied of people. But for many of the refugees there was nowhere to hide. The quayside, courtyards and public gardens remained crowded with displaced people.

By mid-afternoon, discipline had completely broken down in Kemal's regular army and commanders found themselves with little or no authority over men brutalised by years of war. Some of the troops – their passions fuelled by alcohol – were committing atrocities in full public view. British mariners stationed aboard the warships in the bay were witness to many shocking events on that Monday afternoon. Charles Howes was monitoring the violence through his field glasses and was sickened by what was taking place just a few hundred yards from his ship. 'Two young women were seized by the Turks and, after being raped, their breasts were cut off and they were laid in the roadway outside the Oriental Works – a British business house where our naval force was headquartered and had its billet.'

Other corpses were thrown into the sea, whence they were carried by the current towards the British fleet. One seaman serving on the HMS *Serapis* recalled a dead body, floating in an upright position, repeatedly banging against the side of the ship. '[It was] tied in a sack, which was evidently weighted at the bottom.' The captain ordered the corpse to be properly weighted, at which point it sank.

At four o'clock, a small group of senior American officials managed to secure an audience with General Noureddin, yet found him in no mood to discuss the deteriorating situation. Indeed, the good humour he had displayed towards MacLachlan had been replaced by an obstinate unwillingness to listen.

Among those present at the meeting was Major Claflin Davis of the American Red Cross. He pressed upon the Turkish general the absolute necessity of restoring order and helping the refugees return to their homes in the interior. Only this course of action, he said, could prevent a humanitarian disaster on a scale of which the world had never yet witnessed. There were by now several thousand refugees camped out on the quayside and at the mercy of the ill-disciplined Turkish troops. Elsewhere in the city, every public space thronged with hungry fugitives. Davis was convinced that the situation would deteriorate still further, as hundreds of thousands more people were reported as being en route to Smyrna.

General Noureddin was irked by Major Davis's comments. 'Take them away,' he interjected. 'Bring ships and take them out of the country. That is the only solution.'

Davis left the meeting with little doubt that a human tragedy of gigantic proportions was now inevitable. In a memo to

Admiral Bristol, he warned that Noureddin had refused to guarantee the safety of a single refugee. '[I] believe this is a final decision [of the] Nationalist Government as [a] solution of [the] race problem,' he wrote.

As dusk fell over Smyrna, George Horton was taken aboard the USS *Litchfield* in order to spend the hours of darkness in safety. The ship's commander had watched the unrest move ever closer to the European quarter of the city and was no longer prepared to take any chances. He did not want Horton to become one of the Turkish army's victims.

As Horton tried to relax in the ship's wardroom, he listened to the two American journalists – Constantine Brown and John Clayton – reliving the terrible events they had witnessed that day. One of the men read aloud the page he had just typed before emitting a long sigh and tearing the sheet out of the machine. 'I can't send this stuff,' he said to his colleague. 'It'll queer me at Constantinople.'

The men exchanged notes before agreeing that Admiral Bristol would be furious if he read such stories. He had made it absolutely clear that he wanted the world to be kept in ignorance about any Turkish atrocities that might take place in Smyrna, and Brown and Clayton had promised to protect American interests as a condition of their passage to the city. They put away their notebooks and decided instead 'to get busy on Greek atrocities'.

Horton was horrified by what he was hearing. 'It struck me as curious,' he later wrote, 'that men in the presence of one of the most spectacular dramas of history should think it their duty to hurry away in order to find something that would offset it . . . I don't know what the game is, nor who is back of it.'

The stories that the two journalists filed that evening were at shocking variance with every other eyewitness account of that day. 'The discipline and order of the Turkish troops have been excellent,' wrote Clayton in a report that would be published in the *Daily Telegraph*. 'When one considers they have just marched through a country laid waste by the Greek army, with thousands of Moslems slain, this is nothing short of remarkable.'

In an even more extraordinary phrase, he added: 'The apprehension of fear-ridden Smyrna has turned to amazement. After forty-eight hours of the Turkish occupation, the population has begun to realise there are not going to be any massacres.'

Reverend Charles Dobson had every reason to disagree. Late that Monday night, a group of highly distressed women knocked on the doors of the Anglican church and begged him to follow them down the street. '[They] took me to show me carts in which were the bodies of women and babies and also of young girls who had patently been violated before being killed.'

Later still, another member of the clergy – the Armenian priest, Abraham Hartunian – witnessed an even more sinister development. 'I saw with my own eyes the Turks taking bombs, gunpowder, kerosene and everything necessary to start fires, in wagonfulls here and there through the streets.'

He suspected that the Turkish military was planning to set the city on fire.

Tuesday, 12 September 1922

When Rose Berberian awoke on Tuesday morning, she had to pinch herself to confirm that she was still alive. The previous twelve hours had been the most distressing of her life and she looked back on that black Monday with the feeling that she had had an extraordinarily lucky escape.

She had spent much of the afternoon and evening hiding in the coal cellar of the house that adjoined Mr Aram's property. For hour after hour she had lain there in silence, listening to distant screaming and gunshots. There was no noise coming from next door and all that she could think about was what had happened to her mother, brother and sister. She feared that they had met the same fate as the hundreds of other Armenians who had remained in this quarter of the city.

At some point during the evening, her loneliness had turned to panic and she rashly shouted out her brother's name. There was a long silence before she heard her own name being called back. It was her brother's voice and it came from a nearby building. He too had escaped from the Turkish guards and was now hiding – along with his mother and sister – in the attic of the house on the far side of Mr Aram's. The building had been temporarily abandoned by its Italian owner, who had raised his nation's flag over the building in the hope that this would prevent it from being sacked.

Rose emerged from her hiding place under the cover of darkness and managed to clamber along the vine-covered trellis that bordered the terraces of all three houses. After much exertion, she was pulled in through the window for a tearful reunion with her family.

The Berberians had also passed a tense night in hiding, their fitful sleep troubled by the now-familiar sounds of looting and gunfire. After exchanging stories of what they had seen and heard, Rose and her mother crept down to the cellar of the building in order to draw water from the old handpump. As they made their way back upstairs, the front door of the house suddenly burst open and they found themselves face to face with several Turkish officers. The soldiers had come to make an inspection of the building, accompanied by the Italian owner. They wanted to be absolutely sure that he was not concealing any Armenians.

The Italian immediately protested his innocence and Rose's mother had little option but to admit that they had broken into the building after being driven out of their own home. Rose – a headstrong and outspoken girl – added that they had done so because they had seen Turkish soldiers killing men and violating women.

Her words infuriated one of the officers, who slapped her so hard around the face that Rose began shaking uncontrollably. When one of the men asked her what was wrong with her, she told the man that she was sick. 'I have no shoes, no clothes,' she said. 'Please let me go to my aunt's house – it is just down the street – to get some clothes before you take me to the police.' She did not have an aunt down the street but, quick-thinking as ever, she has an idea of how she might rescue her family.

Her ploy worked, possibly because the Turkish soldiers did not wish to appear too menacing in the company of the Italian man. The officer in charge ordered one of his colleagues to accompany Rose to her aunt's house and then return immediately.

Rose was appalled by the scenes of carnage that greeted her. 'It was the first time I had stepped outside for four days,' she later recalled, 'and when I saw the street, I was more terrified than before. Dead bodies, swollen, lay all about on the stoops and stairs of the houses and across the narrow streets. I had to step over them. If I had an aunt down the street, she would surely have been killed by now; the officer knew that. If I walk into a building, I thought, this soldier will probably kill me.'

Rose continued down the street, aware that her one hope of salvation lay at the distant junction. The walled compound of the American Collegiate Institute bordered the eastern edge of the Armenian quarter. If Rose could attract the attention of someone inside, she might yet be able to save herself and her family.

She approached the main gate – still accompanied by the Turkish officer – but saw that it was locked. She then rang the bell next to the side gate; when an American marine poked his head through an open window she shouted in English, 'I'm a student here. Please let me in – quickly.' The soldier retorted that he needed permission from Miss Mills, the acting head, and disappeared from view. Rose was about to give up hope when the gate suddenly opened and Miss Mills appeared in person.

'Oh, Miss Mills,' said Rose. 'This man behind me . . . he is going to kill me. Please let me in.' She quickly explained how her family were in a house down the street, adding that the Turks were certain to kill them and begging that an American sailor be sent to rescue them.

Only now did the Turkish officer realise that he had been duped by the young Armenian girl in his charge. He also knew that he was powerless to intervene. He could not lead Rose away, for he was being watched by American marines, yet neither did he wish to return to his commanding officer empty-handed. While he considered his options, the forthright Miss Mills took control of the situation. She despatched an American marine to the house where the Berberians were being held and told him to bring them back to the relative safety of the American Collegiate Institute.

Rose's sharp wits had saved her family from almost certain death. For the time being, the Berberians were safe.

The Berberians were not alone in finding themselves homeless and dependent on others. By mid-morning on Tuesday, Smyrna was housing as many as 150,000 refugees – most of them from the war-torn countryside around the city. The last of the Greek evacuation ships had set sail three days earlier. Now, flight from Smyrna was impossible for all except foreign nationals. The 500,000 Greeks and Armenians left behind had fallen into a dangerous trap.

What made a difficult situation even worse was the fact that refugees continued to arrive in their tens of thousands. There was no longer anywhere for them to find shelter; they had to camp out in the streets and pray that they would not become victims to the lawless elements of the Turkish army.

'Pitiable objects,' wrote the American officer, Lieutenant Commander Knauss, in his daily report. A guard of the American sentry headquarters, he was increasingly concerned by the ever-growing numbers of refugees. 'For two days they have been huddled in small heaps,' he wrote, 'never stirring except when one of their number approaches with a guard for fresh water. If the Turks come through, their faces express more than fear. They are terror-stricken and as I feared a stampede would ensue in case of panic, I made all preparations for running down the iron screen promptly.'

Their sense of panic was fully justified; Knauss watched in disbelief as a band of Turkish soldiers grabbed a man and dragged him away. 'Today, I have seen during my rounds over a hundred dead and four people killed in cold blood.'

If the situation was tense at US headquarters, it was even more critical at the YWCA. More than 500 women and children had already sought refuge there and many more were asking for asylum. 'They were jammed in there so tight there wasn't an inch to move,' recalled Melvin Johnson, an American sentry. 'But then more of 'em would push up against the doors – crying – and, well, we weren't supposed to but we'd let them in.' At some point that morning, Johnson and a colleague stepped outside in the hope of finding a bakery. 'That's when we saw the victims. They were lying all over in the sun, swelling up with the heat. Two of 'em was women. We couldn't take but one look.'

Refugees sought shelter wherever there was an American, Italian or French flag, aware that these three nations were favoured by Kemal's Turkish army. Thousands of Greeks and Armenians had pitched camp outside the American consulate, while the American International College and American Collegiate Institute were other points of refuge. By midday on Tuesday, at least 1,500 people were being housed in the latter institution. Eight babies had been born in the previous two days and an increasing number of inmates were falling sick. All were terrified that the Turkish army would force the gates and take them prisoner.

'This day, there was a rumour that there would be an attack upon the College,' wrote the Armenian priest, Abraham Hartunian. 'This night, there was another, that in a little while Turkish officials would enter the building and take all the men away for deportation.'

George Ward Price had spent the morning trying to secure an interview with Mustafa Kemal. His persistence eventually paid off; Kemal agreed to meet him and talk about his terms for a lasting peace. 'He talked for half an hour in fluent French,' wrote Ward Price, 'quickly, but with emphasis. One gold medal on his khaki tunic was the only decoration he wore.' Ward Price asked him whether the war against the Greeks was now over. 'There is nothing to fight about any more,' responded Kemal, 'and I earnestly desire peace. I did not want to launch this last offensive but there was no other way of persuading the Greeks to evacuate Asia Minor.' When Ward Price pressed Kemal on his territorial demands, he was told that the nationalists claimed 'all the areas of our country that are principally populated by the Turkish race'. This included all of Asia Minor, parts of Thrace and Constantinople.

This latter demand was of special interest to Ward Price, since there were still some 7,000 British troops in control of the capital. Ward Price asked Kemal what he would do if the British refused to leave. Kemal did not mince his words. 'We must have our capital and if the Western Powers will not hand it over, I shall be obliged to march on Constantinople. I would rather obtain possession by negotiation, though, naturally, I cannot wait indefinitely.'

Ward Price left the interview with the impression that Kemal was fully in command of the situation. The *Daily Mail* ran the interview in full and gave its support to Kemal, arguing that Britain would be wrong to oppose the nationalist army.

Kemal himself was increasingly confident that he could wrest control of Constantinople by a mixture of diplomacy and muscle. That afternoon, he ordered some of his troops to march northwards towards the neutral zone that surrounded the capital and was patrolled by British forces. Kemal wanted to call their bluff and see whether Lloyd George's government was prepared to fight his army.

Ward Price reported Kemal's bellicose comments to Sir Harry Lamb. Alarmed by what he heard, he too arranged a meeting with Kemal in order to obtain clarification. 'Technically, Turkey is still at war with Great Britain,' was Kemal's response. 'I should be entitled to intern all British subject in Smyrna, but I am not going to do so.'

When the admiral of the British fleet, Sir Osmond de Beauvoir Brock, learned this, he decided to send his chief of staff ashore in order to further quiz Kemal as to his intentions, although the British still refused to believe that Kemal represented a serious threat. Brock asked his colleague whether he intended to wear a sword for the meeting. 'A sword for that fellow?' replied the impulsive chief of staff. 'I should think not. I shall carry a walking stick.'

Six miles away in Bournabat, Hortense Wood faced a long and lonely Tuesday afternoon. Her nephew, Fernand, had headed back to Smyrna, leaving her amidst charred and smouldering ruins. She was entirely alone and completely cut off from the outside world. 'A cordon of secrecy is maintained all around Bournabat,' she wrote in her diary that morning. 'No trains run, no telegrams can be sent to town. We are quite isolated.'

Charlton Whittall and his family felt no less isolated. They had spent the previous two nights hiding in the flood drain, listening to the sounds of gunfire and looting. At one point they were joined by a Greek family, from whom they learned that more than 2,000 Greeks from Bournabat had been killed by the Turkish army.

The family's young child cried for much of the morning, leading Charlton to decide that it was no longer safe to remain in their hiding place. He felt that this was the moment for the family to make their escape. When they at last crept out, crawling along on hands and knees through the shrubbery at the bottom of Herbert Octavius's garden, they could see irregular soldiers ransacking the Big House. 'The Whittall family house [was] all illuminated,' recalled Willem, 'with Turks moving about and one, dead drunk, trying to dance with a stuffed bear made up as a hat stand.'

Charlton and his family eventually made their way to Smyrna and were given refuge aboard the *King George V*.

The rest of the extended Whittall and Giraud families were trying to make sense of everything that had happened. Herbert Octavius and his children were by now safely aboard a British warship in the bay of Smyrna, but many of his brothers and sisters were still living at Edmund Giraud's summer house on Long Island. Edmund's wife, Ruth, was doing her utmost to cater for everyone during her husband's temporary absence in England, although supplies were running short. When the larder was finally empty, the various uncles, aunts and cousins climbed onto the *Helen May* and headed back to Smyrna, where they took shelter with friends who had elected to remain in the city.

It was a frightening time for the youngsters. 'I wish I could say that I felt courageous at this point,' recalled Ruth's daughter, Mary. 'But the truth is, I was terrified . . . the uncles would drop in of an evening to post Mother with all the scenes of horror that they had witnessed, with no concern for little ears that were taking it all in. I know that I used to go to bed and shake with fright till Mother joined me in the double bed.'

Ruth Giraud repeatedly turned down the offer of sanctuary aboard one of the British warships in the bay, determined to remain in Smyrna, come what may. Yet Tuesday was a turning point for many who had vowed to stay behind. It was on this day that people realised the violence was no longer sporadic, nor was it going to die down. Mustafa Kemal's army – which had entered the city with such discipline – was completely out of control.

Grace Williamson had long been an enthusiastic supporter of the Turks, but when she came to write her diary that Tuesday afternoon her sympathies were on the turn. 'This day, I think, has been the worst,' she wrote. 'All day there has been a black cloud over us . . . you have read of atrocities . . . They are too bad to [be] spoken of and they are taking place all around. The Turk's vengeance has been smouldering for three years and he is having his fling now. It seems they have spared very few houses in Bournabat.'

Grace began to be concerned for her own safety, although she resolutely refused to leave Smyrna. 'Everyone advises us to clear,' she wrote. 'But I, at least, must stop behind. I gave my word to the staff that I would stick by them whatever happens.' Although she no longer dared to venture outside, she did clamber onto the roof of the English Nursing Home in order to survey the city. '[Smyrna] looks dreadful,' she wrote. 'No end of dead and rubbish all together.'

This was the understatement of the day. When the Reverend Charles Dobson made a tour of the city that Tuesday afternoon, he was witness to a city that had been plunged into anarchy. 'There was desultory shooting, looting and rape all over the place,' he wrote. He saw corpses lying in doorways and alleys in every district, although the carnage was at its worst in the Armenian quarter. 'I was particularly struck with one group consisting of women and babies; and a young girl, almost nude, shot through the breast and with clotted blood on her thighs and genital organs that spoke only too clearly of her fate before death.'

Dobson showed remarkable courage in the face of danger, making his way slowly through the city in order to compile a report on the atrocities. 'There was constantly shooting in the back streets, followed by screams and panic-stricken running,' he wrote. 'The Turks were openly looting everywhere. One man was shot through both thighs, one of which was fractured, his screams were unheeded by the terror-stricken people.'

George Horton also compiled a report about the savagery that afternoon. 'The loot was now being driven out of the bazaars and the Armenian quarter by the cartload,' he wrote, 'and cartloads of corpses, as of beef or sheep, were being sent into the country.' What made these scenes so incongruous was the fact that tens of thousands of refugees were still camping out on the streets, alongside cadavers, dead horses and broken furniture.

In the midst of all the carnage, a most eccentric spectacle unfolded that afternoon on the quayside of Smyrna. A small group of British mariners, armed with antiquated swords and cutlasses, could be seen landing at the northern end of the quay. At their head was an officer in full dress uniform, including frock coat and cocked hat.

The officer in question was Duncan Wallace, formerly of the Royal Navy and a long-term inhabitant of Smyrna. He had been summoned to service aboard the *Iron Duke* by Admiral Brock, who realised that Wallace had local knowledge that might prove invaluable.

Wallace informed the admiral of everything he had seen and confided his fears for his elderly aunt, Alithea Whittall, who refused to leave the nursing home that she owned. He also expressed his concern for the safety of his Greek servants, who had chosen to remain in the family's summer house, and asked whether he might be permitted to go ashore and rescue them.

Brock was reluctant to spare any senior officers or weapons, but he allowed Wallace to gather a small landing party and head to the port. Wallace knew that he could not hope to fight any Turks who might impede his way so he decided to make a psychological impact by dressing in the most extravagant uniform he could find. According to Wallace's son, Ian, 'this improbable force, with my father at their head, stepped onto the quay and marched through the burning town full of drunken Turkish soldiery and looters.'

Wallace reached his summer house only to find that all of the family's maids had been butchered. The situation was less grim at the nursing home, where Alithea Whittall was busily caring for dozens of sick and wounded. Wallace informed her of the dangers of remaining in Smyrna and managed to talk her into leaving. Alithea's only condition was that she could take her patients with her. 'It was now getting dark,' wrote Ian Wallace, 'and the party . . . endeavouring to convey an impression of official importance and confidence to the expedition, and with Alithea Whittall shepherding her patients behind him, mercifully reached the British ships without being molested.'

The 5,000 Armenians still sheltering inside the prelacy were awaiting their fate in absolute silence. Ever since the grenade attack forty-eight hours earlier, there had been an expectation that the Turkish soldiers would soon return. 'People [were] huddled together waiting for hostilities to start anew . . .' wrote Hovakim Uregian, who was still inside the building. 'Food was distributed – thank God we seemed to have plenty of that – and everybody had a good ration. Few, however, had the appetite to eat much during those days of terror and suspense.'

By Tuesday afternoon, there was growing consent among those taking shelter there that it was time to negotiate with the Turkish military. Conditions were becoming increasingly unsanitary and few people had managed to sleep. They were still discussing a plan of action when a Catholic priest named Don Scaliarini visited the prelacy, announcing that he had been in talks with the Turkish military and had secured permission to guide everyone to the quayside under the protection of twelve French sailors. The only conditions attached to the evacuation was that all weapons must be left behind and that every evacuee would be subject to an inspection as he or she left the building.

Don Scaliarini's initiative had been prompted by his desire to help fellow Christians; he felt sure that they would all be massacred if they remained in the prelacy. His offer was put to the vote and the overwhelming majority of Armenians decided to chance their luck on the quayside. Uregian thought they were making a terrible mistake and feared for everyone's safety once they were outside its walls.

The gates to the prelacy were soon opened and the refugees began filing out. As they left the building, a group of Turkish soldiers frisked and searched them. 'At first they pretended to look for arms,' wrote Uregian, 'but if they found a watch or some other valuable object, they would try to pocket it while the overseeing French sailor was looking in some other direction.'

The situation deteriorated when the Turkish soldiers were joined by a group of irregulars, who saw the evacuation as an opportunity to fleece the refugees of everything of value. 'As the crowed in the Prelacy was getting less and less, the Turks were getting greedier, tougher and more violent and unreasonable,' observed Uregian. 'Even the shoes were now considered "potentially offensive weapons" and the last few to come out, I learned from eyewitnesses, were allowed through with barely their pants and shirt on.'

Once the refugees were assembled outside the building, Don Scaliarini attempted to lead them down to the quayside, but it quickly became apparent that the Armenians – having been relieved of their arms – were now considered fair game by the Turkish irregulars loitering in the streets. 'On every corner and on every turn, armed Turks, looking like a pack of wolves, would start firing and menacing, asking for valuables and young girls.'

Don Scaliarini did his best to protect the refugees. 'The poor *mon père* was running all around, reproaching the Turks and exposing himself to real danger in defence of a crowd who were not even his flock.'

Although a fortunate few managed to seek refuge in the precincts of the French and Italian consulates, which flanked the quayside, the vast majority had little option but to settle themselves on the cobbled ground, wherever there was space.

'Any foreign flag or sign was a valuable symbol to hold above a group of people to discourage attacks by the continually harassing and marauding Turks.'

Uregian noted that by the time dusk descended on that Tuesday, 'thousands of Christians were huddled against the walls of the quay, looking for boats to carry them to some foreign ship out in the bay.' Their search was in vain. The local fishing skiffs had long since headed to the nearby Greek islands and the foreign vessels were still under strict orders not to take off any Greeks or Armenians.

Uregian had no intention of remaining with his compatriots on the quayside. He felt it would be safer to find a hiding place in the city – either in an abandoned building or one of the numerous enclosed courtyards. He discarded his hat, which betrayed him as an Armenian, and acquired a red fez, complete with a badge displaying Kemal's photograph. 'I still failed to look like a Turk, because the bone structure of my face was so very far from resembling the Mongoloid Turkish facial structure.' With head bowed, he hurried off to the inner districts of the city.

'I started to walk with a confident pace,' he wrote, 'determined to survive the night, no matter what happened.' He eventually came across a crowd of refugees who were pouring into a courtyard. 'There were old buildings all around and all the people were Greek. I mixed with them and nobody seemed to mind so I decided to spend the night in that courtyard.'

Only now did he realise that he had not eaten or drunk anything all day, but there was no food to be found and Uregian had to endure acute hunger and thirst. He snatched a few hours' rest, reliving the terrible events of the last few days. Although haunted by what he had seen, he knew that his ordeals were shared by many others.

'Thousands of people went through the same experiences . . .' he wrote. 'Night after night, people had to huddle together under walls or next to their bags, screaming whenever the Turks approached and struggling in vain when some girl was kidnapped. Many a father and mother met their death trying to defend the honour of their daughter.'

As the refugees tried to sleep, few noticed that the breeze had freshened and stiffened. It was no longer blowing off the sea, as it had been ever since the arrival of the Turkish army. By the early hours of Wednesday morning, it was blowing from the land. If a fire was to be started now, the Greek, Armenian and European areas of Smyrna would be in grave danger.

Wednesday, 13 September 1922

Wednesday dawned clear and beautiful; it was to be another glorious day. Yet the autumn sunshine did little to mask the reality of the situation inside Smyrna. Mustafa Kemal's victorious army was out of control and the city's population – which had now swelled to 700,000 or more – was in imminent peril.

Sir Harry Lamb had seen enough bloodshed on the previous evening to convince him that it was no longer safe for any British nationals to remain in the city. Most had already heeded his advice and accepted sanctuary aboard one of the British ships in the bay. Nevertheless, 800 or more had stubbornly refused to leave and their lives were now at risk.

Sir Harry took his breakfast at the consulate, as was his custom, and then ventured outside in order to visit the British maternity hospital. He wanted to inform the nurses of his decision and he also hoped to meet the Reverend Charles Dobson. Lamb needed the vicar's help in tracking down all the remaining British nationals in the city.

Dobson readily offered his services. He had already shown remarkable courage over the previous three days, roaming the streets in his efforts to care for the wounded and homeless. Now, he once again took his life into his hands and set out to visit all the addresses where he knew British nationals to be staying.

'The narrower streets were choked by running masses of people carrying their children in their arms,' he later recalled. 'In one of the streets, a man was dragging himself across the road on his elbows. He was shot through both thighs, one of which was fractured. The panic was so great that nobody answered his appeals.'

Dobson picked his way through the streets, methodically bringing news of the impending evacuation to all the British nationals he could find. The remaining members of the Whittall family, the Girauds, the Wood family, the Patersons and Hadkinsons – all were informed that lighters would be despatched from the British battleships later that afternoon to take them to safety. All who wanted to leave would be collected from the quayside; it was their last chance to get out of Smyrna.

To this day, Alfred Simes remembers those last few hours in the city. 'The consulate gave every British family a Union Jack to hang outside their home,' he said. 'It was supposed to offer some sort of protection against attack.' Alfred also recalls his mother casting her gaze across the bay to the waiting battleships. 'There were so many of them in the harbour . . . as a small boy I remember being particularly impressed by the huge turrets. I'd never seen ships like the ones gathered in the bay.' As he watched the vessels from the roof of the family home, his mother hastily gathered together a few belongings. 'We were told to bring jewellery and hand luggage. Everything else was to be left behind.'

The Brussalis family were also preparing their flight. 'My father was well connected with the French community in Smyrna,' recalls Petros. 'He was well liked by the Catholic sisters who ran my school and through them he began making arrangements for us to be transferred to a French battleship.' Petros's parents spent much of Wednesday locking away their valuables; they were to leave the city that night.

Most European nationals in Smyrna – including the entire

Levantine community – realised that it was time to get out while they still had the chance. But in Bournabat, Hortense Wood still refused to countenance the idea of abandoning her home. She was doggedly determined to protect her villa against any Turkish irregulars who dared to come near.

'We have been very anxious [about] Hortense,' wrote one of her sisters in a letter that Wednesday afternoon. She need not have worried; Hortense was more than capable of looking after herself, although her decision to remain in her own home was to have unexpected consequences over the days that followed.

The distressing scenes witnessed by the Reverend Dobson that morning were nothing to the carnage that had been seen by members of the Smyrna fire brigade. The firemen were a mixed company of Greeks and Turks whose station was partly financed by the London insurance firms. These firms had underwritten many of the most prestigious properties in Smyrna, so it was in their interests to protect these properties against fire.

The firemen had already answered several calls during the early hours of Wednesday morning. Now, at 10.30 a.m., a new blaze was reported on Suyane Street, in the Armenian quarter. One of those sent to tackle the flames was Sergeant Tchorbadjis, an old hand in the Smyrna brigade and someone who had seen many harrowing scenes during his long years as a fireman. But nothing prepared him for the horrors that were to greet him that Wednesday morning.

'In all the houses I went into, I saw dead bodies,' he said. 'In one house, I followed a trail of blood that led me to a cupboard. My curiosity forced me to open this cupboard – and my hair stood on end. Inside was the naked body of a girl with her breasts cut off . . .'

When he stepped back outside, Sergeant Tchorbadjis found the streets awash with Turkish military. 'There were plenty of armed soldiers going about. One of them went in where there was an Armenian family hiding and massacred the lot. When he came out, his scimitar was dripping with blood. He cleaned it on his boots and leggings.'

Reports of the ever-worsening violence were by now flooding into the American consulate, where George Horton was keeping a careful note of each new wave of attacks. The missionaries at the American Murray Institute were growing increasingly concerned for their safety, even though they had several marines guarding the building. 'The looting and murder went on steadily under our eyes,' wrote one. 'Fierce chetas [irregulars] were breaking in doors of houses, shooting the poor cowering inhabitants, looting, etc.'

Although Horton was still under strict orders from Admiral Bristol not to evacuate American citizens, by noon on Wednesday he knew that he could no longer obey. American lives were now at risk and he had little option but to follow Sir Harry Lamb's lead. He informed all American nationals that they were to start assembling at the main theatre on Smyrna's quayside. At some point that afternoon, everyone was to be evacuated.

At the same time that George Horton committed himself to evacuating the American population of Smyrna, a teacher named Krikor Baghdjian – who was hiding on the roof of the Armenian Club on Rechidie Street – was witness to a most alarming sight. At the far end of the street, a band of troops was busily unloading what appeared to be large barrels of petroleum. 'I did not see their content,' he wrote, 'but judging by their colour and shape, they were identical to barrels of the Petroleum Company of Smyrna. Each barrel was guarded by two or three Turkish soldiers and they were being carted all along Rechidie Street towards the Armenian Prelacy. I felt a chill on my spine as I realised the purpose of all these preparations.'

As he and his friends watched these disturbing events from their rooftop hideaway, they saw more and more barrels being wheeled into the Armenian quarter. 'Each barrel was placed 200m apart, [and] when all the barrels were in position . . . I heard what I can only describe as "sounds of rain falling on a roof."' The Turkish soldiers were spraying the buildings with petrol.

'We felt drops falling on us,' wrote Krikor, '[and] soldiers in the street below threw up the walls a liquid with buckets. As soon as I got the smell of this liquid from my wet clothes, I had no doubt it was petroleum.'

Flames were spotted shortly afterwards. One of the first people to notice the outbreak of fire was Miss Minnie Mills, the director of the American Collegiate Institute for Girls. She had just finished her lunch when she noticed that one of the neighbouring buildings was burning. She stood up to have a closer look and was shocked by what she witnessed. 'I saw with my own eyes a Turkish officer enter a house with small tins of petroleum or benzine and in a few minutes the house was in flames.'

She was not the only one at the institute to see the outbreak of fire. 'Our teachers and girls saw Turks in regular soldiers' uniforms and in several cases in officers' uniforms, using long sticks with rags at the end which were dipped in a can of liquid and carried into houses which were soon burning.'

Just minutes after Miss Mills had made these observations, Mrs King Birge – the wife of an American missionary – noticed a thin column of smoke rising from the Armenian quarter. 'I went up into the tower of the American College of Paradise and with a pair of field glasses could plainly see Turkish soldiers setting fire to houses.'

Numerous reliable witnesses would later testify to the role of Kemal's troops in starting the fire. Claflin Davis of the American Red Cross saw Turks sprinkling flammable liquid along a street that lay in the path of the fire. Monsieur Joubert, director of the Crédit Foncier Bank in Smyrna, plucked up the courage to ask a band of Turkish soldiers what they were doing. 'They replied impassively that they were under orders to blow up and burn all the houses of the area.' Another senior French businessman – whose business interests required him to testify on condition of anonymity – said that all the shops of Hadji Stamon Street were set alight by soldiers acting under the direction of the former head of Turkish police in Cordelio, a man whose identity he did not reveal but who was known to him personally.

To this day, most Turkish historians persist in claiming that the fire – which was soon to assume terrifying proportions – was an act of sabotage on the part of the Greeks and Armenians. Yet there are scores of impartial accounts that testify to the fact that the Turkish army deliberately set fire to Smyrna. Some of the witnesses were men working for the Smyrna Fire Brigade. They were later called to the Royal Courts of Justice in order to give evidence under oath in a trial brought by the Guardian Assurance Company.

One of them was Sergeant Tchorbadjis, who was on the scene shortly after the first fire broke out. He arrived in Tchoukour Street and made his way onto one of the rooftops in order to get a better idea of the scale of the fire. 'Then I went down into one of the rooms and saw a Turkish soldier well armed. He was setting fire to the interior of a drawer. He looked rather fiercely at me when he saw me but he left. I caught the strong smell of petroleum.'

Sergeant Tchorbadjis's colleague, Emmanuel Katsaros, had a similar experience. He was dousing the Armenian Club with water in an effort to halt the advance of the flames when he saw two Turkish soldiers enter the building with drums of petroleum. He protested when he saw one of them sluicing petrol across the floor.

'On the one hand we are trying to stop the fires and on the other you are setting them,' he said.

'You have your orders,' replied the soldier, 'and we have ours. This is Armenian property. Our orders are to set fire to it.'

Elsewhere, the firemen found themselves unable to fight the flames because their hoses had been cut. There was little they could do but wait for the fire to burn itself out. However, this looked increasingly unlikely for the wind – already strong – was now blowing sharply from the east. The three separate fires spotted by witnesses shortly after noon had, by 1.30 p.m., become one large conflagration that was raging throughout the Armenian quarter. When Garabed Hatcherian climbed onto the roof terrace of the Verkines' house, he thought that the fire looked out of control. 'A huge cloud of smoke is seen rising from the Haynots direction,' he wrote. 'The fire is spreading on two flanks . . . these two flanks are separated and it is evident that the fire has been deliberately set to several places simultaneously.' Hatcherian realised that the blaze would cause even greater human misery, since hundreds of people were being forced onto the streets.

Some of the city's inhabitants left their homes before the fire could cut off their escape routes. The Catholic fathers of the Mechitharist order vacated their monastery and made their way to the French consulate. As they skirted the edge of the Armenian quarter, they saw ample evidence of arson. 'On route, we saw empty drums of petrol and benzine scattered here and there and liquid running down the street,' wrote one of the fathers. 'It was definitely petrol or benzine; we saw Turkish soldiers in an automobile who, with the aid of a pump, were sprinkling all the houses they passed with these flammable liquids.'

By 2 p.m., most of the Armenian quarter was in flames. The churches of Sourp Sdepannos and Aghia Paraskevi, the Armenian hospital and Basmahane station were all reported as being on fire, along with hundreds of houses, cafés and stores.

George Horton had spent much of the morning at the American consulate and had not given much thought to the fire, but shortly after finishing his lunch, he decided to see with his own eyes the extent of the conflagration. 'I went up on the terrace of the consulate to look,' he wrote. 'The spectacle was one of vast dark clouds of smoke arising from a wide area.'

Although Smyrna's streets and boulevards were lined with imposing, stone-built *hôtels particuliers*, they were more flammable than they looked. 'The city had suffered in times past from earthquakes,' wrote Horton, 'and the stone and plaster walls contained a skeleton of wooden beams and timbers to prevent their being easily shaken down. When a wall became very hot from a contiguous fire, these wooden timbers caught inside the plaster and the masonry crumbled.'

The Armenian quarter ought to have been resistant to the flames. Many of the buildings had been rebuilt after a devastating blaze in the late nineteenth century and the streets had been widened to prevent flames leaping from one block to the next. However, such a precaution was of little use in a situation where buildings had been liberally doused with petrol.

As Hatcherian had predicted, the blaze was soon so widespread that many thousands of people had little option but to head to the wide quayside. 'As the conflagration spread and swept on down toward the quay . . .' wrote Horton, 'the people poured in a rapidly increasing flood to the waterfront, old, young, women, children, sick as well. Those who were unable to walk were carried in stretchers, or on the shoulders of relatives.'

Among them was an acquaintance of his – an elderly Greek physician named Doctor Arghyropolos – for whom the stress of the fire was to prove too much. He suffered a heart attack and died shortly after arriving on the quayside.

'The last Miltonic touch was now added to a scene of unparalleled horror and human suffering,' wrote Horton. 'These thousands were crowded on a narrow street between the city and the deep waters of the bay.'

Horton noticed that the stiff wind was sweeping the flames

westwards, towards the European quarter of town. 'Great clouds of smoke were by this time beginning to pour down upon the consulate,' he wrote. 'The crowd in the street before this building, as well as that upon the quay, was now so dense that the commanding officer told me I should not be able to get through.'

Mustafa Kemal had not been seen since the outbreak of the fire. Indeed, he had not appeared in public for almost forty-eight hours. Halide Edib had last seen him on the previous Sunday when she had found him in joyous mood. He had been introduced to a beautiful young girl called Latife – the daughter of a wealthy and well-connected Turkish merchant, Muammer Usakizade.

Latife had been studying law in France, where her family were temporarily residing, but she had returned to Turkey after Kemal's victory at Sakaria and was living in her parents' mansion, chaperoned by her grandmother. She did not hide her affections for Kemal. He told Halide Edib:

'She carried a locket around her neck with my picture in it. She came near me and showing the locket said to me, 'Do you mind?'

'Why should I mind?'

He chuckled delightedly . . . He was already imagining her in love with him.

Edib found Latife to be wistfully beautiful and quietly deter-mined. 'Although she was said to be only twenty-four at the time, she had the quiet manners and the maturer ways of a much older person. Her graceful *salaam* had both dignity and Old World charm.'

She certainly gave every indication of being old beyond her years. 'Although the tight and thin lips indicated an unusual force and will-power, not very feminine, her eyes were most beautiful, grave and lustrous and dominated by intelligence.'

Kemal's advisors were already debating whether she would make him a suitable wife.

The distraction caused by Latife could not disguise the fact that large areas of Smyrna were by now ablaze. Colonel Ismet, Kemal's most successful battlefield commander, was saddened by the extent of the fire. 'We have taken Izmir,' he said. 'But what's the use? The city and half of Anatolia have been reduced to ruins.'

Kemal disagreed. He called it 'a disagreeable incident' and assured Ismet that the damage could be repaired. He had little affection for the old city. When he had first visited Smyrna in 1905, he had been offended by the numbers of Greeks and other Christians living here. 'I saw this beautiful quayside full of members of a race which was our sworn enemy and I concluded that Izmir had slipped away from the hands of its true and noble Turkish inhabitants.' From his point of view, the burning of this infidel city was a small and necessary price to pay for the liberation of his country.

As the fire raged, George Horton's priority was to evacuate the American Collegiate Institute, which was closest to the Armenian quarter, but he was faced with a logistical problem. There were more than 2,000 refugees inside the institute – Greeks and Armenians – who were demanding safe passage to one or another of the American battleships.

Even if this was desirable, it would have been impossible to execute. There were scores of Turkish soldiers and irregulars loitering outside the building and they were most unlikely to allow the refugees to leave. Miss Mills reluctantly agreed to the suggestion that only American nationals should be evacuated – discreetly ushered out of the institute in the company of American marines.

However, this plan of action was to prove an impossible under-taking. The teachers refused to be separated from their wives, children and domestics – most of whom were not American nationals – while the refugees themselves created a stampede at the main gate to the compound. 'I had to use the butt of my gun to keep the people away from the door,' wrote Petty Officer James Webster.

The refugees pleaded to be allowed to leave with the bona fide Americans. The marines were torn between obeying orders and listening to their consciences. In the end, they did both. One group of marines helped the American nationals into a truck and drove them to the waterfront. Another group, consisting of James Webster and six comrades, remained behind in order to escort the refugees to the quayside.

Webster led the way, followed by a large crowd of men, women and children. The Americans were unsure of the quickest route to the waterfront and at every turn their path was blocked by burning buildings or piles of rubble. Their entourage had not gone far when Turkish soldiers began shooting into the crowd. Webster and his men responded by firing their guns into the air.

The gunfire caused absolute panic among the refugees. Women and children screamed as the shots rang out; babies were dropped and trampled underfoot. At one point Anita Chakerian – one of the refugees – stumbled and fell. She was fortunate to be helped to her feet by one of the marines. 'To this day, I still wonder who he was . . .' she later wrote. 'God bless him for saving my life.'

Another of those caught up in the maelstrom was young Rose Berberian, who had left the institute with her mother. They had already been through a terrible ordeal over the previous few days. Now, they had to contend with leaping flames, crum-bling masonry and burning cinders that were raining down from the sky. They followed the American marines until they came to a building that was flying the French tricolour. Rose recognised it as the French consulate and suggested to her mother that they ask for asylum. It was their best hope of saving their lives.

'I was in rags,' she later recalled, 'no shoes, my dress torn, my face and arms black with dirt and dust. I had found two pairs of men's socks – white ones – in the attic of the Italian family and I was wearing these, one pair on top of the other. They were now black too.'

Rose was fortunate to speak good French. She approached one of the French marines posted at the main entrance to the consulate and pleaded with him to give refuge to her and her mother. '*Pour l'amour de Dieu, laissez moi entrer.* I am French. They killed my family. I have no papers, they were destroyed in the fire.'

The marine lifted his arm to let Rose and her mother inside. But at the very moment when they thought they were safe, an alarm bell sounded. It was the order to evacuate. The fire was by now so close to the consulate that everyone was told to leave the building. Rose and her mother found themselves back on the streets, jostling with crowds of refugees.

This time, however, they had the advantage of organised military protection. Everyone inside the consulate was escorted to a building on the quayside, where they were told to line up and present their papers. Rose's turn came soon enough. She informed the consular official of her name and age, and then explained how they had lost all their papers in the fire.

'"You speak French very well," the man said, smiling. "Where did you go to school?" And he handed me the paper authorising our passage to a French battleship.'

Rose was awaiting further instructions when she sighted her sister, from whom she had been separated for several days. After a tearful reunion, the sister explained how she had managed to escape from the Armenian quarter. Their brother had also made it to the quayside and decided to chance his luck by swimming out to one of the battleships in the harbour.

Rose, her mother and sisters were meanwhile rescued by a French lighter and taken to one of the warships in the bay.

The other refugees from the American Collegiate Institute were still battling their way down to the waterfront. James Webster and his fellow marines had taken more than an hour to cover half a mile. In the confusion of gunfire and collapsing buildings they had managed to lose most of the refugees. Of the original 2,000, there were just forty in tow by the time they reached the harbour. One of these was fifteen-year-old Charles Kassabian, who later recalled how he lost his parents during that terrible march. 'So we're running out from the school and I lose them because I'm watching that sailor and when he goes this way, I go this way. And there are thousands – if I say millions, it won't make any difference, because it's that crowded – and the streets are burning all over. Buildings burning. Every place burning. Every place!'

When Charles finally got to the quayside, he pleaded with an American sailor to be taken aboard one of the lighters waiting to evacuate American nationals. '"Brother in America," I say. "Passport". And maybe that makes the difference because he waves his hand. "OK, come on," and all of us run to the boat. So pretty soon we're safe and alive on this big American ship.'

While the marines were helping to evacuate the institute, George Horton was struggling to extricate the last American citizens from Paradise. Anna Birge and a dozen or so others had been picked up from their homes by an American truck, but when they tried to reach the quayside theatre – the point of assembly for American nationals – they found their path blocked by Turkish soldiers. 'I uttered a few English words and tried to look as calm as I thought an American would,' wrote Birge.

'Then they cleared our way ... and we rushed past in safety. Among the many dead bodies, we saw men, women and children shot to death, bodies drawn up in horribly strained postures, with expressions portraying the endurance of excruciating pain.'

Horton was desperately trying to finish the mountain of paperwork demanded by the Turks before they would allow any American nationals to leave the city. By late afternoon, he realised that time was fast running out. 'Great clouds of smoke were by this time beginning to pour down upon the consulate. The crowd in the street before this building, as well as that upon the quay, was now so dense that the commanding naval officer told me that in ten minutes more I should not be able to get through.'

There was indeed a real urgency to getting the American nationals onto the waiting vessels. Edward Fisher, director of the YMCA, burst into Horton's office and warned him 'that he had seen with his own eyes wide streams of kerosene running through the street on which the American Consulate was located'.

Fisher was not mistaken. When Claflin Davis scraped up some mud in the street, 'it smelled like petroleum and gasoline mixed.' He was sure that the Turks were preparing to fire all the buildings close to the waterfront.

American lighters and landing craft had by this time been drawn up alongside the quay. Without a moment to lose, the assembled Americans were led out through the crowd and down to the waterfront. This was not easy, for the streets were blocked by thousands of refugees who were also trying to jostle their way towards the American landing craft. One of those who was helping his fellow nationals aboard – and fighting off the other refugees – was Melvin Johnson. 'As we were pulling out I'll never forget the screams,' he later recalled. 'As far as we could go, you could hear 'em screaming and hollering, and the fire was going on ... [the] most pitiable thing you ever saw in your life ... the only way the people could go [was] toward the waterfront. A lot of 'em were jumping in, committing suicide.'

The Americans were not alone in evacuating their nationals. The French, Italians and British were all engaged in a desperate attempt to rescue the last of their people before it was too late. Earlier that afternoon, Sir Harry Lamb had wired the warships in the bay, asking for lighters to be sent with immediate effect. As soon as they were docked at the quayside, the remaining British nationals were led through the crowds of refugees by their indefatigable vicar, Charles Dobson. 'Nothing – no words – can describe the awful effect of the city,' he later wrote. 'One appalling mass of flames, the water front covered with dark masses of despairing humanity.'

Not everyone accepted the offer of a place on the British vessels. The Giraud family had discovered to their amazement that the *Helen May* – Edmund's beloved motor cruiser – was still tied up in the harbour. They forced their way through the masses and eventually reached the boat. For young Mary Giraud it was a most terrifying experience. 'A flaming town in the background, a port full of English warships ... and ourselves, far enough away from it all not to have to witness more than an overall picture of the chaotic horror of war.'

Yet she saw enough harrowing scenes to haunt her for a long time to come. 'This picture remained with me for many years and my sleep was inevitably broken by nightmares of war. This lasted well into my teens, till finally the horror faded.'

For the British mariners involved in the rescue mission, it was a most testing afternoon's work. 'We had some dreadful moments,' recalled Duncan Wallace, 'especially when we wondered if we could save the inmates of the Maternity Home, whose gallant head, Miss Williamson, when we arrived with stretchers, simply said, "Thank God you came in time. I could not have left my post."'

Grace Williamson later wrote her own account of the rescue. She recalled fifty British troops arriving at the nursing home and forming a human square reinforced with oars. When all the staff and patients had assembled inside this square, the sailors forced a passage through the crowds. Grace finally made it to the *Iron Duke*, where she was received by the ship's admiral. 'From the deck of the *Iron Duke*, we watched Smyrna burn, [and] the fire seemed to reach very near our home.'

For many, the experience of finally reaching the safety of a British warship was too much to bear. One of the Whittall children recalled how her mother broke down in tears. '[She] sat quietly weeping, hardly trying to check her tears with her handkerchief. I had never seen her in tears before and it seemed to me, as I went to her side, that something unbearable had happened.'

Fernand de Cramer had not managed to make the rendezvous for British nationals. He now found himself struggling through the crowds, trying to work out how to get his invalid mother, Lucy, to one of the waiting lighters. 'Picture to yourself a crowd so dense that you could scarcely touch the ground with your feet and you turned upon yourself like grains of sand in a whirlwind. Amid piercing shrieks and blows, people falling into the sea, a smoke so hot that upon my word I thought my entrails were on fire.'

Fernand was at a loss as to know what to do. He knew that, given his mother's weak heart, she was unlikely to survive in a crowd 'so horrible, atrocious, compact and panic-stricken'. Yet the house where she was currently lodged lay directly in the path of the flames and would soon be consumed by fire.

In the end, he bundled her outside, physically manhandled her through the crowds and finally handed her over to a British officer standing by a lighter. 'I told him that she was a born English woman and that her life was entirely in his hands.' The officer promised to do his best, but Fernand had his doubts as

317

to whether she would live. 'She left in an absolute fainting condition,' he wrote.

Lucy de Cramer did indeed survive and would later write her own recollection of the events of that Wednesday afternoon. 'The fright of the population in the streets and on the quays was indescribable!' she wrote. 'Bombs and petroleum were thrown. The flames finished by licking the quays [which] were crowded with the poor people waiting their turn to be saved. Everything that one can say of the horror of that night is not exaggerated!'

Just a few hours earlier, Lucy had deposited the family fortune in the safe belonging to the Paterson family. Now, from the safety of a British warship, she watched the Patersons' property explode in a fireball. 'We are all ruined!' she wrote. 'Complete disaster and ruin.'

Ernest Paterson – Lucy's brother-in-law – also realised that it was the end of an era. '[He] is beside himself,' wrote Lucy. 'His bank, stores and other property reduced to ashes.'

He was not alone in having lost everything. The assets of almost all of the Levantine dynasties were tied up in property and their money was held in local banks. Now, those banks were all in flames. The Levantines watched from afar as all their businesses, possessions and fortunes went up in smoke. Two centuries of inherited wealth, paintings and priceless objets d'art were lost in the great fire of Smyrna.

One of the last British nationals to board the waiting lighters was Percy Hadkinson. He would later write to the British High Commissioner in Constantinople, chronicling everything he saw that night. 'If Your Excellency could only have heard the cries for help and seen defenceless women and children unmercifully shot down or rushed into the sea to be drowned like rats, or back into the flames to be burned to death, you would fully have realised the horror and extreme gravity of the situation.'

The Smyrna quayside had indeed become a scene of abject

human misery. Almost two miles long – and wider than a football pitch – it was large enough to accommodate hundreds of thousands of homeless people. The transformation into a makeshift refugee camp had been rapid and dramatic. Just a few days earlier, the waterfront had been alive to the sound of gypsy orchestras and brass bands. Now, the gaiety had been replaced by rank squalor. The same people who had only recently spent their evenings sauntering up and down in their evening finery were now camped out in the open air with neither privacy nor provisions.

By the time dusk fell on that terrible Wednesday, the quayside was crowded with almost half a million refugees. They stood in real danger of being burned alive for the fire had by now reached the waterfront – a scalding, pulsating heat that was transmitted from building to building by the liberal use of benzine. The Théâtre de Smyrne had erupted into flames shortly after the American nationals had been evacuated. Just minutes later, the American consulate had burst into a wall of fire. George Horton had left in the nick of time. He managed to save the consulate archives but his cherished library was devoured by the flames. The heat was soon so intense that the mooring lines of the ships closest to the waterfront began to burn. All the vessels moved 250 yards out from the quayside, yet the heat was still overwhelming.

'The flames leaped higher and higher,' wrote Oran Raber, a tourist who had arrived in Smyrna just a few days earlier. 'The screams of the frantic mob on the quay could easily be heard a mile distant. There was a choice of three kinds of death: the fire behind, the Turks waiting at the side streets and the ocean in front . . . in modern chronicles, there has probably been nothing to compare with the night of September 13 in Smyrna.'

On board the *Iron Duke*, Admiral Sir Osmond de Beauvoir Brock insisted that the daily routine continue as normal. George

Ward Price recalled how the officers dressed for dinner in their white mess jackets that evening, despite the unfolding vision of hell. When the screams from the distant quayside grew too loud to be ignored, the captain ordered the ship's band to strike up tunes. Other ships followed suit and the shrill cries of the desperate refugees were soon overlaid with a medley of sea shanties.

'One of the strangest experiences that night was to hear the band playing while the town was burning and cries and the roar of the fire filled the air,' wrote Duncan Wallace. Another observer recalled the ship's phonographs blasting out 'the sweet strains of familiar records, including "Humoresque" and the swelling tones of Caruso in Pagliacci floating over the waters'. It was almost possible to lose oneself in the music, were it not for the fact that the quieter arias 'were suddenly drowned in that frightful chorus of shrieks from the Smyrna quay'.

Many of the sailors involved in the evacuation of British nationals had returned to their vessels with tales of horror and cruelty. As their stories spread through the lower decks, there was a growing feeling that something should be done – and done immediately – to help those on the quayside.

Charles Howes was one of those who had taken part in the evacuation; he would remember for the rest of his life the scenes he witnessed. 'Shrieking women calling to unresponsive children who were beyond answering. Children of tender age calling for parents . . . now and again, a cavalry man would take a fancy to a young girl of fifteen or sixteen and drag her away and then a ghostly scream would tell its own story.'

One of Howes' colleagues, a seaman named Bunter, saw hundreds of Greeks clinging to the quayside in an effort to escape the heat of the fire. He then watched Turkish soldiers arriving 'and deliberately severing the victims' arms, resulting in hundreds of bodies falling to their deaths in the sea'.

Once dinner aboard the *Iron Duke* was finished, the officers went on deck to survey the scenes through their binoculars. One of them, Major Arthur Maxwell, watched Turkish soldiers pouring buckets of liquid over the refugees. He thought they were attempting to douse the flames, until he saw a sheet of fire flare up at exactly that point on the quay.

'My God,' he cried to his colleagues, 'they're trying to burn the refugees.'

George Ward Price joined the officers on deck in order to watch the conflagration.

What I see, as I stand on the deck of *HMS Iron Duke*, is an unbroken wall of fire, two miles long, in which twenty distinct volcanoes of raging flame are throwing up jagged, writhing tongues to a height of a hundred feet.

All Smyrna's rich warehouses, business-buildings and European residences are burning like furious torches. From this intensely glowing mass of yellow, orange and crimson fire pour up thick, clotted coils of oily black smoke that hide the moon at its zenith.

The unease felt by many British mariners at their lack of action was mirrored by the crews on board the American warships. On the *Litchfield*, Claflin Davis of the Red Cross approached Captain Hepburn and pleaded for two large lighters, which were moored to the farthest end of the harbour, to be towed to the quayside. In that way, several thousand people could be saved from the worst heat of the flames. Hepburn was unable to oblige. The water was choppy, even in the harbour, and the lighters could be moved only with power launches. However, he had none at his disposal: only the British and French were equipped with such vessels.

Davis persuaded Hepburn to allow him to row over to the Allied vessels and ask for their help, but none was forthcoming. The French admiral was still ashore and out of contact, and the British were less than helpful. Admiral Brock informed Davis that he had repeatedly assured General Noureddin of Britain's absolute neutrality. He could not – and would not – allow his men to take part in the rescue of Greek and Armenian civilians.

Nonetheless, at around midnight, the British admiral had a dramatic change of heart. The cause of his volte-face is unknown; it may be that his conscience was pricked by the attitude of the men under his command. Whatever the reason, his decision to help rescue the refugees led to a sudden flurry of action. Ward Price was on deck when the order was given for all the available picket boats, cutters and whalers to be lowered into the water and despatched to the quayside.

'The scene changed in an instant,' he wrote. 'A shrill piping; a shouting of orders; a trampling of feet. Half the mess-jacketed officers disappear. In three minutes they are on deck again in blue uniforms, with mufflers around their necks and truncheons in their hands to beat back rushes for the boats.' Within minutes, the first of the boats was rowing towards the quayside.

The sight that greeted the British seamen when they arrived at the quayside was worse than anyone expected. More than half a million people were crammed onto the waterfront and they had no possibility of escape. Machine-gun posts at the northern and southern ends of the waterfront prevented them from fleeing, while the fire formed an impenetrable barrier on the land side.

One of the first to reach the quay was Charles Howes. Shortly afterwards, he was joined by Lieutenant Charles Drage of the HMS *Cardiff*. Their initial task was to create a heavily armed cordon on the landing area so that the crowd could not rush the boat.

'Prentice and some men jumped out and tried to clear a place,' wrote Drage, '[but] they were swept back into the boat and literally submerged in a pile of terrified people.' Hundreds rushed forwards and threw themselves into the whaler; the British sailors had no option but to use force to hold them back. 'I only got away by beating them on the head with a tiller.'

Ward Price had accompanied one of the boats to the quay-side to see the evacuation with his own eyes. 'The bow touches the quay and a fighting, shrieking, terrified torrent of humanity pours over it. "Women and children only!" roar the officers, fighting with fists and sticks to keep back the men. It is as unavailing as pushing at an avalanche. The only thing to do is to back out directly the picket boat is full, literally to overflowing.'

Lieutenant Drage managed to push back from the quayside and, as he began rowing towards the British fleet stationed farther out in the bay, he noticed that the water was thick with corpses, among them a baby floating upside down. Drage pulled it out and, seeing a flicker of life, slapped it hard. After a few minutes, it began breathing again.

Howes was meanwhile loading a second boat with refugees; he was sweating profusely from the heat of the flames. 'Right along the sea front was a wall of unbroken fire with flames 100 feet high casting a lurid glow in the sky. The night was rendered at intervals by loud explosions and all the while the people in the rear were being massacred.'

The vision was apocalyptic in its horror: 'The stench of human flesh burning was appalling,' wrote Howes, 'and the streets were stacked with dead. Men, women, children and dogs . . . the heavens were lit by the flames and myriads of sparks flew skywards, the crackling of the wood and the collapsing of the houses sounded like a salvo of guns. The whole of Smyrna, except the Turkish quarter, was now in the grip of the greedy fire . . . [and] as hard as our boats and sailors worked during the night in rescues we did not seem to make much impression in diminishing the crowd.'

Howes was momentarily distracted by Turkish soldiers

throwing the corpses of adults and children into the flames, but soon there were even more terrible sights to claim his attention. 'One of the saddest cases I met was that of a little girl of nine who, with her father and mother and baby in arms, were making their way to the boats when their parents were shot dead. This little girl picked the baby up off the ground and, dashing through the flames, reached the boat.' Howes and his men rescued her and treated the burns on her legs.

'I don't think the majority of English reading people will believe this narrative and will say I exaggerate,' wrote Howes. 'Well, here is the truth. Think of the old time torture, add to them the modern appliances for the destruction of mankind, exaggerate it as much as you like and you will not realise half the horrors of the evacuation of Smyrna.'

And so the night progressed, until more than 2,000 Greeks and Armenians had been taken aboard the *Iron Duke*. Another 2,000 were on the American vessel *Winona*. The *Litchfield* was also full to overflowing. One by one, each of the great battleships in the bay of Smyrna was loaded with a cargo of terrified humanity. On board the Italian ship, *Sardegna*, Oran Raber watched the rescue mission continue into the early hours. 'Women half clothed and pregnant were dragged up the ladder only to fall exhausted on the deck. Children, haggard and half dead, were crying for bread, while young mothers sat on the decks trying to squeeze out a few drops of milk from their own impoverished bodies.' On board the *Bavarian*, the Reverend Charles Dobson was attempting to comfort a mother and daughter who had been gang-raped by fifteen Turkish soldiers.

The Chicago news reporter, John Clayton, suddenly realised that he could no longer bring himself to write the sort of reports expected of him by Admiral Mark Bristol. The scale of the disaster was such that he was at long last forced to admit the truth about what was taking place in Smyrna. 'The loss of life is impossible to compute,' he wrote. 'The streets are littered with dead . . . Except for the squalid Turkish quarter, Smyrna has ceased to exist . . . the problem of the minorities is here solved for all time.' In a sentence that was guaranteed to provoke Admiral Bristol's wrath, he added: 'no doubt remains as to the origin of the fire . . . the torch was applied by Turkish regular soldiers.'

Ward Price's account for the *Daily Mail* – written in the early hours of the morning – was even more graphic:

> Smyrna has been practically destroyed by a gigantic fire . . . without exaggeration, tonight's holocaust is one of the biggest fires in the world's history. The damage is incalculable and there has been great loss of life among the native population . . . many thousands of refugees [are] huddled on the narrow quay, between the advancing fiery death behind and the deep water in front, [and there] comes continuously such frantic screaming of sheer terror as can be heard miles away . . . picture a constant projection into a red-hot sky of gigantic incandescent balloons, burning oil spots in the Aegean, the air filled with nauseous smell, while parching clouds, cinders and sparks drift across us – and you can but have a glimmering of the scene of appalling and majestic destruction which we are watching.

On board the *Simpson*, George Horton took his last glimpse of the city as the battleship slowly steamed out of the bay.

> As the destroyer moved away from the fearful scene and darkness descended, the flames, raging now over a vast area, grew brighter and brighter, presenting a scene of awful and sinister beauty . . . nothing was lacking in the way of atrocity, lust, cruelty and all that fury of human passion which, given their full play, degrade the human race to a

level lower than the vilest and cruellest of beasts . . . one of the keenest impressions which I brought away with me from Smyrna was a feeling of shame that I belonged to the human race.

Thursday, 14 September 1922

All night long the fire raged and all night long the rescue mission continued. Yet the sailors and officers knew that there was a grim arithmetic to the situation in which they found themselves. There were some half a million people on the quayside but there was space on board the battleships for less than one tenth of that number.

Admiral Bristol's intelligence officer, Lieutenant Merrill, arrived in the bay of Smyrna a few hours before dawn aboard the *Edsall*, having spent a few days conferring with his boss in Constantinople. When he stepped out onto the bridge of the vessel, he was surprised to find that the night air had been so heated by the fire that all the mariners on deck were in short sleeves. He felt desperately sorry for the refugees. 'Thousands of homeless were surging back and forth along the blistering quay, panic-stricken to the point of insanity . . .' he wrote. 'Fortunately, the quay wall never got actually hot enough to roast these unfortunate people alive but the heat must have been terrific there to have been felt on the ships two hundred yards away.'

By morning, the furnace was so intense that the captain of HMS *Serapis* – which was anchored closest to the shore – feared that the flammable liquids aboard his vessel would burst into flames. He ordered a shifting of moorings and told the crew to haul her chains aboard. This routine operation was a harrowing one for those involved. 'People clinging to them were precipitated into the water,' wrote one, 'whilst scores of people were swimming round the ship imploring to be saved . . . one man hung to the anchor cable and he was eventually hauled inboard.'

One of the crew helping to weigh anchor found his eye drawn to the seawall, where a horse had caught fire and was chasing wildly across the quayside trampling down children, its hind quarters engulfed in flames. '[It] galloped madly into the crowd,' he wrote, 'its end was not seen.'

By about 5 a.m., the *Serapis* could house no more refugees. 'We had on board about as many as we could hold – the forecastle, upper deck and all the mess decks were full and there were also people in the boiler and engine rooms.' Yet a headcount revealed that just 1,000 souls had been saved – a tiny dent in the crowds camped out on the quayside.

Other vessels were also filling up. When Lieutenant Charles Drage was sent to the SS *Karnak* he found its lower decks so full that he had difficulty jostling his way through. He finally reached the boat deck, where a makeshift infirmary had been established, and where he noted: 'One old lady dying of nervous exhaustion, one man shot in the stomach and dying of peritonitis, one man dying of a cut throat, one with an amputated leg dying of gangrene.'

As Drage made his inspection of the ship, he came across several members of the Whittall family, who told him how grateful they were to have been offered sanctuary aboard the vessel. 'All night they have heard screams, usually ending in gurgles, while through glasses they have seen men and women cut down and shot and girls raped.'

Six miles away in Bournabat, Hortense Wood's sleep was disturbed by a deep-orange tinge to the night sky. It did not take her long to realise what was happening. 'The town [has been] set on fire,' she wrote in her diary. 'We can see the red glow illuminating the sky and glowing smoke ascending ever higher. Bombs are continually exploding and the sound reaches us very distinctly.'

Isolated from Smyrna – and unsure of the scale of the unfolding tragedy – her first thought was for her family. 'I am anxious about my people,' she wrote, 'although I am sure they are safe on board. No communications whatever with the town. No trains. Only military autos.' She had little option but to sit at home and wait for news.

Her only reliable source of information was her nephew, Fernand, who had spent Wednesday night in one of the de Cramers' as yet unburned town houses. Fernand assumed that everyone else in the family had managed to find safety aboard one or other of the British battleships in the bay. However, when he ventured outside on that Thursday morning, he could scarcely believe his eyes. 'I met Aunt Harriet!' he wrote. 'Alone! Having spent all night equally in that hideous crowd. She was half crazed with fright, hunger and fatigue.'

Fernand jostled his aunt through the refugees – avoiding several bands of drunken irregulars – and eventually reached the Point. After much effort and anxiety, he managed to secure her passage aboard a British destroyer.

For the Levantines and Europeans of Smyrna, the worst of their ordeal was almost at an end. But for the city's 320,000 Greeks, and their homeless compatriots, the immediate future looked grim indeed. Georgios Tsoubariotis, an eleven-year-old Greek lad, had spent the night hiding in the church of Haghia Yiannis, along with his mother, father, sister and many refugees. Yet as the fire advanced relentlessly towards the building – and dawn broke the sky – so a new menace arose. 'A dozen brigands appeared, carrying knives,' recalled Georgios when interviewed many years later. 'They began to threaten people, one by one ... they shouted *tsikar paragini*, *tsikar saatini* (take out your money, take out your watch).'

His father handed over all his money, but the man next to them had nothing to give. 'They slashed his shoulder with a knife. The poor man rolled around on the ground, groaning with pain and died, quivering, before our eyes.'

As soon as the brigands had gone, the Tsoubariotis family decided to flee the church. Georgios's father had no desire to join the crowds on the quayside, especially as his eighteen-year-old daughter was extremely attractive. He led his family to one of the city's Greek cemeteries and forced open a family tomb in which he hoped to hide. They were not alone in seeking sanctuary there. 'It was full of people. Almost all the tombs had been opened by parents to hide their girls.' The family were to remain in hiding for the rest of the day and night before making their next move.

The Alexiou family had also spent the night in hiding, seeking shelter in an abandoned building on the outskirts of the city, one that had so far escaped the fire. At one point in the early hours, young Alexis − a twelve-year-old − needed to relieve himself.

We lit matches and my father was looking for the toilet ...The match went out and at the same time, I tripped on something soft. I screamed. My father lit another match and walked towards me. In the trembling light of the match we saw, with horror, that I'd tripped on a severed arm and a bit further on I caught a glimpse of a woman's body. There had been a carnage in there. My father said not to tell my mother about what we'd seen.

The family abandoned their hiding place at dawn and made their way down to the quayside, determined to fight their way onto one of the British or American lighters. Alexis's desperation to get aboard so angered an American marine that he smashed the lad over the head with an iron pole. 'My neck swelled up and hurt unbearably,' he later wrote. Nonetheless, he got aboard the boat, as did his mother, although she tried to hurl herself into the sea when she learned that her husband had been left behind.

'And in all of this,' wrote Alexis, 'I watched Smyrna burn from the ship that slowly sailed away.' Mother and son were taken to Mytilene, where the whole family – including Alexis's father – were eventually reunited.

Dr Garabed Hatcherian had spent the night with the Verkine family, helping to nurse Mrs Verkine's baby, who had been born two days earlier. However, by mid-morning, the house looked set to be engulfed by the flames. Clearly, it was too dangerous to remain there any longer. The respective families bid tearful farewells to each other, packed up a few belongings and prepared to join the refugees on the quayside.

'The fire continues its devastation and has swallowed everything up to the Swedish consulate,' wrote Garabed, who had spent the previous twenty-four hours indoors. 'We find ourselves trapped between three deadly elements: fire, sword and water. We are in a completely desperate situation.'

For days, the family had been sheltered from the worst of the reality of what was taking place in the city. Now, realising that they were no better off than anyone else on the quayside, Hatcherian's wife and children broke down in tears. 'I join their lamentation,' wrote Garabed, 'and confess that I am the only one to be blamed and, with tearful eyes, I ask for forgiveness . . . We have given up hope of swimming. The fire, the shootings and the cudgel of the Turks have squeezed the Christian crowd from three sides. If there is a ray of hope, it is the sea.'

The Hatcherians fought their way through to the sea wall, where an Italian lighter was taking off refugees. 'We implore

331

the seamen in French to accept us as well,' wrote Garabed. 'But they turn a deaf ear to our pleas and soldiers lined in double rows throw us out readily.'

He was most upset to see a film crew making a movie from the safety of one of the warships and was even more disgusted to see them refusing to help those who had swum out to their ship. 'They reject those who approach them even by swimming or rowing to ask for refuge, just because they want to demonstrate their political neutrality.'

Hatcherian was at an absolute loss as to what to do. The family had very little food or water and no prospect of any shelter that night. The air was still ferociously hot and great clouds of acrid smoke hung over the quayside. For three hours, the Hatcherians pushed through the crowds of refugees, begging to be rescued by one of the few foreign lighters still involved in the relief operation. But each time they were met with a blank refusal.

Hatcherian feared for his little daughter, Vartouhi, anxious that she might not survive the ordeal. 'Until midday we wander along the shore under the burning rays of the sun, hungry and thirsty,' he wrote. 'We realise that there is no way out from here. We are dead tired and unable to walk.'

The scale of the devastation left him stunned. All the once-grandiose consulates, clubhouses and theatres were now burned-out shells. Even the Grand Hotel Kraemer Palace had been engulfed by the fire and thick black smoke was still pouring out of its upper windows.

'Amongst the charred buildings, our attention is drawn to the gutted Théâtre de Smyrne which, even as a skeleton, still holds high its imposing façade . . . We pass by it in horror and haste, fearing that its sudden collapse could crush our desperate heads.'

Yet amidst the devastation, a few lone buildings had escaped the flames. At the Point, in the north of the city, a short row of waterfront buildings remained unscathed. Elsewhere, single houses or offices remained upright in defiance of the fireball. There was no obvious reason why they had been spared: a sudden change in the wind's direction, perhaps, or thick retaining walls that had managed to resist the flames. Each of these buildings was crowded with refugees – men, women and children who preferred to remain inside than chance their lives on the quayside.

Garabed wished that he had been able to remain in the relative safety of the Verkines' house, although that too might even now be in flames. He and his family spent another hour pushing their way through the crowds, wondering whether they would ever find safety. 'On the quay, along with household items, one can see valuable objects and human corpses strewn everywhere and we walk through, almost stepping on them. Our noble feelings are worn out, and selfishness has become the only force guiding our existence.'

The wind had whipped up a gale and sheets of spray were blowing in off the sea, providing some relief from the intense heat of the fire. As the Hatcherians dodged bands of irregulars who were menacing the refugees, Garabed reflected on the wretched turn of events that had engulfed his family and friends who were lost among the crowds of the quayside. 'Only a few hours ago, most of these unfortunate people had all the means of livelihood and enjoyments,' he wrote; 'now, deprived from everything, they have been cast into the streets without protection and without hope.'

At teatime that afternoon, as she sat alone with silence all around her, Hortense Wood had a most surprising visitor to her mansion in Bournabat. 'Arrival of Fazil [Fevzi] Pasha and his staff,' she recorded in her diary. 'Ask for rooms for himself and eight officers.'

This was an extraordinary request from an extraordinary man.

Fevzi Pasha had joined Mustafa Kemal's staff two years earlier, serving as Minister for Defence and deputy prime minister for the nationalists in Angora. Now he was marshal of the Turkish army and had come to Smyrna to help Kemal plan his drive northwards towards Constantinople.

Most people would have been flattered to have such a guest staying. Not so Hortense. 'I said I expected the return of my people in a day or two,' she told him, 'and could not give up my sisters' rooms.'

Fevzi Pasha's reaction to this refusal is nowhere recorded; he was perhaps bemused by the indefatigable Hortense. Yet he persisted in his request, aware that most of the other great houses in Bournabat had been reduced to smouldering ruins. In the end, Hortense relented, telling him that she 'could only place two rooms at his disposal'.

Fevzi Pasha gratefully accepted and informed his staff that they would have to find lodgings elsewhere. 'He did not wish to annoy me, he said.' Nevertheless, Hortense left him in no doubt that she found his request somewhat intrusive. 'I had to give up Ernest's room,' she wrote with more than a hint of indignation in her diary, '*and* the two rooms I had already offered him.'

However, she changed her tune when she realised why Fevzi Pasha had chosen her house. Over the coming days, it was to become the central meeting point for Mustafa Kemal and all his senior advisors. Hortense would find herself playing host to the builders of modern Turkey.

As the afternoon wore on, more and more of the warships slipped away from Smyrna. Some headed for the nearby Greek islands, where they offloaded their cargo of distressed refugees. Others – like the American destroyer, *Simpson* – headed for Salonica or Piraeus.

'I found Piraeus, as well as Athens, already crowded to

saturation with refugees from Turkey,' wrote George Horton. He rightly foresaw another humanitarian disaster. Greece, teetering on the brink of bankruptcy after more than three years of war with Turkey, was simply not equipped to deal with an influx of tens – and perhaps hundreds – of thousands of refugees.

The sight of the departing ships filled those left behind with a sense of foreboding. They were being abandoned by the great powers and left to the mercy of the Turkish army. Hovakim Uregian toyed with the idea of organising some sort of resistance, reasoning that if he and a few others could overpower some armed Turks and steal their guns, then they might be able to fight back. In the end, his idea came to nothing. 'My Greek is very limited,' he wrote, 'and very few Greeks speak any Armenian. We could communicate in Turkish but the continued attacks of the Turks and the need to keep shifting to survive give us little opportunity to organise this sort of action.'

Krikor Baghdjian – who had seen the Turks setting the fire from the roof of the Armenian clubhouse – had decided to do everything in his power to make his escape. His first attempt to reach a British destroyer ended in disaster when the lighter, filled to overflowing, capsized and sunk. Baghdjian was fortunate to be a strong swimmer and to make it back to the shore. His second attempt was more successful. He bribed his way onto a little rowing boat that soon approached an Italian merchant vessel.

'At long last we reached its side,' he later recalled, 'but, to our horror, we saw the rope ladder being pulled up. Two of us climbed up the side of the ship and I caught the ladder. Two people caught hold of my legs and we were hung up in the air for a while looking down.'

Krikor began to lose his grip, on account of the weight of the people clinging to his legs. 'But my father pushed them up from the boat as it reached the top of a wave and I secured a better grip. More boat passengers started to climb up the side of the ship and finally, Italian seamen helped us all reach the deck.'

When Krikor was finally on board, his legs gave way beneath him. Others, too, collapsed from the exertion. 'We all lay exhausted on our backs, breathing and looking at the reddening evening sky, as we thanked our lucky stars for having finally made it – to safety and freedom.'

By the time that darkness fell on that Thursday evening, some 20,000 souls had been plucked from the quayside, yet this had made scarcely a dent in the multitude still camped out. Nor did the savagery show any signs of abating. When the American vice-consul, Maynard Barnes, ventured ashore briefly that evening, he witnessed five separate groups of Turks, armed with blood-smeared clubs, prowling through the crowd. 'The proceeding was brutal beyond belief,' he recalled when inter-viewed after the event. 'We were within ten feet of the assailants when the last blow was struck, and I doubt there was a bone unbroken left in the body when it was dropped over the edge of the quay and kicked into the sea.'

The fire was still burning fiercely, even though many parts of the city had been reduced to rubble. The wind had shifted direction once again that evening, driving the flames into areas that had hitherto escaped the inferno. 'At the time when we weighed anchor,' wrote Helena van der Zee of that Thursday evening, 'the city of Smyrna was nothing but a vast blaze. Our offices were burning also. Corpses were floating around our boat. It was a macabre spectacle.'

Like the Whittalls and the Girauds, the van der Zee family had done much to create this once-vibrant city. Now, the work of three generations had come to an abrupt and violent end, and Helena had serious doubts as to whether the family would

ever return to Smyrna. 'And thus was said farewell to this
diabolical spectacle and to this poor city,' she wrote, 'where life
had always been so sweet that it had long been known as the
Pearl of the Orient.'

Friday, 15 September – Monday, 18 September 1922

Dawn arrived late on Friday, 15 September. A dense pall of smoke hung over Smyrna, obscuring the morning sunshine. The fire still raged with terrific intensity in the farthest-flung quarters of the city. Elsewhere, there was little left to burn. Apart from a few lone buildings, fully three-quarters of the city was no longer standing. Only the railway sidings at the Point, the Standard Oil refinery and the Turkish quarter remained intact.

The rescue operation – now into its second night – had continued throughout the small hours, yet the quayside was still densely packed with people. It is hard to compute with any certainty the exact number who remained trapped there on Friday morning. In his report to Washington, Admiral Mark Bristol reckoned that there were less than a third of a million, even though the number of refugees who had entered the city over the previous days was considerably higher than this. Bristol had also neglected to factor in the city's Christian population – perhaps 300,000-strong at the time of Kemal's entry – many of whom were now homeless. According to many eyewitnesses, there were as many as half a million refugees still awaiting their fate on the quayside.

Many had been driven to distraction by hunger and thirst, living off the meagre supplies that they had managed to salvage from their homes. Others were surviving by eating scraps of refuse that were strewn across the quay. There were some for whom the continued predations of the Turkish military had proved too much to bear; quite a number had thrown themselves into the sea in order to escape the horror. When Georgios Tsoubariotis left his graveyard hiding place that Friday morning and made his way to the quayside, his eyes met with a most disturbing sight. 'The sea was full of bodies . . .' he wrote. 'There were so many that if you fell into the water you wouldn't sink because all those bodies would keep you on the surface. And you could see on every body the belly swollen, curving above the surface.'

Even more gruesome was the fact that dozens of young Turkish boys were swimming among the corpses in order to rob them of anything of worth. 'Their noses were covered by scarves tied on the back of their heads, so they wouldn't breathe in the stench of rotting bodies,' he wrote. 'They held a sharp knife and skilfully cut from the bodies the fingers that wore rings, and the ends of the ears that wore earrings, to take those jewels. They took bracelets and anything of worth they might find around people's necks.'

Hovakim Uregian awoke that morning to the smell of burning flesh. 'Curious, I thought, how we had come to think of hell as an inferno of fire and blood, but totally neglected the continuous torture to the human mind that the stench of burned flesh, human flesh in particular, could cause.' Uregian was still hiding in an enclosed courtyard that lay in a quarter of the city that had yet to be devoured by the fire. Nevertheless, he knew that it was only a matter of time before he – and all the Greeks hiding with him – would be flushed out.

The endgame arrived soon enough. Turkish soldiers entered the courtyard, taking prisoner all the males aged between fifteen and fifty, including Uregian.

The reason for their arrest soon became apparent. That

morning, Mustafa Kemal decreed that any refugee still in Smyrna on 1 October would be deported to central Anatolia. In theory, they were to be given two weeks to find passage to Greece or elsewhere, but in practice the deportations began immediately. Any Christians of military age were deemed to be enemies of the Turkish nationalists. As such, they were to be held as prisoners of war.

The treatment of these newly arrested prisoners during their detention was brutal in the extreme. Uregian and the others were marched across the ruined city to a large military barracks that lay in the unburned Turkish quarter, and were housed in its outside courtyard along with many others who had been seized several days earlier. 'Hundreds of them were lying on the sandy ground under the blazing sun,' wrote Uregian. 'Their clothing reduced to rags, no shoes, no hats – everything stolen by the marauding, greedy Turks.'

The soldiers guarding them were irregulars from the Anatolian hinterland – men who had little respect for human life, carried whips made of barbed wire and indulged in cruel psychological games. There was one tap in the centre of the courtyard and this would be turned on during the worst heat of the day, but no one was allowed to approach the cool stream of flowing water. 'The poor prisoners were not only prevented from quenching their thirst, but under the threat of whips they would sadistically be pushed over to the sunny side of the yard.'

The sound of the splashing water drove some men crazy. Uregian watched one prisoner, who had been deprived of water for several days, rush to the tap in desperation. As he lapped the liquid from the ground, three guards started beating him with their barbed-wire whips. They continued until his back was raw and then carted him away. He was never seen again.

Although Uregian fully expected to meet a similar fate, for there seemed to be no hope of getting out of the barracks alive, he was to be saved by a most unexpected intervention on the part of one of the commanding officers. At some point that Saturday afternoon, all the men aged eighteen or younger were told to stand up and form a line. Uregian guessed that everyone below fighting age was going to be released and he therefore joined the line, even though he was actually twenty-two.

'I rubbed my cheeks,' he wrote, 'knowing that a flushed appearance made me look more boyish.' His ploy saved his life. He and a few others were led back into the main building and told that they were free to go. 'I looked into the yard to see the prisoners,' he wrote. 'I almost felt guilty for "abandoning" them now.'

Uregian's luck was to continue that night. After almost being beaten to death by two Turkish irregulars on the quayside, he managed to jostle his way aboard a British freighter. After a terrifying week, he found himself a free man.

His was one of the few uplifting stories to emerge from that terrible weekend. Many thousands of others – Greeks and Armenians – were marched into the interior of the country and either killed or held as prisoners of war.

Among them was a young Greek man named Panagiotis Marselos. He was told that he was being taken to Magnesia, some thirty miles from Smyrna, along with 5,000 other prisoners. The forced march resembled the deportation of the Armenians seven years earlier. Every few miles, the guards would lead a group of men away from the roadside and shoot them.

'The slaughter didn't stop,' he wrote. 'We headed to Bournabasi, which we reached at night, and they put us in a barbed wire enclosure. They started taking five at a time and killed them.' Marselos escaped the death squads but he and his fellow survivors were deprived of food and water for three long days. When they finally came to a river, they were given a few minutes to slake their thirst in water that was contaminated by a putrefying corpse. 'I couldn't resist my thirst,' recalled Marselos.

'I drank . . . and my brother drank too, and our lips were sticky from the fat secreted by the broken body.'

This was to be their only stop for water. When Marselos and his dwindling band of fellow Christians finally reached Magnesia, they were once again desperate for water. Their thirst was intensified by the fact that they were locked in a dusty warehouse. '[It] was made of limestone,' wrote Marselos. 'As we moved about, the dust rose and we breathed it in. We had burns on our lips and in our mouths. All you could hear was the phrase: "My God, water!"'

Within a week of leaving Smyrna, fewer than 500 of the prisoners were still alive. The guards forced these hardy survivors to harm themselves and their comrades. When one of the guards saw that Marselos had a gold filling, he made him knock the tooth out with a rock. Next, Marselos was ordered to bite off another man's ear, which he was unable to do. The unfortunate victim – left in terrible pain – was eventually shot by the guard. Marselos then had all his remaining teeth pulled out by another prisoner.

For three long months, Marselos was to suffer great cruelty. The prisoners were marched from village to village, occasionally being sold off as slaves to local Turks. These were often tortured and killed in revenge for the excesses committed by the Greek army. Marselos was witness to the murder of one of his comrades. '[They] cut off his nose, ears and other bits and then drove a sharp stick into the ground and forced him onto it. The stick went through him and then they set him on fire and burnt him.'

It was not until the spring of 1923 that both Marselos and his brother – who had also cheated death – were finally freed under the terms of a deal struck between the Greek and Turkish governments. They made their way to Piraeus before settling in Greece and rebuilding their lives in the countryside around Patras.

★　　★　　★

Everyone still stranded in Smyrna over that weekend would later have his own story of suffering. For many, survival was a combination of quick thinking and good luck. This was certainly the case for Aristotle Onassis, the eighteen-year-old son of Socrates Onassis, one of Smyrna's wealthiest merchants.

Socrates had been arrested by the military some two days earlier and was being held in a prison in the Turkish quarter. Aristotle had meanwhile been allowed to remain in the family villa at Karatash, a cosmopolitan suburb that was connected to Smyrna by ferry. Even so, he knew that it was not safe to stay for much longer. His favourite uncle, Alexander, had been hanged in Kasaba; two other uncles, Yannis and Vasilis, had been deported into the interior. Aristotle suspected that it would be only a matter of time before he would meet a similar fate.

He was starting to plot his escape from Smyrna when a Turkish general pitched up at the villa and decreed that the building was to be commandeered for his headquarters. Young Aristotle displayed a pluck and sharp-wittedness that was to save his life. He suggested to the general that he be allowed to remain in the house in order to service the temperamental heating and plumbing systems; he added that through his father's Turkish business contacts he had access to the latest gramophone cylinders, as well as the finest cigars and whisky.

None of this was true, yet it bought him time. The general allowed Aristotle to stay on the condition that he could fulfil these promises. He also gave the lad a military pass that gave him freedom to all areas of the ruined city, unmolested by the Turkish military.

The pass proved invaluable to young Aristotle. He was able to visit his father, from whom he learned about the scale of the deportations. And, with the help of one of his father's Turkish business contacts, he began to lobby for Socrates' release. Although his father was not freed for many weeks, he was assured by the prison governor that he would not be harmed.

Much of the Onassis family's money had been held in the safes of their head office. The building itself had been burned in the fire, but Socrates thought it possible that the heavy metal safes might have survived since they were specifically designed to withstand fire. Following his father's advice, Aristotle made his way through the ruined city until he located the burned-out shell of the Grand Vizier Han. He managed to ease his way inside the building, clambering over timbers and fallen masonry until he finally located two of his father's safes. Upon opening them, he found that many wads of Turkish banknotes had indeed survived the flames. He stuffed them into his jacket, shirt and trousers; later that day, he managed to smuggle some of the money into prison. Socrates used it to buy better food, treatment and – eventually – his freedom.

Aristotle himself realised that life in Smyrna was becoming too dangerous for comfort. Knowing that he was unable to fulfil his promises to the Turkish general living in his family's house, he decided that it was time to make a hasty exit. He made contact with America's vice-consul, James Loder Park, and managed to secure a passage aboard the American vessel, *Edsall*. Money and connections made his escape from Smyrna rather easier than it was proving for the majority of refugees.

The general who commandeered the Onassis family villa was not alone in seeking suitable quarters for himself and his staff. All of Mustafa Kemal's senior aides and advisors had been looking for accommodation – most of them in the unburned bourgeois suburbs. Kemal himself was drawn to Bournabat, where the beautiful villa belonging to Hortense Wood proved an irresistible temptation. He decided to hold his first military meeting here, in the house where his senior army marshal, Fevzi Pasha, was still lodging.

'Arrival of Kemal Pasha in our house,' wrote Hortense on

Saturday, 16 September, 'together with Ismet Pasha and other generals, and the famous Turkish lady, Halide Edib.'

Hortense had long harboured an unstinting admiration for Kemal and it remained undimmed by the destruction of Bournabat. She blamed the irregulars for all of the ongoing violence; as far as she was concerned Kemal himself remained above criticism. 'I so admire [him],' she wrote. She chatted with him for a quarter of an hour before Kemal asked whether he could use her house as a temporary headquarters. Hortense duly obliged, no longer clinging to the pretence that her sisters would be returning any day.

'[Kemal] with five others went upstairs to discuss the answer to the allies [regarding Constantinople],' wrote Hortense. She was delighted to have so many young generals in her house, especially as they were discussing matters that would decide the future of Turkey. 'The fate of the empire was being discussed just outside my bedroom door, near the piano.'

Kemal was planning his next move with great care. The British were utterly opposed to withdrawing their forces from the neutral zone around Constantinople. At a cabinet meeting on the previous Friday, Lloyd George was adamant that British forces would not 'run away before Mustafa Kemal'. He was supported by Winston Churchill, who requested that reinforcements be sent to Constantinople with immediate effect. But when the Allied governments were asked to send troops too, there was a lukewarm response. And when British ministers appealed to the empire for help, they were met by a wall of silence. Only New Zealand was prepared to come to Britain's aid.

Knowing that Lloyd George was becoming increasingly isolated, Kemal held several secret meetings with representatives of Britain's allies. He played his hand with skill, appealing for a diplomatic solution to the crisis while threatening force to get what he wanted. When the French High Commissioner urged Kemal to call off the advance on Constantinople, Kemal replied that he was unable to stop his triumphant soldiers. 'Our victorious armies . . .' he said with a chuckle once the High Commissioner had left the room. 'I don't even know where they are. Who knows how long it would take us to reassemble them.'

Kemal had neither the desire not the inclination to fight for Constantinople, for he remained convinced that he could win the country's capital by other means. 'We are pursuing a very calculating and moderate policy . . .' he wrote to one of his generals. 'We are trying to isolate the British.'

After hours of discussion in the upper rooms of Hortense Wood's house, Kemal and his entourage emerged and asked for something to eat. 'These gentlemen dined here,' wrote Hortense proudly, 'and later on Kemal asked for a bath. He had one, after which we renewed our conversation. He promised to come again.'

On the following day, the Turkish high command issued a decree, informing all of Bournabat's surviving Greek families that they were free to return to their homes. Many were confused by the mixed signals coming from the Turkish high command, especially as they had only recently learned that Kemal intended to deport all Christian refugees within a fortnight. '[They] are still timid and frightened,' wrote Hortense after having wandered through the rubble-littered streets of Bournabat. 'Most of their belongings have been stolen and their houses wrecked.'

Later that afternoon, Kemal and his generals gathered once again at Hortense's villa. 'They assemble in Ernest's room,' she wrote, 'and discuss the political situation and [then] leave to visit Noureddin.' Fernand de Cramer arrived from Smyrna while Kemal was still there and was introduced to him. He was impressed with the Turkish leader's ability to deal with his aunt, 'complimenting [her] and kissing her hands. He is a real charmer.'

Kemal's generals had by now commandeered all of the

remaining villas in Bournabat that remained undamaged. 'Emin [is] staying at Edward Whittall's,' wrote Hortense, 'Ismet is staying at Mary Giraud's.' Kemal himself had moved into Latife's house, which was also in Bournabat. On Monday, 18 September, Latife and her grandmother invited a select group of senior nationalists to dine with them. In the seclusion of the spectacular walled garden, it was almost possible to forget the fact that Smyrna no longer existed. 'We passed through a pleasant old Turkish garden which overlooked the blue waters of the bay,' wrote Halide Edib, who was one of the guests. 'The steps leading up to the veranda and the veranda itself were muffled with ivy, wisteria, jasmine and roses in charming profusion and disorder.'

At some point in the afternoon, Kemal left the ladies for a few minutes, only to reappear in a beautiful white suit. Latife gazed at him admiringly. 'She was dazzled by him and he was frankly in love. So the strong current of human attraction between the two enlivened the evening.'

Kemal, in an ebullient mood, was delighted that, with Smyrna in nationalist hands, his long battle was nearly over.

'We are celebrating Smyrna,' [he said to Latife that evening]. 'You must drink with us.'

'I have never touched raki, Pasha — but I will drink champagne to celebrate.'

As he raised his tiny decanter of raki, he pointed at me, [wrote Halide Edib] and said: 'This is the first time I have drunk raki in the presence of this Hanun Effendi: we were always a bit uneasy in her presence.'

I raised the champagne glass and wished him happiness.

While the Turkish generals plotted their next move, Garabed Hatcherian had temporarily managed to escape from the quayside. Among the few homes that had escaped the fire he found one that belonged to his friends, the Sivrihissarian family. He returned to fetch his family and the Hatcherians made their way to the house, where they were given a warm welcome.

They were not alone in seeking shelter. Scores of other refugees – all friends and acquaintances of the family – had taken refuge here. One of these informed Hatcherian that a number of houses on Chalgidji Bashi Street had also escaped the fire. Since this was where he had lived – and he was anxious to gather a few treasured belongings before leaving the city – Hatcherian decided to see whether the rumour was true. He and a friend disguised themselves as Turks and set off through the smouldering city.

They soon grasped the impossibility of their mission. 'Out of the ruins of the buildings, smoke and flames are still rising . . .' he wrote. 'The fire has been much more extensive than we thought.' He realised that there was no chance of finding his house intact; in the Armenian quarter scarcely a wall remained standing. 'Only a few of us have witnessed the utter devastation caused by the fire,' he wrote. 'Its horrendous impression will be indelibly retained in our memories.'

As Hatcherian and his friend made their way back to the quayside they were stopped at gunpoint by a Turkish soldier. He quizzed them about their nationality and – not believing their claim to be Turkish – arrested them, taking them to a military bureau in the unburned section of Basmakhanien train station. Here they were interrogated before being led to a detention centre. For the next twelve hours, they were held in a crowded room along with forty other prisoners.

'Near the door of the room, there is a petrol tank filled with water and a small tin bowl,' wrote Hatcherian. 'Only after constant begging are the prisoners allowed to drink water. As for the natural needs, it is very difficult to get the permission to go downstairs, and only under police supervision.'

Every few minutes, more prisoners were led into the room, which was soon packed and claustrophobic. As darkness fell, a new horror emerged. 'After midnight . . . my attention is drawn to the begging voice of a woman coming from the floor below,' wrote Hatcherian. 'Her voice is mixed with the threatening voice of a Turkish soldier and the plaintive screaming of a three to four year old. The woman, whose voice sounds young, implores the soldier to spare her honour.'

Her pleas went unanswered. She was repeatedly raped — at least twelve times — before dawn brought an end to her ordeal.

On the following morning, Hatcherian and his friend were told to line up and were then led outside. As they reached the gate of the building, they watched a cart passing by, piled high with human corpses. 'Many of them are beyond recognition,' wrote Hatcherian. 'Some are bloated and different body parts are charred. This loathsome picture makes me shudder.'

Under armed guard, the men were marched through the Turkish quarter, then herded inside a large military compound and told to find a space in the courtyard, alongside the other prisoners.

'The barrack square is rife with filth,' wrote Hatcherian. 'The prisoners . . . relieve themselves wherever they can, so that urine and excrement flow all over the place.' Throughout the day, hundreds more people were brought to the barracks prior to their deportation to the interior. With each new batch of arrivals, the conditions — already bad when Garabed arrived — became increasingly intolerable.

'It is not possible to breathe the fetid air of the square,' he wrote. 'The stench causes nausea, we become dizzy and can hardly stand straight.' The men were continually hassled and abused by their guards, who would grab prisoners at random and lead them outside the compound. None was ever seen again.

'It is impossible to describe the horror and the emotional chills we felt each time we saw a soldier approaching us,' wrote

Hatcherian. 'Not even for a minute did we close our eyes, and the hours felt like months.'

Senior American officials spent the weekend trying to persuade the Greek government to send a fleet of vessels to rescue the crowds on the quayside before it was too late. But the Greeks would only agree to this if the safety of their ships would be guaranteed by the Turks. Such an assurance was not forthcoming. According to a telegram sent to Admiral Mark Bristol in Constantinople, 'Kemal . . . said he would not take responsibility to allow Greek ships into the harbour.'

Bristol himself was coming under increasing pressure to send more vessels to Smyrna in order to speed up the humanitarian relief effort, yet he remained extremely reluctant to get involved, fearing that it would jeopardise American interests and potential future oil deals. His policy came under much criticism in Constantinople. The former consul-general to Persia was so disgusted that he launched a stinging attack on Bristol in an interview for the *New York Times*. 'The United States,' he said, 'cannot afford to have its fair name besmirched and befouled by allowing such a man to speak for the American soul and conscience.' He informed the newspaper's readers how Bristol had once told him: 'I hate the Greeks, I hate the Armenians and I hate the Jews. The Turks are fine fellows.'

Although no American vessels pulled into the bay of Smyrna that weekend, a few other ships made an appearance. Among them was a little freighter called the *Dotch*, which arrived on Sunday with a delivery of food and supplies for the American Relief Committee. This had been established, against all the odds, at the farthest end of the quayside.

On board the *Dotch* was an American doctor named Esther Lovejoy, who had volunteered to come to Smyrna in order to help with the relief effort. She had visited the city once before, in 1904, and had fond memories of its Edwardian charm. Now, a rather different sight greeted her eyes. 'The destruction was complete,' she wrote. 'The ruin somehow reminded me of trees I had seen in Belleau Wood [site of a ferocious battle in France in 1918], with all the branches shot away.'

Lovejoy estimated that there were still 300,000 refugees on the quayside, all of whom were in a terrible condition. 'The people squatting on that quay were filthy,' she wrote. 'They had no means of keeping clean. They dared not go back into the ruins of the city for any purpose lest they lost their lives. In less than two weeks, the quay had become a reeking sewer in which the refugees sat and waited for deliverance. When the crowd stirred, the stench was beyond belief.'

Lovejoy realised the absolute urgency of getting these people off the quayside. Just thirteen days remained before all who were still alive would be deported to the interior. And this, she knew, was considered by everyone to be 'a short life sentence to slavery under brutal masters, ended by mysterious death'.

If their lives were to be saved, it would be achieved only by a monumental effort. Although she could not do it by herself, she knew that there was someone on hand to help.

Tuesday, 19 September –
Saturday, 30 September 1922

A sa Jennings had scarcely slept in six nights. As an employee of Smyrna's YMCA, and a man with a clear sense of duty, he was proving extraordinarily resourceful in a time of crisis. As soon as the fire had begun to burn itself out on the previous weekend, he commandeered two intact and unoccupied houses that were situated in the far north of the city. One of the buildings was transformed into an emergency maternity hospital; the other was converted into a supply depot to feed the hungry and needy.

This alone was a remarkable achievement, given that large numbers of out-of-control Turkish irregulars were roaming the burned-out city. However, Jennings was soon to perform far greater feats. He would lead what must rank as the most extraordinary rescue operation of the entire twentieth century.

He was, according to most accounts, a shy and unprepossessing individual. Scarcely five feet tall, and diminutive of build, he wore large glasses and had an uncommonly large mouth. When he smiled, he looked like a frog. A devout Methodist minister from New York, Asa had worked for the YMCA in several foreign countries but had singularly failed to make much of an impression. Now forty-five years of age, he had come to

Smyrna with his wife and two sons in order to take up his appointment as Boys' Works Secretary.

He had been in the job for only a few weeks when he found himself caught up in a crisis of unprecedented proportions. When the killings began in earnest, he was urged to follow the example of his fellow Americans and retreat to the safety of one of the destroyers in the bay. Nevertheless, Jennings refused to be intimidated by the Turkish irregulars and vowed instead to do everything in his power to save the refugees on the quayside. He hoisted the American flag over the two properties that he had appropriated and told the marines on shore to bring pregnant women and orphaned children into his care. Within hours, he had more than 1,000 people in what he labelled — somewhat unfortunately — his 'concentration camps'.

His work won him no plaudits from the American navy. Commander Halsley Powell of the *Edsall* told him that his humanitarian work was 'irresponsible' and ordered him to remove the American flag from the quayside buildings. Jennings duly obliged, but he had no intention of stopping his rescue mission. 'I have seen men, women and children whipped, robbed, shot, stabbed and drowned in the sea,' he wrote, 'and while I helped save some it seemed like nothing as compared with the great need. It seemed as though the awful, agonising, hopeless shrieks for help would forever haunt me.'

He had already saved several lives during his occasional visits to the *Edsall* and the experience had taught him that individuals could make a very real difference in such a desperate situation. On one occasion, he was standing on deck when he heard a low cry from the water. When he peered over the rail, he saw a refugee floundering around in the sea, too cold and exhausted to reach the ship. The sailors on board were prepared to let the person drown, but Jennings gave them a public dressing down and ordered them to drop a line into the water. The refugee — a little boy, naked and freezing — was hauled aboard and given warm clothes.

A few minutes later, a second person could be seen attempting to reach the destroyer. The ship's lights were making the swimmer a target for Turkish snipers on shore and so they were turned off, yet once again the sailors refused to lift a finger to rescue the refugee.

'For pity's sake,' said Jennings, 'why don't you lower a boat?'

The men told him that it would be a breach of American neutrality and added that they could not do such a thing without specific orders.

'Well, I'll order it,' said Jennings. 'Push off that boat.'

The men meekly obeyed, rowing across to the swimmer and fishing out a bedraggled young girl. She was brought on deck and handed over to Jennings, who wrapped her in blankets. Although she slowly began to revive, she was clearly dazed by her long swim. 'She looked at us with a wild expression in her eyes . . .' wrote Jennings, '[but] finally she realised she was with friends who would protect her, and such a look of joy and thankfulness came over her face as I shall never forget.'

When the pain of her suffering suddenly returned, she began to sob and call out someone's name. Jennings did not speak Greek so he decided to ask the rescued boy – who knew a little English – whether he might translate what she was saying. 'Suddenly,' wrote Jennings, 'I felt the boy's grip tighten in mine, the little fellow bounded from my side and threw himself on the girl. Then, from her lips, there burst the name she had been moaning before in grief. He was her brother, and there on the deck of that ship we had reunited them.'

By Tuesday, 19 September, the humanitarian crisis on the quayside had become a sanitary crisis as well. Corpses had lain on the cobblestones for almost a week and were in an advanced state of putrefaction. Many of the refugees were suffering from fevers and acute diarrhoea, a result of living off contaminated water and food. When Esther Lovejoy peered into the harbour that morning, she was sickened to see that the current had drawn the carcasses of hundreds of horses towards the water's edge. 'As the mass washed to and fro with the waves against the stonework,' she wrote, 'a bloated human body occasionally appeared and this sickening spectacle was augmented by the liberation of offensive gases peculiar to putrefying flesh.'

A little later that morning, she was talking to a young Greek girl when a peculiar noise arose from the mass of refugees. 'There was a strange murmur of many voices rising and falling along the waterfront,' she wrote. 'The sound was mournful, like the moaning of the sea, increasing in volume as the darkness deepened. The language was unfamiliar, the tone minor and the effect weird and indescribably uncanny. "What are they doing?" I asked this girl. "Praying" she answered simply. "Praying for ships."'

Jennings joined them in their prayers that relief would soon be at hand, but the hoped-for vessels never arrived. Whilst the Allied ships already in the harbour took away as many refugees as possible, they never returned for more. George Horton had met the captain of one of these vessels, the *Winona*, in Piraeus and begged him to return to Smyrna. The captain refused. 'By the time I get there,' he said, 'all the thousands standing on the quay will be dead of thirst and hunger.'

On the morning of 20 September, Jennings suddenly awoke to the reality that there would be no more ships. Neither America, nor the other Allied powers, had any intention of lifting a finger to save the masses trapped between the Turks and the sea. If nothing was done – and done soon – they would either die of disease or be deported into the interior of Anatolia, no doubt to an almost-certain death. Jennings later described how he was seized with 'an uncontrollable urge' to do something. He had made up his mind to risk his life for those who needed help.

There was still a number of vessels in the bay and Jennings

decided to visit each one in turn in order to persuade the captain to take a cargo of refugees to the nearby Greek island of Mytilene. After being granted permission to borrow the *Edsall's* launch, he rowed across to the French vessel, *Pierre Loti*. But when he asked the captain to take refugees, he was met with a blank refusal. The captain said that he was bound by his government's neutrality. He would not save the life of a single refugee.

Next, Jennings rowed over to an Italian cargo ship, the *Constantinapoli*, and talked to its captain. He, too, refused to join the relief effort. He said that he was under strict orders not to help those on the quayside.

Jennings challenged the man, asking whether the Italian consul could overrule such an order. The captain admitted that this was indeed the case, at which point Jennings offered the man 6,000 lire if he agreed to take 2,000 refugees to Mytilene. He then returned ashore and confronted the Italian consul, pleading with such conviction that the official was shamed into agreeing. Jennings next approached the Turkish authorities and – after introducing himself as head of the American Relief Operation – told them of what he intended to do. The Turks were disarmed by this strange man, who was tiny of stature yet spoke with such authority. They granted him permission to take away women and children, but said that he was forbidden from embarking men of military age.

The boarding began on the following morning, Thursday, 21 September, and was overseen by Jennings himself. He assembled 2,000 of the refugees in one of his quayside houses and then led them down to the jetty. The whole operation was carried out under the watchful eye of the Turkish military, who were on the lookout for men who had disguised themselves as women in the hope of getting away.

'It was heart-breaking to see the grief of loved ones when these ruses were discovered and soldiers pulled the men back from the ships,' wrote Jennings, but he was powerless to intervene. 'It was either play the game as the Turks said or not play it at all.'

By late afternoon on Thursday, the agreed number of refugees were all aboard the *Constantinapoli*. Jennings joined them, for he intended to accompany the captain to Mytilene in order to ensure that he fulfilled his part of the deal. No sooner had the ship weighed anchor than the refugees, charged with emotion after their long days on the quayside, began crowding around Jennings in order to show their gratitude. 'They kissed my hands and my clothing and many actually grabbed me and fell at my feet and kissed my shoes. This was too much for me.' Jennings hid himself in his cabin and did not emerge until the vessel arrived at its destination.

It was dark by the time the *Constantinapoli* entered the harbour, yet the lights of the town revealed the silhouettes of no fewer than twenty-five empty Greek passenger ships — part of the fleet that had been used to evacuate the defeated Greek army from its Asia Minor adventure. Jennings suddenly saw his opportunity: he went ashore and summoned a conference of all the Greek naval commanders, along with the British consul and other prominent citizens. He announced that he wanted permission to use these vessels to evacuate the refugees from Smyrna.

The most senior official in Mytilene was General Frankos, commander of the vanquished Sixth Army, who was effectively in charge of the fleet at anchor in the bay. The general listened to what Jennings had to say and agreed in principle to the loan of six ships, but he wanted a written guarantee to the effect that they would be protected by the American military. He also wanted an assurance that the Turkish authorities would allow the ships to return to Mytilene.

Jennings hurried back to Smyrna and managed to secure a written agreement of sorts from Commander Halsley Powell. The American commander offered to 'escort the ships in and out of the harbour', although he stopped short of offering to protect them if they were to come under attack. General Frankos was not reassured by the American offer; he could not afford to take the risk of losing his ships to the Turks.

Jennings, realising that he would get no further with the Greek general, decided to take a different approach, contacting the captain of a Greek ship, *Kilkis* – an old destroyer that had formerly been in the service of the American navy – and pleading for his support. 'Somehow,' wrote Jennings, 'I had the strange confidence that through her I could get help.'

He was right. The captain of the *Kilkis* welcomed Jennings on board and agreed to his suggestion that they send a telegram to the authorities in Athens. 'In the name of humanity,' read their message, 'send twenty ships now idle here to evacuate starving Greek refugees from Smyrna without delay.' The telegram was signed 'Asa Jennings, American citizen'.

An answer was received just minutes later. The Athens authorities wanted to know more about Asa Jennings. Who was he? And on whose behalf was he acting?

'I identified myself as Chairman of the American Relief Committee in Mytilene,' Jennings later recalled. 'I didn't bother to explain that I held the position solely by virtue of the fact that I was the only American there.'

Although he did not know it at the time, Jennings' telegram had acted as a wake-up call for a Greek government that was caught in complete paralysis in the wake of its army's defeat in Anatolia. The prime minister called a crisis meeting of his cabinet in order to decide whether or not they should intervene in the humanitarian crisis, even though this carried the risk of renewed fighting with the Turks. Everyone at the meeting agreed to the principle of sending ships, but, like General Frankos, they wanted an American guarantee that the vessels would be protected if the Turks attempted to seize them. This was something that Jennings could not promise. 'No time to discuss details of exactly how ships will be

protected,' was his response to the ministers. 'Stated guarantees should be entirely satisfactory.'

These 'guarantees' did nothing to reassure the Greek cabinet,
who continued to vacillate for much of the day. Ministers feared
not merely a renewed confrontation with the Turks; they were
also alarmed at the prospect of having to cope with the influx
to Greece of half a million refugees. By mid-afternoon on
Saturday, Jennings had still received no answer and so he decided
to play his final card.

I threw caution to the winds [and] staked everything on
this one. I told them that if I did not receive a favourable
reply by six o'clock that evening I would wire openly,
without code, so that the message could be picked up by
any wireless station in the vicinity, that the Turkish authorities had given their permission, that the American Navy
had guaranteed protection, and that the Greek government
would not permit Greek ships to save Greek and Armenian
refugees awaiting certain death, or worse.

To his astonishment, his bluff worked. Less than two hours
later, he received an answer. 'All ships in the Aegean placed
under your command to remove refugees from Smyrna.' Asa
Jennings had been appointed an admiral of the Greek navy.

He could scarcely believe his ears and would later smile at
the sheer ludicrousness of the situation. 'All I knew about ships,'
he said, 'was to be sick in them.' But he was brought swiftly
back to reality when the captain of the *Kilkis* asked for orders
from his new admiral.

Jennings' appointment was met with rather less enthusiasm
by the captains of the other ships in Mytilene harbour. None
of them had any desire to sail to Smyrna and one by one they
reported that their vessels were not seaworthy. Jennings, refusing
to allow a few lily-livered Greek captains to scupper his rescue

mission, informed them that he would be sending naval engineers aboard every vessel that reported itself unseaworthy. If this was found not to be the case, there would be a court-martial of the captain that very night, followed by a possible execution in the morning.

Jennings' bluff once again had the desired effect. By midnight on Saturday, 23 September, all the ships in the bay were reported with steam up and ready to sail. Admiral Jennings took his position on the bridge of the *Propondis*, which he had chosen as his flagship, a decision that had caused the captain much amusement. 'He was tickled to death to think that his ship had been selected,' said Jennings. 'At twelve o'clock I was ready and, ordering the Greek flag run down, an American flag flown in its stead and a signal flag that meant "follow me" run up aft. I mounted the bridge and ordered full steam ahead.'

When the flotilla was met by the USS *Lawrence*, which was on route from Mytilene to Smyrna, the captain of the American vessel wired Jennings to ask whether he would prefer to come aboard the destroyer. Jennings hesitated but felt duty bound to remain on his flagship. '[I] saw my nine ships following in good order and, remembering my promise to the Greek cabinet that I would go with the first ship, declined with thanks and remained on the bridge.'

The little convoy pushed on through the night, slowly chugging its way towards Smyrna. It was dawn by the time the *Propondis* slipped into the harbour, followed by the other vessels of Jennings' fleet.

Jennings had been in the city throughout the crisis and had witnessed terrible scenes of death and destruction, yet the human misery that greeted him on that Sunday morning still shocked him to the core:

At the water's edge, stretching for miles, was what looked like a lifeless black border. Yet I knew that it was a border not of death but of living sufferers waiting, hoping, praying for ships − ships − ships! As we approached and the shore spread out before us, it seemed as if every face on that quay was turned towards us, and every arm outstretched to bring us in. Indeed, I thought that the whole shore was moving out to grasp us. The air was filled with the cries of those thousands, cries of such transcendent joy that the sound pierced to the very marrow of my bones.

While Jennings had been arranging the fleet of rescue ships, Esther Lovejoy had been trying to work out how to get all of the refugees away from Smyrna. The logistics were frightening. More than a third of a million people needed to be evacuated in the space of six days. That meant boarding some 50,000 people each day. Whilst the Turkish authorities had at long last agreed to allow women and children off the quayside − along with men who were not of military age − it quickly became apparent that they intended to put every possible obstruction in the way. Jennings' ships were allowed to dock only at the end of the railroad pier − a narrow walkway that was not designed to cope with large crowds. The walkway was enclosed by metal fences and divided into three long sections, each of which had its own narrow gate. These gates were guarded by a double line of Turkish soldiers, while at the entrance to the pier there was a large crowd of senior officers.

'The purpose of these fences was to force the refugees to pass through the narrow gates,' wrote Lovejoy, 'where they could be carefully scrutinised and all men who appeared to be of military age detained for "deportation to the interior."'

The sight of Asa Jennings' fleet sailing into the harbour triggered a mixture of exhilaration and dread among the refugees. There was elation at the thought that they might finally be rescued but absolute terror that they might be left behind. As soon as the first vessel docked, the crowd struggled to its feet and, in one great wave, pushed forwards towards the walkway. 'The description of that frantic rush to reach the ships is beyond the possibility of language,' wrote Lovejoy. 'Pain, anguish, fear, fright, despair and that dumb endurance beyond despair, cannot be expressed in words.'

When she later came to relive these events – and set them down on paper – she was struck by the dogged determination of the human spirit. It seemed to her extraordinary how men, women and children who had experienced unspeakable atrocities nevertheless clung to life with hope and conviction for the future:

> Fortunately, there seems to be a point at which human beings become incapable of further suffering. A point where reason and sensation fail, and faith, cooperating with the instincts of self-preservation and race preservation, takes control, releasing sub-human and super-human reservoirs of strength and endurance which are not called upon under civilised conditions of life.

The Turkish military permitted a handful of British and American marines to come ashore in order to help supervise the evacuation, but the sheer numbers of displaced people meant that order and discipline quickly broke down as the crowds surged forwards.

'Thousands and thousands of refugees, with heavy bundles upon their backs, pressed forward along the quay, struggling to reach and pass through the first gate,' wrote Lovejoy. 'The Turkish soldiers beat them back with the butts of their guns to make them come more slowly, but they seemed insensible to pain and their greatest fear in the daylight was the fear of not reaching the ships.'

In such a throng, it was a case of survival of the fittest. Those who fell were trampled underfoot; those who were sick were abandoned to their fate. Lovejoy, who was standing close to the land end of the pier, felt helpless in the face of such misery:

> Many of the women ... were pushed off the quay into the shallow water, near that floating mass of carrion which washed against the stonework.
>
> No effort was made to help them out of the water. Such an effort would have necessitated the putting down of bundles, or children, and every person in that crowd strong enough to carry anything was carrying a pack or a child, or helping the sick and old of his own family.
>
> So these women stood in the water waist deep, holding up their little ones, until they were able to scramble out and join the crowd, with nothing in the world left to them but the wet rags on their backs.

The crush was worst at the first gate, where tens of thousands of refugees created a bottleneck. Women lost shoes and clothes in the scrum. Hair was torn out and couples separated. Lovejoy saw one elderly grandmother who had lost almost all her clothes. Naked from the waist down – and unconscious of the fact – she was wailing for her family. Another woman encouraged her young child through the pier gate, only to find her own path blocked by soldiers. She pushed them away, but was beaten back by the butts of their rifles.

> The mother's instinct is hard to control [wrote Lovejoy]. With a wild expression of countenance she turned, dropped her bundle and went over that iron picket fence, which was at least seven feet high, like an orang-outang.
>
> A soldier was ordered to stop her, and he cornered her between the fence and a small building on the inside, beat her with the butt of his gun, and finally pinned her against the building with the muzzle of it, in an effort to make

her listen to reason and obey orders. But that poor mother had reverted to the lower animals and was acting on instinct. She couldn't be controlled by a gun unless it was fired. With her eyes on her child, who was being pushed along with the crowd in the distance, she broke away and the soldier shrugged his shoulders impotently, as much as to say, 'What is the use of trying to manage such a crazy creature.'

Many women were in such desperation to get away that they attempted to climb the fences that divided the pier into separate sections. Several got caught on the sharp metal pickets and were unable to get down. Children lacerated their feet on the broken glass that was strewn across the pier, and mothers were beaten by one or other of the numerous Turkish soldiers who were loitering at the various gates. Lovejoy watched officers join in the robbery, fleecing the refugees of any last money, jewellery or gold fillings that they might still have.

'Individual soldiers would seize the more prosperous-appearing women, drag them out of the line and rob them in broad daylight,' she wrote. Any men of military age who attempted to escape with their families were given even rougher treatment. They were severely beaten, then officially arrested and placed with the group of prisoners awaiting deportation to the interior.

'As family after family passed through those gates, the father of perhaps 42 years of age, carrying a sick child or other burden, or a young son, and sometimes both father and son, would be seized.'

Lovejoy found it heart-rending to see these families – so close to freedom – being separated, probably for ever.

In a frenzy of grief, the mother and children would cling to this father and son, weeping, begging and praying for mercy, but there was no mercy. With the butts of their guns, the Turkish soldiers beat these men backward into the prison groups and drove the women toward the ships, pushing them with their guns, striking them with straps or canes, and urging them forward like a herd of animals, with the expression, '*Haide! Haide!*' which means 'Begone! Begone!'.

The British and American sailors were allowed to watch – but not to help – the refugees along the pier. For some, however, the scenes proved so distressing that they were goaded into action. One Royal Navy surgeon attended several emergencies at the far end of the pier, while Lovejoy herself did her utmost to help any pregnant women.

'In a city with so large a population there were, of course, a great many expectant mothers,' she wrote, 'and these terrible experiences precipitated their labours in many instances. Children were born upon the quay and upon the pier, and one woman who had been in the crush at the first gate for hours, finally staggered through holding her just-born child in her hands.'

By the end of that first day, Lovejoy had seen such harrowing incidents that they would remain with her for the rest of her life. 'Children fell off the pier and were drowned, young men committed suicide, old people died of exhaustion and, at the end of the pier, when two or three ships were loading at the same time, children were lost and their mothers ran to and fro frantically calling for their little ones, and great was the joy if the lost were found.'

Among those fighting their way to the quayside were Garabed Hatcherian and his family. Garabed had been released from his prison barracks three days earlier, having been informed by the Turkish soldiers that he was considered too old to be worth deporting.

As soon as he was free, he made his way to the house of his friends, the Sivrihissarians, which still stood intact amidst an area of the city that lay almost entirely in ruins. He was fearful that the house would have been forcibly entered by the military yet, for some inexplicable reason, it had been left untouched. Garabed knocked on the door and was ushered into the hallway, which was crowded with dozens of friends and relatives of the Sivrihissarians.

'Anxiously I search for my wife,' he wrote, 'who I was afraid might have suffered mental collapse during my absence, for she had shown some signs of nervous breakdown when we were parting.' He was delighted to find that she was alive and well, 'although extremely emaciated and pale'.

At four o'clock in the afternoon, Garabed decided that it was time for his family to make their bid for freedom. They said their farewells to the Sivrihissarians and – with a wistful glance back at the house – pushed their way deep into the heaving masses in an attempt to reach the first gate of the pier.

[We] are mingled in the huge crowd as we all attempt to reach the door of mercy . . . I am squashed at my back and at my chest and I fear that Vartouhi [his baby daughter] may choke. Some critical minutes pass and I mobilise all my physical strength to save my poor girl from certain death . . . I lose my balance and I fall down. Fear over-comes me that the crowd will stampede Vartouhi and me and we will be smothered. But I manage to get up, making a superhuman effort.

After hours of jostling and heaving, the Hatcherian family at long last found themselves approaching the first gate of the pier. Garabed himself was helped through the gate by an American marine. When a Turkish soldier prevented his wife and children from following him, he bribed the man with a small bundle of banknotes.

It was unfortunate that this exchange of money was witnessed by another Turkish soldier. Garabed quickly offered a bribe to this second soldier but was met with a chilling refusal. 'With the end of a bayonet on my breast, he orders me back through the door. The children scream and cry. My wife begs him with tears.'

The Turkish soldier continued to force him and his family back to the first gate, where a new American marine was just taking up his position. 'With my poor English, I beg the American guard to have mercy at least with the innocent child in my arms and to intervene. "That is not my business," was his cool reply.'

The Hatcherians were almost back on the quayside when the Turkish soldier had a sudden change of heart and let them go. 'Blinded by [the] number of bills in my wife's hand, [he] grabs the money and disappears. I am free from the clutches of the beast. But I am totally worn of torment and agony; I become dizzy, my eyes see black, I hardly manage to sit on a rock and faint.'

After a few minutes, Garabed recovered consciousness. He stood up and, supported by his wife, tried to push his way back into the crowd. However, after a few steps he felt as if he were going to collapse again. He summoned all his might and, aided by some hidden inner force, managed to propel his family forward through the remaining gates. Although at several points he stumbled and fell, the sight of a vessel docked just a few hundred yards ahead focused his mind.

'I mobilise all my strength and with Vartouhi in my arms, I take off towards the dock, where the last Turkish guard is in control. My wife and my children follow me. Exhausted and with a throbbing heart, I arrive before the guard. I go by him, pale and with my head lowered.'

The guard scrutinised the family carefully before allowing them through the barrier. 'I stop for an instant and check to see whether there is anyone missing. We are all here, eight people, including the maid.'

One final push and Garabed found himself on the deck of the ship. '[I] manage to drag each of my family members up on the ship, one by one. We are all miraculously freed. After so much hardship and suffering, my being alive is an absolute miracle.'

The Hatcherian family were finally free but for many others on the quayside Jennings' vessels were as far away as ever. As dusk descended on Sunday evening, the sense of panic intensified. The Turks had announced that the pier was to be closed during the hours of darkness. Any refugees who had not been taken aboard one of the ships would have to try again on the following day.

'There was nothing the refugees seemed to dread more than to be overtaken by darkness,' wrote Lovejoy, '. . . after struggling all day to reach that point, it was sometimes impossible to embark, or to get back to a place of comparative safety, within range of the searchlights, before darkness settled.'

As night closed in, Jennings had every reason to congratulate himself on a successful day's work. Some 15,000 refugees had been saved from certain death – each one of whom owed his or her life to the tiny Methodist minister from New York. It was an insignificant number in comparison to those still on the quayside, but it was a beginning.

For those on board the ships, it was a blessed release from a terrible ordeal. As Jennings' fleet headed out of Smyrna harbour towards Mytilene, Garabed Hatcherian stood on deck and cast his gaze back towards the home he had once loved.

'With tears in our eyes and our hearts full of emotion, we

watch the crowds huddle on the quay and consider ourselves lucky that, finally, we are free from this infernal city.'

He never wanted to set foot in Smyrna again.

While Asa Jennings was spiriting away his first batch of refugees, Kemal and his senior staff were celebrating the capture of Smyrna at a party in the grounds of Latife's mansion. Kemal was in the best possible humour. Dressed in a white-belted Russian shirt, he took an active lead in the evening's folk dancing and even sang songs about his native Rumelia. One of the guests at the party was the Turkish journalist, Falih Rifki, a close associate of Kemal. He remembered Kemal being in buoyant mood that evening, although he was careful not to betray his jubilation. 'His movements were masculine and dignified. He avoided unnecessary gestures. His manner was not *alla franca* (European like) but Western; not *alla turca* (Turkish like) but genuinely Turkish.'

Kemal spoke at length that evening on many different subjects – of war, love and pity. 'The discussion brought home to me for the first time that this determined warrior and calculating politician was also a very human man of the world.'

While Kemal and his generals partied into the early hours, momentous events were unfolding in Greece. On Thursday, 21 September, two senior-ranking army colonels had staged an anti-royalist coup on the island of Mytilene. Five days later, the rebellion spread to Athens. The Greek navy mutinied and joined the revolution. Shortly after, King Constantine abdicated and a new revolutionary government replaced the discredited old regime.

Jennings was deeply concerned when he was brought news of the revolution in Athens. His first fear was that it would make his task even more difficult, especially as the government that had appointed him admiral of the fleet was no longer in power. However, the new regime gave him their unstinting support, declaring that his rescue mission should continue 'without hesitation'.

369

This was music to Jennings' ears. After landing his 15,000 refugees in Mytilene, he returned to Smyrna on Tuesday, 26 September. This time he had an armada of seventeen ships and many more people willing to help. Esther Lovejoy once again spent her waking hours nursing the sick and pregnant and helping them aboard the ships in the bay. Although aware that they were engaged in a race against the clock, she felt that it was a race they were beginning to win. By the end of Tuesday evening, Jennings had managed to spirit away another 43,000 souls.

His heroic rescue mission made a deep impression on the American and Allied commanders still in Smyrna. Realising that there would still be many refugees left on the quayside by 1 October – in spite of Jennings' superhuman effort – they requested that General Noureddin extend his deadline by another eight days. To their surprise, he agreed – and he also granted permission for British ships to enter the harbours of Urla, Chesme and Ayvalik in order to take away the tens of thousands of Christian refugees gathered there. The Turkish general had suddenly grasped that it was in his interests to co-operate with the Allied powers. They had become the instruments of the nationalists' domestic policy: to rid Turkey once and for all of its troublesome minorities.

The rescue operation continued daily, overseen at all times by Jennings and Lovejoy. By nightfall on 27 September, the number of refugees had fallen to below 200,000. Just two days later, less than half that number remained. Esther Lovejoy embarked on the USS *Litchfield* on the last day of September in order to head to America and raise funds for the homeless and destitute. By the time she left, there were fewer than 50,000 refugees still awaiting rescue from the charnel house of Smyrna.

'From the deck of the *Litchfield* after dark, the ruins of Smyrna seemed as spectral and fantastic as a nightmare,' she wrote. 'I could not see the public huddled at the north end of the quay in the angle they dreaded so terribly, but I knew they were there and that later in the night they would shriek for search lights.'

She also knew that their suffering was almost at an end, and that they would have only a few more days to wait before they would finally be free.

Aftermath

Esther Lovejoy was correct in thinking that the remaining refugees on the quayside would soon be rescued. Within days of her departure, the last of them were finally liberated. For the first time since 6 September, silence reigned over the Smyrna waterfront. The only reminders of the horrors that had taken place were the corpses, the piles of discarded belongings and the haunting backdrop of the burned-out city.

The total death toll is hard to compute with any certainty. According to Edward Hale Bierstadt – executive of the United States Emergency Committee – approximately 100,000 people were killed and another 160,000 deported into the interior. 'It is a picture too large and too fearful to be painted,' he wrote in his 1924 study of the disaster, *The Great Betrayal*, although he did his best, interviewing numerous eyewitnesses and collecting their testimonies. Other estimates were more conservative, claiming that 190,000 souls were unaccounted for by the end of September. It is unclear how many of these had been killed and how many deported, although Greek sources suggest that at least 100,000 Christians were marched into the interior of the country. Most of these were never seen again. Among those who did eventually make it to Greece were Panagiotis Marselos and his brother who had suffered a terrible ordeal at the hands of their Turkish guards. They made their way to Piraeus before settling in the countryside around Patras.

Almost all of Smyrna's other survivors were also taken to Greece where they hoped to build their lives afresh, but their initial optimism was quickly replaced by a grim reality. They were penniless, unemployed and homeless; most were treated as third-class citizens.

Athens bore the brunt of the influx; makeshift encampments sprang up right across the city and were to remain in situ for many years to come. 'Public schools were turned into hospitals [and] town halls were used as barracks,' wrote Henry Morgenthau, America's former ambassador to Turkey. 'Even the beautiful National Opera House ... was filled with refugees, each of which had its velvet-lined boxes becoming the home of a whole family.'

Morgenthau described once-prosperous families who were now walking around in 'shoes made of pieces of discarded auto-mobile tyres'. Their clothing, cobbled together from flour sacks, 'was a fashion born of necessity'.

The refugees found it difficult to settle in Athens, which was a fraction of the size of Smyrna and had none of its charm. There were many, particularly among the Armenian commu-nity, who felt that they would be better off building their lives in a different country. They would eventually emigrate to America, Canada or elsewhere in Europe where they founded little communities that they named after their former neigh-bourhoods in Smyrna.

Rose Berberian and her family went to Marseilles, where they were helped out of their penury by the Sisters of Mercy. They shared and relived the stories of their momentous last days in Smyrna. Rose's brother told how he had swum out to a British destroyer, only to have scalding water thrown over him by the crew. He had then swum farther out into the bay, to an Italian vessel, where he was finally given sanctuary. Rose, her brother and sister were young enough to put the terrible events behind them, but Rose's mother continued to mourn the death of a husband she had last seen on Friday, 8 September 1922.

Garabed Hatcherian and his family headed to Salonica, where Garabed eventually found work as a physician. They lived there until the 1950s, when the family emigrated to Argentina. Forty years were to pass before Garabed's granddaughter, Dora, learned of the existence of his diary, describing the last days of Smyrna. She was so moved by what she read that she published the manuscript – first in Armenian and then in an English translation.

Aristotle Onassis fared rather better than many of Smyrna's refugees. He stayed in Greece where he would later become famous as one of the world's richest shipping tycoons. He returned briefly to Smyrna in 1955 in order to make a pilgrimage to the family's villa in the suburb of Karatash. The house had been taken over by a Turkish family who invited him inside. Aristotle was surprised to find that the rooms were still furnished with the belongings of his childhood.

The Smyrna refugees who remained in Athens would eventually congregate in an area of the city that they called Néa Smírni (New Smyrna). Yet there was none of the liveliness of the old city and poverty remained a constant worry. Many never recovered from the loss of all their wordly possessions. Three generations later, Néa Smírni is still one of Athens' poorest quarters.

Venizelos's maligned city governor, Aristeidis Stergiadis, did not dare to return to Greece and face the wrath of his motherland. After escaping from Smyrna, he headed to the South of France where he lived the rest of his life in exile. He became a convenient scapegoat for Venizelos's failed foreign adventure. To this day, he remains a reviled figure in Greece.

The other senior Greek politicians and generals involved in the latter stages of the Asia Minor campaign were arrested and put on trial. Eight were accused of high treason; six of them were sentenced to death by firing squad. Among them was the half-deranged General Hatzianestis, who had spent so much of his time decorating his waterfront mansion in Smyrna.

Venizelos himself managed to escape censure for his role in the Asia Minor debacle. Chimerical as ever, he argued that everything had gone according to plan while he had been at the helm. His political career was far from over; in the coming weeks and months, he was to play a leading role in negotiations with Kemal's nationalists.

The other principal players in the Smyrna catastrophe found their lives transformed by what they had seen. George Horton returned to America and began writing a highly personal account of everything he had witnessed. The resulting book, *The Blight of Asia*, was published in 1926. It was forthright in its criticism both of the Turks and of the policy of the American government. Not surprisingly, Horton's book was heavily criticised by the American establishment.

Horton's *bête noire*, Admiral Mark Bristol, remained pro-Turkish to the end, urging the State Department not to get involved in the refugee crisis in Greece. American bureaucrats read his memos with interest and declared themselves 'inclined to agree'. Much of their aid went to Mustafa Kemal's Turkey.

A handful of people decided to return to Smyrna. Grace Williamson went back in October 1922 in order to restart her nursing work, but shortly after landing in the city she was arrested by the Turkish military and then locked up in the police headquarters. She was fortunate to escape with her life. 'I am now very certain that we shall not be able to live in Smyrna for years, if ever,' she wrote.

Alexander MacLachlan fared a little better. Despite almost losing his life in the events of 1922, he returned to the city in order to re-establish the American International College. However, he found his work hampered at every turn; in the hastily rebuilt city of Izmir, there was no place for foreign-run institutions. MacLachlan decided to quit in 1926. Just a few years later, the board of trustees voted to close down the college.

Hortense Wood was one of the few to remain in Bournabat in the weeks that followed the destruction of Smyrna. Although she remained stoic in the face of disaster, after a few months of loneliness her nerve broke. Bournabat remained deserted. The Levantines, Greeks and Armenians had all left and showed no signs of returning. Even her beloved cat, Topsy, had moved on to another world. Hortense found him dead in the garden, his head dashed to pieces with a rock. She vowed to remain in Bournabat, and would live there until her death in 1924, yet she felt terribly, desperately alone. 'The gates of the houses [are] left wide open,' she wrote in her diary. 'The houses looted and deserted, the streets empty. The village abandoned by all former residents and our friends. Will they ever return!'

It was a pertinent question and one that many of the Levantines were asking themselves. The Whittalls, Girauds and Patersons – along with many of their former neighbours – were turning their thoughts to the future. It seemed inconceivable that they would not go back to the city that had been their virtual fiefdom for centuries, yet even the most bullish of Levantine patriarchs had to admit that the immediate future looked bleak indeed. Some had been taken to Cyprus, where they were eking out an existence of sorts in makeshift accommodation. Others had been shipped to Malta, where they were lodged in a disused military barracks at the Lazaretto. Among this latter batch was Herbert Octavius Whittall, along with many members of his extended family. They were accorded no respect by the British government in whose care they now found themselves. The barracks were damp and unsanitary, and the military rations virtually inedible. 'The food is getting worse and worse,' wrote Herbert Octavius. 'Not fit for a dog.'

He, like all the other Levantine refugees in Malta, felt betrayed and abandoned by Britain. The Whittalls were proud of their British roots and throughout their long years in Turkey they had always viewed Britain as the mother country. Now, they discovered that the feeling was not reciprocated.

As Herbert Octavius reflected on his plight, it suddenly dawned on him that everything he cared about – everything that he had taken for granted – had been swept away. 'I am,' he admitted, 'feeling very low.' It was a moment of truth for a man who had never worn his emotions on his sleeve.

The extended Wood family – including Hortense's elderly sisters – had fared somewhat better than the refugees in Malta. They had made their way to Cyprus, where they were living in a cheap hotel in Larnaca. 'For the moment we will stay here,' wrote Lucy de Cramer, Fernand's mother. 'It is a primitive place. Bad hotel. Food good enough. My head is confused. I write without clear ideas! My glasses I left at Smyrna! I can hardly see!'

She was surrounded by old friends from Bournabat but there were no servants to attend to her needs and the gaiety of their carefree social occasions was a thing of the past. 'To live in a bedroom [and] make mutual visits . . . is not diverting.' There was a growing feeling that the old way of life had disappeared for ever. The summer balls, the tea dances, the yachting and family picnics of just a few weeks previously already seemed to belong to another era.

Several of Lucy Wood's oldest friends had already decided not to return to Bournabat. Even her sister, Louise, vowed not to go back, but when she was asked where she would live, she merely shrugged her shoulders. Smyrna was the only home she knew.

In the general upheaval and overwhelming human suffering, the fate of the Smyrniot Levantines seemed an irrelevance. They had not been raped or killed – that had been the fate of their servants. Nor had they had to face the horrors of the quayside. Yet most were ultimately to share the sufferings of exile. Everything they had striven to create had been destroyed: their magnificent homes, their profitable businesses and the city of Smyrna itself.

Few in Britain had any sympathy for a class of individuals who had lived privileged lives for centuries. Even fewer in Turkey mourned their loss. Indeed, many saw them as the authors of their own downfall. At the same time that soldiers had been marching to their deaths in central Anatolia, the Levantines of Smyrna had been busily preparing their annual spring balls. 'We could not know how precarious was the basis of our ordered life,' wrote one of Herbert Octavius's great-nieces. '[It was] the end of the family as a tribal authority . . . the end of the family greatness [and] of their wealth, and everything they stood for.'

Most would never again set foot in Turkey. Herbert Octavius himself went to Tunis and retired from business. He never worked again. Other members of the Whittall dynasty went to America, Canada or colonial Central Africa. At least one of Magdalen's great-grandsons managed to rediscover the family's Midas touch. James Whittall headed to Rhodesia – now Zimbabwe – and turned 65,000 acres of semi-desert into rich dairy farmland. A 1966 article in the *Daily Express* gave James much of the credit. 'It is the result of the tough pioneering spirit of the British race,' it said. 'Of the grit and intelligence of the Whittall family.'

Most of the Whittalls' neighbours in Bournabat also headed to foreign climes. The Giraud family was among the little contingent that chose to return to Turkey and chance their luck in Ataturk's modern republic. Almost nine decades after the catastrophe, Brian Giraud is still engaged in a legal battle to get compensation for the land and property that was confiscated by Ataturk's new state.

As the Levantine refugees took stock of their situation, a tragedy of far greater magnitude was unfolding in Turkey. The catalyst was Mustafa Kemal's march on the neutral zone around Constantinople, which was guarded by British troops. Kemal played his cards with skill, entering the zone with his army but declining to fight the British. At the same time, he negotiated a secret deal with the French – Britain's half-hearted ally – that gave him much of what he wanted. This included eastern Thrace and the city of Constantinople.

When Kemal's initiative was made public, it took the wind out of Lloyd George's sails. Since he could not lead Britain into war against a nation that was holding out the olive branch of peace, he was left with little option but to agree to armistice talks. They were held at Mudanya, on the Sea of Marmara, and Kemal would walk away from the conference with a full deck of cards.

Lloyd George was simultaneously being relieved of his. He had already been facing serious criticism of his policy towards Smyrna from many of the Unionists in his coalition government. Now, the party's rank and file joined the chorus of dissent.

Lloyd George was normally a consummate reader of men's minds, yet on this occasion he had seriously misread the mood of his own politicians. Over the next week, there was intense behind-the-scenes lobbying to remove him from power. The Unionists held a meeting at the Carlton Club and voted overwhelmingly to bring down the coalition. Lloyd George was brought the news immediately. He resigned from office later that day.

He was not alone in his downfall. In the aftermath of the Mudanya armistice, Sultan Mehmet VI Vahdettin also found himself a spent force. For more than two years he had been the figurehead of a discredited regime that had willingly co-operated with the Allied powers. Now, he had to face the consequences of that co-operation.

On 4 November, the sultan's government saw the writing on the wall and resigned en masse. The following day, all the old Ottoman ministries were shut down. Turkey was henceforth to be ruled from Angora. The sultan still clung to his throne, but the brutal murder of one of his most outspoken ex-ministers left him in fear for his life. On 16 November 1922, he asked the British for help in escaping from Constantinople.

The British were willing to oblige. At dawn on the following morning, the sultan, his young son and a handful of courtiers were smuggled out of the imperial palace in two army ambulances. They were driven down to the waterfront where the HMS *Malaga* was waiting. The sultan was taken to Malta and thence to Mecca. He eventually settled in San Remo with three of his wives and remained there until his death in 1926, never again setting foot in Turkey. His departure marked the end of a dynasty that had occupied the throne for 469 years.

The realisation that the Turkish nationalists now controlled the reins of power caused absolute panic among the huge Christian population still living in Asia Minor. On the Aegean coast, in central Anatolia, in the Black Sea cities of Samsun and Trebizond, and elsewhere in the Christian enclave of the Pontus, there was a sudden and massive exodus of Greeks and Armenians. All had seen the way the wind was blowing. In the wake of Greece's military disaster, they understood that it was no longer safe to remain in their hereditary homes.

These families left empty-handed, abandoning houses, churches and monasteries that had been a part of their lives since Byzantine times. They took flight in every place where nationalist forces now held sway, even in the European areas of Turkey. As the defeated Greek army retreated through eastern Thrace, the local population had very little option but to leave. Old men, pregnant women, children and babies – all took to the road, abandoning their farms, their crops, their livestock.

One of those reporting on their flight was Ernest Hemingway, a young journalist working for the *Toronto Star*. He had not been in Smyrna, as is often claimed, and the short story that he later wrote about the scenes on the quayside was derived from the testimonies of those who had been there. However, Hemingway was on hand to witness the exodus from other parts of Turkey:

> Exhausted, staggering men, women and children, blankets over their heads, walking blindingly along in the rain beside their worldly goods . . . It is a silent procession. Nobody even grunts. It is all they can do to keep moving . . .
>
> No matter how long it takes this letter to reach Toronto, as you read it in the *Star* you may be sure that the same ghastly, shambling procession of people being driven from their homes is filing in unbroken line along the muddy road to Macedonia.

One of those involved in helping the refugees was Asa Jennings. After leaving Smyrna, he had headed to Macronissa, a bleak and uninhabited island off the coast of Attica. This had become one of many quarantine stations for newly arrived refugees. All had to be checked for infectious diseases before being allowed to land in mainland Greece.

Jennings was joined by Esther Lovejoy, who had returned to Greece after her successful fund-raising initiative in the United States. She was overwhelmed by the scale of what was taking place. Greece had already had to absorb the entire population of Smyrna and its hinterland. Now, hundreds more ships docked each day to discharge their human cargo. The arrival of these vessels was preceded by a telegram that varied only in the number of people on board. 'Four thousand refugees. No water. No food. Smallpox and typhus aboard.' Many of those on the ships were so sick that they died soon after landing, 'most of them from exhaustion due to lack of food and water and other hardships incident to this terrible migration'.

The exodus from Asia Minor was on a biblical scale and it was to continue for many months. To Esther Lovejoy's eyes, it was 'the greatest migration in the history of mankind'.

The migration was eventually enshrined in law in 1923, when Kemal put his signature to the Treaty of Lausanne. All of Turkey's remaining 1.2 million Orthodox Christians were to be uprooted from their ancestral homes and moved to Greece. And the 400,000 Muslims living in Greece were to be removed from their houses and transported to Turkey. It was ethnic cleansing without parallel.

The only exception was the Greek population of Constantinople. A special clause exempted the city's Christians – along with the Greek Orthodox Patriarchate – from having to leave. Many remained there until 1955, when an outbreak of sectarian violence convinced most of them that it was time to pack their bags. These days, Patriarch Bartholomeus presides over a dwindling flock that numbers a few hundred.

The supreme irony of the Treaty of Lausanne is that the chief negotiator for the Greeks was none other than Eleftherios Venizelos. He might have been expected to baulk at dismantling his dream of a mighty Greek empire in Asia Minor, yet Venizelos remained buoyant in the face of disaster, arguing that the influx of refugees presented a unique opportunity for his beleaguered nation. '[It] will enable us . . . to ensure, despite the collapse of a Greater Greece, the consolidation of a Great Greece.'

Venizelos had also come to realise that Greece could not regard Turkey as an enemy in perpetuity. Although his nation had been vanquished in war, the two countries had deep ties and shared a mutual border. Greece's veteran politician swallowed his pride and made his peace with Mustafa Kemal.

He would eventually take his policy of reconciliation one step further. In 1930, when he was once again prime minister of Greece, he travelled to Ankara in order to hold face-to-face talks with Kemal. The two men had much in common and found themselves getting along well together. At a splendid dinner, they talked about forging a joint foreign policy concerning the Mediterranean and even discussed the possibility of a federation of the two countries.

As Venizelos left the soirée, he was met by a quite extraordinary sight. The streets of Ankara had been decked with bunting and flags, all in the blue-and-white colours of Greece. For a brief moment, it was as if the impossible had happened. It was as if the Megali Idea had indeed triumphed.

Turkey itself was to change irrevocably in the wake of the exchange of populations. Less than nine months later, Mustafa Kemal was elected president of the new republic. Soon after, the last vestiges of Ottoman rule were swept away in a series of radical reforms that were intended to bring modernity to Turkey. The caliphate was abolished and the Western alphabet introduced. The fez, which had for so long symbolised the old Turkey, was summarily banned. The yashmak – the veil that women traditionally wore over their faces – also began to disappear.

All Turks were henceforth to take family names in the Western tradition: Kemal himself chose the name Ataturk, Father of the Turks.

Kemal had already offered a further taste of the changes that were to come when he married Latife in January 1923. His young Smyrniot bride surprised many by appearing unveiled at the wedding ceremony. The Kemals looked the epitome of a modern European couple. Eyes widened still further when Latife travelled back to Angora, dressed in riding breeches, high boots and spurs. George Ward Price, who was there at the time, noted that Turkish onlookers 'were startled by this costume, which no other woman in Turkey would have dared to adopt'.

Bornova, January 2006. I am sitting in Hortense Wood's conservatory, drinking Nescafé Gold Blend with Hortense's elderly great-niece, Renée Steinbuchel. We discuss the old times, when

Bornova was still Bournabat; when a Greek butler served coffee on a chased silver tray. Outside, the garden is waist-high in weeds. In the house itself, the cavernous salons and drawing rooms are all in semi-darkness.

'Ah, Hortense,' says Renée with a sad smile. 'A clever lady. Fluent in seven languages and a talented pianist. She was taught by Franz Liszt, you know. And she was a suffragette. Very modern.'

Renée produces her great-aunt's last diary – 155 pages of clipped prose – and starts to read a few extracts. In among tales of coffee mornings, tea parties and dances, there are snippets about Mustafa Kemal, Herbert Octavius, Topsy the cat and Calliope the Greek maid. Like all good diarists, Hortense reveals much about herself; I find myself listening to a women who is witty, haughty and opinionated. Little escaped her notice; even less escaped her censure. This little book is, in its own way, a masterpiece of literature. It is perhaps the truest representation of Levantine Smyrna at the beginning of the twentieth century.

Renée was born in the aftermath of 1922, yet her thoughts and sentiments seem to belong to another world. She speaks of her great-aunt as if she has just popped out to cut some jasmine; she talks of Ataturk's visits as if they took place only a few days previously. However, her answer to one of my questions brings me sharply back to reality. When I ask to see the room where Mustafa Kemal planned modern Turkey, she tells me that the ceiling is fragile and at risk of crashing down. The entire house – the bricks and mortar of old Bournabat – is in the process of collapsing.

It is a similar story elsewhere in Bornova. The Anglican parish that bears Magdalen Whittall's name presents a sorry picture of decline. The church was restored after the destruction of 1922 but the stained-glass windows have once again been smashed by local Turkish boys and the graveyard resembles a jungle. Of the Whittall family tombs, nothing whatsoever remains.

The loggia where Magdalen once held court has also gone

and the botanical gardens have been turned over to high-rise apartments. Even the palatial villas have for the most part disappeared. Most of the houses that survived the destruction of 1922 were eventually knocked down in the 1970s. The Lane family's magnificent villa was demolished in 1973. Edmund Giraud's Italianate palazzo was destroyed in the following year. The Patersons' thirty-eight-room mansion was bulldozed too, its site used to build an industrial carpet factory.

The nearby Big House – magnificent domain of Herbert Octavius – was one of the few villas to be restored after being ransacked in 1922. The house was given to Izmir's Ege University and became the official headquarters of the chancellor.

Only one mansion is still redolent of glories past. In its heyday, Edward Whittall's villa had had 'the unstudied charm and graciousness which comes from the daily use of beautiful things'. Three generations later, it stands defiant against the tide of history.

It remains surrounded by the spectacular botanical garden that Edward himself laid out. This was where he spent his long hours of leisure, clipping topiary and creating new and wonderful hybrids. These days, the garden is tended by Brian Giraud, Edward's great-grandson. Against all the odds, Brian has preserved a glimpse of paradise in an otherwise fallen world.

The stone lions may no longer spout water. The hothouses may no longer be filled with pelargoniums. Yet there is still an air of magic to the place. Rare magnolias, lilacs and wisteria – many of them planted by Edward himself – fill the evening air with a heady, odoriferous scent. And great banks of roses in pinks, mauves and lemon-yellows still tumble down the old balustrade.

Six miles away in the brash modern city of Izmir, the first rays of a weak winter sun are breaking out from behind the rocky bulk of Mount Pagos. It is Friday, 6 January, a working day for most of the inhabitants of Turkey's third largest city. Shopkeepers are unlocking their doors; bars and cafés are already busy. But to the few Turks who are out and about, a novel and incongruous sight is taking place on the quayside. A little procession of Greeks is making its way towards the pier, under the stern gaze of a monumental bronze Ataturk.

For the first time in eighty-four years, Izmir's tiny Greek community – mostly consular staff – is being allowed to celebrate the great church feast of Epiphany: the Blessing of the Waters. All are aware of the symbolism of the feast.

The priest reaches the end of the pier and raises his crucifix high above his head. Then, with a dramatic flourish, he flings it deep into the water. Seconds later, one of the men plunges into the icy Aegean and retrieves the cross from the bottom of the sea. It is a ritual that was once performed in front of hundreds of thousands of exultant faithful. Now, the little group intone a final prayer and quietly make the sign of the cross. It is a first sign of rapprochement between the two nations.

In 2007, the Greeks hoped to perform the ceremony again. They were denied permission.

Notes and Sources

Each book is given a full reference where first mentioned. Thereafter, it is referred to in abbreviated form. The place and date of publication is given wherever possible.

n.d.	no date of publication
n.a.	no author recorded
BL	British Library
NA	National Archives
IWM	Imperial War Museum

PART ONE: PARADISE

Wheel of Fortune

PP. 3–7
Alexander MacLachlan's 1938 memoirs have never been published. Parts of them are accessible at www.levantine.plus.com under the title 'A Potpourri of Sidelights and Shadows from Turkey', henceforth referred to as MacLachlan, 'Potpourri'. I printed them on 25 January 2006. Letters and memos written

by MacLachlan and others – and now held in the NA – confirm all the principal episodes that are described in his diary. The most informative are listed in the relevant sections below.

Smyrna's early history stretches back into antiquity; it was already an ancient city when Christianity arrived in the first century: see The Revelation of St John the Divine, Chapter 1, verse 11.

Hortense Wood's manuscript last diary, henceforth referred to as 'Last Diary', is a day-by-day account of events in Bournabat and Smyrna, covering the period from June 1922 until May 1923. The original is still in the possession of Hortense's great-niece, Renée Steinbuchel.

Grace Williamson's fascinating account has never been published. It is also available on www.levantine.plus.com under the title 'Grace Williamson's Diary of the September 1922 Events in Smyrna', henceforth referred to as Williamson, 'Diary'. I printed it on 25 January 2006. This, too, is complemented by records in the NA.

PP. 7–17

I interviewed Petros Brussalis at his home in Athens on 2 November 2005.

The description of Smyrna's various quarters in the years prior to the First World War is based on the many accounts listed below.

Laurence Abensur-hazan, *Smyrne: Evocation d'une échelle du Levant, XIX-XX siècles*, France 2004, is an excellent book with many citations from foreign travellers.

Annuaire Oriental, Commerce, Industrie, Administration, Magistrature de l'Orient, The Annuaire Oriental and Printing Company Ltd, Constantinople, 1913; this is a most useful resource as it details every aspect of the city's population, as well as listing all the different businesses in the city.

Karl Baedeker, *Baedeker's Mediterranean*, Leipzig, 1911; Fred

Burnaby, *On Horseback through Asia Minor*, London, 1898; Gaston Deschamps, *Sur les routes d'Asie*, Paris, 1894; Hervé Georgelin, 'Aperçu sur les relations entre millets à Smyrne à la fin de l'empire ottoman, d'après les sources diplomatiques', published in the 2004 edition (no. 14) of *Deltio Kentrou Mikrasiatikon Spoudon* (Bulletin of the Centre for Asia Minor Studies). Georgelin is also the author of the excellent *La fin de Smyrne: du cosmopolitisme aux nationalismes*, Paris, 2005.

Louis de Launay, *La turquie que l'on voit*, Paris, 1913; *Macmillan's Guide to the Eastern Mediterranean*, London, 1906; Mirtil Marcel, *Le Tour du Monde*, G. N. Michail, *Smyrna before the Catastrophe* (in Greek), Athens, 1992. This is a re-edited facsimile of a 1920 Greek-language city guide.

John Murray, *Murray's Handbook for Travellers in Turkey in Asia*, London, 1878; Bülent Senoçak, *Levant'in Yildizi: Izmir*, Izmir, 2003. Senoçak kindly met me in Izmir and gave me a detailed and large-scale map of Smyrna's different quarters in the period prior to the First World War.

Marie-Carmen Smyrnelis, *Smyrne, la ville oubliée, 1830–1930: Mémoires d'un grand port ottoman*, Paris, 2006, is a most useful collection of essays on all the different communities that had made Smyrna their home. Sir Charles Wilson, *Murray's Handbook for Travellers in Asia Minor*, London, 1895.

I interviewed Alfred Simes at the British consulate in Izmir on 28 April 2006.

Garabed Hatcherian's chronicle was published in English in Canada in 1997 under the title: *An Armenian Doctor in Turkey* (ed. Dora Sakayan).

There is much of interest about Smyrna's American community in George Horton, *The Blight of Asia*, Indianapolis, 1926, republished by Taderon Publishers, London, in 2003. For more background information on the role of American charity workers in the declining Ottoman empire, see James Barton, *Story of Near East Relief*, New York, 1930; and Robert L. Daniel, *American*

Philanthropy in the Near East, 1915–1930, Athens, Ohio, 1970.

I interviewed Esma Dino Deyer in Izmir on 24 April 2006. She kindly granted me access to her private collection of documents, including letters written by Rahmi Bey, Liman von Sanders, Admiral Peirse, Talaat Bey and Enver Pasha.

PP. 17–28

The descriptions of life in Levantine Bournabat, both here and elsewhere in the book, are taken from memoirs, both published and unpublished. The most evocative is Ray Turrell's *Scrap-book*, privately printed by Richard Bell, n.d.

Other accounts of interest are as follows: Samuel Bird, *And Unto Smyrna: The Story of a Church in Asia Minor*, London, 1956; Edward Alfred Edwards, *Family Notes*, 1974; Edmund Giraud, *Days off with Rod and Gun*, n.d.; Eldon James Giraud, *Days of my Years*, 1971; Tom Rees, *Merchant Adventurers in the Levant*, 2003; Mary Whittall, 'A Book of Thoughts: Memories of my Childhood in Turkey', unpublished manuscript. I was kindly sent this by Barbara Jackson, a Whittall descendant now living in Canada. I(an) Richard Wookey, *Fortuna*; he remembered the Big House when it had a team of forty gardeners. A. C. Wratislaw, *A Consul in the East*, 1924, contains many anecdotes about the British Levantines.

A very good essay on the Levantine community is Oliver Jens Schmitt's, 'Levantins, Européens et jeux d'identité', in *Smyrne, la ville oubliée*, Marie-Carmen Smyrnelis, 2006. Another excellent essay is A. J. Hobbins, 'Paradise Lost: The Merchant Princes and the Destruction of Smyrna', published in Fontanus, vol. XI, 2003. I am most grateful to John Hobbins for his advice and help.

A most interesting, though dated, guide to the remaining houses of old Bournabat is Evelyn Lyle Kalças, *Gateways to the Past: Houses and Gardens of Old Bornova*, Izmir, 1983. A more recent article about the Giraud family's garden can be found in Rosemary Baldwin, 'A Garden in the Levant', *Cornucopia*, 1992, vol. 1.

Among the many books in Brian Giraud's private collection are those relating to the Anglican community of Smyrna and its suburbs: 'St Mary Magdalene Anglican Church, Bornova' (unpublished), 'Vestry Minutes Book, 1871–1930' (unpublished): 'Miss Gladys Routh's Buca Notes and Correspondence' (unpublished), circa 1958; Donald H. Simpson, *Anglican Church Life in Smyrna and its Neighbourhood, 1636–1952*, 1952; 'Buca: General Meetings and Special Meetings of the Congregation, 1897–1957' (unpublished).

A scholarly background to the Levantine business magnates can be found in E. Frangakis-Syrett, *The Commerce of Smyrna in the 18th Century*, Athens, 1992.

My account of the Whittall family is based on the above accounts, as well as the following: 'Whittall Family of Smyrna', (family papers), Exeter University Library (Special Collections): MS 259. See also 'Trading in the Levant: Centenary of C. Whittall and Co., Smyrna', which is in this file.

Gertrude Bell's letters and papers are held at the University of Newcastle. They can be found online at www.gerty.nel.ac.uk. See especially her letters of 3, 4, 11 and 19 March 1902, and 3 April 1907. See also Edmund H. Giraud, *Family Records*, n.d.; Betty Ann McKernan, *The Genealogy of the Whittall Family of Turkey*, privately published, 1996; Yolande Whittall and Benjamin Perkins, *The Genealogy of the Whittall Family of Turkey*, privately published, 1967; *The Whittalls of Turkey, 1809–1973*, n.a., n.d.

The Great Idea

PP. 29–33
William Childs' description of his journey through Anatolia is to be found in his 1917 account, *On Foot Through Asia Minor* published by Blackwood, Edinburgh. For background on Childs, see John Fisher, *Gentlemen Spies*, London, 1952.

For more on the Greeks of Asia Minor, see Gerasimos Augustinos, *The Greeks of Asia Minor*, Ohio, 1992; Burnaby, *On Horseback; Foreign Office, Peace Handbooks (No. 59), Anatolia*. This was one of numerous Foreign Office publications prepared for diplomats attending the Paris Peace Conference of 1919. Louis de Launay, *Chez les grecs de turque*, Paris, 1897; Deschamps, *Sur les routes*; A. J. Toynbee, *The Western Question in Greece and Turkey*, London, 1922; and Wilson, *Murray's Handbook*.

For a scholarly analysis of the situation, see Dr Karl Dieterich, *Hellenism in Asia Minor*, 1918; Paschalis M. Kitromilides, 'Greek Irredentism in Asia Minor and Cyprus', published in *Middle Eastern Studies*, vol. 26, no. 1, 1990.

PP. 33–39
The best and most detailed study of Lloyd George's foreign policy towards Greece and Turkey (and, indeed, Greece's own foreign policy towards Asia Minor) is Michael Llewellyn Smith, *Ionian Vision*, London, 1973 (republished with an extended bibliography in 1998).

For more on Lloyd George, see John Grigg's excellent four-volume biography, *The Young Lloyd George; Lloyd George: The People's Champion; Lloyd George: From Peace to War; Lloyd George: War Leader*, London, 1978–2002. The author died before completing the final volumes of his work. For the end of Lloyd George's career, see Lord Beaverbrook, *The Decline and Fall of Lloyd George*, London, 1963. See also Kenneth O'Morgan, *The Age of Lloyd George*, London, 1971. For Lloyd George's own version of events, see *The Truth about the Peace Treaties* (2 vols), London, 1938. Frances Stevenson, *Lloyd George: A Diary*, London, 1971, provides interesting insights into Lloyd George's character.

See Sir John Stavridi's papers in St Anthony's College, Oxford, particularly the following entries in his diary: 10 November 1912, 31 January 1913, 2 February 1913, 12 March 1915, 15 April 1915, 22 May 1915 and 24 June 1915.

For more on Venizelos, see Llewellyn Smith, *Ionian Vision*; Doros Alastos, *Venizelos: Patriot, Statesman, Revolutionary*, London, 1942. Many of Venizelos's speeches and writings were published in English by the Anglo-Hellenic League.

PP. 39–44

See the reference sources for pp. 17–28.

PP. 44–48

My account of Rahmi Bey is derived from the following: Horton, *The Blight of Asia*; references in letters written by the Whittall and Giraud families; an interview with his daughter-in-law; and numerous references in the National Archives. A brief but interesting account of Rahmi Bey and the sumptuous dinners of the Levantines is to be found in Paul Jeancard, *L'Anatolie*, Paris, 1919.

For more on George Horton's early career, see Marjorie Housepain Dobkin's essay 'George Horton and Mark L. Bristol: Opposing Forces in U.S. Domestic Policy, 1919–1923', *Deltio*, (Bulletin of the Centre for Asia Minor Studies), vol. 4, Athens, 1983. (This was a special issue on the Asia Minor catastrophe.) For more on friendly relations between Smyrniot Greeks and other nationalities, see Georgelin, *La fin*, pp. 115ff.

Scherzer's visit to the city can be found in Charles de Scherzer, *La province de smyrne*, Vienna, 1873.

PP. 48–53

Many original diplomatic documents are cited in Georgelin, *La fin*, pp. 192ff. For the events on Long Island, see Giraud, *Days off*. I consulted five other accounts of interest: 'Le sac de Phocée et l'expulsion des grec ottomans d'asie mineure en juin 1914', n.a., published in *Revue des Deux Mondes*, vol. 24, 15 December, 1914; Edouard Chapuisat, 'L'opinion genevoise contre les persé-cutions anti-grecques', *Les Etudes Franco-Grecques*, July 1918;

'L'oeuvre germano-turque d'extermination en Asie Mineure', n.a., *Les Etudes Franco-Grecques*, April 1920; 'Les persécutions anti-helléniques en turquie', n.a., published by Centre des Liberaux Hellènes de Lausanne, 1918; and Archimandrite Alexander Papadopoulos, 'Persecutions of the Greeks in Turkey before the European War', American-Hellenic Society, no. 6, 1919.

Enemy Aliens

PP. 54–57

A full account of the *Sultan Osman I* debacle can be found in Richard Hough, *The Big Battleship*, London, 1966. See also Winston Churchill, *The World Crisis: The Aftermath*, London, 1929.

Much of the information in this chapter was gleaned from local newspapers, especially the *Newcastle Daily Chronicle* (31 July 1914, 6 August 1914); the *Newcastle Daily Journal* (30 July 1914, 3/4/5/6 August 1914); the *Newcastle Weekly Chronicle* (11 July 1914).

PP. 57–61

The best general study of the ailing Ottoman empire is Alan Palmer, *Decline and Fall of the Ottoman Empire*, London, 1992. See also N. M. Turfan, *The Rise of the Young Turks*, London, 1999; F. Ahmad, *The Young Turks*, Oxford, 1969.

A most interesting account – and enlivened with diplomatic gossip – is Henry Morgenthau, *Ambassador Morgenthau's Story*, 1918, republished in 2003 by Sterndale Classics, London. See also his often amusing *Secrets of the Bosphorus*, 1918.

For more on German military involvement in Turkey, see Liman von Sanders, *Five Years in Turkey*, Annapolis, 1927. See also Ulrich Trumpener, *Germany and the Ottoman Empire, 1914–1918*, Princeton, 1968. This excellent volume also offers some interesting information about von Sanders. Another worthwhile volume is Edward Meade Earle, *The Great Powers and the Bagdad Railway*, New York, 1923.

PP. 61–65
The most poignant memory of the declaration of war is found in Mary Whittall's 'A Book'. See also Giraud, *Days off*.

Clifford Heathcote-Smith's correspondence is scattered through various files in the National Archives. See FO195/2460 for despatches on the outbreak of war. There are also letters and memos from George Horton; of particular interest are FO383/81/1401 and 16918.

PP. 65–68
George Horton wrote at some length about Rahmi Bey in *The Blight of Asia*. For more on anti-Greek propaganda, see Georgelin, *La fin*.

Rahmi's Double Game

PP. 69–74
The story of Whittall's Union Jack is in Wookey, *Fortuna*. Other family stories from this time are taken from Mary Whittall, 'A Book'. There are many references to Rahmi Bey's benevolence in the National Archives. See especially FO383/91/251, 1401, 16918 and 31782. See also Horton, *The Blight of Asia*.

PP. 74–77
Enver Pasha's offensive in the Caucasus is one of the less well-known campaigns of the First World War. My account was drawn from the following: W. E. D. Allen and Paul Muratoff, *Caucasian*

Battlefields, Cambridge, 1953; *Source Records of World War I* (7 vols), ed. Charles Horne, vol. 3, 1923. This contains eyewitness accounts of the fighting. Edward Erickson, *Ordered to Die: A History of the Ottoman Army in the First World War*, London, 2001, pp. 52–63. *History of the First World War*, ed. Barry Pitt, in 128 parts issued in eight volumes; see vols 15 and 16, 1970–72. Ward Rutherford, *The Russian Army in World War I*, London 1975, especially pp. 92–8. An excellent eyewitness account of the army's preparations for battle is to be found in Clarence D. Ussher, *An American Physician in Turkey*, 1917, republished in 2002 by Sterndale Classics, London.

PP. 77–84
For more on Sir Edward Grey's memo, see Llewellyn Smith, *Ionian Vision*. See also NA: FO371/2242. Rahmi Bey's negotiations with Admiral Peirse are in Horton, *The Blight of Asia*. See also J. Corbett and H. Newbolt, *Naval Operations*, vol. 2, pp. 196ff., London, 1929; Paul G. Halpern, *The Naval War in the Mediterranean, 1914–1918*, London, 1987.

Numerous memoirs support Brussalis' and Simes's assertion that the war years were a time of abundant food.

PP. 84–88
There is an extensive and growing literature on the Armenian genocide. Walter Geddes' account is in Horton, *The Blight of Asia*; Morgenthau's in *Ambassador Morgenthau's Story*. See also Trumpener, *Germany*; Johannes Lepsius's influential *Le rapport secret du Dr Johannes Lepsius sur les massacres d'Arménie*, Paris, 1918; James Bryce and Arnold Toynbee, *The Treatment of Armenians in the Ottoman Empire, 1915–1916*, originally published in 1916 and republished in 2000 by Taderon Press, New Jersey. See also Ussher, *An American Physician in Turkey*.

Three excellent eyewitness accounts are: Raphael de Nogale, *Four Years Beneath the Crescent*, London, 1926; Lewis Einstein,

Inside Constantinople, London, 1917; and Harry Stuermer, *Two War Years in Constantinople*, 1917.

'The Ten Commandments' document is in the National Archives, FO:341/4172/31307. There is a most interesting explanatory note by Heathcote-Smith, detailing how he acquired the document.

Saving the Enemy

PP. 89–94

There is much about the British bombing raids in the National Archives. See FO383/234, especially documents 103912, 104400, 105783, 111886, 112718, 114371, 119636, 126381, 131038 and 137673 (on the detention of Levantines). See also Horton, *The Blight of Asia*. For more on the Levantine internment, see Whittall, 'A Book'.

PP. 94–96

On the capture of Long Island, see Liman von Sanders, *Five Years*; and Horton, *The Blight of Asia*.

PP. 97–99

See Horton, *The Blight of Asia*. For general background, see John Keegan, *The First World War*, London, 1998.

For more on the deportations, see the reference sources for pp. 84–88; also, Toynbee, *The Western Question*; and an essay entitled 'Turks and Greeks in Asia Minor', by Félix Sartiaux, *New Europe*, 19 February 1920. See also *Persecutions of the Greek Population in Turkey since the Beginning of the European War*, Greek Ministry of Foreign Affairs, London, 1918; and *The Black Book of the Sufferings of the Greek People in Turkey from the Armistice to the End of 1920*, Constantinople, 1920. The story of the hidden deserter is in Turrell, *Scrap-book*.

PP. 99–102
See Horton, *The Blight of Asia*, and *Recollections* Grave and Gay, Indianapolis, 1927. For mid-war Bournabat, see Turrell, *Scrapbook*, and Eldon Giraud, *Days of my Years*.

PP. 102–108
For more on Salonica, see Horton, *Recollections*, and the following: Alan Palmer, *The Gardeners of Salonika*, London, 1965; Mark Mazower, *Salonica: City of Ghosts*, London, 2004.

Rahmi's plot against the central government is in NA: FO371/3448. See especially document 167738.

PART TWO: SERPENTS IN PARADISE

Peace and War

PP. 111–114
Lieutenant Colonel John Barker's manuscript is in the IWM, manuscript 96/36/1. See also Captain Gilbert Rogers' account in IWM: 92/36/1. There are many other fascinating documents covering the period 1918–22; to my knowledge, none of these has ever been cited before.

On the British prisoners of war, see NA: FO383/458/119437. See also FO371/3421 and FO383/534. This latter includes letters of thanks for the role played by Herbert Octavius Whittall.

PP. 114–118
For Dixon's arrival, see NA: FO371/415722090 and 22088. For British intelligence reports, and information on the unsettled countryside, see reports by Lieutenant Colonel Ian Smith, W. Lewis

Bailey and the British Chamber of Commerce in Smyrna, all in FO371/4157.

Annie Marshall's account was published under the title 'Impressions of Smyrna in War-Time', *The Contemporary Review*, March 1919; David Forbes's report is in NA: FO371/4165.

The story of Alp Arslan's abduction was recounted to me by Rahmi Bey's daughter-in-law. See also Eldon Giraud, *Days*, and Arslan's own account, published in French in *Tempo Magazine*, no. 19, April 1988.

PP. 118–124

The best general account of the occupation is Philip Mansel, *Constantinople: City of the World's Desire*, London, 1995. See also Harold Armstrong, *Turkey in Travail*, London, 1925, pp. 73–107; J. G. Bennett, *Witness*, London, 1962; Neville Henderson, *Water Under the Bridges*, London, 1945.

Lord Curzon's 'The Future of Constantinople' is in the BL, see MSS EUR, F112/268. See also Erik Goldstein, 'Holy Wisdom and British Foreign Policy', *Byzantine and Modern Greek Studies*, vol. XV, 1991. On the Allied occupation, see the manuscript entitled 'The Occupation of Constantinople', by Brigadier General Sir James Edwards, NA: WO161/85.

Ward Price's account of Kemal is in George Ward Price, *Extra-Special Correspondent*, London, 1957, p. 104. For more on this period of Kemal's life, see Andrew Mango, *Ataturk*, London, 1999, and Lord Kinross, *Ataturk: The Rebirth of a Nation*, London, 1964.

PP. 124–134

The best general account of the Paris peace conference is Margaret Macmillan, *Peacemakers*, London, 2001. For more specific information on the Greek perspective, see N. Petsalis-Diomidis, *Greece at the Paris Peace Conference, 1919*, Institute for Balkan Studies, 1978. See also NA: FO371/4165, especially 52429,

which describes a meeting between Clifford Heathcote-Smith
and Metropolitan Chrysostom.

Other documents of interest include *Mémoire soumise à la
conférence pour le Patriarcat Oecuménique*, Paris, 1919; Eleftherios
Venizelos, *Greece Before the Peace Congress of 1919*, American-
Hellenic Society, 1919; *Hellas and Unredeemed Hellenism*,
American-Hellenic Society, 1920 (this includes two interesting
essays, 'Smyrna, a Greek City' by Charles Vellay, and 'Hellenism
in Asia Minor in the Middle Ages' by Charles Diehl). See also
NA: FO608/89/1 for documents sent to Paris by Greek communities living in towns across Anatolia.

See also Harold Nicolson's gossip-filled account, *Peacemaking,
1919*, London, 1933.

For more on Wilson, see C. E. Callwell, *Field Marshal Sir
Henry Wilson* (2 vols), London, 1927.

Blood on the Quayside

PP. 135–148
See Eldon Giraud, *Days*, for more about Bournabat.

The best and most detailed account of the Greek occupa-
tion and subsequent administration of Smyrna is Victoria
Solomonides, 'The Greek Administration of the Vilayet of Aidin,
1919–1922' (unpublished doctoral thesis). A copy of this is held
in the Institute of Historical Research in London. See also
A. A. Palles, *Greece's Anatolian Venture and After*, London, 1937;
George Glasgow, 'The Greeks in Smyrna', *The New Europe*, 25
March 1920. Winston Churchill's quotation is from *The World
Crisis: The Aftermath*, London, 1929.

Ian Smith's intelligence report is in NA: FO371/4231. See
especially document 14564. On the general situation in Smyrna,
see James Morgan's report in NA: FO371/4157.

There are many eyewitness accounts of the Greek landing.

Of particular interest are those by Alfred van der Zee, Donald Whittall, George Perry, Ahmed Feizi, Commander R. L. Berry, Dr Alexander MacLachlan and the commanding officer of the USS *Arizona*. These are all in NA: FO406/41.

See also Lieutenant Lycett Gardner, IWM: PP/MCR/84; and 'An Authentic Account of the Occurrences in Smyrna', FO371/5140/E1448 (this file includes several other accounts). FO371/4231 also has a report by Mr D. Forbes and information about the various British attempts to deal with Colonel Zafiriou. For British reactions to the occupation, see FO371/4201. See also *The Times*, 9, 19 and 24 March 1919; and the *Address of W. A. Lloyd*, Anglo-Hellenic League, 1920. The account by Phanis Kleanthis, published in Greek under the title *Hellenic Smyrna*, is cited in Georgelin, 'Aperçu'.

PP. 148–151
The account of the protest meeting is taken from Halide Edib, *Turkish Ordeal*, London, 1928. Other Turkish and British reactions can be found in NA: FO406/80101. This includes letters written by the grand vizier and various reports by British intelligence agents serving in Turkey.

Ex Oriente Lux

PP. 152–158
Colonel Toby Rawlinson's escapades are admirably described in his *Adventures in the Near East, 1918–1922*, London, 1923.

Kemal's activities are set out in Mango, *Ataturk*; Kinross, *Ataturk*; and Edib, *Turkish Ordeal*. Also useful is Heathcote-Smith's unpublished manuscript, 'History of the Nationalist Movement', NA: WO32/5733/2737/2. There is much of interest in FO371/4158. This file includes Rawlinson's reports from Anatolia and Captain Hurst's intelligence reports of Kemal's movements.

PP. 158–170

Toynbee's account of Stergiadis is in *The Western Question*. Horton, *The Blight of Asia*, also has many interesting facts about the Greek governor. Much more detailed information is to be found in Solomonides, 'Greek Administration', and Llewellyn Smith, *Ionian Vision*.

For more about Smyrna at this time, see Bennett, *Witness*; Sir Tom Bridges, *Alarms and Excursions: Reminiscences of a Soldier*, London, 1938; and Eldon Giraud, *Days*. Helena van der Zee's account was given to me in unpublished typed manuscript by Willy Buttigieg. It is lacking a title page – and has no attributed author – but references within the text suggest that it could only have been written by Helena. It will be hitherto referred to as van der Zee, 'Memoirs'. There is an interesting picture of the city in late 1919 in *L'image de la grèce: Smyrne*, Frederic Boissonas, Editions d'Art Boissonnas, Geneva, 1919.

Horton's report on Stergiadis's governorship is in *Report on Turkey: USA Consular Documents*, Athens, 1985. The Greek perspective, as seen from inside Smyrna, is best represented by E. Dourmoussis, *La Vérité sur un Drame Historique: La Catastrophe de Smyrne, Septembre 1922*, Paris, 1928.

For a detailed eyewitness account of the Greek army's advance into Aidin, and the preceding massacre, see W. A. Lloyd, 'More Turkish Massacres in Asia Minor', *Review of Reviews*, December 1919. Lloyd was a New Zealander who travelled to Smyrna to investigate conditions under the Greek administration.

The Shattered Vase

PP. 171–180

Edib's account of the British occupation of Constantinople, and subsequent events, is in *Turkish Ordeal*. For the British perspective, see Andrew Ryan, *Last of the Dragomans*, London, 1951. For a detailed analysis of events unfolding in Anatolia, see Mango, *Ataturk*. See also A. L. Macfie, 'British Views of the Turkish Nationalist Movement in Anatolia, 1919–1922', *Middle Eastern Studies*, vol. 38, no. 3, July 2002.

For more on Rahmi Bey's arrest, including petitions for his release, see NA: FO608/109, especially documents 345/369/408/460/461. See also FO371/6502; Briton Cooper Busch, *Mudros to Lausanne, 1918–23*, New York, 1976; and Compton Mackenzie, *Greek Memories*, London, 1932.

On the Greek advance, see Llewellyn Smith, *Ionian Vision*, and Toynbee, *The Western Question*. Winston Churchill's analysis of the situation is in his *World Crisis*.

PP. 180–184 AND 186–189
See Giraud, *Days off*; Giraud, *Days of my Years*; Turrell, *Scrap-book*.

PP. 184–186
See Llewellyn Smith, *Ionian Vision*; see also E. Chivers Davis, 'Election Week in Athens', *The Balkan Review*, vol. 4, no. 5, 1920.

PP. 189–197
This is drawn from Llewellyn Smith, *Ionian Vision*; Toynbee, *The Western Question*; Edib, *Turkish Ordeal*.

Into the Desert

PP. 198–202
My account of the atrocities was drawn from three principal sources: a parliamentary paper (HMSO, 1921) entitled *Reports on Atrocities in the District of Yalova and Guemlek and in the Ismid Peninsula*; Maurice Gehri, 'Mission d'enquête en Anatolie, 12–22 May, 1921', *Revue Internationale de la Croix-Rouge*, no. 31, Geneva, 1921; Toynbee, *The Western Question*.

PP. 203–217

For NA references to Rahmi Bey, see references listed above. For information about conditions and daily life in Smyrna, see NA: FO369/1745/K11622; FO371/6552/E1299; FO371/6491/E1301. Monroe's report is to be found at FO371/6491/E3931 and E2005. An account of consular drunkenness is to be found at FO369/1745/K11367.

For more on King Constantine's visit, see Llewellyn Smith, *Ionian Vision*; and Nash and Grayson (eds.), *A King's Private Letters*, London, 1925. The Winston Churchill quote is in his *World Crisis*; the account of the Greek military offensive is taken from Toynbee, *The Western Question*; Llewellyn Smith, *Ionian Vision*; Edib, *Turkish Ordeal*. An excellent account of the military campaign is to be found in HRH Prince Andrew of Greece, *Towards Disaster*, London, 1930. See also Palles, *Greece's Anatolian Venture*.

There are many interesting records in the NA. See FO421/302/no. 47, a report by Colonel Hoare Nairne and, in the same file, his second report. He speaks of Hatzianestis' insanity and compares him to 'a well-dressed Don Quixote'.

PART THREE: PARADISE LOST

I have listed below the most frequently consulted general works – those used to provide a backdrop to almost all the day-by-day chapters. More specific references are included in the appropriate place.

A. Andreades, *La Destruction de Smyrne et les dernières atrocités turques en asie mineure*, Athens, 1923, is a detailed account of the unfolding catastrophe.

Edward Hale Bierstadt, *The Great Betrayal*, London, 1924. A damning indictment of the Turkish army's role in the destruction, Bierstadt's book met with a hostile response from the

American establishment when first published. It contains many eyewitness accounts, published in full at the end.

Marjorie Housepain Dobkin's *Smyrna 1922: The Destruction of a City*, New York, 1972, reissued with a new introduction in 1988, is an excellent and invaluable reference book. Dobkin interviewed many American servicemen serving in Smyrna, as well as Armenian survivors who later rebuilt their lives in America. It has three shortcomings: many new accounts have come to light in recent years; there is a strong focus on the Armenian community (the Levantines – and, indeed, Greeks – are little mentioned); and the atrocities committed by the retreating Greek army are underplayed. My account of Rose Berberian's extraordinary escape is taken from this book, as are several of the observations made by American service personnel.

Constantine G. Hatzdimitrou, *American Accounts Documenting the Destruction of Smyrna*, New York, 2005. This excellent collection, published during the course of my research, includes newspaper reports, intelligence briefings and personal testimonies.

Dr Lysimachos Oeconomos, *The Martyrdom of Smyrna and Eastern Christendom*, London, 1922, is a collection of contemporary newspaper reports and personal testimonies.

La Mort de Smyrne, Paris, 1922, and *Les derniers jours de Smyrne*, Paris, 1923, both by René Puaux. These accounts are drawn from the testimonies of eyewitnesses and contain important information not found elsewhere.

Wednesday, 6 September 1922

PP. 221–231

Hortense Wood's account of the Greek army's retreat is in 'Last Diary'. For a day-by-day account of the growing concern about the Greek army's defeat, see NA: FO371/7886, which contains numerous consular accounts and intelligence reports. Other sources include Horton, *The Blight of Asia*; Edib, *Turkish Ordeal*; Oeconomos, *Martyrdom* (this includes the anonymous Manchester businessman's testimony). See also Williamson, 'Diary'.

Garabed Hatcherian's fascinating, if terrible, account is published under the title *An Armenian Doctor in Turkey: Garabed Hatcherian: My Smyrna Ordeal of 1922*, ed. Dora Sakayan, Montreal, 1997. See also Turrell, *Scrap-book*, and MacLachlan, 'Potpourri'. Dobson's important 'Report' is in NA: FO371/7949/E12182. Charles Howes' harrowing account is one of a number of manuscripts in the IWM: 'Diary of C. J. Howes', 84/14/1.

Thursday, 7 September 1922

PP. 232–239
See Wood, 'Last Diary'. Charlton Whittall's return and subsequent escape is recounted in an unpublished manuscript written by his son, Willem ('Vim') Whittall in November 1986. This will henceforth be referred to as Whittall, 'Escape'. Vim decided to write his account when he realised that he was 'the last surviving offspring of any of the children of my grandparents, James and Magdalen'. See also Mary Giraud, *Book of Thoughts*; Williamson, 'Diary'. There is much about Admiral Mark Bristol in Dobkin, *Smyrna 1922*, but see also her essay on George Horton, listed in the references for pp. oo–oo. See also Ward Price, *Extra-Special Correspondent*. On the departure of the Greek administration, see Horton, *The Blight of Asia*, and Hatcherian, *An Armenian Doctor in Turkey*.

Friday, 8 September 1922

PP. 240–248
See Wood, 'Last Diary'. Many other details, both here and elsewhere, are to be found in a collection of unpublished letters written by Hortense Wood, Fernand de Cramer and other members of the extended Wood family. I am most grateful to Renée Steinbuchel for allowing me to photocopy these unique and fascinating accounts. Henceforth, they are referred to as Wood, 'Family Letters'. See also Williamson, 'Diary'; Ward Price, *Extra-Special Correspondent*; Horton, *The Blight of Asia*. The account written by Hovakim Uregian was published in 1982 – along with a second account by Krikor Baghdjian – under the title, 'Two Unpublished Eyewitness Accounts of the Holocaust of Smyrna', *Armenian Review*, September 1922, pp. 362–89, henceforth referred to as Uregian–Baghdjian, 'Unpublished'. Lieutenant Merrill was one of the many servicemen interviewed by Dobkin, in *Smyrna 1922*.

Saturday, 9 September 1922

PP. 249–260
See Williamson, 'Diary'; MacLachlan, 'Potpourri'; Wood, 'Family Letters'; Whittall, 'Escape'; Horton, *The Blight of Asia*. Anna Birge's account is published in Hatzidimitrou, *American Accounts*. See also Howes, 'Diary'; Hatcherian, *An Armenian Doctor in Turkey*; van der Zee, 'Memoirs'. Abraham Hartunian's story is in Dobkin, *Smyrna 1922*.

Sunday, 10 September 1922

PP. 261–273
See Uregian – Baghdjian 'Unpublished'; Hatcherian, *An Armenian Doctor in Turkey*. Another most important source for the destruction of Armenian Smyrna is an almost unknown document entitled 'A Brief Report Concering the Smyrna Disaster', written by Smyrna's Armenian bishop, Ghevont Tourian, henceforth referred to as Tourian, 'Brief Report'. I am most grateful to George Hintlian in Jerusalem for informing me of the manuscript's existence and to Ara Melkonian for translating it into English.

Kemal's entry into Smyrna is to be found in Mango, *Ataturk*, and Edib, *Turkish Ordeal*. See also Ward Price, *Extra-Special Correspondent*; MacLachlan, 'Potpourri'. For Chrysostom's brutal murder, see Puaux's two works and Tourian, 'Brief Report'. Details about the murder of Mr and Mrs de Jongh are in Oeconomos, *Martyrdom*. For events in Bournabat, see Wood, 'Last Diary', and Whittall, 'Escape'. Dr Murphy's murder is in many accounts, especially Wood, 'Last Diary', and Oeconomos, *Martyrdom*.

Monday, 11 September 1922

PP. 274–287
See Whittall, 'Escape'; Wood, 'Last Diary'; Wood, 'Family Letters'; MacLachlan, 'Potpourri'; Williamson, 'Diary'; Hatcherian, *An Armenian Doctor in Turkey*; Horton, *The Blight of Asia*; Dobkin, *Smyrna 1922*. The best source for the attack on MacLachlan by the Turkish irregulars is to be found in the NA. See the 'Statement by Dr Alexander MacLachlan', FO371/7902/E10810. This file includes several other accounts of the incident. See also MacLachlan, 'Potpourri'. The story about Kemal's hotel visit is in Mango,

Ataturk. For Charles Howes' observations, see his unpublished 'Diary'. Horton's story about the two American journalists is in *The Blight of Asia.* See also Revd Charles Dobson's 'Report'.

Tuesday, 12 September 1922

PP. 288–301

See Dobkin, *Smyrna 1922,* for the Berberian story and for quotes from the American marines. See also Mango, *Ataturk;* Ward Price's despatches are in Oeconomos, *Martyrdom.* See also Wood, 'Last Diary'; Whittall, 'Escape'; Giraud, *Book;* Williamson, 'Diary'; Dobson, 'Report'. The manuscript account of Ian Duncan Wallace's rescue mission has never been published. I was given a copy of these memoirs, entitled 'Evacuation of Smyrna, 1922', by Barbara Jackson. See also Uregian–Baghdjian, 'Unpublished'; Tourian, 'Brief Report'.

Wednesday, 13 September 1922

PP. 302–326

Sir Harry Lamb's despatches are in the NA. Of particular interest are the following files: FO371/7890; FO371/7888; FO371/7898. See especially the document E10382, Percy Hadkinson's report to the British High Commission. I also made much use of British vice-consul Edwyn Hole's unpublished 'Memorandum by Mr Hole on Events in Smyrna', NA: FO371/7894/E9883. A second report can be found at FO371/7890/E9557. See also Dobson, 'Report'. Alfred Simes was one of the few Levantines to go back to the new city of Izmir. He lives there to this day.

See also Wood, 'Last Diary'. The testimonies of the firemen, cited in Dobkin, *Smyrna 1922,* are from the trial held in December

1924 at the Royal Courts of Justice in London. See also the following: Uregian–Baghdjian, 'Unpublished'; Minnie Mills' testimony, along with others, is in Hatzdimitrou, *American Accounts*. See also Puaux's two books for the accounts of the French witnesses. In addition I have drawn on Hatcherian, *An Armenian Doctor in Turkey*; Horton, *The Blight of Asia*; Edib, *Turkish Ordeal*; Mango, *Ataturk*.

James Webster's quotes – and those of other Americans cited in this chapter – are found in Dobkin, *Smyrna 1922*. See also Dobson, 'Report'. For the Girauds' escape, see Mary Giraud, *Book*. Other accounts are taken from Williamson, 'Diary'; Wood, 'Family Letters'. Oran Raber's account is in Hatzdimitrou, *American Accounts*. Lieutenant Charles Hardinge Drage's unpublished manuscript is in IWM under the title 'The 1914–1933 Diaries of Commander C. H. Drage'.

I also made use of the anonymous and untitled manuscript MISC97 (1473), written by a mariner serving on HMS *Serapis*; and T. W. Bunter's untitled account, 87/22/1. He was serving on the hospital ship, *Maine*, in the bay of Smyrna.

Ward Price's despatches have been reprinted several times. I used the version in Oeconomos, *Martyrdom*.

Thursday, 14 September 1922

PP. 327–337

The account of the *Serapis* is in IWM: MISC97 (1473). See also Drage, 'Diaries'; Wood, 'Last Diary'; Wood, 'Family Letters'. Georgios Tsoubariotis's account is published in Demetrios Archigenes, *Martyries apo te Mikrasiatike katastrophe*, Athens, 1973. This is a fascinating collection of Greek eyewitness accounts of the unfolding disaster. Unfortunately, it has not been published in English.

The account of the experiences of the Alexiou family is

published in the first volume of *I Exodos*, ed. F. D. Apostolopoulou, published in Athens in 1980 by the Centre for Asia Minor Studies.

See also Hatcherian, *An Armenian Doctor in Turkey*; Horton, *The Blight of Asia*; Uregian–Baghdjian, 'Unpublished'. Maynard Barnes' short account is in Dobkin, *Smyrna 1922*.

Friday, 15 September – Monday, 18 September 1922

PP. 338–351

For figures on the numbers of dead and deported, see Bierdstadt, *The Great Betrayal*. For more on Georgios Tsoubariotis, see *Martyries*. For Uregian's story, see Uregian–Baghdjian, 'Unpublished'. Panagiotis Marselos's harrowing account is published in *I Exodos*. See also Tourian, 'Brief Report', for more about the deported Greeks. The story of Onassis's time in Smyrna is taken from Nicholas Gage, *Greek Fire*, New York, 2000.

See also Wood, 'Last Diary'; Mango, *Ataturk*; Edib, *Turkish Ordeal*; Hatcherian, *An Armenian Doctor in Turkey*. There are many references to Admiral Bristol, as well as copies of his telegrams, in Hatzdimitrou, *American Accounts*. Esther Pohl Lovejoy's excellent account was published in New York under the title *Certain Samaritans*, 1927.

Tuesday, 19 September – Saturday, 30 September 1922

PP. 352–371

Asa Jennings' extraordinary rescue attempt is drawn from two sources. One is R. W. Abernathy, *The Spirit of the Game*, London, 1926. Abernathy sailed to Smyrna with Jennings in 1924 and the latter recounted to him the entire rescue operation. The other is William T. Ellis, 'Jennings of Smyrna', *Scribner's Magazine*, vol. 84, August 1928. Jennings' own report – and other papers relating to the YMCA operations in Smyrna – are in the National Archives in the Library of Congress and the YMCA Historical Reference Library in New York. For Jennings' subsequent career, see Robert Daniel, *American Philanthropy in the Near East*, Ohio, 1970. See also Lovejoy, *Certain Samaritans*; Hatcherian, *An Armenian Doctor in Turkey*.

The story of Kemal's celebrations are in Mango, *Ataturk*. For more on the coup in Greece, see Llewellyn Smith, *Ionian Vision*.

Aftermath

PP. 372–386

See Bierstadt, *The Great Betrayal*. Henry Morgenthau, *An International Drama*, London, 1930, has much information on the refugees in Greece; see also Hatcherian, *An Armenian Doctor in Turkey*. The story of Onassis's subsequent career is in Gage, *Greek Fire*. Grace Williamson's attempted return to Smyrna is to be found in NA: FO371/7949/E12328; MacLachlan outlines his own return in 'Potpourri'. See also an unpublished account about Smyrna in February 1923, written by Captain Casper Swinley of HMS *Curaçao*, in IWM: 83/44/11.

Hortense Wood's diary continues until June 1923 and is an interesting source on the aftermath. For more on the Levantine refugees in Malta, see the account written by the Bishop of Gibraltar, John Greig, published in *Gibraltan Diocesan Gazette*, vol. 6, no. 3, November 1922. See also Herbert Octavius's letters in NA: FO369/1817/K16250. The *Daily Express* article is reprinted in full in *The Whittalls of Turkey*, 1809–1973, n.a., n.d.

Kemal's moves in the aftermath of the destruction of Smyrna are best outlined in Mango, *Ataturk*, and Kinross, *Ataturk*, but for a much more detailed account of the march on

Constantinople, see David Walder, *The Chanak Affair*, London 1969. Ernest Hemingway's newspaper articles are available in the anthology, *Dateline: Toronto: The Complete 'Toronto Star' Despatches, 1920–1924*, ed. William White, New York, 1985.

Asa Jennings' work won him no recognition from the American government. The Greek government was more generous, awarding him the highest civilian honour, the Golden Cross of St Xavier, and the highest war honour, the Medal of Military Merit.

One of the best books on the aftermath of 1922 – and with particular focus on the population exchange – is Bruce Clark, *Twice a Stranger: How Mass Expulsion Forged Modern Greece and Turkey*, London, 2006. Arnold Toynbee's assessment of the situation can be found in 'The Denouement in the Near East', *The Contemporary Review*, October 1922. Lovejoy's continued work is detailed in *Certain Samaritans*. For the end of Lloyd George's career, see O'Morgan, *The Age of Lloyd George*; and Beaverbrook, *The Decline and Fall of Lloyd George*.

Picture Acknowledgements

Petros Brussalis, Corbis, Halidé Edib *The Turkish Ordeal* 1928, Grace Ellison *An English Woman in Angora* 1923, Craig Encer/www.levantine.plus.com, Hervé Georgelin *La Fin de Smyrne*/Collection Michel Paboudjian, Getty Images/Hulton Archive, HRH Prince Andrew of Greece *Towards Disaster* 1930, George Horton *The Blight of Asia* 1926, Roger Jennings, Betty McKernan, www.smyrnialbum.s5.com (reproduced photographs are reduced copies of the originals published on the *Memories from Smyrni 1900–1922* website by Konstantinos N. Chatzikyriakos), Yolande Whittall. Contemporary postcards and photographs in private collections.

Index